WO**M**EN IN S̶ ̶ LOAN
A Fe**M**inist List edited by
Jo Campling

Editorial Advisory Group

Phillida Bunckle, *Victoria University, Wellington, New Zealand;* Miriam David, *South Bank University*; Leonore Davidoff, *University of Essex*; Janet Finch, *University of Keele*; Jalna Hanmer, *University of Bradford*; Beverley Kingston, *University of New South Wales, Australia*; Hilary Land, *University of Bristol*; Diana Leonard, *University of London Institute of Education*; Susan Lonsdale, *Department of Health*; Jean O'Barr, *Duke University, North Carolina, USA*; Arlene Tigar McLaren, *Simon Fraser University, British Columbia, Canada*; Hilary Rose, *University of Bradford*; Susan Sellers, *University of St Andrews*; Pat Thane, *University of Sussex*; Clare Ungerson, *University of Southampton*.

The last two decades have seen an explosion of publishing by, about and for women. This list is designed to make a particular contribution to this continuing process by commissioning and publishing books which consolidate and advance feminist research and debate in key areas in a form suitable for students, academics and researchers but also accessible to a broader general readership.

As far as possible, the books adopt an international perspective, incorporating comparative material from a range of countries where this is illuminating. Above all, they are interdisciplinary, aiming to put women's studies and feminist discussion firmly on the agenda in subject areas as disparate as law, literature, art and social policy.

Please see overleaf for a full list of published titles

WOMEN IN SOCIETY
A Feminist List edited by
Jo Campling

Published

Christy Adair **Women and Dance: sylphs and sirens**

Sheila Allen and Carol Wolkowitz **Homeworking: myths and realities**

Ros Ballaster, Margaret Beetham, Elizabeth Frazer and Sandra Hebron **Women's Worlds: ideology, femininity and the woman's magazine**

Jennifer Breen **In Her Own Write: twentieth-century women's fiction**

Valerie Bryson **Feminist Political Theory: an introduction**

Ruth Carter and Gill Kirkup **Women in Engineering: a good place to be?**

Joan Chandler **Women without Husbands: an exploration of the margins of marriage**

Gillian Dalley **Ideologies of Caring: rethinking community and collectivism** (2nd edn)

Emily Driver and Audrey Droisen (*editors*) **Child Sexual Abuse: feminist perspectives**

Elizabeth Ettorre **Women and Substance Use**

Elizabeth Fallaize **French Women's Writing: recent fiction**

Lesley Ferris **Acting Women: images of women in theatre**

Diana Gittins **The Family in Question: changing households and familiar ideologies** (2nd edn)

Tuula Gordon **Feminist Mothers**

Tuula Gordon **Single Women: on the margins?**

Frances Gray **Women and Laughter**

Eileen Green, Diana Woodward and Sandra Hebron **Women's Leisure, What Leisure?**

Frances Heidensohn **Women and Crime** (2nd edn)

Ursula King **Women and Spirituality: voices of protest and promise** (2nd edn)

Susan Lonsdale **Women and Disability: the experience of physical disability among women**

Mavis Maclean **Surviving Divorce: women's resources after separation**

Shelley Pennington and Belinda Westover **A Hidden Workforce: homeworkers in England, 1850–1985**

Vicky Randall **Women and Politics: an international perspective** (2nd edn)

Diane Richardson **Women, Motherhood and Childrearing**

Susan Sellers **Language and Sexual Difference: feminist writing in France**

Patricia Spallone **Beyond Conception: the new politics of reproduction**

Taking Liberties Collective **Learning the Hard Way: women's oppression and men's education**

Clare Ungerson and Mary Kember (*editors*) **Women and Social Policy**: a reader (2nd edn)

Kitty Warnock **Land before Honour: Palestinian women in the Occupied Territories**

Annie Woodhouse **Fantastic Women: sex, gender and transvestism**

Women and Social Policy

A Reader

Second Edition

Edited by

Clare Ungerson and Mary Kember

MACMILLAN

First edition 1985
Reprinted 1990, 1991
Second edition 1997

Published by
MACMILLAN PRESS LTD
Houndmills, Basingstoke, Hampshire RG21 6XS
and London
Companies and representatives
throughout the world

ISBN 0–333–60186–6 hardcover
ISBN 0–333–60187–4 paperback

A catalogue record for this book is available from the British Library.

This book is printed on paper suitable for recycling and made from fully managed and sustained forest sources.

10   9   8   7   6   5   4   3
06   05   04   03   02   01   00

Printed in China

Contents

Acknowledgements

The authors and publishers wish to thank the following for permission to use copyright material:

Avebury Press for Clare Ungerson, 'Payment for Caring – Mapping a Territory' in *The Costs of Welfare* by R. Page and N. Deakin (eds) (1993), pp. 149–64.

Blackwell Publishers for material from Jennifer Strickler, 'The New Reproductive Technology: Problem or Solution?' in *Sociology of Health and Illness*, 14(1) (1992), pp. 111–28; and Rose Wiles, 'Women and Private Medicine' in *Sociology of Health and Illness*, 15(1) (1993), pp. 68–85.

Hilary Brown and Helen Smith for material from, 'Women Caring for People: The Mismatch Between Rhetoric and Women's Reality' in *Policy and Politics*, 21(3) (1993), pp. 185–93.

Carfax Publishing Company, Abingdon, for material from Miriam David, 'A Gender Agenda: Women and Family in the New ERA?' in *British Journal of Sociology of Education*, 12(4) (1991), pp. 433–46; Rosemary Deem, 'The New School Governing Bodies – Are Gender and Race on the Agenda?' in *Gender and Education* 1(3) (1989), pp. 250–8; and Lis Sperling, 'Can the Barriers be Breached? Mature Women's Access to Higher Education' in *Gender and Education*, 3(2) (1991), pp. 199–212.

Office for Official Publications of the European Communities for data included in *Eurostat* publications.

Feminist Studies Inc., c/o Women's Studies Program, University of Maryland, for material from Jane Lewis and Gertrude Åström, 'Equality, Difference and State Welfare: Labour Market and Family Policies in Sweden' in *Feminist Studies*, 18(1) (1992), pp. 59–85.

The Geographical Association for material from Sophie Bowlby, 'Women, Work, and the Family: Control and Constraints' in *Geography*, 75(1) (1990), pp. 17–26.

Harvester Wheatsheaf for material from Hilary Graham, *Hardship and Health in Women's Lives* (1993), pp. 55–71; and John Baker, *Lone Parenthood: Coping with Constraints and Making Opportunities* (1992), pp. 110–25.

Institute for Public Policy Research for material from Anna Coote, Harriet Harman and Patricia Hewitt, *The Family Way* (1990), pp. 39–42.

The Controller of HMSO and the Office for National Statistics for Crown copyright material.

Jessica Kingsley Publishers for material from Rosalind Edwards, 'Access and Assets: The Experience of Mature Mother-students in Higher Education' in *Journal of Access Studies*, 5(2) (1990), pp. 191–4.

Roderick J. Lawrence for figures from *Housing, Dwellings and Homes: Design Theory Research and Practice* (1987) John Wiley. Copyright © Roderick J. Lawrence.

Ruth Lister for material from 'Tracing the Contours of Women's Citizenship' in *Policy and Politics*, 21(1) (1993), pp. 3–16.

Liverpool University Press for material from Sylvia Trench, Taner Oc and Steven Tiesdell, 'Safer Cities for Women: Perceived Risks and Planning Measures' in *Town Planning Review*, 63(3) (1992), pp. 279–96.

Locke Science Publishing Company Inc. for material from Ruth Madigan and Moira Munro, 'Gender, House and Home: Social Meanings and Domestic Architecture in Britain' in *The Journal of Architecture and Planning Research*, 8(2) (1991), pp. 116–32.

Longman Group for material from Gill Whitting, 'Women and 1992: Opportunity or Disaster?' in *Social Policy Review 1989–90*, pp. 214–27; and Angela Dale, 'Women in the Labour Market: Policy in Perspective' in *Social Policy Review 1990–91*, pp. 207–20.

Macmillan Press Ltd for material from Jenny Morris, *Independent Lives: Community Care and Disabled People* (1993), pp. 40–9.

Jane Millar for 'State, Family and Personal Responsibility: The Changing Balance for Lone Mothers in the UK' in *Feminist Review*, 48 (1994), pp. 24–40.

National Westminster Bank for material from Tim Walsh, 'Part-time Employment and Labour Market Policies' in *National Westminster Bank Quarterly Review*, May (1989), pp. 43–55.

Routledge for material from Mary Langan, 'Who Cares?' in *Women, Oppression and Social Work* by M. Langan and L. Day; and Julia Brannen and Peter Moss, *Managing Mothers* (1991) Unwin Hyman, pp. 29–32.

Random House UK Ltd for material from Michelle Stanworth, 'Just Three Quiet Girls' in *Gender and Schooling* (1981) Hutchinson.

Sage Publications for material from Sara Arber and Jay Ginn, *Gender and Later Life* (1991), pp. 129–52.

Every effort has been made to trace the copyright-holders, but if any have been inadvertently overlooked the publishers will be pleased to make the necessary arrangement at the first opportunity.

Introduction to the Second Edition

CLARE UNGERSON AND MARY KEMBER

It is over ten years since the first edition of this book was published. This second edition is very nearly completely new: only one of the excerpts from the first book has been retained, and the introductions to the sections are completely rewritten. In addition, Mary Kember is joint editor of this volume, and has been responsible for the sections on the labour market, lone mothers, child care and education. Nevertheless, the basic structure of the previous edition is maintained, in the sense that social policy is considered in relation to women (rather than gender) and divided along the traditional service delivery lines of social security, education, health, housing and personal social services. Three new sections are added – on the labour market, on child care, on lone mothers – while a fourth – on informal care – follows a pattern, set by the previous edition, of considering an issue that has played a very important part in the development of the British feminist perspective on social policy.

The reasons for changing almost the entire contents of this reader will be obvious to anyone who has followed the development of the feminist perspective on social policy as it has happened over the past decade. As with other disciplines in the social sciences and the humanities, the feminist social policy literature has grown enormously. Indeed, one of the many problems in putting this book together has been the sheer weight of material that had to be taken as the basis for the selection of the excerpts, and the long process of deciding just which pieces were the most appropriate for the themes we wished to tackle. The growth in the literature has been fuelled by two factors: the first is the development of a gendered perspective in all the traditional areas of social policy analysis, such that it is now very difficult to envisage research within the mainstream of social policy that does not, at least, pay *some* attention to gendered issues. Secondly, the feminist analysis of social policy has continued to break new ground and focus social policy analysis in areas previously untrodden. For example, the analysis, by feminists, of the implications of a sexed and gendered domestic life has brought into prominence the question of how to underwrite citizenship for women when social rights, since the inception of the British welfare state, have been dependent on full and continuous labour market participation. Similarly, the analysis of 'care' and the question of how to build social policies that both recognise the gendered nature of caring, and the need to empower all those involved in the caring relationship, was originally opened up as an issue by feminists and has now been taken much further by disabled feminists. While both these issues of citizenship and care had been formulated when the first edition of this book was put together, the literature on both these topics, and on many others, has gone deeper and wider, producing sets of literature that have been influential well beyond Britain. This is a real cause for celebration. Inevitably, though, it means that no single collection of readings can possibly do justice to that range and richness of literature. It is to be hoped that the excerpts of published work included here will serve as an introduction and a structure, rather than present the 'last word' on what is important when thinking about the relationship between women and social policy.

Thus, on the one hand, we wish to pre-empt those who will argue that we have underplayed or overlooked particular issues. We suggest that no single book can cover all the topics that are important, let alone all the literature that is of value. It is the legitimate aim of libraries, not collections of readings, to be comprehensive. On the other hand, though, we have clearly been working to some criteria of selection which we should be clear about. One aim is obvious enough: to reflect changes, both in feminism itself and in social policy analysis and social policies, that have taken place over the last decade. Feminist analysis, which has its origins in the idea of women as the 'other' in relation to men, has itself become increasingly focused on differences between women and the way in which some women – particularly black women and women with disabilities – have been implicitly defined as 'other' by the predominantly white, well-educated and able-bodied women of early second wave feminism. Increasingly, feminist social policy analysis reflects, and attempts to integrate, the idea of difference between women, particularly along the dimensions of race, class, disability and sexuality (Williams, 1992; 1995). During the selection process, we tried to find readings that reflect this development, although it has to be said that it has sometimes proved difficult to find literature that fits well with the particular themes we wished to cover. As far as social policy analysis is concerned, we have been anxious to include readings that reflect two major changes of the past decade: first, the impact of marketisation on the British welfare state, and, second, the development of a specifically European perspective, both within social policy analysis, and within the direction of social policy itself. Many of the readings, therefore, consider the likely impact of the changes in the British welfare state, especially as that process has developed since 1988; some of these readings cover the position of women as workers and volunteers within the changing service delivery systems, as well as their position as users of those services. In order to reflect the growth in political and economic importance of the European Union most of the comparative readings are concerned with member states of the EU.

The book begins with a section on social security and citizenship, and then moves on to consider women in relation to the labour market, and the related issue of child care provision. These sections cover the basic need of women for an independent income, whether it comes to them through the functions of caring or through their earnings via participation in the labour market. The sections on the labour market and on child care follow on from the discussion of women's relation to social security and economic independence, since they tackle the question of the source of women's financial autonomy and the way in which social policy acts as one of many determinants of women's economic opportunity. The position of women without men raises particular issues about the appropriate source of women's income within a 'male breadwinner model' welfare state; thus the section on lone mothers continues and develops the theme of the appropriate source of women's income. However, while adequate and independent income is obviously a basic need, so too is accommodation located within a safe environment and the section on housing and planning tackles this issue. The following sections on education, health, the personal social services and informal care follow the traditional service delivery pattern of social policy analysis, and the structure of the first edition of this reader.

At the end of each section there is a bibliography that refers to all the authors cited in the excerpts and in the section introduction. We hope these bibliographies will prove useful guides to further reading.

Finally, of course, our thanks are due to our patient publishers especially Jo Campling, Frances Arnold and Catherine Gray, our families, and the contributors who gave permission for their work to be reproduced within these pages. None of them bears responsibility for the pages that follow.

Bibliography

Williams, F. (1992) 'Somewhere over the Rainbow: Universality   and Diversity in Social Policy', in N. Manning and R. Page (eds)   *Social Policy Review*, 4, Canterbury: Social Policy Association.

Williams, F. (1995) 'Race/Ethnicity, Gender and Class in Welfare   States: A Framework for Comparative Analysis', *Social Politics*, Summer, pp. 127–59.

I

Women, Social Security and Citizenship

Introduction

CLARE UNGERSON

The first edition of this book divided the section on women and social security into two halves: one centred on 'motherhood', the other on 'marriage'. The purpose of this division was twofold. Partially, it was to reflect the way in which the feminist analysis of women and social security had developed in Britain by the early 1980s, but, secondly, it was also to reflect the way in which feminist politics surrounding welfare issues had developed during the same period. In academic social policy the central contribution of feminist *analysis* of the welfare state in the 1970s had been to identify the assumptions about the nature of marriage, and women's dependency on their husbands, which had been built into the British social security system since the Beveridge report and the post Second World War welfare settlement. Much of this work was pioneered by Hilary Land (Land, 1975; 1976; 1978; 1980). It made sense to have a subsection entitled 'Marriage' which used Land's work to identify these assumptions, and also looked at the way such assumptions in turn impacted on the social security treatment of single women who entered cohabiting, but unmarried, relationships with men.

The section on 'Motherhood' more closely reflected the feminist *politics* of social security as they had emerged during the 1970s. Here the campaigns surrounding Family Allowances, or, as they later came to be called, after the 1975 Child Benefit Act, Child Benefit, had brought women together in their defence. In the light of the possibility that these allowances might be paid to men through the taxation system rather than to mothers through the Post Office, women across and beyond class divides had protested that a universal benefit, payable to mothers for the care of their

7

children, was an essential 'lifeline' for mothers who had limited earnings, or had inadequate financial support from their men (Walsh and Lister, 1985).

The section on social security in this new edition no longer bears this division between the two statuses of marriage and motherhood. There are a number of reasons for this, not least that it failed then, and even more does so now, to reflect the complex reality of women's lives. The point is that most women operate within three worlds of marriage (or a relationship with a man), motherhood and/or caring, and paid work. Each one of these three statuses of wife, mother, worker brings with it its own source of income. As a wife or cohabitee, a woman gains resources (or at least the law expects her male partner to provide resources) through the pooled incomes of the household which are usually predominated by the man's earnings or his social security rights, treating her as his dependant (Pahl, 1989). As a mother, she gains an income, albeit a very small one, through Child Benefit payable to her, and, if she is a lone mother without paid work and with low enough income and capital, she gains a basic minimum income through the social security benefit of means tested Income Support, and/or maintenance from the father/s of the children she cares for. As a worker she gains an income through her personal earnings which, if low enough, can be topped up with means tested social security benefits, in particular Family Credit. Many women find that they spend their lives juggling these three statuses, living each one in segments of their days – the wife at night, the mother in the early morning and at the school gate, the worker during the times when the children can be cared for by someone else – and they try to find a satisfactory and satisfying path through the emotional and financial complexities of an over-busy life. It is important to try to capture this combination of statuses or roles by treating them together; hence the division between 'marriage' and 'motherhood' has been abandoned in the pages of this reader, and instead they are treated together, with a separate section later in the book on women in the labour market.

There are, of course, some costs to this procedure. If one does not make these conceptual divisions between marriage, motherhood and paid labour as sources of income for women, or to put it another way, between the statuses and roles of wife, mother and worker, one fails to capture completely the complexity, contradictions, and stubbornness of the British social security system when it comes to the treatment of women. It is the case, for example, that the British system remains obstinately wedded to the original idea, enshrined in the Beveridge report, that women are essentially the dependants of their men. This has been termed the 'male bread-winner model' of welfare by a number of feminist commentators (Langan and Ostner, 1991; Lewis, 1992). This model of welfare can be seen in a wide variety of measures, including and especially the Child Support Act 1991. This demands that biological fathers make financial contribution to the costs of keeping their children and uses an assessment formula which also expects fathers to make a contribution to the maintenance of their children's 'primary carers' – in other words their children's mothers (or as will be the case in the majority of cases, their ex-wives or partners), thus, in effect, continuing the idea that women are economically dependent on men (Lister, 1994). Nevertheless, there are contradictions here: it is also the case that the 'male breadwinner model' is becoming distinctly frayed at the edges as the Conservative government (writing in 1995) struggles to withdraw from social security provision by encouraging women with children to enter the labour market – largely by reducing the number of hours workers have to work per week in order to qualify for the means tested Family Credit which tops up the earnings of low-paid workers. But even this is not without its contradictions since the desire to see mothers in paid work is not presently backed up by adequate child care provision (see Section III of this book) and mothers with children under 16 years of age do not, as men do, have to be available for work in order to claim Income Support.

What is important to bear in mind is that women operate within the overlapping worlds of marriage, family and paid work, and that governments and political parties have views about which one of these arenas is the most appropriate place for women to be. However, these views of both political parties and policy-makers are presently in flux, and at one and the same time commentators on both the left and the right can hold contradictory opinions as to whether 'women' are best construed as wives, mothers or workers. Some of these contradictions reflect debates that presently divide both the major political parties in Britain. These debates are not easily encapsulated as 'left' or 'right' wing – there are the odd bedfellows of the 'new' right and the old 'ethical socialists', both apparently yearning for the 1950s when mother stayed at home and father went to work, and arguing for more difficult divorce and much less encouragement of women into the labour market (Dennis and Erdos, 1992 present the 'ethical socialist' point of view; Morgan, 1994 presents the 'new right' view). Yet others on the right want to see more women, particularly lone mothers, off benefit and into work, in order to discourage a 'dependency culture', with the state, in its maintenance through income support of women on their own, acting as a surrogate husband (Anderson, 1992). The argument that women, including lone mothers, should be construed as workers also finds favour among the centre left. Here the argument is distinguishable from that of the right, since the argument on the left is that this construction of women as workers could only take place within a labour market regulated by the state. The state would both regulate the labour market and use incentives to encourage employers to introduce 'family friendly' employment practices; at the same time, the state would provide adequate social insurance cover for part-time workers, thus allowing women to combine, without enormous cost, the roles of worker and carer. However, the argument on the centre left has recently begun to move beyond a focus on women only: in order to resolve the problem of parenting and other forms of care within the home and simultaneously maintain sexual equality, it is argued that *men* should also be construed as carers, through the introduction of paternity leaves (Commission on Social Justice, 1994). The result of these debates is that at all points along the political spectrum, policies concerning the appropriate source of income for women twist and turn, and show little sign of settling down. Increasingly, too, the focus turns towards the sexual division of labour in the home, and how social policy might be used to encourage greater equality in the division of caring tasks between women and men.

It is also the case that since the 1980s the feminist analysis of women's position both in relation to the economy and to the polity has broadened out into a much wider issue of how to guarantee 'women's citizenship'. This follows the literature of feminist political theorists such as Carole Pateman who have argued that the development of democratic societies has been profoundly and intrinsically gendered and that welfare states are similarly gendered (Pateman, 1988a; 1988b; 1989). Political scientists have developed this citizenship analysis to look particularly at the political representation and political participation of women in modern democracies (Phillips, 1991b; Lovenduski and Randall, 1993), while feminist analysts writing within a social policy framework have argued for a version of citizenship that stresses in particular the question of how to underwrite women's economic independence (Lister, 1990b; 1995; and for a discussion of the theoretical issues within a comparative framework, see O'Connor, 1993). In all these writings the central question is whether women's full citizenship consists in treating them as the same as men or as essentially different from them (Bock and James, 1992). If women are construed as the 'same' as men then the correct way to proceed towards equality between the sexes is to unlock the discriminatory practices that exclude women from full political participation and full economic opportunity and independence. If women are construed as essentially different from men then the best way to proceed is to revalue women's essential qualities of nurturing and responsibility (Gilligan, 1982; Larrabee, 1993; Tronto, 1993) and elevate these private and particularistic values into the public sphere. In social policy terms, the question comes down to whether women should be treated, within social security systems, as workers, in precisely the same way as men are, or whether they should be treated as mothers and wives. If they are treated as workers, then they would be expected to be 'available for work' just as men are expected to be, irrespective of 'domestic responsibilities' such as the presence of children; if they are treated as mothers and wives, then they would be expected to remain at home, and the social security system would be oriented towards treating women as their men's dependants, and treating mothers as the organisers and providers of care within the household.

The excerpt by Ruth Lister reproduced here draws attention to the complex realities of women's lives and the social rights, or lack of them, that women in Britain can attain. She suggests that the term 'woman' or 'women' is somewhat misleading, in the sense that it assumes that all women are in the same position, while it is really the case that there are considerable differences between women, particularly along lines of class and race. Nevertheless, she argues that the continuing assumption of all women's economic dependence on their men runs like a thread through the British social security system. The impact of this assumption is to affect fundamentally the structured opportunities for autonomy available to all women but especially those without a male partner, such as lone mothers, and those, such as lesbians, who have no desire to enter a long-term relationship with a man. The excerpt by Jane Lewis and Gertrude Åström tells a rather different story. Here, in the Swedish example, is a welfare state that is unequivocal in its assumption that women are both carers and workers. It also takes the view that social policy should encourage men to take an active role in child care, particularly in the months immediately following the birth of their children. The construction of social security policies, and policies for child care, based on the idea that women are primarily workers and that, *through paid work*, women should acquire rights to leave to care for their children and other dependants, has had a profound effect on women's participation rates in Sweden. But as Lewis and Åström point out, this policy of treating women, not as exactly like men but rather as having 'two roles', has not been entirely successful in underwriting equality. Women have entered particular areas of the labour market – notably the child care sector of the welfare state – and have opted to work shorter hours than men, thus reducing their earnings in relation to those of men. Thus, even in welfare states which have tried to put care and citizenship together, there remain intractibilities in the domestic division of labour, which mean that social rights, in practice, continue to be divided along gendered lines. It is unlikely that the issue of gendered citizenship will be resolved until the problem of the unequal division of responsibility for care is itself untangled, and both men and women citizens come to be construed as both workers and carers.

Tracing the Contours of Women's Citizenship

RUTH LISTER

Introduction

The language of citizenship is once again fashionable in academic and political circles, with the main British political parties vying with each other to be the party of the citizen.

The gender-neutrality of this language helps to obscure both the gender-blindness and gender-bias of much that has been written and said in the name of the citizen. This is hardly a novel phenomenon. The classical status of citizen was explicitly defined so as to exclude women. Through much of history, women were regarded as lacking the qualities necessary to be responsible citizens in the public sphere of the polis (Jones, 1988).

Whether or not the concept of citizenship can be reformulated so as satisfactorily to include women is a question which this chapter attempts to begin to address. It is part of a wider question, referred to by Stuart Hall and David Held (1989) as the 'irreconcilable tension' between the ideals of equality and universality embodied in the very idea of the citizen on the one hand and the 'post-modern' emphasis on difference and diversity on the other. Given that those ideals represented a false equality and a false universalism (Williams, 1989) the tension, in fact, goes to the heart of 'the very idea of the citizen'.

Gender is only one element in that tension. In focusing on women's relationship to citizenship, it is important to remember that women themselves are not a monolithic group. Women's

From Ruth Lister, 'Tracing the Contours of Women's Citizenship', *Policy and Politics*, 21 (1993).

position as citizens will be mediated by other factors such as 'race', ethnicity, class, disability, age and sexual orientation. The image of a polyhedron, 'reflecting different and changing experiences' has been put forward by Fiona Williams (1991, p. 12) to provide 'a more multi-faceted and interrelated model of the divisions through which people's lives are constituted'.

Another question mark raised over the concept of citizenship relates to the limitations of the nation-state to which it is linked, in the face of the erosion of national sovereignty and the threat of ecological disaster (Heater, 1990; Held, 1991).

The concept, nevertheless, remains an important one in analysing the relationship between the individual and the state in any one nation. This chapter focuses on the UK but the constraints on women's citizenship that it identifies operate elsewhere, even if not in precisely the same forms. Its starting point is the 'public–private' divide which underpins the very meaning of citizenship. In this particular formulation of the 'public–private' divide, the 'private' refers to the domestic within what Carol Pateman (1989, p. 183) has dubbed the 'patriarchal separation'.

David Marquand (1989) has observed that 'citizenship is nothing if it is not public'. On this basis, he has argued (1991) that it is unreasonable to expect the notion of citizenship to address questions concerning the 'private' sphere of the home and family.

This stance reflects a very long tradition in political theory, which treats as an irrelevance whatever occurs in the 'private' sphere. In this way, the division drawn between the 'public' and the 'private', which upholds the power of male citizens, disappears out of the focus of what constitutes political theory. It becomes, instead, a boundary around it.

Yet the 'public' and the 'private' are not absolutely separate spheres and the dividing line between them is not a natural given. Where it is drawn is a political act. It is also a culture-specific line (Yuval-Davis, 1991) and is one which is drawn in different places for different groups according to the amount of power they wield. Thus, for example, disabled people and those in poverty and/or without a home can find that their privacy is treated with rather less respect than that of other groups.

If women's relationship to citizenship is to be understood and changed, the 'public–private' divide has to be brought into sharp focus. In doing so, it is helpful to employ Nancy Fraser's (1990) tripartite division of the public sphere into the state, the 'official-economy of paid employment' and what she refers to as the 'arenas of public discourse'. As Anne Phillips (1991, p. 87) has observed, 'the new emphasis on our role and aspirations *as citizens* . . . helps us to look again at the relationship between the political, economic and social spheres' as well as that between the 'public' and the 'private'.

The official economy of paid employment

Writers such as Carol Pateman (1989, p. 186) have noted that employment has replaced military service as the 'key to citizenship'. Women and men have a very different relationship to paid employment, with implications for their role as citizens *vis-à-vis* both the state and the polity.

Part of the difference lies in the perception of the differential meaning of the wage for women and men. The ideology of the family wage still runs deep despite women's increased labour market participation and the growth in the number of female-headed households. Even where women's earnings are making a significant contribution to household income there is a tendency to devalue them and to treat them as marginal (Brannen and Moss, 1991).

The ideology of the family wage shapes women's opportunities in the official economy of paid employment, irrespective of the presence or absence of a 'male breadwinner' capable of earning a 'family wage'. As Jane Millar (1989, p. 313) has observed, 'the increasing construction of women as secondary earners makes it much more difficult for women who have to support themselves (and their dependants) as primary or sole earners to do so'.

In her study of solo women in the European Community, Millar (1990) noted that, like married women, they 'tended to be concentrated in service sector employment and thus in lower paid jobs'. Both neo-classical and radical labour market theories 'suggest that, firstly, even solo women will be disadvantaged at the point of entry to employment because employers treat all women as a class; and secondly, that the experiences of all women before entry to the labour market (in education, socialisation) are based on the idea that women as a class become wives and mothers' (ibid., p. 38–9).

This view is supported by an analysis by Heather Joshi (1991) which attempted to assess the relative importance of motherhood and gender in accounting for women's low pay. Her conclusion was that 'the direct consequences of motherhood play a relatively minor part in accounting for mothers' low pay' (ibid., p. 187).

At the same time, women and men enter the labour market under very different conditions. By and large, not only do men enter it unencumbered by responsibility for the physical care of children or adults, but they are also serviced domestically. They are thus free to be full-time wage-earning citizens and, if they so choose, active political citizens.

Most women, on the other hand, at some stage or stages of their lives, are either excluded completely from the official economy of paid employment by the care of young children or of adults or they stagger under what Kollontai dubbed the triple burden of child care (and/or increasingly adult care), domestic labour and paid work.

Some women with money can ease the burden – sometimes by buying the services of women without money (Ungerson, 1990) – but it is still generally the woman's responsibility and the woman's money. For women without money, the burdens are accordingly that much greater.

The public spheres of the economy and the state have not seen it as their responsibility to ease the burden on women with domestic responsibilities in the UK. In contrast with most other European countries, particularly Scandinavian ones, the care of children is seen as essentially a private matter (Cohen, 1988; Moss, 1988–9).

Of more concern to the government have been the *obligations* of citizenship in the 'official economy of paid employment'. Thus, for example, at the 1988 Conservative party conference, John Moore (1988) set the party the task of

> correcting the balance of the citizenship equation. In a free society, the equation that has rights on one side must have responsibilities on the other. For more than a quarter of a century, public focus has been on the citizens' rights and it is now past time to redress the balance.

This reflects, in part, the influence of New Right theorists from the United States to whom the Thatcher government looked for inspiration. The theme of citizen obligations was pursued most explicitly by Lawrence Mead (1986) in his book *Beyond Entitlement: The Social Obligations of Citizenship*. Its central thesis was that the enforcement of work obligations on the poor is 'as much a badge of citizenship as rights' (ibid., p. 229).

Traditionally, the obligation to take paid employment has implicitly been construed as primarily a male obligation. However, the growing reliance of female-headed lone parent families on welfare, at a time when their total numbers have also been growing, has resulted in questions being raised about the relationship of lone mothers to the labour market.

Recent policy developments in the UK have, in fact, been geared only indirectly (and not always consistently) to encouraging lone mothers into paid employment. They have instead concentrated on the maintenance obligations of fathers. In this way, it has been possible to side-step questions about the proper place for mothers – not an easy question for a Tory party which cannot decide whether it is their children or the economy which needs women more. Nevertheless, the White Paper *Children Come First* makes it clear that the government sees payment of maintenance, together with various modifications to the social security scheme, as a bridge across which lone mothers can enter into full-time paid work (now defined as 16 hours a week).

In contrast, in the United States, female-headed families, including those containing very young children, have been the primary target for 'workfare' policies designed to enforce citizenship obligations. Writers such as Mead and Michael Novak (1987) appeal to notions of the 'common good' in their treatises on the citizenship obligations of the poor to take what, Mead himself has made clear, are usually low-paid, often dirty and unpleasant jobs. The justice of such an appeal is questionable in a deeply divided society such as the Unites States or the UK (Lister, 1990a).

Similarly, whilst there may appear to be a certain logic in arguing that, if men and women are to be treated as equals, they should face the same work obligations, we do have to stop and consider the constraints under which lone mothers enter the labour market and the burden of unpaid work in the home that they carry. Thus, Joan Brown (1989, p. 72), in her research paper for the Social Security Advisory Committee, concluded:

> the lesson from the U.S. is not that workfare or other forms of compulsion are worthy of imitation, but that programmes to induce a return to the labour force have to be focussed on the

real needs of the individual lone mother and must be backed by child care and by other supportive measures.

Moreover, questions about equal obligations to take paid work raise questions about the division of unpaid work. This theme has been developed by Peter Taylor-Gooby (1991), using the notion of 'moral hazard' to describe men's evasion of caring work.

The sexual division of labour, which places no obligation on men to undertake caring and domestic work and which governs the relationship of women and men to both paid and unpaid work, also has implications for their respective positions as citizens in the other two areas of the public sphere: the state and the polity.

The state

It is through the state that social rights of citizenship are determined and allocated. T. H. Marshall (1952) identified as key to social citizenship a 'universal right to real income which is not proportionate to the market value of the claimant' (p. 47). Nevertheless, the allocation of income maintenance rights to women is heavily influenced by the manner in which those rights are tied to labour market position as well as by the ideology of women's economic dependency.

Economic dependency

The full or partial economic dependency of many women on men and the ideology underpinning it are at the nub of any assessment of women's citizenship (Lister, 1990b). One of the criticisms that has been made of Marshall's work on citizenship is his failure to treat as problematic the relationship between citizenship and dependency within the family in the same way that he did the relationship between citizenship and social class (Pascall, 1986).

The ideal of citizenship enshrined in the Beveridge report incorporated into it assumptions about married women's economic dependency. It was criticised for doing so at the time in a feminist critique of the Beveridge report (Abbott and Bompas, 1943). The harmful effects on many women (and children) of the economic dependency of those living with men was one of the

arguments used in the campaign for the Endowment of Motherhood and for the payment of family allowances, when introduced,
to women.

Contemporary research suggests that those harmful effects cannot simply be dismissed as history. Three aspects can be highlighted
as particularly significant in shaping the contours of women's
citizenship.

First is lack of control over resources. Research has shown how
some separated and divorced women prefer the poverty of lone
parenthood to their economic position within marriage (Graham,
1987; Bradshaw and Millar, 1991). Women on their own can have
greater control both over their access to the resources entering into
the household and over how those resources are allocated and
consumed.

Second, beyond a general mutual duty of financial support (Pahl,
1989), a women has no real enforceable rights to a share in her
male partner's income so long as she is living with him. This
contrasts with the increased emphasis on the financial obligations
of absent fathers. As Robert E. Goodin (1985, p. 37) has warned
'depending on their families for assistance subjects beneficiaries to
the arbitrary will of another'. It also affects power relationships
generally within the family as Jan Pahl's research has demonstrated
(Pahl, 1989).

Pahl's work has also pointed to a third consequence of economic
dependency: a sense of obligation both towards the economic
provider and with regard to what the money should be spent on
(ibid., p. 209).

Her research underlined the importance to many women of
having 'money you know is your own' (ibid., p. 200). In the same
vein, the authors of a Department of Employment study of unemployed women commented on 'the strength of the need among
married women to achieve a measure of financial independence –
especially in that majority of households where financial control
was not fully shared' (Cragg and Dawson, 1982, p. 53).

Similarly, Eithne MacLaughlin (1991) has observed the value
that carers attach to the invalid care allowance, as providing
them with money of their own, although this value can be compro-
mised where the benefit does not represent an increase in total
family income. Four-fifths of respondents in her study of the
invalid care allowance felt that having an independent income
was very or fairly important. The particular importance for black

women of access to an independent income has been highlighted in a study by Nicki Thorogood (1987).

The lack of security, rights and autonomy involved in a personal relationship of economic dependency and the sense of deference it can create are corrosive of any notion of citizenship rights.

The extent of women's economic dependency is partly a function of their position in the life-cycle. It will also vary according to factors such as 'race' class and disability. For example, Afro-Caribbean women are less likely to be economically dependent upon a man, and black women generally are more likely to be working full rather than part time (Amos and Parmar, 1984; Cook and Watt, 1987; Bruegel, 1989). The whole issue of dependency can be particularly problematic for disabled women who 'face the threat of psychological, physical and material dependency' and for whom access to the usual means of economic independence is 'limited in different ways and to a greater extent than it is for most other people' (Lonsdale, 1990, pp. 82, 141; see also Campling, 1981). This reflects women's particular relationship to the disabling socio-economic environment in which disabled people live (Morris, 1991).

A growing number of women are achieving at least a degree of economic independence through the labour market; indeed it has been pointed out that fewer than a fifth of adult women are totally dependent on the earnings of a man with whom they live (Glendinning and Millar, 1991). Nevertheless, economic dependency is still a fact for a significant minority who are at home full-time caring for young children or elderly or disabled relatives. Moreover, the degree of economic independence achieved through (often insecure) part-time work, the typical option for (white) mothers, is limited (Lister, 1992a). The findings of the ESRC Social Change and Economic Life study suggest that:

> Financial equality depends upon a wife's full-time employment, since part-time work simply operates to reduce calls on the husband's wage, without increasing wives' influence over finances – equality in household financial arrangements depends crucially on women's full-time employment rather than simply on employment, *per se*. (Vogler, 1989, p. 24)

Furthermore, as noted earlier, the ideology of women's economic dependency still has a firm grip. Like most ideologies it is highly convenient for those who benefit from it. As Glendinning and Millar (1987, p. 25) argue, it underpins the sexual division of labour and 'does more than simply describe the economic circumstances of very many women. It also creates and legitimates gender inequality' inside and outside the home. In this way the ideology can shape the lives even of those not directly dependent upon a man, for example lesbian women or Afro-Caribbean female heads of households. Thus, while white feminists have too glibly assumed that the issue of economic dependency is a central one for all women, failing to recognise the problematic nature of the concept of dependency for many black feminists (Carby, 1982), it is not totally irrelevant even to black women who are not economically dependent on a man.

The ideology is also convenient in that it helps to obscure other elements of dependency and the interdependence of which it is a part, namely, men's dependency upon their female partners for the care and servicing of themselves and their families (Graham, 1983). Indeed, Bettina Cass (1990) has argued that public policy should therefore be identifying not women's dependence as the problematic but men's independence, with its consequences for welfare.

This is an important point. However, the problematising of men's independence does not mean that women's economic dependency ceases to be an issue for public policy. Indeed, it is arguably becoming even more important as an issue in those countries such as the UK and the US where public policy is attempting to shift economic dependency from the public to the private sphere in the name of 'reducing dependency on the benefits culture' and encouraging 'independence, self-reliance and personal responsibility' (Moore, 1988).

An example of this trend is the UK government's policy on maintenance. Presented as a policy to enforce absent parents' (primarily fathers) financial obligations towards their children, it also places new obligations upon them to provide for the caring parent. As a result of an unremarked amendment to the Social Security Act 1990, the maintenance formula now includes the caring parent's income support allowance. In this way, women's economic dependency on men that they do not even live with is being enforced. Bradshaw and Millar's (1991) research for the DSS found absent fathers much less willing to pay maintenance for their former partners than for their children. The attitudes of the women were not elicited.

Another example has been the introduction of the social fund. This discretionary, cash-limited system of primarily loans replaced lump sum grants for those living on social assistance. There is evidence, from the DSS-sponsored evaluation of the social fund, as well as from a number of small-scale pieces of research, that claimants are having to turn to private sources of help such as family, charities and money-lenders in the face of refusals from the social fund or a reluctance to be indebted to it (Craig and Glendinning, 1990; Cohen, 1991; Smith, 1991a; Cohen *et al.*, 1992; Huby and Dix, 1992). Some of this research suggests that it is women who are bearing the main brunt of this shift in dependency as part of the more general burden they bear of managing poverty. As against this, the social fund does seem to have provided assistance for women leaving violent relationships (although this may become less common as the fund comes under greater financial pressure).

Social rights and the labour market

As women have to some extent strengthened their position in the labour market, so they have gradually occupied a slightly stronger position in the national insurance scheme. This process has been assisted by the removal of direct sex discrimination in social security as a result of the EEC Directive. More recently, though, it has been partially undermined by the imposition of more restrictive contribution conditions, which have particularly disadvantaged women (Lister, 1992a).

More fundamentally, as noted earlier, women's position in the labour market is still inferior to that of men. So, therefore, is their position in a social security system in which entitlement, by way of contribution tests, depends on previous employment status and favours male employment patterns (Land, 1988).

This is not just a British phenomenon. For example, Arnlaug Leira (1989) has written of Norway that a dual concept of citizenship is at work: 'one associated with citizen the wage-earner, the other with citizen the carer', the former attracting 'the more generous and institutionalised benefits' (ibid., pp. 33–4).

This is exemplified in the UK social security system by the way in which the non-contributory social security benefits, intended to fill some of the gaps left by the contributory system, are deliberately maintained at a lower level than the contributory. In this way they do not undermine the cherished contributory principle which privileges 'citizen the wage-earner'. Indeed, it is not uncommon for this principle to be upheld as the very epitome of universal social citizenship rights (see e.g. Ignatieff, 1989).

The consequences of the link between labour market position and social rights are long term, with many women facing poverty in old age because they have not 'earned' adequate pensions (Walker, 1987; Groves, 1991; Joshi, 1991; Smith, 1991b). Of relevance here is the other public–private split, that between the state and the private market welfare sector (the latter, of course, being subsidised by the state).

Fred Twine (1992) has suggested that occupational and private pensions should be regarded as providing a 'civil opportunity' rather than a social right – a civil opportunity which favours those in secure, continuous well-paid employment throughout the life-course. He writes 'as long as civil opportunity takes precedence over social rights, those absent from or harshly treated by the labour market slip into poverty at various points in their pre-retirement life course and in consequence in old age. This is particularly true for women' (ibid., p. 174). Therefore, he argues, strengthening social rights through state provision 'is essential if women are to be included in citizenship in old age' (ibid., p. 172). This conclusion is supported by an EOC report on women and pensions (Davies and Ward, 1992).

The Beveridge report was quite explicit that married women's claim to social citizenship attached to their maternal role, and an imperialistic one at that (Williams, 1989). This claim, though, gave them only indirect social citizenship rights through their husbands, thereby reinforcing their economic dependency upon men. This was then mitigated slightly through the social rights attached to their children in the form of the Family Allowance.

Social rights that come second hand, mediated by a third party, are not genuine rights of social citizenship. Indeed, they undermine the notion of citizenship. And, while the Family Allowance (now Child Benefit) is a very important (if still inadequate) right of social citizenship, it is essentially a benefit for the child and not the mother, even if for mothers without a wage it is normally their only independent source of income (supplemented now in some cases by Family Credit).

Lone mothers, other than widows, were excluded from the Beveridge social insurance scheme altogether. They have therefore had to rely on the inferior rights afforded by means-tested assistance. Nevertheless, inadequate as they are, such rights have enabled women to live independently of men. There has been some limited progress in recognising women's social citizenship rights (Pateman, 1989; Cass, 1990).

Despite this limited progress, the social security system still fails to deal adequately with women's poverty (Glendinning and Millar, 1992). Some of this poverty is hidden within the family where income is not shared fairly. There is a growing body of evidence to suggest that women and children do not always receive a fair share of a male 'breadwinner's' income (Brannen and Wilson, 1987; Vogler, 1989).

Poverty itself can spell exclusion from full rights of citizenship and undermine people's ability to meet their citizenship obligations (Lister, 1990a). Women's poverty is one example of how the intersection of different inequalities compounds the erosion of citizenship rights. Other examples include the impact of racism and the particular vulnerability of disabled women to poverty.

Women also tend to take the main responsibility for managing poverty and for mediating on behalf of their families with welfare institutions. The launch by the UK Prime Minister of the Citizen's Charter to provide 'one of the central themes of public life in the 1990s' (Major, 1991, p. 2) is therefore potentially of particular significance for them. The Charter promises 'more power to the citizen'; it does not address the question of women's lack of power as citizens. It promises 'to raise the standard of public services'; in so far as it achieves this promise, women, as the main users of public services, should benefit. However, without the backing of any new resources, it remains to be seen how effective the Charter will be.

That the particular needs of women citizens are not addressed in the Charter is not surprising; it reflects a deeper failure in the political system. Although women played an important role in early campaigns around the welfare state, ultimately they lacked the political power to shape it according to their needs. The same has been said of the more advanced, 'woman-friendly' welfare states of Scandinavia where women have still 'been the objects of welfare policy and not its creators' (Hernes, 1987b, p. 86). The lesson drawn by Scandinavian feminist theorists is that 'it is necessary that women participate in the determination of what their social needs and political interests actually are' (Borchorst and Siim, 1987, p. 154).

Equality, Difference and State Welfare: Labour Market and Family Policies in Sweden

JANE LEWIS AND GERTRUDE ÅSTRÖM

Many feminists regard Sweden as a progressive paradise, in terms of both its levels of social provision and its degree of gender equality. Although it is commonly appreciated that virtually all Swedish women are in the labour market and that public sector day care provisions are better than in most Western countries, the way in which this has been achieved is less well known. For example, many English-speaking feminists are surprised to learn that Sweden does not rely on equal opportunity legislation to promote equal pay or to counter sex discrimination.

In Sweden, women's rights and entitlements are structured differently from other modern welfare states. Most states operate a gendered model of welfare entitlements that defines and treats women as wives and/or mothers. Their labour market position then becomes a matter of individual 'choice', with greater or lesser opportunity for legal redress in cases of sex discrimination. In Sweden, the definition of women's entitlements to welfare in family policies has changed dramatically since the early 1970s, away from the provision of benefits to them as mothers and towards benefits that they draw by virtue of their labour market status. Yet, paradoxically, the outcome of this shift has been the strengthening of policies that recognise women's needs as mothers. The framework of equal treatment on the basis of labour market participation supported by a full employment policy seems to have made possible the greater recognition of women's caring work in the family.

From 'Equality Difference and State Welfare: Labour Market and Family Policies in Sweden', *Feminist Studies*, 18(1) (1992).

Many feminists have addressed the difficult issue of the basis
for women's claims on the state, the fundamental choice appearing
to be that between equality and difference. In policy terms, this has
translated into claims based on women's status as paid workers or
on their status as mothers. As Joan Scott has argued, this is an
impossible choice. An option for equality means acceptance that
difference is antithetical to it, and an option for difference means
admitting that equality is unattainable (Scott, 1988). Furthermore,
it is a choice that women reformers have historically sought to
avoid, using both arguments strategically (Lewis, 1991). Yet when
Alice Kessler-Harris suggested (in her Sears' case evidence) that
women's claims might be premised on either equality with men or
difference, depending on the particular historical moment and
group of women concerned, the court found such ambiguity uncon-
vincing as a legal argument (Kessler-Harris, 1989). Writers like
Scott urge us to transcend the dichotomy of equality and difference, but it is hard in policy terms to know what this means.
Although it is by no means clear that Swedish policy has
succeeded in 'transcending' the dichotomy, it has constructed a
distinctive equal opportunity strategy by grafting the right to
make a claim on the basis of difference on to a policy based on
equal treatment.

The Swedish example also serves to address a second crucial
question for feminists: what can be hoped for from the state?
Many feminist policy analysts in Britain and the United States
remain ambivalent at best as to their expectations of state action,
given women's weak institutional position and the historical tendency of most welfare states to make assumptions about the reality
and desirability of female dependence on men when formulating
welfare policies. Although recognising that the outcomes of welfare
policies have changed familial and other structures in society, such
that male power has been challenged, state policies have also served
to perpetuate patriarchal structures. At best, English-speaking feminist policy analysts view state patriarchy as patriarchy at a remove
and thus preferable to dependence on individual men (Graham,
1982; Oakley, 1986; Pateman, 1988). In contrast, the Scandinavian
literature on women and the state has grown increasingly optimistic
about the possibility of a 'woman-friendly state'. (Hernes, 1987a)
This is in part a product of the nature of policies delivered in
Scandinavian countries and in part due to the rapid increase in
women's formal political representation. All Nordic parliaments

(with the exception of Iceland) have a critical mass of women members.

This chapter will argue that the Swedish model has resulted in significant gains for women but that its story is also something of a cautionary tale. The Swedish government played the major part in promoting the early 1970s' legislation that resulted in women's independent treatment as workers. This makes an assessment of its motives important; what the state gives may be taken away, although such reversals have not been a significant characteristic of the Swedish experience to date. Furthermore, serious problems remain within the Swedish model, centring on the unequal division of unpaid work and sexual segregation in paid employment. Despite a public commitment to achieving greater equality in the work of women and men, the Swedish system of promoting equal opportunities has only changed the position of women, leaving that of men relatively untouched. In addition, it is still not clear that women are in a position to make a genuine choice between paid and unpaid work.

Welfare state regimes and the basis of social entitlement

All Western countries have developed policies of social ameliora-tion over the last century. The mainstream literature on the devel-opment of welfare states addresses the economic, institutional, political, and class variables that may explain this but often ignores gender and race. The older functionalist arguments which viewed the emergence of social policies as part of the logic of industrialism go some way towards suggesting why modern states took steps to rehabilitate the injured, facilitate labour mobility, and protect skilled (male) workers against sickness and unemployment (Wilensky and Lebeaux, 1958). Many more recent left-wing writers on the emergence of welfare states have also stressed the degree to which the survival of capitalism requires a degree of social protec-tion (Esping-Andersen, 1987).

But the timing and instruments of social protection differ widely between nation-states. Explanations of this variation have focused much more on actors and politics, with the arguments falling into two broad camps: either that social provision has been imposed 'from above' or extracted by working people 'from below'. Theda Skocpol has made a forceful attempt to 'bring the state back in' and to argue for the importance of states and bureaucracies as autonomous actors (Evans, Ruescheneyer and Skocpol, 1985). But the majority of the participants in the debate focus on the importance of social class. Frances Fox Piven and Richard A. Cloward, for example, have argued that elites made concessions to the poor to prevent or respond to social unrest but that the gains were substantially weakened when peace was restored (Piven and Cloward, 1971). The social democratic 'power resources' model emanating from Sweden has argued for the importance of working-class strength and the way in which wage earners were able to use the democratic state to displace class struggles from the workplace into the political arena (Korpi, 1978). More recent work has emphasised the importance of alliances between the working and middle classes in the creation of 'solidaristic' welfare states that offer universal, tax-based provision (Baldwin, 1990).

Women tend not to figure in these accounts of the development of welfare provision, in part because they focus on state-provided welfare to the exclusion of provision by the family and voluntary organizations. Seth Koven and Sonya Michel have suggested that in the weakly centralised late nineteenth-century states of Britain and the United States women were able to exert considerable influence through their philanthropic work, and they compare this favourably to women's lack of power in the late twentieth-century corporatist Swedish state (Koven and Michel, 1990). This is difficult to prove, however, as the field of influence (measured by the amount of legislative change) secured by even famous women philanthropists remained small. Moreover, the vast majority of nineteenth-century British and American women remained poor, and, because philanthropic effort was patchy, such benefits as they acquired were unevenly distributed. Furthermore, although Swedish women, like women in other welfare states, were not a major force in post-war social policy-making, they have acquired much more political power in recent decades (Pedersen, 1989). This may provide some support for Laura Balbo's suggestion that strong welfare states provide women with political entitlements (Balbo, 1987).

Welfare states developed varied structures which have had very different implications for women (Esping-Andersen, 1990). The Scandinavian (social democratic) countries and, to some extent, Britain, emerged from World War II with a commitment to universally provided benefits and services, based on citizenship rights and full employment. The conservative/Catholic countries (Austria, Belgium, France, Germany) emerged with a commitment to making the state a compensator of first resort through social insurance programs designed to maintain status differentials between occupational groups, and between men as breadwinners and women as wives and mothers. The principle of 'subsidiarity' also ensured that the state only intervened to provide services when family resources were used up. The United States, to some extent Canada and Australia, and, by the end of the 1980s, Britain, developed 'liberal' welfare regimes, characterised by means tested benefits and a residual role for the state (Marmor, 1990).

Few scholars have attempted to introduce gender into the analysis of welfare regimes (Langan and Ostner, 1991; Shaver, 1991). The major commitment of both conservative and liberal welfare regimes in the twentieth century has been to the development of insurance schemes which work via the labour market. Core welfare programmes have thus been above all the prerogative of the regularly employed, who have been predominantly male. In most welfare systems, women's rights to welfare have therefore been indirect, a function of their presumed dependence on a male breadwinner. This has meant, first, that women's substantial contributions to welfare, both paid and unpaid, have been ignored and with them the direct entitlements that should have been women's due; and, second, that women's needs have been defined in terms of motherhood as a social function rather than on the basis of individual need (Land, 1978; Riley, 1981).

Although potential or actual motherhood provided the justification for making the grounds of women's social entitlement different from those of men, in most states' social security systems women have qualified for benefits as wives rather than as mothers. Women have thus been provided for via their husbands in accordance with assumptions regarding the family wage and the bourgeois family form. Women with children and without men have historically posed a particularly difficult problem. Over time, governments have oscillated between treating these women as mothers, or, given that they lack a male breadwinner to depend upon, as workers. The current swing in liberal welfare regimes toward treating them as workers (under 'workfare' schemes in the United States) has more in common with nineteenth than with mid-twentieth-century social policy. In liberal welfare regimes, where a dual insurance/assistance model operates, first-class (insurance) benefits tend to go to men and second-class (welfare) benefits to women (Nelson, 1990).

The definition of social citizenship entitlements is thus linked firmly to the independent status of wage-earner. Nowhere has government attached a significant value to the unpaid work of caring that women do for the young and old within the family. To this extent, gender regimes tend to cut across other ways of categorising welfare systems. The Swedish welfare regime also grounds welfare provision in a citizen worker model, but it is arguably unique in respect to gender. Women gain social welfare entitlements on the same basis as men, that is, as workers; and, crucially, virtually all women and men have the right to work. The basis of the Swedish welfare structure is therefore 'equality' rather than 'difference', but given that the recognition of difference has been grafted on to the model, the issue becomes the extent to which the model has succeeded in securing substantive equality between women and men.

Legislating the basis of women's social entitlements in Sweden

Swedish Social Democratic governments are usually seen as a leading force promoting equality between women and men in recent decades. But the meaning of equality in Sweden is significantly different from the 'equal to men' formulation which is implicitly (and explicitly in regard to legislation on matters such as workfare) favoured by U.S. governments. Before the 1960s, Swedish social democracy was more profoundly influenced by arguments about improving the position of women based on difference than by those based on equality. This helps to explain the particular mix of policies adopted since the 1970s, which bears no relation to the kind of equal opportunity legislation familiar in Britain and the United States.

Pre-World War II Swedish social democracy embraced the idea of difference in its thinking about the relations between women and men. This was largely due to the influence of Ellen Key, who accepted the view of nineteenth-century medical and social scientists that women were essentially different and who argued that women's special knowledge as mothers should be the basis for their contribution to society (Key, 1912; 1914). The central importance Key attached to motherhood led her to adopt a radical stance in regard to all women's (married or unmarried) right to give birth. Difference played a large (Karen Offen (1988) has argued a dominant) role in other European feminists' thinking in the late nineteenth century. In Sweden, Key's ideas also helped shape the social democratic movement's views as to what was 'good and rightful' in everyday life. The most powerful image in Swedish social democracy has been that of building 'the people's home'. This encompasses both the idea of society and state as a good family home, where no one is privileged, all cooperate, and no one tries to gain advantage at another's expense; and, also, of ensuring that productive capacity is used to the advantage of people and their families. In 1927, the chairman of the Social Democrats and later long-time prime minister, Per Albin Hansson, sketched out women's part in the social democratic project: 'We have come so far that we have been able to begin preparing the big People's Home. It is a matter of creating comfort and well-being there, making it good and warm, light and cheerful and free. To a woman there should be no more attractive mission' (Hirdman 1987). Whether in the big People's Home of state and society or the small People's Home of individual household and family, women's contributions (and rewards) were allocated on the basis of motherhood (Steedman, 1990).

During the 1930s and 1940s, social democracy's conceptualisation of women's place in society was challenged by the writing of Alva and Gunnar Myrdal, themselves Social Democrats. In 1935, the Myrdals published their bestseller, *Kris i Befolkningsfrågan* (Crisis in the Population Question), (Myrdal and Myrdal, 1935) the same year that in Great Britain Enid Charles predicted that by the year 2000 the population of England and Wales would be reduced to that of London. The common 1930s' theme of 'national suicide' was profoundly conservative and the Myrdals, like prophets of doom in other countries, advocated eugenic social engineering (Charles, 1934). However, the Myrdals' insistence on 'democratic' population planning differentiated them from the extremes of national socialism and made their work, published in the 1940s, influential in policy-making circles beyond Sweden (Titmuss, 1938).

In the Myrdals' conception of 'preventive social policy', children had to be wanted and reared to be productive adults, which meant that society had to invest in their welfare and that of their families. The Myrdals argued that governments must recognise that society's greatest asset was its human resources and exercise appropriate control over that asset. But the state planning component in their thinking existed alongside the strong belief that state policies should aim to realise the potential of each individual, albeit that the justification for this belief remained the promotion of the social good. Thus, although women's role as mothers had 'national' significance, the Myrdals also insisted that women had the right to develop their talents to the fullest in other fields and particularly in paid employment. They argued that if the state wanted babies from middle-class mothers it must make it possible for them to keep their jobs (Hirdman, 1989). During the late 1940s, Alva Myrdal developed, with Viola Klein, her extremely influential idea of 'women's two roles', whereby women ideally entered the labour market from school and remained until the birth of their first child, returning again when the children left school. Myrdal and Klein demanded state support for motherhood and flexibility from employers to accommodate this bimodal career pattern (Myrdal and Klein, 1956; Lewis, 1990). Thus, Myrdal's policy inheritance within Sweden had three components: first, she sought to reconcile the claims of equality and difference within a single strategy; second, her main justification for this strategy was the nation's need for the talents women could bring to the labour market and for more babies, rather than women's own needs; and, third, she was content to change women's lives without pressing for concomitant changes in those of men.

During the 1950s and early 1960s, the labour force participation rate of women over 15 remained constant at about 30 per cent. As in most Western countries, married women in the childbearing years had lower participation rates, consistent with the 'dualroles' model. During this period, women were entitled to six months maternity leave, and, from 1954, flat-rate benefits as mothers, with employed women receiving an additional subsidy for 90 days (Abukhanfusa, 1987). But beginning in the early 1960s, the desirability of the dual-roles model was questioned, first within the Liberal party and then by the social democratic movement. In 1968, a joint task force report on equal opportunity by the trade union confederation (LO) and the Social Democratic party concluded that 'there are thus strong reasons for making the two-breadwinner family the norm in planning long-term changes within the social insurance system' (Hirdman, 1989).

During the late 1960s and early 1970s, the social democratic governments took conscious steps, first, to make the dual-breadwinner family a reality by increasing the incentives for married women to work all their adult lives; and, second, to change the basis of women's entitlement to social benefits from that of mother to worker. The active use of both labour market and family policies to change women's position in Swedish society was consistent with the broader pattern of development of the Swedish welfare state, which prioritised full employment and which also demanded that those qualifying for its most generous benefits manifest their readiness to work (in return the 1974 Security of Employment Act and Promotion of Employment Act provided strong job security for both women and men). The (very small) number of unemployed have historically received minimal welfare benefits. Although women's pension entitlement was equal to that of men, other benefits, paid to them as mothers, were substantially lower than wage rates. The decisions made in the early 1970s, which treated women as workers for the purposes of social entitlements, raised women's compensation for their work as mothers to the rates they could command as members of the labour force.

The most important change designed to promote women's employment was the introduction of separate taxation, first on a voluntary basis in 1968, and then in law in 1971. Separate taxation, together with high marginal tax rates, makes it more favourable for family income for a woman to go out to work than for her husband to add extra overtime hours. In the United States or Britain (where separate taxation was introduced only in 1989), the labour market effects for women are not the same because of the less progressive tax system. In Sweden, both marginal and average tax rates have been higher for the one-earner than for the two-earner family. Thus, for a full-time industrial male worker who earned SEK 70 000 in 1981 (US\$ 13 333) the marginal tax rate was 90 per cent for the one-earner family as opposed to 68 per cent for the two-earner family (Gustafsson, 1983). From this point it therefore became more profitable for any extra income to be earned by the woman.

The second major change promoting female employment was the increase in the number of places in public day care, both in day care centres and with registered child care providers. Prior to the late 1960s, the most important element of public expenditure on family policy was that of the child allowance, but by the late 1970s this accounted for only 25 per cent of such spending, largely because of the growth in day care (Olsson, 1986). In 1968, 5 per cent of children under school age (7 years) had places in public day care and 4.6 per cent with child care providers. At the 1975 Congress of the Social Democratic party, a five-year plan was presented which promised a substantial increase in day care provision, and by 1979, 27 per cent of below school age children were accommodated by the public child care system. By 1987 this had risen again to 47 per cent (29 per cent in day care), with priority being given to the children of employed mothers. Nevertheless, at the end of the 1980s it was clear that the 1982 promise by the Social Democrats of a place for *all* preschool children over 18 months by 1991 would not be fulfilled.

The responsibility for providing child care rests with local government and both access and, to a lesser extent, cost to the parents vary substantially between local communities. In Stockholm, in 1989, 75 per cent of children were accommodated at a cost of SEK 1105 (US$ 187) a month for one child and SEK 1420 (US$ 240) for two or more children for parents whose income exceeds SEK 14 000 (US $2372) a month (the average wage for a male worker). Day care is therefore relatively cheap. In other communities as few as 25 per cent of children may have places and at 50 per cent greater cost to parents. Such wide differentials cannot be wholly explained by regional differences in women's labour participation rate (which ranges from 75 per cent to just over 90 per cent), although Stockholm, which has the most places, also has the greatest percentage of women in full-time employment. These differentials in availability and cost have benefited middle-class parents disproportionately (Leira, 1989). In 1984–5, 19 per cent of children whose parents were members of the mainly manual workers trade union confederation had child care places, compared with 32 per cent of lower middle-class, white-collar parents and 44 per cent of the children of academics. The estimated cost for a day care place is twice that of an early primary school place, but Siv Gustafsson and Frank Stafford have calculated that the payoff in terms of women's labour market productivity allows the policy to pass the kind of cost–benefit tests that have increasingly been imposed on social policies during the 1980s (Gustafsson and Stafford, 1988).

In 1974, a scheme of parental insurance was introduced. Rather than women being given flat-rate maternity benefits, they were offered compensation for loss of market earnings. Men were also offered the same 90 per cent replacement of earnings if they chose to care for children. Also in 1974, legislation was passed giving a parental leave of six months to be taken before the child reached age 4 together with a ten-day-per-year child sick leave entitlement, available until the child reached age 10. For those (few) claimants with no job, benefits were fixed at a relatively low flat rate. The parental leave was extended in 1975 to seven months, in 1978 to eight months, and in July 1980 to 12 months, with nine months at 90 per cent replacement earnings and three months at the flat-rate level. In 1980 the number of child sick leave days was also increased to 60. No further significant extensions of either form of leave occurred until 1989, when parents became entitled to 12 months' leave under the insurance scheme with a further three months at the flat-rate level, and 90 days' child sick leave. The parental leave was projected to rise to 18 months over 1990–1 and the number of child sick leave days to 120, but these plans were frozen during the political crisis of January 1990. Also, in 1979, parents with children under 8 years gained the right to reduce their working day (at their own expense) from eight to six hours. However, repeated demands from women's groups for a legislated six-hour day for all workers have not been met.

The vast majority of women claim virtually the whole amount of permitted parental leave at the 90 per cent replacement of income rate, but only one-half of the three months available at the flat rate, which demonstrates the importance to the family economy of replacing income. However, only one man in five applies for leave in the child's first year and for an average of only six weeks. Over a 15 year period, the percentage of parental leave claimed by men has remained constant at between 5.5. and 6.5 per cent. Only men in higher paid, public sector jobs are likely to opt for parental leave. Applications for child sick leave days are shared much more equally between women and men, although on average only 6.9 days a year are taken by any family (Näsman, 1986) and as many as 50 per cent of families claim no sick leave days at all. This provision has become an effective means of providing a caring subsidy to dual-earner families with children with special needs.

Sweden is way ahead of the rest of Europe in its parental leave legislation. Several other states provide limited paid, or more generous unpaid, leave, but the politics of parental leave have been fiercely fought. By the late 1980s, the European Commission had prepared a draft directive on the subject. However, this has been opposed by the British government, which views it as a costly and undesirable piece of state interference.

Not surprisingly, the labour market participation rate of women in Sweden has increased dramatically since the 1960s. This has been true of most Western countries and has to do with the demand for female labour by service industries, women's increased desire for employment, and families' increasing need for two incomes. However, the Swedish increase has been more dramatic both because participation rates were lower during the 1950s and early 1960s than in countries such as the United States or Britain and because of the very high participation rates achieved by women with young children. By 1986, 89.8 per cent of women aged 25 to 54 (only 5 per cent less than men of comparable age) were in the labour market and 85.6 per cent of women with children under 7 worked compared with 55 per cent in the United States and 28 per cent in Britain. By 1984, only 7 per cent of Swedish women between 25 and 54 were classified as 'housewives'. However, many women work part-time, 43 per cent in 1989, compared with 37 per cent in Britain and 24 per cent in the United States, although most Swedish women are working three-quarters' time. In 1986, only 10.9 per cent of women 25 to 54 worked under 19 hours a week (Persson, 1988). Swedish policies have been effective in getting women both to work outside the home and to have children. Compared with West Germany, for example, more than twice as many Swedish mothers of pre-school children work, although in 1984, the West German fertility rate was 1.27 and the Swedish rate was 1.61.

Interpreting the policy changes: implications for women

The official view of the change in social policies affecting women that began in 1968 was:

> The aim of a long-term programme for women must be that every individual, irrespective of sex, shall have the same practical opportunities, not only for education and employment but also in principle the same responsibility for his or her own mainte-nance as well as a shared responsibility for the up-bringing of children and the upkeep of the home. (Gladh and Gustafsson, 1981)

Swedish ministers thus spoke the language of equal opportunity, yet their policy approach differed profoundly from that in both the

United States and Britain, where governments also expressed a commitment to achieving equal opportunity during the late 1960s and early 1970s.

In part, the Swedish approach was due to a different conception of equality. British and US legislation sought to secure women's equality with men in the public world of employment. Under equal opportunity legislation, if a woman received less pay than an equivalently employed man, or if she suffered discrimination in hiring, promotion, or layoffs, she could seek legal redress (Meehan, 1985). The legislation was premised on the idea of securing formal equality between women and men at work. In contrast, Sweden had a considerably stronger and better institutionalised tradition (dating back to the policies framed by the Myrdals) for also recognising women's needs as mothers. This, together with the active labour market policy at the core of the Swedish welfare system, enabled women to synchronise family and labour market work. Sweden did not pass equal opportunity legislation on US and British lines until 1980 (as a result of an initiative by the parties the Swedish term 'bourgeois') but the legislation lacks adequate enforcement provisions and has been little used (Dahlberg, 1982). Rather, the Swedish equal opportunities strategy has involved, first, defining all adults as workers and providing incentives to ensure that women enter the labour market and, second, providing compensation to women and men for lost earnings with generous recognition of the needs of parents. To this extent the Swedish system moved beyond the severely formal equality on men's terms offered in Britain and the United States to encompass women's needs as mothers.

However, the aim of the strategy as stated in 1968 was to do more than accommodate women's 'two roles'. It also was intended to provide a substantive equality: women and men were now able to share the work of the public and the private sphere equally. However, this has not yet occurred. The opportunity strategy was couched in gender-neutral language (Eduards, 1991), yet the outcome of the reforms has been to exaggerate gender divisions. Because the legal changes (in tax, daycare provision, and parental insurance) focused entirely on the supply side, there was no reduction in the degree of sexual segregation in the workplace; indeed, Sweden has one of the most sexually segregated labour markets in the Western world (Jonung, 1984). The vast majority of women work in the public sector, and many are paid for the kind of work they would formerly have done at home. Between 1965 and 1984 the number of public sector jobs expanded from 700,000 to 1.4 million, and 75 per cent of these were taken by women. This is not to say, as one leading liberal Swedish economist has argued, that all caring work has (in his view, unfortunately) entered the public sector (Lindbeck, 1986). The figures still show women devoting 60 per cent of their time to non-market work. According to data from the National Board for Consumer Policies, the full-time Swedish working mother works an average of 73 hours, of which 34 are unpaid; the Swedish father works 65 hours of which 18 are unpaid (Persson, 1988).

Because unpaid work is still performed disproportionately by women in Sweden, women tend to become part-time workers with the birth of a first child (Bernhardt, 1987). However, a large proportion of part-timers work full-time in jobs with good benefits but exercise their right to reduce their hours from eight to six. Together with the occupational segregation that restricts women's access to high-status, high-paying jobs, this means that in 1989 women's earnings for full-time work averaged only 77 per cent of men's. The solidaristic wage policy of the Swedish trade union movement has proved successful in securing 90 per cent of the male wage for women in manufacturing jobs, but very few women are so employed. Solidaristic wage bargaining made formal legislation on equal pay in large measure unnecessary but has in and of itself failed to secure equal earnings. Thus, Swedish women are able to combine paid and unpaid work more easily than women in Britain or the United States, but they remain poorer than men both in regard to money and time (Land, 1991; Hernes, 1987a).

Arguably, the Swedish strategy was not gender-neutral at all. Rather, it may be seen as an updated version of Myrdal's vision of women combining motherhood and paid employment. It has, however, profoundly changed the balance between these, in part as a result of the Swedish interpretation of feminist demands for equality but also as a result of the government's desire to see a change in the way *women* used their time. During the 1960s, Sweden experienced severe labour market shortages and when the government decided in 1966 not to encourage large-scale immigration (as Britain, for example, did), it became imperative to increase married women's labour market participation (Eduards *et al.*, 1985; Hammar, 1985). The first steps in the Swedish equal opportunity strategy – separate taxation and increased day care provision – were supply-side measures, designed to pull women into the labour market. But women took the kind of low-paid, low-status service sector jobs that were held in many other countries by married women and people of colour. The second major step in the strategy – parental insurance – was directed at both women and men, but although women were 'forced' to be workers by dint of both the effects of the tax changes and by the changed basis of women's entitlement to benefits, men were not 'forced' to be carers. Even the promise of 90 per cent replacement of income failed to change men's behaviour significantly.

Further evidence that the measure, despite its gender-neutral language, was designed primarily with women in mind comes, first, from the minimal, flat-rate benefit for those not in employment; second, from the fact that men were not (until 1986) eligible for parental leave unless their partners were in paid work; and, third, from the way in which government policy-makers voiced their anxiety about the policy's potentially detrimental effect on *women's* labour market behaviour. By 1980, the extension of parental leave had reached the point beyond which it would pull women out of, rather than push them into, the labour market. The scheme therefore remained untouched during the 1980s. Recent promises to extend it further may well be linked to the government's failure to achieve a sufficient expansion of day care places and therefore to its need once more to shift the balance between women's paid and unpaid work.

If the main aim of the Swedish policies was to allow women to take a greater share in the work of the public sphere, the *nature* of the work was not a matter of concern. In 1972, Olof Palme, the Social Democrat prime minister, contemplated the mass entry of women into primarily public sector service jobs with equanimity (Hirdman, 1987). Although this was achieved via the collectivisation of child care and the establishment of parental leaves, men's lives in both the public sphere of work and the private sphere of the family remained virtually untouched. Indeed, it is arguable that the parental insurance scheme, which despite its gender-neutral language was aimed at women, served to reinforce job segregation. Elisabeth Näsman has shown that many of the (relatively few) women working in male-dominated jobs actively search for work in female-dominated occupations, where their postpartum behaviour – in terms of claiming parental leave and opting to reduce their working hours to six per day – will not be at variance with other workers. It is significant that the demand for a six-hour day for *all* women and men raised by the Social Democratic Women's League in the early 1970s as part of an equal opportunity package and again during the Social Democratic party conference of 1987, was not met. This measure alone could force a substantial change in the way men allocate their time and arguably is a necessary prerequisite for changing the sexual segregation of paid work. However, the aim of Swedish policies has been, like the British and American, to permit the reorganisation of women's lives rather than to promote substantive equality between women and men. As in other countries, Swedish women are thus doing much more work in the public sphere, and the vast majority of men are not doing more work in the private sphere. The extent to which men change the balance between unpaid and paid work in their lives is determined by private negotiation within the household and the outcome depends on the women's bargaining power. Thus, as Näsman has shown, it is in families where the woman has higher education (a proxy for high-status, high-paid work) that the man is most likely to take parental leave (Näsman, 1990).

Nevertheless, the Swedish equal opportunity strategy allows women to make a claim on the basis of difference, as well as a large measure of equal treatment as workers. This distinguishes the Swedish strategy from East European models of female citizenship, which were also based on equal paid worker status with men. Since the early 1970s, Swedish women have first had to become workers to qualify for parental leave at a favourable benefit level, but, paradoxically, having taken a job, they could then exert a claim as mothers and stay at home for what has proved to be a steadily lengthening period. An increasing number of women are opting to have a second child within two-and-a-half years of the first, thus maximising their time off. Thus, Swedish social policies have succeeded in changing women's behaviour, but women have, to some extent, also managed to manipulate the policies to their advantage.

Bibliography to Section I

Abbott, E. and Bompas, K. (1943) 'The Woman Citizen and Social Security', in J. Clarke, A. Cochrane and C. Smart (eds) (1987) *Ideologies of Welfare*, London: Hutchinson.

Abukhanfusa, K. (1987) *Piskan oh Moroten*, Stockholm: Carlssons, pp. 185–95.

Amos, V. and Parmar, P. (1984) 'Challenging Imperial Feminism', *Feminist Review*, 17.

Anderson, D. (1992) (ed.) *The Loss of Virtue: Moral Confusion and Social Disorder in Britain and America*, London: Social Affairs Unit.

Andrews, G. (ed.) (1991) *Citizenship*, London: Lawrence & Wishart.

Balbo, L. (1987) 'Family, Women and the State: Notes Towards a Typology of Family Roles and Public Intervention', in C. S. Maier (ed.) *Changing Boundaries of the Political: Essays on Evolving Balance between the State and Society, Public and Private in Europe*, Cambridge: Cambridge University Press, pp. 201–19.

Baldwin, P. (1990) *The Politics of Social Solidarity: Class Bases of the European Welfare State, 1875–1975*, Cambridge: Cambridge University Press.

Bernhardt, E. M. (1987) 'The Choice of Part-time Work among Swedish One-child Mothers', Stockholm Research Reports in Demography, no. 40, Stockholm: Stockholm University.

Bock, G. and James, S. (eds) (1992) *Beyond Equality and Difference: Citizenship, Feminist Politics and Female Subjectivity*, London: Routledge.

Borchorst, A. and Siim, B. (1987) 'Women and the Advanced Welfare State: A New Kind of Patriarchal Power?', in A. Showstack Sassoon (ed.) *Women and the State*, London: Hutchinson.

Bradshaw, J. and Millar, J. (1991) *Lone Parent Families in the UK*, London: DSS/HMSO.

Brannen, J. and Moss, P. (1991) *Managing Mothers: Dual Earner Households after Maternity Leave*, London: Unwin Hyman.

Brannen, J. and Wilson, G. (eds) (1987) *Give and Take in Families*, London: Allen & Unwin.

Brown, J. (1989) *Why don't they go out to work? Mothers on benefit*, Social Security Advisory Committee Research Paper 2, London: HMSO.

Bruegel, I. (1989) 'Sex and Race in the Labour Market', *Feminist Review*, 32.

Campling, J. (1981) *Images of Ourselves*, London: Routledge & Kegan Paul.

Carby, H. (1982) 'White Women Listen! Black Feminism and the Boundaries of Sisterhood', in the Centre for Contemporary Cultural Studies, *The Empire Strikes Back*, London: Hutchinson.

Cass, B. (1990) 'Gender and Citizenship. Women's Claims to Citizenship in the 1990s', paper given at Social Policy Association Conference, Bath.

Charles, E. (1934) *The Twilight of Parenthood*, London: Watts.

Cohen, B. (1988) *Caring for Children*, London: EEC.

Cohen, R. (1991) *Just about Surviving: Life on Income Support*, London: Family Service Unit.

Cohen, R., Coxall, J., Craig, G. and Sadiq-Sangster, A. (1992) *Hardship Britain*, London: Child Poverty Action Group.

Commission on Social Justice (1994) *Social Justice: Strategies for National Renewal*, London: Vintage.

Cook, J. and Watt, S. (1987) 'Racism, Women and Poverty', in C. Glendinning and J. Millar (eds) *Women and Poverty in Britain*, Brighton: Wheatsheaf.

Cragg, A. and Dawson, T. (1982) *Unemployed Women: A Case Study of Attitudes and Experiences*, London: Department of Employment.

Craig, G. and Glendinning, C. (1990) *The Impact of Social Security Changes*, Ilford: Barnardos.

Dahlberg, A. (1982) 'The Equality Act', Arbetslivscentrum Working Papers, F11, Stockholm.

Davies, B. and Ward, S. (1992) *Women and Personal Pensions*, London: EOC/HMSO.

Dennis, N. and Erdos, G. (1992) *Families without Fatherhood*, London: IEA Health and Welfare Unit.

Eduards, M. *et al.* (1985) 'Equality How Equal?', in E. Haavio-Mannila *et al.* (eds) *Unfinished Democracy: Women in Nordic Politics*, Oxford: Pergamon.

Eduards, M. L. (1991) 'Towards a Third Way: Women's Politics and Welfare Policies in Sweden', *Social Research*, 58, Fall, pp. 677–705.

Esping-Andersen, G. (1987) 'The Comparison of Policy Regimes: An Introduction', in M. Rein, G. Esping-Andersen and L. Rainwater, *Stagnation and Renewal in Social Policy: The Rise and Fall of Policy Regimes*, New York: M. E. Sharpe.

Esping-Andersen, G. (1990) *The Three Worlds of Welfare Capitalism*, Cambridge: Polity Press.

Evans, P. B., Ruescheneyer, D. and Skocpol, T. (eds) (1985) *Bringing the State Back In*, Cambridge: Cambridge University Press.

Fraser, N. (1990) *Rethinking the Public Sphere: A Contribution to the Critique of Actually Existing Democracy*, World Sociological Conference, Madrid.

Gilligan, C. (1982) *In a Different Voice: Psychological Theory and Women's Development*, Cambridge, Mass.: Harvard University Press.

Gladh, L. and Gustafsson, S. (1981) 'Labour Market Policy Related to Women and Employment in Sweden', Arbetslivscentrum Working Papers, F8, Stockholm.

Glendinning, C. and Millar, J. (1987) (eds) *Women and Poverty in Britain*, Brighton: Wheatsheaf.

Glendinning, C. and Millar, J. (1991) 'Poverty: The Forgotten English-woman – Reconstructing Research and Policy on Poverty', in M. Maclean and D. Groves (eds) *Women's Issues in Social Policy*, London: Routledge.

Glendinning, C. and Millar, J. (1992) *Women and Poverty in Britain: the 1990s*, Hemel Hempstead: Harvester Wheatsheaf.

Goodin, R. E. (1985) 'Self Reliance v. the Welfare State', *Journal of Social Policy*, 14(1), pp. 25–47.

Graham, H. (1983) 'Caring: A Labour of Love', in J. Finch and D. Groves (eds) *A Labour of Love: Women, Work and Caring*, London: Routledge & Kegan Paul.

Graham, H. (1987) 'Being Poor: Perceptions of Coping Strategies of Lone Mothers', in C. Glendinning and J. Millar (eds) *Women and Poverty in Britain, the 1990s*, Hemel Hempstead: Harvester Wheatsheaf.

Groves, D. (1991) 'Women and Financial Provision for Old Age', in M. Maclean and D. Groves (eds) *Women's Issues in Social Policy*, London: Routledge.

Gustafsson, S. (1983) 'Equal Opportunity Policies in Sweden', Arbetslivs-centrum Working Papers, F18, Stockholm.

Gustafsson, S. and Stafford, F. (1988) 'Daycare Subsidies and Labour Supply in Sweden', Centre for Economic Policy Research Discussion Paper, no. 279, London.

Hall, S. and Held, D. (1989) 'Left and Rights', *Marxism Today*, June.

Hammar, T. (1985) *European Immigration Policy*, Cambridge: Cambridge University Press.

Heater, D. (1990) *Citizenship: The Civil Ideal in World History, Politics and Education*, London: Longman.

Held, D. (1991) 'Between State and Civil Society: Citizenship', in G. Andrews, (ed) *Citizenship*, London: Lawrence & Wishart.

Hernes, H. (1987a) *Welfare State and Woman Power: Essays in State Feminism*, Oslo: Norwegian University Press.

Hernes, H. (1987b) 'Women and the Welfare State: The Transition from Private to Public Dependence', in A. Showstack Sassoon (ed.) *Women and the State*, London: Hutchinson.

Hirdman, Y. (1987) 'The Swedish Welfare State and the Gender System: A Theoretical and Empirical Sketch', The Study of Power and Democracy in Sweden, English Series, Report no. 7, Stockholm.

Hirdman, Y. (1989) *Atta Lägga Livet till Rätta: Studier i Svensk Folkem-spolitic*, Stockholm: Carlssons.

Huby, M. and Dix, G. (1992) *Evaluating the Social Fund*, London: DSS/HMSO.

Ignatieff, M. (1989) 'Citizenship and Moral Narcissism', *Political Quarterly*, 60 (1), pp. 63–74.

Jones, K. B. (1988) 'Towards the Revision of Politics', in K. B. Jones and A. G. Jonsdottir (eds) *The Political Interests of Gender*, London: Sage.

Jonung, C. (1984) 'Patterns of Occupational Segregation in the Labour Market', in G. Schmid and R. Weitzel (eds) *Sex Discrimination and Equal Opportunities*, London: Gower.

Joshi, H. (1991) 'Sex and Motherhood as Handicaps in the Labour Market', in M. Maclean and D. Groves (eds) *Women's Issues in Social Policy*, London: Routledge.

Kessler-Harris, A. (1989) 'Gender Ideology in Historical Reconstruction: A Case Study from the 1930s', *Gender and History*, 1, Spring, pp. 31–44.

Key, E. (1912) *The Woman Movement*, New York: G. P. Putnam's Sons.

Key, E. (1914) *The Renaissance of Motherhood*, New York: G. P. Putnam's Sons.

Korpi, W. (1978) *The Working Class in Welfare Capitalism: Work, Unions and Politics in Sweden*, London: Routledge & Kegan Paul.

Koven, S. and Michel, S. (1990) 'Womanly Duties: Maternalist Politics and the Emergence of Welfare States in France, Germany, Great Britain and the United States, 1880–1920', *American Historical Review*, 95, Autumn, pp. 1076–108.

Land, H. (1975) 'The Myth of the Male Breadwinner', *New Society*, 9, October.

Land, H. (1976) 'Women: Supporters or Supported?', in D. L. Barker and S. Allen (eds) *Sexual Divisions and Society: Process and Change*, London: Tavistock.

Land, H. (1978) 'Who Cares for the Family?', *Journal of Social Policy*, 7(3).

Land, H. (1980) 'The Family Wage', *Feminist Review*, 6.

Land, H. (1988) 'Women, Money and Independence', *Poverty*, 70 (Child Poverty Action Group).

Land, H. (1991) 'Time to Care', in M. MacLean and D. Groves (eds) *Women's Issues in Social Policy*, London: Routledge.

Langan, M. and Ostner, I. (1991) 'Gender and Welfare', in G. Room (ed.) *Towards a European Welfare State*, Bristol: School of Advanced Urban Studies.

Larabee, M. J. (1993) (ed.) *An Ethic of Care: Feminist and Interdisciplinary Perspectives*, New York: Routledge.

Leira, A. (1989) *Models of Motherhood*, Oslo: Institutt for Samfunns Forskning.

Lewis, J. (1990) 'Women's Two Roles: Myrdal, Klein and Post-war Feminism', in H. Smith (ed.) *British Feminism in the Twentieth Century*, Cheltenham: Edward Elgar.

Lewis, J. (1991) *Women and Social Action in Victorian and Edwardian England*, Stanford: Stanford University Press.

Lewis, J. (1992) 'Gender and the Development of Welfare Regimes', *Journal of European Social Policy*, 2(3), pp. 159–73.

Lindbeck, A. (1986) 'Limits to the Welfare State', *Challenge*, 28, January/February, pp. 31–44.

Lister, R. (1990a) *The Exclusive Society: Citizenship and the Poor*, London: Child Poverty Action Group.

Lister, R. (1990b) 'Women, Economic Dependency and Citizenship', *Journal of Social Policy*, 19(4), pp. 445–67.

Lister, R. (1992) *Women's Economic Dependency and Social Security*, Manchester: Equal Opportunities Commission.

Lister, R. (1994) 'The Child Support Act: Shifting Family Financial Obligations in the United Kingdom', *Social Politics*, 1(2).

Lister, R. (1995) 'Dilemmas in Engendering Citizenship', *Economy and Society*, 24(1), pp. 1–40.

Lonsdale, S. (1990) *Women and Disability*, London: Macmillan.

Lovenduski, J. and Randall, V. (1993) *Contemporary Feminist Politics: Women and Power in Britain*, Oxford: Oxford University Press.

McLaughlin, E. (1991) *Social Security and Community Care: The Case of the Invalid Care Allowance*, London: DSS/HMSO.

Maclean, M. and Groves, D. (eds) (1991) *Women's Issues in Social Policy*, London: Routledge.

Major, J. (1991) Foreword to *The Citizen's Charter*, London: HMSO.

Marmor, T. R. (1990) *America's Misunderstood Welfare State*, New York: Basic Books.

Marquand, D. (1989) 'Subversive Language of Citizenship', *The Guardian*, 2 January.

Marquand, D. (1991) 'Deaf to duty's call' *New Statesman and Society*, 25 January

Marshall, T. H. (1952) *Citizenship and Social Class*, Cambridge: Cambridge University Press.

Mead, L. (1986) *Beyond Entitlement: The Social Obligations of Citizenship*, New York: Free Press.

Meehan, E. (1985) *Women's Rights at Work: Campaigns and Policies in Britain and the United States*, London: Macmillan.

Millar, J. (1989) 'Social Security, Equality and Women in the UK', *Policy and Politics*, 17(4), pp. 311–20.

Millar, J. (1990) 'The Socio-economic Situation of Single Women in Europe', in M. O'Brien, L. Hantrais and S. Mangen (eds) *Women, Equal Opportunities and Welfare*, Birmingham: Cross-National Research Group.

Moore, J. (1988) Conservative Party Conference, 12 October.

Morgan, P, (1994) 'Double Income, No Kids: The Case for a Family Wage', in C. Quest (ed) *Liberating Women . . . From Modern Feminism*, London: IEA Health and Welfare Unit.

Morris, J. (1991) *Pride against Prejudice*, London: Women's Press.

Moss, P. (1988–9) 'The Indirect Costs of Parenthood: A Neglected Issue in Social Policy', *Critical Social Policy*, 24.

Myrdal, A. and Klein, V. (1956) *Women's Two Roles*, London: Routledge & Kegan Paul.

Myrdal, A. and Myrdal, G. (1935) *Kris i Befolkningsfrägen*, Stockholm: Albert Bonniers Forlag.

Näsman, E. (1986) 'Work and Family – a Combination Made Possible by Part-time Work and Parental Leaves?', Arbetslivscentrum Working Papers, F24, Stockholm.

Näsman, E. (1990) *Föräldraledighetslagen i tillämpning*, Stockholm: Arbetslivscentrum.

Nelson, B. (1990) 'The Origins of the Two-channel Welfare State: Workmen's Compensation and Mothers' Aid', in L. Gordon (ed.) *Women, the State and Welfare*, Madison: University of Wisconsin Press, pp. 123–51.

Novak, M. *et al.* (1987) *A Community of Self-Reliance: The New Consensus on Family and Welfare*, Milwaukee: American Enterprise Institute for Public Policy Research.

Oakley, A. (1986) 'Social Welfare and the Position of Women', Titmuss Memorial Lecture, Hebrew University of Jerusalem.

O'Connor, J. (1993) 'Gender, Class and Citizenship in the Comparative Analysis of Welfare State Regimes: Theoretical and Methodological Issues', *British Journal of Sociology*, 44(3), pp. 501–18.

Offen, K. (1988) 'Defining Feminism: A Comparative Historical Approach', *Signs*, 14, Autumn, pp. 119–57.

Olsson, S. E. (1986) 'Sweden', in P. Flora (ed.) *Growth to Limits: The Western European Welfare States since World War II*, Florence and Berlin: Walter de Gruyter, pp. 4–116.

Pahl, J. (1989) *Money and Marriage*, London: Macmillan.

Pascall, G. (1986) *Social Policy: A Feminist Analysis*, London: Tavistock.

Pateman, C. (1988a) *The Sexual Contract*, Cambridge: Polity Press.

Pateman, C. (1988b) 'The Patriarchal Welfare State', in A. Gutman (ed.) *Democracy and the Welfare State*, Princeton: Princeton University Press.

Pateman, C. (1989) *The Disorder of Women*, Cambridge: Polity Press.

Pedersen, S. (1989) 'The Failure of Feminism in the Making of the British Welfare State', *Radical History Review*, 43, Winter, pp. 86–110.

Persson, I. (1988) 'The Third Dimension – Equal Status between Swedish Women and Men.' The Study of Power and Democracy in Sweden, TS, Stockholm.

Phillips, A. (1991a) 'Citizenship and Feminist Politics', in G. Andrews (ed.) *Citizenship*, London: Lawrence & Wishart.

Phillips, A. (1991b) *Engendering Democracy*, Cambridge: Polity Press.

Piven, F. F. and Cloward, R. A., (1971) *Regulating the Poor*, New York: Pantheon Books.

Riley, D. (1981) 'The Free Mothers: Pronatalism and Women Workers in Industry at the End of the First World War in Britain', *History Workshop Journal*, 11, Spring, pp. 59–118.

Scott, J. (1988) *Gender and the Politics of History*, New York: Columbia University Press, pp. 167–77.

Shaver, S. (1991) 'Social Policy Regimes: Gender, Race and the Welfare State', Centre for Social Policy Research, University of New South Wales, Sydney, Australia.

Smith, R. (1991a) *Under the Breadline*, London: The Children's Society.

Smith, S. (ed.) (1991b) *Economic Policy and the Division of Income within the Family*, London: Institute for Fiscal Studies.

Steedman, C. (1990) *Childhood, Culture and Class in Britain: Margaret McMillan, 1860–1931*, London: Virago.

Taylor-Gooby, P. (1991) *Social Change, Social Science and Social Welfare*, Brighton: Wheatsheaf.

Thorogood, N. (1987) 'Race, Class and Gender: The Politics of House-work', in J. Brannen and G. Wilson (eds) *Give and Take in Families*, London: Allen & Unwin.

Titmuss, R. M. (1938) *Poverty and Population*, London: Macmillan.

Tronto, J. C. (1993) *Moral Boundaries: A Political Argument for an Ethic of Care*, London: Routledge.

Twine, F. (1992) 'Citizenship: Opportunities, Rights and Routes to Welfare in Old Age', *Journal of Social Policy*, 21 (2).

Ungerson, C. (1990) 'Rich Women, Poor Women? Some Notes on Labour Market Trends', paper given at HSFR Conference, Stockholm.

Vogler, C. (1989) *Labour Market Changes and Patterns of Financial Allocation within Households*, Oxford: Nuffield College.

Walker, A. (1987) 'The Poor Relation: Poverty among Old Women', in C. Glendinning and J. Millar (eds) *Women and Poverty in Britain: the 1990s*, Hemel Hempstead: Harvester Wheatsheaf.

Walsh, A. and Lister, R. (1985) *Mother's Life Line: A Survey of How Women Use and Value Child Benefit*, London: Child Poverty Action Group.

Wilensky, H. and Lebeaux, C. N. (1958) *Industrial Society and State Welfare*, New York: Russell Sage Foundation.

Williams, F. (1989) *Social Policy: A Critical Introduction*, Cambridge: Polity Press.

Williams, F. (1991) 'Somewhere Over the Rainbow: Universality and Selectivity in Social Policy', Social Policy Association Annual Conference, Nottingham, 9–11 July. Published under same title in Manning, N. and Page, R. (eds) (1992), *Social Policy Review* 4, Canterbury: Social Policy Association.

Yuval-Davis, N. (1991) 'The Citizenship Debate: Women, Ethnic Processes and the State', *Feminist Review*, 39.

II

Women and the Labour Market

Introduction

MARY KEMBER

Participation in the labour force on equal terms with men was hailed by sections of the Women's Movement in the 1970s and 1980s as the major way in which women, through financial independence, would 'liberate' themselves. Increased participation in higher education by women, equality legislation and employment initiatives (such as the Women into Science and Engineering campaign) to break down stereotypical images of what was perceived as 'men's' work and what was 'women's' work were seen as significant steps in the march towards equality of opportunity for women.

Women's participation in the labour force has substantially increased over the past 30 years. Over half of all UK women of working age were economically active in 1993, with three out of four active amongst 35 to 44 year olds (Central Statistical Office, 1994). In 1991, economic activity rates amongst UK women were the second highest in the European Community. Paid employment, at least at some stage in their life-cycle, is accepted as a normal part of most women's lives.

Yet a look at women's current position on the labour market, as outlined in the article here by Angela Dale, demonstrates the discrepancy between the ideas of equality of opportunity and the reality of continued sex segmentation in the labour market. Figures from the Equal Opportunities Commission in 1992 showed that women earned only 69 per cent of the male gross hourly earnings for manual workers and 55 per cent of the gross monthly earnings for male non-manual earnings in 1990 – with the UK second in the league of EC countries for the widest earnings differentials between men and women (*The Guardian*, 20 October 1992). Nearly one out of two women in employment works part time (Central Statistical

Office, 1994) and women tend to be concentrated in certain sectors of employment such as retailing, the hotel and catering industries health, financial services and education. The Winter 1992–3 Labour Force Survey showed that 83 per cent of women in employment were employed in the service sector compared with 56 per cent of men (*Employment Gazette*, November 1993). While some professions which traditionally barred women – such as banking, medicine and dentistry – do now have almost equal entry (Crompton and Sanderson, 1986), the labour market remains highly sex-differentiated. Lonsdale (1992) suggests that the consequences of this occupational segregation are that differing wage structures have grown up for men and women, that the frequently very different nature of work done by men and women has been an excuse for keeping women's jobs from equal pay legislation, and that men and women typically have differing expectations about their own jobs – leading to a sometimes surprising acceptance by women of their own low pay and low prospects (Hakim, 1991). At the same time, the inability of women to climb to the top of career ladders because of the so-called 'glass ceiling' (the point at which, in an organisation, women do not seem to be able to rise any further) has been well documented. In 1991, only 4 per cent of middle and senior management in the UK were women, with the figure falling to 1 or 2 per cent in top management (*The Guardian*, 22 October 1991). Women are segregated both horizontally and vertically from male workers.

While women have undoubtedly increased their participation in the labour force in recent years, the sexual division of labour ensures that women's relationship to paid labour is different from that of men's. Women's participation in domestic labour affects and reinforces their role in paid employment (Dale, 1987). While jobs women typically carry out in the paid labour market tend to replicate the work they do at home – such as catering, cleaning, caring, hairdressing (Lonsdale, 1992) – their lack of power in the labour market is carried with them into the household and thence back into the labour market, setting up a cycle of powerlessness which is hard to break (Dale, 1987). Women's domestic role – above all as mothers – affects their position in the labour market: women's economic activity and whether they work full or part time is largely determined by their age and the age of their youngest dependent child. In 1992–3, only half of women of working age with a youngest child between the ages of 0 and 4 were economically active compared to 72 per cent and 80 per cent for women with a youngest child 5–10 years and 11–15 years, respectively (Labour Force Survey: *Employment Gazette*, November 1993). That women enter a pattern of downward occupational mobility on returning to work after childbirth has been discussed by Martin and Roberts (1984), Dale (1987), Dex (1987). Even though increasing numbers of women are returning to work straight after the period of their maternity leave, it does not appear to be closing the gap in occupational status between men and women – and thus the disparity in their pay. Lack of child care provision inevitably means that for most women the solution is to return to work on a part-time basis. The financial costs to women of breaks in employment to bring up children and the likely return to part-time work are high: Heather Joshi (1991) estimates around a half of potential earnings are lost after bearing the first of two children – through lost seniority, lost experience and lost training opportunities. On top of lost future earnings potential, women are likely to lose pension rights as well.

Part-time work is a major feature of women's employment and is responsible not only for much occupational segregation but also for the perpetuation of many of the inequities of the labour market in terms of rates of pay and employment conditions. Most of the increase in women's employment has been in part-time work: between 1951 and 1989, the number of women working part-time increased from 3/4 million to nearly 5 million (Lonsdale, 1992). Of women in employment in winter 1992/3, 43 per cent worked part-time (Labour Force Survey: *Employment Gazette*, November 1993). That women as part-time workers are seriously disadvantaged has been well discussed (Beechey and Perkins, 1987; Grant, 1991). Yet employers claim that women are attracted to jobs which offer them 'flexibility' – a word which, Ursula Huws argues, 'like so many others...has been hijacked from the libertarian left and given a new meaning by the right' (Huws, 1989). But while a particular *form* of flexibility – that allows women to meet children from school, take time off during school holidays etc. – may well be what some women want from their paid employment, that determined by the employer 'which requires varying amounts of work at unpredictable times and brings fluctuating rewards, far from increasing choice for an individual worker, actually *decreases* it' (Huws, Hurstfield and Holtmaat, 1989). Linda Grant (1991) reports one shop steward in a drinks manufacturing company as saying: 'You've hit the magic word management love to use –

flexibility. Flexibility, nowadays, is a dirty word to most of the workforce.' So while job opportunities have increased for women, so has the primacy of women's domestic role tacitly been reinforced over their role as paid worker. As, increasingly, households move away from their traditional formation, large numbers of women who are sole or main breadwinners are inevitably left in poverty by this situation.

Tim Walsh, in the article reproduced here, argues that current employment protection serves a shrinking section of the working population – and protects few of those who are in the most vulnerable position on the labour force. At the same time, the social security system – based on the model of male as breadwinner/ female as primary carer – is increasingly inadequate to serve the needs of a population where large numbers of people are, for a variety of reasons, able to participate in the labour force only on a part-time basis, while being the sole breadwinner in the household (many of whom are women caring for sick or elderly relatives, or lone mothers). The reduction of weekly hours from 24 to 16 for entitlement to Family Credit was a concession to the poverty suffered by many people working part-time – but many more fall far short of this. As Lewis and Piachaud (1992) say, 'the assumption that married women should be financially dependent on their husbands has meant state policy has been used further to restrict their access to benefits' – thus reinforcing the male as breadwinner and marginalising women as earners.

Part-time work, then, advocated on the one hand by government as a way of reducing women's poverty and taking them off benefits – but at the same time not challenging their primary domestic role – only serves to increase sexual segregation on the labour market and to perpetuate women's poverty. Yet Heather Joshi (1991) demonstrates that motherhood is not necessarily the primary factor in women's low pay and prospects. In a study in the 1970s, childless women with comparable 'human capital' to men were shown to earn substantially less than men. Gender is still reason in itself, it would seem, for women's unequal place on the labour market.

Discussion of the labour market in the UK cannot take place now without consideration of the influence of the European Union – however much national governments want to limit the influence of Brussels. As the 1980s drew to a close and 1992, the date of implementation of the European Single Market came closer, there was much speculation in Europe as to what effect the Single Market might have upon women's employment. It seemed that there were some grounds for optimism. With trade barriers brought down and restrictions lifted, it was thought that job opportunities would increase, and women, as well as men, would be able to take advantage of new opportunities. Demographic changes across much of the Community meant that fewer young women would be available to enter the job market in the 1990s and the shortfall would be made up by employers taking on greater numbers of older women returning to the labour force. The majority of new jobs were part-time and would allow women the opportunity to combine domestic responsibilities with paid labour, and expansion in the service sector meant that opportunities were increasing in areas of work where women had traditionally predominated (jobs in the services accounted for 60 per cent of total employment in the Community in 1991). Trends in the late 1980s in the European labour market certainly appeared to benefit women.

Yet there tends to be pessimism amongst women about the real advantages of the Single Market. Across Europe, as in the UK, women start from a worse economic base than men: they are paid less, are more likely to be unemployed, are concentrated in a few particular sectors and are less likely to be economically active. Predicted labour market benefits to women have already been shown to be more limited than at first anticipated. Recent figures (*Bulletin on Women and Employment in the EC*, No. 3, 1993) show how, despite the advances made by some younger and more educated women to enter higher level and traditionally male job categories, lower-skilled service work has become even more female dominated. As the manufacturing sector has declined, so the service sector has grown – and this is mainly where the new jobs are to be found. It seems that occupational segregation by gender is a persistent feature of all European labour markets.

Angela Glasner (1992) points out how, despite different cultures and traditions, European women are linked by disadvantage. Yet, as Gill Whitting says, European women do not form a homogeneous group whether within the same locality or across the regions of the Community. EU policy does not take into account the very *different* needs of European women. Jane Goldsmith (1990) gives an account of the ways in which black and ethnic minority women may be particularly disadvantaged by the effects of the Single Market: that these women already make up a large proportion of the women carrying out homework, unskilled factory work and piecework suggests their difficulties will be exacerbated by a market increasingly looking for this type of worker without increasing their protection. Likewise, the experience of rural women in the southern Member States is very different from that of women in urban areas. And within each region and group of women there are the more vulnerable – particularly lone mothers (Jo Roll, 1992) and older women. Each of these groups needs particular attention – the Internal Market emphasis on 'flexibility' is likely to make them more vulnerable and insecure rather than less. One scenario has been that for well-trained, mobile women in the Community, opportunities will open up in new and advantageous ways giving them access to other rights and benefits: yet for the *majority* of women there will be little benefit, and even increased *dis*advantage. Thus it is possible that European economic union will increase divisions amongst women rather than decreasing economic differences between *men* and women.

What happens now and how quickly depends to a large extent on attitudes of individual governments. John Major's Conservative government adopted the attitude that the EU is about opening up markets and increasing competitiveness, with the accompanying attitude that protecting the worker increases expense for the employer and thus lessens their competitiveness. Meanwhile, the Labour Party has argued that the development of the EU cannot be left simply to market forces if equality is to be a reality: the Single Market *must* be accompanied by development of the Social Chapter. The prevailing political climate is likely to be highly significant through the 1990s in terms of the extent to which we get a 'social' Europe as well as an 'economic' one.

Women in the Labour Market: Policy and Perspective

ANGELA DALE

Increased levels of female labour market participation

The 1951 Census recorded women's labour market participation at about 42 per cent (Joshi, 1988) and women formed over one-third of the British labour force. A high proportion of women left the labour market either at marriage or family formation, only returning to paid work after a number of years absence, if at all. It was these women who represented the pool of labour which the earlier mentioned studies had identified.

Women's labour market participation has increased dramatically since the 1950s, reaching 70 per cent in 1987 (Table 1). Despite the initial reluctance of employers, the post-war increase in female labour has been almost exclusively through women with dependent children returning to part-time jobs (Joshi, 1988) (Table 2). Only since 1985 have women's full-time employment rates risen to the levels recorded in the 1950s.

An examination of the occupational distribution of male and female full-timers and female part-timers (Table 3) shows clearly the way in which part-time jobs are concentrated at the bottom end of the occupational spectrum. As such, women's part-time work has an occupational distribution which is distinct from both that of women and men working full-time. While these data relate to 1981, they none the less still represent a fairly accurate picture of the occupational distribution of these three groups today. Although large numbers of part-time jobs were created by employers, they have been highly segregated, particularly by gender. There are a

From Angela Dale, 'Women in the Labour Market: Policy and Perspective', *Social Policy Review*, 1990–1, pp. 207–20.

Table 1   *Economic activity rates, women under 60, Great Britain (percentages)*

Year	Full-time	Part-time	Economically active
1901	–	–	34
1931	–	–	38
1951	37	5	42
1961	35	15	50
1971	33	22	56
1973	34	23	60
1975	33	26	62
1979	34	26	64
1981	33	25	64
1983	31	25	62
1985	33	27	66
1986	35	28	69
1987	36	28	70

Sources: Figures for 1901, 1931, 1951, 1961 from Joshi (1988) based on the Census of Population. Figures for 1971–87 from the General Household Survey published reports; self-definitions of full and part-time are used. For years 1931 and 1973–87 the lower age limit is 16. For years 1951–71 the lower age limit is 15.

Table 2   *Economic activity rates of women aged 16–59 (percentages)*

	1971	1975	1979	1983	1985	1987
No dependent children						
Full-time	49	52	51	46	47	50
Part-time	18	17	18	18	21	22
Dependent children						
Full-time	15	16	16	14	17	18
Part-time	26	35	36	32	35	37
Dependent child less than 5 yrs						
Full-time	7	6	6	5	8	11
Part-time	18	22	22	18	22	24

Source: General Household Survey published tables (based on Joshi, 1988).

number of reasons for this. Much of the post-war growth in the economy was in the service sector – particularly in education, health, financial services, and hotel, catering and distribution. These were all areas where women were already highly concentrated and thus generated an increased demand for 'female' jobs

(Oppenheimer, 1970; Hakim, 1979). These jobs tend also to be locally available and therefore fit in with the domestic constraints of women with young children. However, they are also of low status, highly segregated by sex and with low rates of pay.

Table 3 *The occupational distribution of men and women working full-and part-time (percentages)*

	Men (1)	Women FT (2)	Women PT (3)
Professional – barristers, solicitors, accountants, university teachers, doctors, dentists, pharmacists	6	1	0
Teachers – all except university	3	7	2
Nurses – SRN, SEN, auxilliaries, medical technicians paramedicals and social workers	1	8	8
Intermediate – civil servants (EO to Senior Principal) computer programmer, systems analyst, librarian, personnel officer, manager, journalist	19	8	2
Clerical – typists, secretaries, clerks, receptionists, non-retail cashiers, telephonists	7	39	19
Shop workers – sales assistants, reps, petrol pump attendants, check-out operators, cashiers	4	7	16
Skilled manual – hairdressing, cook, baker, weaver, tailor, police officer (RG IIIM)	39	10	6
Semi-skilled factory – assemblers, packers, graders, sorters, inspectors, machine operators, storekeepers	9	11	6
Child care and domestic – school meals supervisors, canteen assistants, waitresses, care attendants	1	5	20
Other semi-skilled – agricultural workers, shelf-fillers, bus conductors, postal workers	6	3	4
Unskilled manual – cleaners, kitchen hands	5	2	16
All working	100 (51112)	100 (20216)	100 (14352)

The occupational classification is that of the Women and Employment Survey.
Part-time work is based upon self-definition.
Data refers to employees only.

Source: Dale (1987).

The effect of part-time work is not simply restricted to earnings ability but also affects employment protection rights and eligibility for an occupational pension. Analysis of the 1984 Labour Force Survey (LFS) showed that 46 per cent of women who were in 'permanent' part-time jobs did not fall within most employment protection legislation, either because of the short hours they worked or the length of time they had been with their employer (Dale and Bamford, 1988); also, only 15 per cent of part-timers were contributing to occupational pension schemes (Dale, 1991). Additionally, of course, many part-time jobs are established on a temporary or casual basis. Even those part-time jobs which are in higher level occupations, e.g. teaching, have typically not been seen as career posts and have not been open to promotion.

It is therefore apparent that, while the number of women in paid work has increased greatly over recent decades, this has done little to reduce gender-based inequalities within the labour market. To the extent that part-time work has been constructed as low level and low paid, the expansion of part-time working amongst women must be a major explanatory factor in gender inequalities within the labour market.

Continuity of labour force participation and downward occupational mobility

Research carried out during the late 1970s and 1980s has demonstrated that, on their first return to work following child-bearing, many women take part-time jobs at a lower level than the job they had held before childbirth. Work history data from the Women and Employment Survey (Martin and Roberts, 1984; Dex, 1987) clearly show how movement into part-time employment following child-bearing is associated with downward occupational mobility. Such jobs, of course, conform to employers' perceptions, discussed earlier, of the kind of work suitable for married women with children.

This downward mobility is also responsible for considerable occupational inequality between men and women, as well as representing a considerable skill wastage. While no comparable data are yet available for men, cross-sectional comparisons suggest that at the stage in the life-course when women are most constrained by domestic and child care responsibilities, men are consolidating and improving their occupational position, typically by gaining professional qualifications and by moving into managerial and supervisory positions (Dale, 1987). Thus, in aggregate, men and women show a widening in occupational status over the life-course with married men moving up into managerial positions while married women move down into part-time personal service sector jobs.

Work in both Britain (Joshi, 1988) and the USA (Corcoran *et al.*, 1983) shows that a break from employment followed by part-time working leads to a fall in income that is not recovered in later life, even if full-time work is taken. This must clearly be one factor which explains why the observed pay differential between men and women is still so high.

Greater continuity of employment over the life-cycle may be expected to help women in retaining their occupations and thereby avoiding downward mobility associated with family formation. The Women and Employment Survey showed that successive cohorts of women are returning to paid work more quickly after child-bearing. Also, the proportion of women returning to work within six months of their first birth has increased from 9 per cent for women with a first birth between 1945–9 to 17 per cent for those with a first birth between 1975–9 (Martin and Roberts, 1984). Although this may suggest that women are increasingly taking advantage of the statutory provision for six months maternity leave, the Women and Employment Survey showed no clear evidence of an increase in the proportion of women returning to full-time work. Rather, there has been an increase in the return of women to part-time work. If the part-time jobs available remain concentrated in the low level occupations shown in Table 3, this will exacerbate rather than reduce the disparity between men and women's employment at this stage of the life-course.

While it is tempting to make the simplistic assumption that part-time work is inevitable for women who have dependent children, this idea is quickly dispelled by international comparisons of women's employment patterns. Figure 1 shows the extent of full- and part-time working among women at five-year age intervals in France and the UK. It is evident that part-time working is much more prevalent in the UK and that it is particularly associated with the years of family formation. French women are more likely to retain a full-time job during the stage of family formation.

Figure 1 *Women's employment patterns in France and the UK*

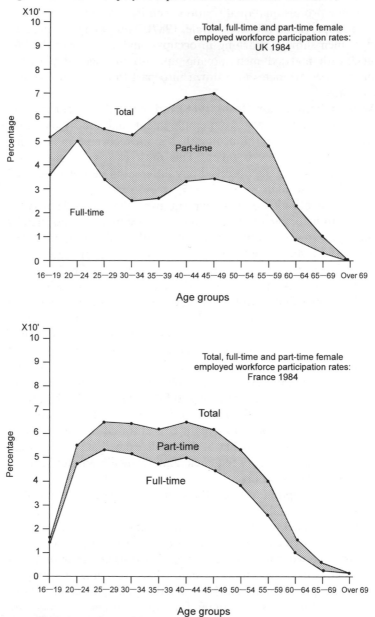

Source: Dale and Glover (1990).

However, discontinuity of employment over the life-course and part-time work is not the sole reason for the observed differences in men's and women's occupational status and earnings. As Beechey (1988) argues, it is important to look beyond the domestic sphere if one wishes to explain gender differences in employment patterns.

Legislation on equal pay and sex discrimination

Legislation introduced in the 1970s was, of course, aimed at providing greater equality of opportunity for women. The Sex Discrimination Act 1975 and the Equal Pay Act 1970, both of which came into effect in 1975, provided a mechanism whereby some of the grosser anomalies of gender discrimination in the labour market could be challenged. While the effectiveness of these Acts is often questioned, they have undoubtedly contributed to a climate of opinion in which it is less acceptable to deny jobs or opportunities to women.

None the less, considerable male-female pay differentials are found not just in Britain but in most other Western industrial countries (OECD, 1985). In Britain, data from the New Earnings Survey (Department of Employment 1988) show that while women's full-time average earnings (exclusive of overtime) as a proportion of men's rose from 63.1 per cent in 1970 to 75.5 per cent in 1977, the 1977 figure represented a peak which has never subsequently been reached. In 1988, women's full-time earnings relative to men's were 75.1 per cent – still 0.4 per cent lower than the peak in 1977. This suggests that, while the Equal Pay Act had an effect on pay differentials immediately after it came into force, little has changed since 1977. It further implies that the 1983 Equal Pay (Amendment) Regulations, which allow a woman to claim equal pay with a man in the same employment provided her work is 'of equal value' to that of that man, has had little effect so far.

To formulate effective policies to promote greater equality for women, it is important to unravel the reasons for this. Is it explained by women occupying jobs that require lower levels of skill or education, or by women being paid at lower rates than men for jobs at similar skill levels? To pose this question raises the further, fundamental question of how skill is assessed and measured. A review of the Greater London Whitley Council job evaluation scheme, quoted by the Low Pay Review (1989), concluded that, when assessing skill level, choice of factors and the weight given to them was biased towards jobs traditionally held by men. Further, the scheme omitted factors that would recognise skills typical of women's jobs in local authorities.

Most research on male-female earnings differences is unable to make comparisons by skill level. However, the Social and Economic Life Initiative (SCELI) collected data on three different measures of skill, relating to (i) human capital (ii) discretion or choice and (iii) job content. Research by Horrell, Rubery and Burchell (1989) drew comparisons between men working full-time and women working full-time and part-time. They found that 'from the specifically financial point of view, the most important issue for women, and in particular for part-timers is to achieve equal pay and equal benefits for jobs of equal skill and job content' (ibid., p. 34). This suggests that the 1983 'Equal Value' amendment may be helpful in obtaining higher wage rates for women. However, the authors go on to point out that, in practice, many of the industries and firms in which women work are highly constrained in their ability to pay higher wage levels and this, indeed, may be related to a policy of employing women.

The extent of occupational segregation by sex in Britain is considerable and strongly related to inequality of earnings. There is ample evidence that women in 'male' jobs have higher earnings than women working in 'female' jobs (Martin and Roberts, 1984). Part-time jobs, overwhelmingly filled by women, are much more highly segregated than full-time work and have considerably lower levels of pay. (In 1988 the average hourly earnings of women working part-time were £2.72 – less than 75 per cent of average earnings for women working full-time (Bryson, 1989).) The 1975 Sex Discrimination Act may be expected to help women gain entry to occupations previously denied to them. However, problems of calculating an index which can provide a reliable measure of change in occupational segregation over time (Siltanen, 1990) mean that there is no firm consensus on whether segregation is increasing or decreasing. It is likely that there has been little consistent reduction in horizontal segregation between 1961–79.

However, changes are always most likely to be evident amongst those groups newly entering or re-entering the labour market. In particular, a comparison of successive cohorts is able to identify changes that may be expected to work their way through the occupational structure over time. The proportion of women entering higher education and the professions shows a steady increase over time which may lead to a change in the occupational distribution of women in the longer term. However, it cannot be assumed that this heralds a major change in patterns of occupational segregation generally. Work by Cynthia Cockburn (1987) suggests that sex stereotyping in YTS schemes is still very much in evidence and offers no prospect of short-term change – despite the fact that one of the explicit aims of YTS was to try to overcome it. Other research (Cross, 1987) has shown that YTS schemes are also reproducing existing forms of racial stereotyping within the labour market.

The greater representation of women in higher education

In the achievement of educational qualifications there is clear evidence that the percentage of women going into higher education is still rising. Thus women are moving towards equality with men in terms of entry to higher education. In 1965–6 women formed 28 per cent of all UK full-time university undergraduate entrants whilst in 1986–7 they formed 42 per cent (Department of Education and Science, 1988). In 1987–8 they formed 49 per cent of all UK full-time polytechnic students (CSO, 1989).

In a number of professions which, in the past, had successfully excluded women, there is now near equality of entry between men and women. Crompton and Sanderson (1986) have recorded the rapidly increasing number of women entering medicine, dentistry, accountancy, banking and pharmacy. The Law Society's statistical report for 1989 reveals that women accounted for 46.6 per cent of solicitors qualifying in 1988–9, 51.9 per cent of candidates passing the solicitors' final exam in 1988 and 52.7 per cent of trainee solicitors registering between August 1988 and July 1989 (*The Guardian*, 18.10.89). This expansion is not only related to the greater number of girls going into higher education and the removal of formal barriers to the entry of women, but also to the rapid growth of these professions, making it difficult to recruit sufficient men, especially in the south-east. The Women into Science and Engineering campaign must surely reflect the dearth of young men seeking to enter these professions, rather than the altruism of employers and professional bodies.

However, it remains to be seen whether the women now entering professions in equal numbers with men will manage to retain that equality at all levels of the career structure. At the moment women are extremely underrepresented at the higher levels of most professions – for example, only about 13 per cent of hospital consultants are women (Allen, 1990).

Recent changes in the 1980s and 1990s, both in the occupational and industrial structure and in the demographic structure, are likely to influence the level of demand, not just in the professions but in all occupations and industries. This in turn will influence the extent to which government and employers are willing to promote women's entry to a wider range of occupations, and to retain women during the period of family formation.

It is important to point out that all the figures so far quoted are national statistics that do not enable the identification of any distinctive patterns by ethnic minority group. No time series data are available on employment participation by ethnic origin, and numbers in non-white groups are generally too small to allow separate analyses. However, the Department of Employment has produced figures which combine three years' data from the Labour Force Survey (with an annual sample size of about 200 000 individuals) which allow reliable employment estimates by ethnic origin (CSO, 1989). These give some indication of the extent to which national statistics submerge the distinctive employment patterns of small ethnic groups.

The labour market experience of ethnic minorities

Estimates from the 1985–7 Labour Force Surveys show the extent of variation amongst women from different ethnic origins; only 18 per cent of those from the Pakistani/Bangladeshi group were economically active compared with 55 per cent of women from the Indian ethnic group, 68 per cent in the 'white' group and 73 per cent in the West Indian/Guyanese group. It is only amongst the 'white' group that part-time working is high – it is less than 30 per cent for the other groups. Rates of unemployment are also considerably higher for the non-white women. It is therefore important to recognise that most of the data discussed here are dominated by the large white ethnic group and may not be an accurate reflection of employment processes amongst minority groups.

During recent years there have been a number of major changes that are likely to have an impact upon women's labour market position in coming years. These changes, with the policy implications or opportunities that arise from them, are discussed below.

Labour market deregulation

Partly as a response to the economic recession of the early 1980s, and partly in line with the Conservative government's preference for market forces, there has been a general reduction in labour market regulation. There has been a widespread adoption of the concept and, to a lesser extent, the practice of 'flexibility' (Atkinson, 1984; Dale and Bamford, 1988; Pollert, 1988). There have been an expansion and promotion of those forms of work which are least subject to statutory regulation – part-time working, temporary contracts and self-employment. Related to this is the move towards privatisation and casualisation – for example, cleaning, catering and waste disposal services in local authority and government must now be tendered for by private contractors. The 1986 Wages Act removed all workers under 21 years of age from the protection of the Wages Council and reduced the power of the Wages Councils for other workers. Self-employment has been heavily promoted by government, with the Enterprise Allowance Scheme providing a financial incentive to the unemployed who wish become self-employed.

There is considerable doubt over whether this opens up new opportunities for groups who might otherwise be excluded from the labour market, or whether it simply exploits the weak labour market position of these groups and thereby reinforces male–female employment differentials. None the less, it is necessary to consider whether greater opportunities for 'flexible' working have made it easier for some women to earn an independent income. Westwood and Bhachu (1988) provide case study evidence of the way in which some women from ethnic minorities have been able to use opportunities for self-employment to achieve greater independence. However, the lack of regulation in the labour market also permits the exploitation of women, particularly from ethnic minorities (Mitter, 1986). As Phizacklea (1983, p. 2) points out, it is important not to adopt a framework where 'dirty, arduous and poorly paid work is represented as a gift from the West to the women of the Third World'.

Cause for concern over the impact of increasing levels of part-time working, particularly in the personal services, also comes from the Social Change and Economic Life Initiative. Generally, there has been an increase in skill levels amongst the workforce, although this has not been the case for those working in the lower levels of the personal service sector (Gallie, 1989). Thus the increase in these jobs has also brought with it deskilling relative to other sections of the workforce. This is particularly notable within part-time employment. Horrell, Rubery and Burchell (1989), also using SCELI data, argue that the growth of part-time work is likely to increase the polarisation within the labour market, with women part-timers having less skilled jobs, less pay and lower benefits than men while women in full-time jobs have similar benefits to men but none the less have lower rates of pay. This concern is supported by data from the New Earnings Survey (Bryson, 1989) which show a growth in the pay differential between women's full-time and part-time earnings since 1977, in both manual and non-manual jobs.

There is, then, evidence that one of the changes in the employment relationship between men and women over recent decades has been an increase in the proportion of women taking low-paid jobs with few prospects of promotion. The projected increase by the Department of Employment in women's participation levels in the age group 25–34, from 64 per cent in 1987 to 70 per cent in 1995, raises the question of whether this will be achieved by even higher levels of part-time working amongst women with dependent children. However, this rather gloomy prospect is tempered by predicted changes in both the demographic and the occupational structure during the 1990s.

The impact of change in the occupational structure and the demographic structure

During the 1990s employment growth is predicted to outstrip supply (Metcalf and Leighton, 1989). Employment forecasts carried out by the Institute for Employment Research (IER) (1988) predict an increase in total employment of about 1.2 millions between 1987 and 1995. At the same time, well-documented changes in the demographic structure predict a fall of 1.3 millions in the labour force aged under 25, by the year 2000 (Department of Employment, 1989). Over the next ten years the proportion of the male workforce aged 16–24 will fall from 22 per cent to 17 per cent (Ermisch, 1990). Although the Department of Employment predicts that the civilian labour force will increase by about one million between mid-1988 and the year 2000, and 90 per cent of this increase will be amongst women, there will still remain a labour shortage. In the same way that the labour shortage of the post-war years caused employers to rethink their employment policies towards married women, the 1990s should witness a much greater recognition of the need to make better use of women's skills. Embryonic schemes to retain women during family formation and to encourage retraining by 'women returners' are already being put into operation in industries already facing shortages (e.g. banking). One of the interesting features of this predicted labour shortfall is that it is higher level occupations which are predicted to expand the fastest. Forecasts by the Institute of Employment identify a 19 per cent increase in 'professional and related' occupations between 1987 and 1995; an increase of 10 per cent in management jobs and 8 per cent in craft and skilled manual work.

Recent changes in the structuring of occupational ladders may also be making it easier for women to advance vertically within higher level occupations. Lovering (1990) has argued that there is now a greater reliance upon objective measures of ability and success, which have replaced some of the traditional bases for promotion, such as length and continuity of service, which tend to militate against women's interests. There is also evidence that employers of professional workers are now less likely to demand frequent geographical mobility as part of the career process. This, again, is particularly helpful to women. What remains to be seen, however, is the extent to which these professional women will retain their occupational positions over the period of family formation or whether they will, like so many earlier generations, find themselves experiencing downward mobility at this stage.

A further question to be answered is whether this expansion of higher level occupations will simply widen the disparities between well qualified women and those women in part-time work, or whether there will be a 'trickle down' effect of benefit to all women.

Policy implications

The expansion of professional and managerial occupations provides an important opportunity for women to gain and retain
higher level jobs. The staff shortages faced by employers should
provide the incentive to introduce a great deal more flexibility and
creativity into structuring jobs, for example by introducing part-
time work into career grades. It also provides a considerable incentive for both government and employers to provide child care for
working mothers. Whilst some progress has been made with the
recent decision to allow companies to claim tax relief on workplace
nurseries, child care provision in Britain is still markedly lower than
in most other European countries. As Metcalf and Leighton (1989)
argue, the extent to which women with dependent children decide
to work will be influenced by their net wage rate and also the cost
of child care. In a situation where women's wage rates are low and
child care costs are high, there may be little economic gain in taking
a paid job. Higher wage rates and low-cost, good quality child care
would cause proportional increases in the labour market participation rates of women.

The predicted shortage in skilled manual and craft occupations
(traditionally 'male' strongholds) may provide scope for reducing
sex segregation. While pressures of adolescent conformity seem to
be one of the factors that prevent young women from entering male
dominated occupations (Cockburn, 1987), older women who are
given the opportunity to retrain in non-traditional jobs may be able
to serve as role models, thereby making it easier for younger
women to take such jobs.

Conclusion

The current relationship between men's and women's employment
needs to be understood not just in terms of the domestic division of
labour, but also in the context of the barriers and control which,
historically, have operated against women's but not men's employment. While it has always been the situation that many married
women have held paid jobs, it is only in post-war years, with the
removal of the marriage bar, that it has been possible for most
women to hold a highly paid or high status job. Placed in this
context, there has been a considerable advancement over the years.

However, the very great rise in part-time working, and the almost total failure for higher level jobs to be constructed on a part-time basis, give rise to considerable concern. A number of policy options are available for increasing equality between men and women in employment, and it is to be hoped that the shortfall of young people now entering the labour market will provide the impetus to ensure that the skills and abilities of both men and women are more fully used.

Part-time Employment and Labour Market Policies

TIM WALSH

Characteristics of part-time employment: research evidence

National statistics

Part-time employment is defined for statistical purposes as persons voluntarily working 30 hours or less per week excluding meal breaks and overtime. On this basis, some 5.1 million workers in Great Britain are engaged on a part-time basis representing about a quarter of the workforce. Part-time working is not simply a characteristic of jobs growth in the 1980s, but has been a significant feature of Britain's employment structure for at least three decades; one in ten workers were part-timers in 1961. Figure I shows that between 1951 and 1981, the number of full-time employees fell by 2.65 million while part-time employment rose by over 4 million and increased its share of total employment from 4 to 21 per cent. Since 1981 the growth of part-time working has continued, rising a further 700 000 by 1987, to 24 per cent of total employment. All recent employment projections forecast that the growth in part-time jobs will continue; the Institute for Employment Research at the University of Warwick has estimated that 28 per cent of all jobs will be part-time by 1995.

Over the period of rising part-time employment in relative and absolute terms there have been important changes in the way part-time workers have been utilised. The hours worked by female part-timers have declined from a weekly average of 19.6 and 20.3 for manual and non-manual respectively in 1972 to 18.8 and 20 hours per week by 1987. More significantly, data on hours distribution show that whereas in 1972 31.2 per cent of manual, and 24.0 per

From Tim Walsh, 'Part-time Employment and Labour Market Policies', *National Westminster Bank Quarterly Review*, May 1989, pp. 43–54.

Figure 1 *Growth of part-time work in Great Britain, 1951–87*

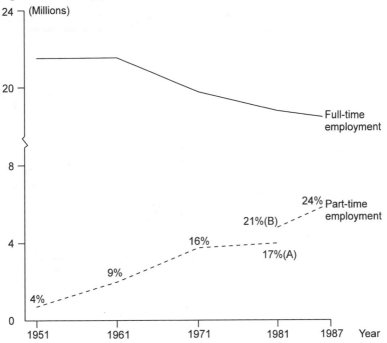

Note: Percentages represent part-time as per cent of all employment.
Sources: Census of Population, 1951, 1961, 1971 and 1981(A); Census of
Employment, 1981(B), and employment estimates for 1987.

cent of non-manual female part-timers worked 16 hours or less a
week, by 1987 the figures had risen to 40.6 per cent and 31.7 per
cent respectively (Table 1). Changing utilisation of part-timers is
also reflected in evidence from the Labour Force Survey which
shows that the proportion of part-timers working on a temporary
basis rose from 10 to 14 per cent between 1981 and 1986.

To examine how changes in part-time employment are mani-
fested at company level, detailed case studies were conducted in
two industries which are substantial employers of part-time staff –
the retail and hotels and catering industries (Figure 2). Employment and pay records from nine large retail and hotel companies
covering 81 000 employees were examined and in-depth interviews
with senior management were held to delineate the reasons behind
part-time employment use. This research has been reported in
detail elsewhere and the principal findings are set out here as the

Figure 2 *Distribution of part-timers by industry (percentages), September 1987*

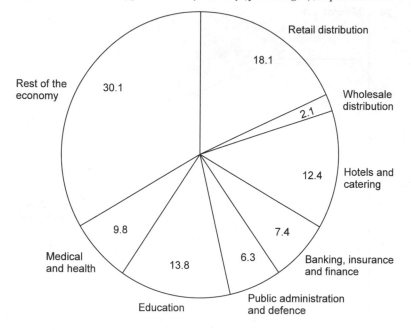

Source: Department of Employment estimate of employees in employment. *Employment Gazette*, March 1988.

basis for discussing some policy implications of part-time jobs growth in the context of labour market deregulation. Table 2 sets out details of the companies studied.

Table 1   *Distribution of normal basic hours of adult female part-timers in all industries and services*

Date of survey	Average weekly hours	Percentage with normal basic hours in the ranges:			
		Not over 8	8–16	16–24	24–30
Manual females					
1972	19.6	9.4	21.8	41.2	27.7
1987	18.8	11.6	29.0	36.8	22.5
Non-manual females					
1972	20.3	7.7	16.3	49.0	27.0
1987	20.0	7.9	23.8	46.7	21.5

Source: NES 1972 (table 149, 153) and 1987 (table 177, 182).

Table 2   *Case study companies visited, April 1984*

Case study	Total employment[1]	% of part-timers
Hotel A, 830 beds	273	28.9
4 Star category		
Hotel B, 298 beds	185	16.2
4 Star category		
Hotel C, 68 beds	44	13.6
3 Star category		
Hotel D, 80 beds	57	14.0
4 Star category		
Hotel E, 316 beds	114	7.9
Retail X, mixed high street chain store	21,152	64.6
Retail Y, department store	1,452	31.5
Retail Z, multiple grocer	57,827	56.9
of which:		
Z1 London branch	350	46.3
Z2 outer London branch	159	66.0

Note: [1] excluding casual staff.

Company level evidence

Part-time employment was significant in most of the companies studied, typically ranging from one-fifth to two-thirds of total employment in the hotel and retailing companies. While the proportions of part-timers were greatest in low-value retail outlets, such as grocery and mixed retailers, part-time employment was central to the business operations of all the establishments visited. Data on working hours, hourly rates, and daily and weekly trading patterns indicated that the chief economic benefit to the company from the utilisation of part-time labour arose from their employment in occupations for which labour needs are less than full-time. Savings in direct labour costs – employment on an 'as needed' basis – coupled with productivity gains (measured by sales per person) and flexibility on an hourly basis were the motive forces behind greater dependence on part-time employees. Savings in indirect labour costs, such as National Insurance, were salient, but not the primary reason for part-time jobs growth, chiefly because of the practical difficulties in matching individual workers' hours to the earnings' thresholds of the National Insurance system. Where 'cut off' criteria involved hours of work (as opposed to the earnings thresholds of the National Insurance scheme), for example the 8 and 16 hour barriers for employment protection legislation, there was wider recognition by employers of the additional savings that could be made in non-wage labour costs by specifically altering employment structures and hours schedules.

The evidence further suggested that part-time employment is regular employment, determined by the pattern of product demand and customer flow and by the type of sales – its growth is not a short-term response to either recession or uncertainty but the outcome of a long-term trend and a permanent feature of the firms' employment structures.

Part-timers' relatively low pay could be accounted for by a combination of lower basic rates (in some cases), their engagement in less diverse occupations and by differences in systems of payments compared to full-timers. For example, differences between rates grew progressively larger for the more highly graded jobs from which part-timers were generally excluded and commission, bonus and 'tronc' (service charges) payments formed a smaller proportion of earnings in occupations where part-timers predominated such as check-out staff and chambermaids. Pay systems did not reward skill, experience or seniority for the bulk of the part-time workforce.

These factors were underpinned by different employers' perceptions of full and part-time workers' income needs. In particular, discussions with personnel managers revealed that despite the 'reliability' of part-time workers, particularly middle-aged married women, they were still viewed as, in some way, 'less committed' to the organisation. Employers expressed the view that the flexible working hours which suited part- timers' own circumstances somehow justified less favourable treatment; the offer of part-time work was viewed by employers as an attractive part of the 'employment package' in itself. The notion that where individuals work less than full-time hours the centrality of work is subordinated, thereby justifying different treatment, thus appeared to underpin employers' perceptions.

While it is the case that convenience of hours is the main reason why individuals work part-time, part-timers worked under the specifications and to the time schedules laid down by the employer. It was not important for retailers and hoteliers to ascertain available hours of work from potential recruits; the companies had certain hours' schedules, 'core hours' or 'standard working times', to be filled.

By the nature of their engagement at peak hours part-timers were central to business operations and were not a poor substitute for full-timers. This, coupled with the fact that they comprised up to two-thirds of the labour force, means that it is unhelpful to categorise such workers as marginal or as 'supplementary recruits' to full-time staff. This terminology is inappropriate for it does not reflect the actual experience and desires of the part-timers themselves nor does it indicate their importance in meeting business objectives and raising productivity. Part-time work may be undervalued but is by no means 'peripheral' to employee or employer alike. Thus the implication of the 'core-periphery' model that only the 'core' workers are indispensable to a company's operations, cannot be supported.

Part-time employment and workers' rights

The growth in part-time jobs and the changing use made of part-timers by employers, reflected in reductions in working hours, carry implications for employee rights and benefits under employment and social welfare legislation, including statutory redundancy rights, provisions relating to guarantee payments, maternity benefit and unfair dismissal. The model of a full-time and continuous relationship between employer and employee is no longer an accurate or typical description of the employment relationship for a large and growing section of the labour force. Indeed, it is arguable whether the concept bore much relevance to the Britain of the nineteenth century. Then, much of the British population sought to evade regular full-time employment and often kept second jobs in agriculture after entering the factory system. It was only the creation of a single occupational labour force that underpinned the full-time employment concept; the formation of a labour force in which workers were expected to be competent in a single occupation made as important a contribution to the concept of full-time employment as the extension of production over the whole of a working day or week of whatever length.

It is in this context that the failure of manpower policies and systems of social protection to adapt to changing labour markets should be understood. Changing employment patterns and ossified institutions that surround the labour market have resulted in ambiguity over employment status, discontinuity in employment rights and uneven social protection between full and part-timers.

Ambiguity over employment status arises from both statute and from common law concepts. For example, the Employment Protection (Consolidation) Act 1978 adopted the primacy of the contract of employment – common law concept of the contract of service – as the basis for qualification, without specifically defining the categories of employment that the Act intended to regulate; only under the Sex Discrimination and Race Relations Acts does protection apply to both contracts for services and contracts of employment.

Under the common law contract of service itself, to qualify for unfair dismissal and other employment rights, part-timers must work at least 16 hours a week or between 8–16 hours for five years unbroken service with the same employer. Yet New Earnings Survey data set out in Table 1 shows that among manual (female) part-timers nearly a third (29 per cent) worked between 8 and 16 hours a week and some 11.6 per cent worked less than 8 hours a week in 1987. A further obstacle to statutory rights, pertinent to part-time employment where hours may vary from week to week, is the interpretation that for continuous service to be met the employee must work more than 16 hours in each week of employment (Corton House Ltd *v.* Skipper 1981), though in some circumstances variation in part-time hours causing them to fall below the 8 or 16 hour thresholds may be treated as 'temporary cessations of work' and so preserve continuity of employment (Secretary of State for Employment *v.* Deary 1984).

Because of the inappropriateness and unreliability of these and other 'tests' of what constitutes a contract of service many part-time workers, who may nevertheless effectively be employed on a permanent basis, fail to qualify for many employment protection rights available to full-timers, often despite the intention of the legislation itself. Clearly, not only is employment protection being provided for a shrinking proportion of the labour force but, as Standing (1986) has commented, it is provided 'only to a small number of those who have the greatest employment insecurity'. Flexibility cannot be viewed in isolation from social and individual welfare. If the workers affected are predominantly women, non-unionised, low paid and with few employment rights, the burdens of flexibility and cost cutting will be borne almost solely by the part-time labour force, many of whom are among the least able in society to bear such costs. Further, because the right to insurance-based social protection is linked to single-income earners in full-time, continuous paid employment, an increasing proportion of the labour force is not entitled to wider social provisions. Where benefit eligibilities are linked to hours of work or earnings levels, such as social security, unemployment benefit, sick pay and pension schemes, many part-time workers, who nevertheless work continuously, may be denied social protection.

The concept of a standard, full-time continuous working week which underpins social protection systems and employment legislation is increasingly obsolete. By failing to develop in line with labour demand an increasing proportion of the labour force is not catered for. The conceptual basis of employment policy, indeed its historical origins in terms of continuous, full-time (manufacturing) employment, is of declining relevance to the modern labour market; the concepts of 'full-time employment' and 'normal' working week in relation to policy are increasingly redundant as the variety in working hours spreads.

Flexibility, part-time jobs and employment policy

Policy developments

Current UK policy views labour flexibility as an essential and necessary condition for enhancing productivity and sustaining economic growth in a modern economy. The 1985 Employment White Paper took the view that the 'biggest single cause' of high unemployment was rigidities in the jobs market and that labour flexibility was the way that 'employers can offer more jobs'. Employment policy as set out in the 1988 White Paper seeks to encourage labour flexibility by removing or reducing labour market rigidities by, for example, reducing real wage and non-wage labour costs, and limiting institutional constraints on labour demand and supply.

Similar measures to encourage part-time and more flexible working have also been introduced throughout Europe. In France a decree of August 1986 eased the restrictions in the Labour Code relating to types of *travail differencié* (peripheral work); the decree lifts certain restrictions on the use of fixed-term and temporary employment contracts and encourages the use of part-timers, and in Belgium the 'Hansenne' working time experiments, designed to create jobs and increase organisation flexibility by waiving legal constraints upon changes in working time organisation, have expanded. Spain, Italy and the Netherlands have all introduced more flexible systems of employment contracts, but only two of the (then) ten European Community (EC) members – United Kingdom and Ireland – made a distinction between part-timers and full-timers with regard to rules concerning dismissal. By contrast, in France an Employment Protection Act (1985) gave part-timers the same legal protection as full-time employees and in Belgium '[a]ll the essential features of the planned Community directive [have been] legally established' since March 1982.

At Community level too, as part of a range of measures on the reduction and reorganisation of working time, the EC has produced a draft directive on part-time work in an attempt to make such work attractive to all workers. The draft directive aims to guarantee part-timers equal rights on a *pro rata* basis and to extend to part-timers the employment rights currently enjoyed by full-timers; part-timers would thus be entitled, *inter alia*, to equal treatment as regards training and promotion and rules governing dismissal and social security rights. However, member states could still operate a threshold in terms of hours or earnings below which part-timers would be exempted from such schemes. The Council of Social and Labour Ministers have failed to adopt the part-time Directive or other measures relating to workers' rights since 1980, indicating perhaps that deregulation is the preferred policy.

Employment implications of part-time jobs growth in the context of labour market deregulation

In the light of the changes taking place in the structure of employment, and the inability of institutions of social and employment protection to cover workers entering the labour market, there are a number of points to be made on employment policy based simply on deregulation and moves to encourage labour flexibility within firms.

First, the characteristics of the new jobs, the preferences of employers and the requirements of the job seeker in terms of earnings, mean that the ability of part-time jobs to absorb displaced full-time workers, say from manufacturing industries, is likely to be severely limited. If part-time jobs are characterised by low and unstable weekly earnings with little employment protection and poor career opportunities, it is unlikely that an individual with skills in a declining industry would easily transfer to part-time jobs without advice, training and financial support. The continued growth in part-time working, very largely in service industries, is likely to generate a need for people, aptitudes and skills not typically held by those currently in full-time work. Moreover, without protection of rights and income, the jobs that are being created may be filled by persons currently outside the labour market who, because of their lack of entitlement to unemployment or other benefits, will take such jobs. A possibility is that under an educational loan system students will increasingly fill part-time jobs (as is often the case in North America, Japan and Australia) rather than those registered as unemployed.

Indeed, the structure of jobs growth in recent years is probably an important factor in explaining why (registered) unemployment remains at historically high levels despite the relatively high economic growth rates prevalent since 1981. Changing labour demand, by mobilising labour supplies from outside the paid labour force, means that the unemployed are bypassed by rising (part-time) employment. Employment policy by ignoring the heterogeneity of labour supply and the permanency of the demands for part-time labour (often in jobs with low hourly and weekly earnings) under-estimates the potential mismatch between supply and demand.

Second, labour market deregulation may assist the growth of part-time employment but, by extending differences in labour uti-lisation between full and part-time workers, this might have an adverse impact on part-timers' productivity and commitment to particular industries or firms. If an industry or occupation comes to be regarded as being one of low status, it might confer low status upon individuals or demographic and social groups who are engaged in it. In the longer term this may be exacerbated by the supply of labour only from these social groups and decline in self-motivation necessary in filling vacancies due to the 'poor image' the jobs present to the job seeker. The status of occupations is partly a function of the continuity of employment, the level of earnings and the scope for career development. Thus, although employers' costs are increased if part-time workers are covered by employment legislation, beneficial effects leading to more systematic recruit-ment, training and retention policies by employers may also be generated. In this way, greater employment security to part-timers can aid rather than hinder industrial performance.

Third, by assuming a simple division between work and non-work, conventional thinking on employment largely ignores the implications for wider public policy of the growth in complete jobs for very much less than normal hours. In particular, policy based on flexibility accentuates the decoupling of 'work for production' from 'work for income'. While there has never been a complete link between the two concepts, the increase in whole jobs, on a less than full-time basis, which meet production requirements, but not income or livelihood needs, poses a major challenge to traditional public policy. Maximum hours are likely to be primarily in the control of the employer, not the employee, and in its present form, part-time working, may provide an unsatisfactory level of economic independence, of limited protection against unemployment and of access to a range of social entitlements. Thus under conditions of employment deregulation, and as employers become increasingly sophisticated in their utilisation of part-timers by refining hours worked, segmentation will be strengthened, and income as a means of livelihood further eroded. By reducing jobs into smaller and smaller parcels it is more likely that individuals will have to rely on a mixture of paid part-time labour and social security benefits to achieve income sufficiency.

The choice of combining paid labour with social benefit is however constrained by present arrangements. A jobless couple, for example, can only earn 19 per cent of their benefit (up to £15 per week between them for couples unemployed for more than two years) before state benefits are withdrawn (in 1948 the same couple could earn up to 75 per cent of their national assistance before state benefit entitlement was affected). The 'earnings-disregard level' for a single person today is a mere £5.00. Thus to avoid loss of benefit £ for £ a person seeking work needs a full-time job (defined in this case as above 24 hours per week) on which family credit can be claimed. There might therefore be a need to weaken the link between full-time (paid) employment and social protection and a case for bringing unemployment benefit, income support systems and developments in employment policy closer together so that the unemployed might be encouraged to take the part-time jobs that are being created.

One pointer in this direction comes from a French scheme (Decree of 5 March 1985) in which persons receiving unemployment benefit, who take up a part-time job on an employment contract of at least 18 hours per week where their earnings are lower than their benefit, will receive a payment to make the pay up to the level of the former benefit. Thus, unlike the British Job Splitting Scheme which encourages employers to create part-time jobs (the French have an equally unsuccessful scheme), this French scheme promotes the mobility of the unemployed into the jobs that are being created, by recognising the link between the new part-time jobs and low weekly earnings associated with less than full-time hours. In Belgium too, the Royal Decree 22 March 1982 entitled persons avoiding unemployment by accepting part-time work to unemployment benefit for the hours they were not working, so that regardless of their particular part-time rotas – whether they work three full days a week or three hours a day – such workers can top up their earnings with unemployment benefit. Partial unemployment benefit in respect of part-time workers is also available in other European countries.

Conclusions

The worker's relationship to employer and income is changing rapidly; working patterns have moved considerably away from the traditional basic work week, yet domestic employment and social policies have been slow to accompany such changes. Employment protection legislation and systems of social protection are still geared to working patterns of continuous full-time employment. A reconsideration of the form of employment law and of systems of social protection that surround labour markets needs to accompany or at least take cognisance of changes in the structure of jobs growth, with perhaps explicit definition of the forms of working arrangements to be covered within the protective legislation. In future the underpinnings of employment will need a variable and organic standard upon which protective legislation can be built – the present fixed and artificial distinctions between hours worked, and status and contract are no longer clear or relevant bases for today's and tomorrow's labour market. Above all, there is a need to provide greater flexibility in the labour market at large – between industries, occupations and full and part-time jobs – and not simply measures to enhance flexibility within internal labour markets.

Greater employment flexibility is desired by employers to ensure business survival in the highly competitive product markets of the single European market and the tighter labour markets of the 1990s. There is likely to be an increasing need for discrete labour use, not continuous full-time employment. Part-time working arrangements may, however, lead either to the extension of inferior employment conditions and a reduction in opportunity, or to the development of greater choice among individuals, within an agreed framework of rights. A social judgement is, therefore, necessary between the rights of workers and society's obligations to employers. 'Flexibility' and employment security need not be mutually exclusive; the scope exists for the benefits of flexibility to be more evenly distributed between employer and worker alike.

Women and '1992': Integration or Segmentation?

GILL WHITTING

Introduction

The drive to achieve full economic and monetary union within the European Union (EU) brings to the forefront those issues historically at the centre of Common Market debates. The question of sovereignty continues to dominate the negotiations; to different degrees Member States have been wary of what they consider unwarranted intrusions into national affairs. Moreover, the economic thrust of the Treaty of Rome has prompted at least two major questions: first, will economic union bring benefits to all, or will it result in additional benefits to those countries, regions and individuals that already enjoy a relatively high level of social and economic integration and prosperity? Second, to what extent do the Treaties of Rome and Maastricht allow for policies that can inject a social dimension to reduce existing irregularities and counter some of the additional 'costs' of an economic-oriented Internal Market?

With regard to the second question, the development of equal treatment legislation is one of the most significant in the evolution of a European social policy. Indeed the promotion of women's rights has been assisted by Article 129 of the Treaty of Rome which imposes a firm legal obligation to implement a policy of 'equal pay for equal work'. And complementary to this chapter, Directives have been passed on equal pay, equal treatment and social security (Docksey, 1987; Meehan, 1987; Szyszczak, 1987). Nevertheless, there are considerable obstacles to the progress of equal treatment between men and women throughout the EU, not the least of which is the attitude of the UK government which has seriously affected European policy, regarding, for example, parental leave and the conditions of part-time work.

The purpose of this chapter is to discuss some of the social and economic consequences of the Internal Market for women. It argues that the Single European Act is significant for women in the way that proposals interact with existing socio-economic structures and trends. For example, if economic integration is successful in its demands for a flexible workforce, the precarious position which women currently occupy in the labour market could intensify; women may remain unequal when compared to men as regards pay, conditions and career prospects; and the reform of the Structural Funds (main EU funds for regional development and training) may reduce rather than enhance the visibility of women in EU expenditure, planning and resource allocation. On the other hand, the Single European Act may provide opportunities for women to enhance their economic position, as European-wide social policies are introduced, sometimes over the heads of reluctant national governments.

The Single European Act

The Single European Act (the Act – sometimes referred to as '1992') aims to remove all remaining barriers to free trade between the 12 Member States of the EU in order to achieve economic integration on a scale that allows the European market to compete more effectively with its Japanese and American counterparts. Some 280 legislative measures were initially proposed to free the movement of capital, goods, services and labour and to remove a number of fiscal barriers. Monetary union is a further aim of the Act. The change from unanimity to qualified majority voting (for a limited number of measures) in the council of Ministers assisted the agreement (of those representing heads of Member States) to some two-thirds of the Internal Market proposals (Cmnd 372, 1988).

The Act is primarily concerned with economic and monetary change. References to social policy and other sectors specify the health and safety of workers, recognising the need to harmonise conditions across the EU, and the promotion of the dialogue between management and labour at the European level. Social cohesion features within the spirit of the Act. This relates to the strengthening of economic and social cohesion within the Community and, in particular, to the reduction of regional inequalities. For this purpose the Act specifies reforms to the way in which the Structural Funds are allocated and managed. Developments in research and technology are also encouraged in the interests of European and international competitiveness and a number of environmental actions are also recommended.

Social policy and social dimension

The Internal Market programme raises wider issues of social policy than those included in the Act. Social policies are required, first, to assist the operation of a European-wide market on the scale intended and, second, to meet the economic and social costs of consolidating the Internal Market. The role of social policy is well documented by the Commission of the European Communities (the Commission) (CEC (1988) 1148, September 1988) and updated in the Green Paper on Social Policy (CEC, September 1993). The Commission recognises that the social implications of the Internal Market require the active participation of both national authorities and Community institutions. A number of priorities are identified, for example, the social policy contribution to establishing a single European labour market; the scope and financial cost of providing social security; action in the field of education, training and job creation; and legislation relating to working conditions and industrial relations. The Commission makes reference to existing high levels of unemployment, growing inequalities in income distribution, the appearance of new forms of poverty and the processes by which particular groups in the population become marginalised and excluded (see Room, Lawson and Laczko, 1989, for a discussion of 'new' poverty).

The social implications of the Internal Market and the more concrete measures that have come forward from the Commission as part of the Social Charter have generated considerable controversy. The UK in particular has a reputation for opposing virtually all forms of EU social legislation. Although the last European elections resulted in a balance of power perhaps more favourable to the development of a 'Social Europe', the current administration in the UK is still strongly opposed to a social Europe because, in its view, this would hinder rather than assist the operation of a free, European-wide market. An EU Social Charter is legitimate only in as far as it deals with job creation and this in turn is viewed as a consequence of wealth creation. Other social policies are perceived as the sole and proper responsibility of Member State governments; therefore the UK government strongly objects to the 'imposition' of legislation and the breaching of sovereignty with respect to existing or future EU legislation that deals with equal treatment, social security, workers' rights, and so on. However, it is interesting to note that one of the radical proposals coming from Europe concerns the introduction of a 'guaranteed minimum income' across the EU (O'Higgins, 1988). Although in its infancy, this proposal is allowing a debate to take place that would not otherwise be present in the UK given the social, economic and political preoccupations of the current administration.

The Maastricht Treaty

The entry into force of the Maastricht Treaty has created a new situation in relation to social policy at European level (CEC, September 1993). In the first instance, there is the existence of the Agreement on Social Policy, adopted by all Member States except the UK and enshrined in the Protocol on Social Policy which is annexed to the treaty.

This Agreement seeks to clarify the kind of areas which the Union's social policy would cover and also establishes new procedures for decision making. The Agreement sets out the following objectives: 'the promotion of employment, improved living and working conditions, proper social protection, dialogue between management and labour, the development of human resources with a view to lasting high employment and the combating of exclusion'.

Two groups of areas of activity are identified, one of which is to be decided on the basis of qualified majority voting and the second, to be decided by unanimity. The two areas cover:

Qualified majority voting

- protecting workers' health and safety;
- working conditions;
- information to and consultation with workers;
- equality between men and women with regard to labour market opportunities and treatment at work;

- the integration of persons excluded from the labour market, without prejudice to Article 127 of the Treaty of Rome.

Unanimity

- social security and social protection of workers;
- protection of workers where their employment is terminated;
- representation and collective defence of workers and employers, including codetermination;
- conditions of employment for third-country nationals legally residing in Community territory;
- financial contributions for promotion of employment and job creation, without prejudice to the provisions relating to the Social Fund.

Actions explicitly excluded from action are pay, the right of association, the right to strike and the right to impose lock-outs.

The Agreement also formalises a process of two-stage consultation with the social partners, which can lead to the negotiation of collective agreements at European level, possibly as a substitute for legislation.

Thus, social policy is now potentially governed by two separate legal frameworks: that of the Treaty of Rome which continues to apply and that of the Agreement on Social Policy which 11 Member States have agreed to operate between them.

The scope of social policy for women

So whilst there has been considerable evolution in the development of a European social policy that could bring about changes in the future for women, the current situation especially for the UK is that the most robust EU policies are focusing on a rather narrow set of issues that obscures the fact that many women cannot compete equally in the labour market.

Women's roles in the family affect their employment experiences, not only in terms of access to work in general, but also in terms of the type of work into which they are channelled and the pay that they receive. Equal value campaigns emphasise this point that women's work is badly paid because the paid work they do is analogous to household employment and undervalued in the market because domestic labour is unpaid (Meehan and Whitting, 1989).

The general issues that question the role of Europe and the prospects of economic and social integration are highly visible in the public debates. The more specific issues that identify the roles of and consequences for women, either as workers or as citizens with basic 'rights', are less visible although the Commission of the European Communities is, however, actively encouraging research and debate at a European level on the consequences for women (Moss, 1988; CEC, 1989; CEC, 1993a). In the UK, the Equal Opportunities Commission (EOC) views the Internal Market as an opportunity to bring 'equal opportunities into the mainstream of British life'. The British government was being asked by the EOC to back its verbal commitment to equal opportunities with tangible support for new initiatives. The EOC strategy called for measures enabling men and women to take an equal share in work and the family; an equal chance for women to have training; a narrowing of the pay gap between the sexes; better protection for part-time workers and greater protection in tax and pensions. It is important for this discussion to note the EOC emphasis on policies at the interface between social and economic problems in the relations between men and women.

Key issues

Any assessment of the Internal Market raises a number of issues. First there is the question of time scale. The initial debate placed too great an emphasis on 31 December 1992 as the date by which it was anticipated that European integration would be completed. Some of the changes took place in advance of 1992: this included the issuing of new guidelines that determined the allocation and management of the European Social Fund, a fund providing essential resources for vocational training initiatives. Many of the less controversial Directives were also approved. These included, for example, the removal of technical barriers to trade of different kinds. By contrast, the more controversial legislation relating, for example, to the free movement of people is less likely to be on the statute books by the end of the 1990s. Realistically, the changes envisaged are likely to be effected far into the next century.

Second, each Member State is unique in terms of existing economic and social laws and policies, the traditions that underpin them, the institutions empowered to enforce or implement them. For example, different countries have different approaches to providing social security and any assessment of the effects of a more competitive job market will need to consider the social security implications and the differences between countries in their ability to respond.

Third, the aims and objectives of the Internal Market will interact with an existing socio-economic and political context. This context includes, for example, trends across the EU in demographic change, unemployment and employment patterns and, in consequence, their challenge to policy-makers in the Member States.

The context for implementing the Single European Act

The most significant factors for the future operation of the Internal Market are the numbers, skills, location and 'flexibility' of workers. Demographic change in the EU will increasingly put pressure on the availability of younger workers. The service sector will continue to expand while the manufacturing sector shrinks and the skills required by employers will continue to change.

It is anticipated that companies may relocate their operations as the opportunities within the wider European market become more visible; this relocation may be determined by the presence of a suitably skilled workforce and/or it may have relocation consequences for workers seeking employment. (One of the fears voiced by the trade union organisations is that relocation decisions may be based on perceptions of geographical areas where trade union organisation is weak or partial and/or where wage rates are low (*Labour Research*, November 1988).) But if new technology predictions are any indication of future work organisation, the location of the worker may be less important as computer operatives can increasingly work from home. Nevertheless the trend is for employment to be more varied with an increasing number of part-time jobs, jobs undertaken by self-employed workers and jobs that are temporary.

It is anticipated that these changes to the location and nature of work will generate economic and social costs which will fall upon particular geographical areas and population groups. For example, the Commission warns that progress towards the Single Market is likely to involve new patterns of 'social exclusion and marginalisation' (CEC [88] 1148, September 1988). Over 40 million people in the EU are currently in poverty (O'Higgins and Jenkins, 1989) and approximately 10.9 per cent of an EU total population of 320 million are currently unemployed (EUROSTAT, March 1994). It is difficult to be precise as to how the Internal Market will affect the labour market; there is, however, no evidence to suggest that those who were vulnerable before '1992' will fare any differently now and for the future. One assessment of the effects of the Act suggests that in the short term jobs will be lost; in the medium term an increase of 1.8 million jobs is forecast; in the long term the forecast is 5 million new jobs created (Cecchini, 1988). But these are rather sweeping figures based on rather controversial and questionable assumptions about the EU economy and the gains from market integration.

The detail of social policies vary from country to country but there are nevertheless common problems. Taking social security as an example, three problems arise (Com (87) 230 Final): the financing of current or projected needs in terms of social protection expenditure; the implications of demographic trends for public expenditure and labour costs; and the problem of marginalisation affecting a considerable number of people in the Member States. Social security financing is affected by the growth in expenditure resulting from persistent high-level unemployment and pressure on old age and sickness insurance sectors, and by a slowing down of incoming revenue. As the population ages, there are increasing demands on public expenditure, particularly on health for older people. The ageing of the working population also has consequences for the cost of labour; geographical and vocational mobility is likely to decline amongst older workers and a sharp drop is anticipated in the rate at which the active population is renewed. There may be a need for a migration policy to encourage labour mobility in the more distant future.

The consequences of the Act for women

The possible consequences for women arise, first, from their economic and social position within the EU labour market as it currently operates, and, second, from the prediction that a more competitive and European-wide market will demand a more flexible response from its future workforce.

Recent trends in the European labour market appear, superficially, to benefit women. Certainly between 1975 and 1991 participation rates for women have increased in all the Member State countries (see Table 1). Except for Ireland, where male activity has continued to show a major increase, women have been the chief agents in the 82 per cent growth in the active population in the EU as a whole (1975–85). This change derives essentially from the rise in the relative number of women seeking work, especially married women who increasingly form an important part of those participating in the labour market (Meulders, 1989). An expansion of the service sector has also contributed to the reorganisation of female work patterns. However, further analysis suggests that the position of the female workforce has not markedly improved. For example:

- Women are not a homogeneous group: age, and other socio-economic factors determine their position and future opportunities in the labour market. Lone mothers and migrant women are two groups which are particularly vulnerable. Older women are also precarious given that their socio-economic position depends on previous work histories and current social protection (especially pension) rights.
- Women face considerable problems arising from long-term unemployment: with the exception of Ireland and the UK, the numbers of women unemployed, according to official statistics, is higher than the numbers of men unemployed (Table 2).
- Throughout the EU, women tend to be confined to certain professions and, despite the Equal Pay legislation, are still likely to earn less pay than men.
- Women's jobs are typified by part-time, temporary and precarious work of many kinds; in the more developed countries part-time work is seen as a major characteristic of the service sector. In Italy, Greece and Portugal part-time work is a feature of the agricultural sector (Table 3 and Figure 1).

On the one hand, it is argued that this current experience may intensify post – 1992. For example, recent evidence from a survey of occupational segregation of women and men in the EU (CEC, 1993a) suggested that increased women's participation has not led to greater equality between the sexes. Rather, that new contours of segmentation and division are emerging between men and women,

Table 1   *Women in the active population*

Country	Mean annual growth rates of active female population 1975–85	Contribution of active female population to growth in total active population (%) 1975–85	Rates of female activity 1975	1985	1991*
Belgium	1.9	145	44.0	50.5	57.7
Denmark	2.3	75	63.5	74.5	84.7
West Germany	0.7	75	49.6	50.4	68.8
Greece (1977–85)	4.0	66	—	41.8	46.7
France	1.8	106	51.0	55.0	68.9
Ireland	2.0	49	34.5	36.6	49.3
Italy	2.6	79	34.6	41.0	51.0
Luxembourg	2.0	200	38.3	43.2	50.5
Netherlands	3.9	76	31.0	41.2	58.7
Portugal	2.1	71	51.5	57.2	67.4
Spain (76–85)	1.1	104	32.4	33.6	46.9
UK	1.4	84	55.1	60.1	71.3
EEC – Twelve	1.6	82			62.4

*Updated using the 1991 Labour Force Survey (EUROSTAT).
Sources: EUROSTAT and OECD. Employment prospects. Compiled by Daniele Meulders, '*Employment*', paper given at a Conference on Evaluation of Community Policy on Equal Opportunities, Toledo, April 1989.

Table 2   *Women out of work*

Country	Overall unemployment rates 1976 M	W	1986 M	W	1991 M	W
Belgium	4.5	10.2	8.9	17.9	6.9	14.2
Denmark	5.1	5.2	5.7	9.8	9.4	11.4
West Germany	3.5	4.9	7.2	9.5	5.7*	6.6*
France	3.3	5.7	9.6	12.4	9.4	13.4
Ireland	10.4	6.6	19.2	16.8	17.2	20.0
Italy	5.2	6.6	11.2	18.6	7.7	17.2
Luxembourg	0.3	0.4	1.2	1.9	2.4	3.9
Netherlands	5.8	5.1	12.2	12.7	7.9	13.2
UK	6.0	3.1	14.0	9.3	12.0	8.1
Spain					19.5	29.1
Portugal					4.9	6.8

*Unified FRG.
Source: EUROSTAT; Meulders (1989). Updated using Labour Force Survey 1991 (EUROSTAT, 1994).

and that there is also a trend towards greater inequality within the female· labour force.

Completing the Internal Market places emphasis on 'flexibility'. For the employer, an existing workforce appears more flexible if workers can be moved from job to job by downgrading skills, contracts and shift patterns; a new workforce is more flexible to the employer if it is part-time, temporary, freelance, home-based, subcontracting, and so on. Many Member States are indeed developing new forms of employment which differ from more 'traditional' jobs: the differences include working days, duration of contracts, hours, workplaces, mode of payment, and so on, preferred because of the advantages they offer to employers. Women's jobs are particularly affected by these developments (Huws, 1989).

Demographic and other future changes are likely to result in fewer people of the appropriate age to participate in the labour force. There are, therefore, considerable opportunities for women from all socio-economic groups to continue to take up work. These issues, however, raise policy questions. Although circumstances differ between different groups of women depending on their socio-economic characteristics, the demands of the Internal Market highlight the need for training – to ensure that all women can take advantage of new work opportunities, especially in new technology industries and non-traditional occupations and for social protection to ensure that the unintended but perhaps inevitable consequences of integration are met.

Table 3 *Proportion of female workers in full-time and part-time employment, 1991*

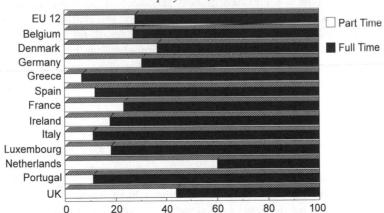

Figure 1 *Proportion of female workers by sector in 1991 – EU12*

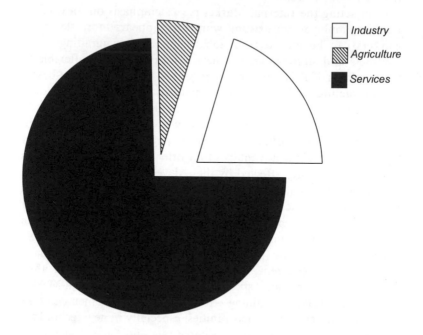

Challenge for social policy

Social policies are required, first, to assist the operation of an European Union integrated market and, second, to meet the economic and social costs arising from economic integration. Policies are required that recognise that women overall require special treatment that will enable them to compete equally with men; however, policies should also consider the differences between women that require differential and not equal treatment. If women are to take advantage of new work opportunities, social policy needs to consider employment barriers, incentives and disincentives. Policies could encourage, for example, the availability of secure and well-paid jobs that can be filled by those with domestic responsibilities; the provision of good quality, affordable and accessible child care; the provision of training to ensure that women have the skills required; the removal of financial disincentives created by the level and structure of social security benefits

(Millar, 1989). To what extent are these issues addressed by EU policies?

Equal treatment

Equal treatment between men and women is addressed by the EU through its equal opportunities legislation and action programmes. The EU's commitment to equality between men and women goes back to Article 119 of the treaty establishing the EEC, with subsequent legislation based on the Social Action Programme of 1974. The aim was to achieve 'equality between men and women as regards access to employment and vocational training and advancement as regards working conditions, including pay... and to ensure that the family responsibilities of all concerned may be reconciled with job aspirations' (Council Resolution 21.2.74).

In legal terms, the EU's commitment to equal opportunities is founded upon three main equality Directives (Docksey, 1987): the Equal Pay Directive adopted in 1975 designed to implement the principle of equal pay for men and women; the Equal Treatment Directive adopted in 1976 guarantees the principle of equal treatment for men and women in access to employment, vocational training and promotion, and working conditions; the 1978 Directive concerns the progressive implementation of the principle of equal treatment for men and women in statutory social security schemes. Two further Directives were adopted in 1986: to extend the principle of equal treatment to occupational social security schemes, and to men and women in self-employed occupations including agriculture, and the protection of self-employed women during pregnancy and maternity. The Commission also drafted a Directive on Parental Leave and Leave for Family Reasons which was not adopted owing mainly to the opposition of the UK government. A proposal for a Directive on the burden of proof in the area of equal pay and equal treatment for women and men (Com (88) 269 Final) was also not adopted due to opposition from the UK. In addition, the Commission was asked to prepare a directive on the prevention of sexual harassment at work which aims to protect workers against the risk of sexual harassment and encourages employers to establish and maintain working environments free of sexual harassment.

The Commission monitors existing legislation and develops existing policy through the establishment of Community Action Programmes on the Promotion of Equal opportunities for Women. There are also networks of independent experts from all Member States which monitor the practical and legal implementation of Directives, and note obstacles and cases of discrimination. There are now five networks covering: the application of the equality Directives, women in the labour force, the diversification of vocational choices, child care, and women in local employment initiatives.

The challenge for social policy is, first, to continue to develop equal opportunities legislation and action at the level of the Community and, second, to assist the full implementation of these Directives and Programmes within Member States. The implementation of equal opportunities legislation relies primarily on the powers which the EU has to influence practices in the Member States. This is particularly so for policy areas, for example, income maintenance, which remain the responsibility for national governments. Where legislation exists, as in the case for equal treatment between men and women, the EU is able to exert greater influence over Member States primarily through the work of the European Court of Justice. But even with this assistance, implementation is a complex, slow and frustrating process. Economic integration presented a prime opportunity to review the scope of legislation and the content of plans and to expand policies and programmes to counter discrimination on the grounds of sex.

Unequal treatment

Social policy needs also to address the implications of the Internal Market for women who, on their own or with children, migrate to an EU country, either from within or outside the existing EU (Prondzynski, 1989). With the completion of the Internal Market, migration is a key area of concern. The situation for migrant women is complicated by at least three factors. First, persons migrating within the Community are provided for under the Treaty of Rome and subsequent legislation, conferring rights in employment, pay and conditions, and social security. In contrast, those persons emigrating from outside the EU are not affected by the Treaty (Sivanandan, 1988); their situation is governed by numerous national laws which differ from one Member State to another. Second, the majority of women enter the country of immigration as dependants, and not as workers in their own right. Third, migrant women are also a heterogeneous group. There are women who migrate alone or with their husbands and who seek employment in the receiving country. Women may join their already emigrated husbands and, in this case, the continuation of residence in the new country often depends on the husband's work and the marriage relationship. There are migrant women who choose not to work but who face problems of social and cultural isolation in the new environment. Women who marry migrants face problems arising from cross-cultural marriages and new problems are added if the migrant decides to return to his home country. Migration also leads to women being left behind with the responsibility for supporting and caring for children.

Migrant women pose a particular challenge for employment and training policies; typically, migrant women are in low paid, insecure employment with little opportunity to gain access to training schemes. Without sufficient attention to these issues, increased mobility in the 1990s and into the twenty-first century may intensify the situation for certain groups of migrant women who, at least initially, are restricted in their independence.

Training

The provision of training plays a vital role in the success of the new, enlarged market; the rate of women's participation in the more secure and better paid jobs will depend on their ability to acquire the necessary skills. Within the EU the major resource for funding vocational training is the European Social Fund (ESF), one of the Structural Funds considerably increased in size to support the Internal Market programme. In the past, these resources have been used in the UK to create and sustain local labour market strategies for vulnerable workers, including women, and to lever other financial resources from government and from the private sector (Whitting and Quinn, 1989).

Changes to the allocation of ESF funds has now moved away from priorities determined by eligible population groups on the basis of submitted projects. Priorities are now determined at the level of regions on the basis of programmes that specify labour market priorities. Because the successful training schemes run by or for women are often small-scale and local organisations, it was feared that the interests of women will be bypassed in the new allocation arrangements. The challenge for social policy is to ensure that area-based programmes filter down to those in the community most in need. In the UK at least it was proposed to prepare a separate women's training operational plan. Other countries, especially the new members of the EU, are less experienced in getting European funds. The organisation and development of women's groups also varies between countries; not all Member States have women's organisations which can initiate and sustain training that is geared to women's needs. One of the results from the EU's Second Programme to Combat Poverty demonstrated how projects successfully met the training needs of lone mothers (Whitting, 1988). In many countries, the projects had initiated training schemes that were tailor-made to the life-style of the lone parent family. For example, schemes provided child care for participants and they were sensitive to the restrictions on a lone mother's time. But more than this, the approach to training and the organisation and direction of courses required careful thinking to avoid a situation where women felt 'put off' or unable to participate, or even to feel a 'failure'. The example of training also emphasises the need for proper monitoring and evaluation of social policy so that initiatives, particularly of the innovative kind referred to here, can be evaluated so that other organisations and future policies benefit from the experience.

Vocational training and the promotion of employment for women is targeted under a Community initiative call NOW – New Opportunities for Women. This initiative provides funding for transnational action programmes, including measures to assist women to set up small businesses and cooperatives, advice and guidance for women returning to work, complementary measures to develop child care facilities, and so on. Resources from the Structural Funds which contribute to NOW totalled ECU 153 million in 1990–3. Actions funded under NOW, and other ESF support for women's training and employment, were recently evaluated in a special edition of *Social Europe* (CEC, 1992) which also serves as a guide for the types of activities that can be pursued with the ESF.

Child care

The European Child Care Network, established as part of the second European Equal Opportunities Programme, has undertaken a study of child care policy and provision throughout the Community, and has made proposals for action to the Commission which in turn is committed to put forward its own proposals for action. The Child Care Network proposals envisage a three part European Strategy consisting of legislation, with Directives on Child Care Services and Employment Rights for Parents, funding for the development of services, primarily in less developed regions, possibly through the use of the Structural Funds; and a European Action Programme on Child Care, involving collaboration and exchanges between Member States. The Coordinator of the Network emphasised (Moss, 1988) that the issue of child care, and more broadly, the issue of reconciling work and family responsibilities, is assuming greater importance in the Commission. This reflects an increasing realisation that discussions of the implementation of the Internal Market have been gender blind. For example, the free movement of labour needs a uniform and high level of child care services and parental employment rights in all countries, if it is to fully benefit women with children. Although there is a serious lack of child care provision in the majority of the Member States, a number of them are responding innovatively to the new opportunities for women and the labour market. In the UK, however, the position is far from favourable; current developments in child care which consist entirely of exhortations to employers may well fail to address adequately a labour market opportunity of major social and economic significance.

Conclusions

It is virtually impossible to identify or predict the outcomes of the Internal Market; essential legislation has yet to be passed. Moreover, the scale of the operation suggests change far into the next century. However, for many in the UK the EU presents a political agenda far more progressive than the current, national policy agenda. In the field of social policy, debates are taking place in Britain which continue to reflect a more collectivist ideology; these are supported in Europe and currently challenge the market-oriented and individualist stance of the current administration. Nevertheless, these more radical social policies are not yet enshrined in the Single European Act and it remains to be seen how much of the social policy agenda at European level can be accomplished. It also remains to be seen to what extent the social dimension of the Internal Market can be translated into legislation and more concrete and robust programmes of action. '1992' was essentially about trade: trade within Europe and between Europe and other world markets. The future of social Europe depends on the decisions of Member State leaders and their commitment to address existing and future inequalities within their own countries. In the UK the responsibility falls on political activists and commentators of many kinds to lobby and campaign for social and economic policies to address the issue of increasing inequality.

As far as women are concerned, the major impact of the Internal Market programme will arise from the demands of economic integration on labour markets. Although different issues will arise for different countries, the changes envisaged may reinforce rather than reduce the precarious and exploitative situation that typifies women's employment in Member State countries. But at the same time, the Internal Market presents an opportunity to raise and resolve issues that effect women's employment opportunities and outcomes. Social policies are required to ensure equal treatment between men and women and to recognise the differences in socioeconomic circumstances and needs of different groups of women. In particular, migration is a key area of concern for 1992 and it is migrant women who are particularly vulnerable when it comes to the question of rights, protection and citizenship.

Bibliography to Section II

Allen, I. (1990) Women Doctors, in S. Macrae (ed.) *Keeping Women In*, London: Policy Studies Institute.

Althauser, R. P. and Kalleburg, A. L. (1981) 'Firms, Occupations and the Structure of the Labour Market', in I. Berg (ed.) *Sociological Perspectives on Labour Markets*, Academic Press, pp. 119–49.

Atkinson, J. (1984) *Flexibility, Uncertainty and Manpower Management*, IMS Report No. 89, London: Institute of Manpower Studies.

Atkinson, J. and Meager, N. (1986) *Changing Working Patterns*, London: NEDO.

Becker, G. (1985) 'Human Capital, Effort and the Sexual Division of Labor', *Journal of Labor Economics*, 3 (1), Pt 2, pp. S33–S58.

Beechey, V. (1988) 'Rethinking the Definition of Work', in J. Jenson, J. *et al.*

Beechey, V. and Perkins, T. (1987) *A Matter of Hours: Part-time Work and the Labour Market* Cambridge: Polity Press.

Blackburn, R. and Mann, M. (1979) *The Working Class in the Labour Market*, London: Macmillan.

Bryson, A. (1989) 'Part-time Working', *Low Pay Review*, 37, London: Low Pay Unit.

Bulmer, M. (ed.) (1975) *Working Class Images of Society*, London: Routledge and Kegan Paul.

CEC (1988) 1148, The Social Dimension of the Internal Market, September, Brussels: Commission for the European Communities.

CEC (1989) Conference Report on Evaluation of Community Policy on Equal Opportunities. Toledo, April, Brussels: Commission for the European Communities.

CEC (1992) 'Evaluation of Women's Involvement in European Social Fund Measures in 1990', in *Social Europe*, Lefebvre M-C., for DGV, Brussels: Commission for the European Communities.

CEC (1993a) 'Occupational Segregation of Women and Men in the European Community' in *Social Europe*, Rubery, J. and Fagan, C for the Equal Opportunities Unit, DGV, Brussels: Commission for the European Communities.

CEC (1993b) *European Social Policy* (Com (93) 551), September, Brussels: Commission for the European Communities.

Cecchini, P. (1988) *1992: The Benefits of a Single Market.*

Central Statistical Office (1989) *Social Trends 19*, London: HMSO.

Central Statistical Office (1994) *Social Trends 24*, London: HMSO.

Cockburn, C. (1987) *Two Track Training: Sex Inequalities and the YTS*, London: Macmillan.

Com (87) 230 Final, 'Problems of Social Security – Common Interests in the Member State.'

Confederation of British Industry (1967) *Employing Women: The Employers' View*, London: CBI.

Corcoran, M., Duncan, G. and Ponza, M. (1983) 'A Longitudinal Analysis of White Women's Wages', *Journal of Human Resources*, XVIII (4), pp. 497–520.

Crompton, R. and Sanderson, K. (1986) 'Credentials and Careers: Some Implications of the Increase in Professional Qualifications among Women', *Sociology*, 20 (1), pp. 25–42.

Cross, M. (1987) 'Black Youth and YTS: The Policy Issues', in M. Cross and D. Smith (eds) *Black Youth Futures*, Leicester: National Youth Bureau.

Dale, A. (1986) 'Labor Market Structure in the United Kingdom', *Work and Occupations*, 15, pp. 558–90.

Dale, A. (1987) 'Occupational Inequality, Gender and Life-cycle', *Work, Employment and Society*, 1 (3), pp. 326–51.

Dale, A. (1991) 'Stratification over the Life-course: Gender Differences within the Household', in G. Payne and P. Abbott (eds) *The Social Mobility of Women*, Brighton: Falmer.

Dale, A. and Bamford, C. (1988) 'Flexibility and the peripheral Workforce', Occasional Papers in Sociology and Social Policy No. 11, Department of Sociology, University of Surrey, Guildford.

Dale, A. and Glover, J. (1990) 'An Analysis of Women's Employment Patterns in the UK, France and the USA: The Value of Survey Based Comparisons', Department of Employment Research Paper No. 75. London: DOE.

Daniel, W. W. (1980) *Maternity Rights: The Experience of Women*, London: Policy Studies Institute.

Department of Employment (1988) 'Pay in Great Britain: Results of the 1988 New Earnings Survey', *Employment Gazette*, November, pp. 601–5.

Department of Employment (1989) 'Labour Force Outlook to 2000', *Employment Gazette*, April, pp. 159–72.

Department of Employment and Science (1988) *Education Statistics for the UK, 1988*, London: HMSO.

Dex, S. (1987) *Women's Occupational Mobility*, London: Macmillan.

Docksey, C. (1987) 'The European Community and the Promotion of Equality', in McCrudden (ed.) *Women, Employment and European Equality Law*, Eclipse.

Employment: The Challenge to the Nation (1985) CMND 9474, London: HMSO.

Equal Opportunities Commission (1986) *Women and Men in Britain: A Statistical Profile*, London: EOC.

Equal Opportunities Commission (1991) *Women and Men in Britain*, London: EOC.

Ermisch, J. (1990) *Fewer Babies, Longer Lives*, York: Joseph Rowntree.

European Industrial Relations Review (1985) June; (1986) June, October.

European Network of Experts on the Situation of Women in the Labour Market, *Bulletin on Women and Employment in the EC*.

European Parliament (1982) *Working Document on Voluntary Part-time Work*, Document 1–540/82, Report 3, September.

EUROSTAT (1993) *Women in the European Community*, Luxemburg: OOPEC.

EUROSTAT (1994) Unemployment 3, March.

Euzeby, A. (1988) 'Part-time Employment and Social Security', *International Labour Review*, 127(5).

Fabian Society (1966) 'Womanpower', Young Fabian Pamphlet No. 11, London.

Gallie, D. (1989) 'Technological Change, Gender and Skill', SCELI Working Paper No. 4.

Glasner, A. (1992) 'Gender and Europe: Cultural and Structural Impediments to Change', in J. Bailey (ed.) *Social Europe*, London: Longman.

Goldsmith, J. (1990) 'The Effects on Women of the Creation of the European Internal Market in 1992, with Particular Reference to the Problems of Black and Ethnic Minority Women in the UK (A preliminary study)', unpublished report for European Parliamentary Labour Party.

Goldthorpe, J., Lockwood, D., Bechhofer, F. and Platt, J. (1969) *The Affluent Worker in the Class Structure*, Cambridge: Cambridge University Press.

Grant, L. (1991) 'Part-time Work. Women Count the Cost', Wycrow Working Paper 2, University of Bradford: Wycrow.

Hakim, C. (1979) 'Occupational Segregation', Department of Employment Research Paper No. 9, London: DOE.

Hakim, C. (1991) 'Grateful Slaves and Self-made Women: Fact and Fantasy in Women's Work Orientations', *European Sociological Review* 7(2) September, pp. 101–21.

Hemeldonck, M. Van (1988) 'Working Document on the Effects of Completion of the Internal Market in 1992 on Women in Europe', Brussels: European Parliament Committee on Women's Rights.

Horrell, Rubery, J. and Burchell, B. (1989) 'Gender and Skills', SCELI Working Paper No. 5.

Huws, U. (1989) 'Danger. Women at Work', *New Statesman and Society*, 17 March, pp. 12–13.

Huws, U., Hurstfield, J. and Holtmaat, R. (1989) *What Price Flexibility? The Casualisation of Women's Employment*, London: Low Pay Unit.

Institute for Employment Research (1988) *Review of the Economy and Employment: Occupational Update 1988*, IER.

Joshi, H. (1988) *Changing Roles of Women in the British Labour Market and the Family*, London: Birkbeck College.

Joshi, H. (1991) 'Sex and Motherhood as Handicaps in the Labour Market', in M. Maclean and D. Groves, *Women's Issues in Social Policy*, London: Routledge.

Joshi, H. (1992) 'The Cost of Caring', in C. Glendinning and J. Millar (eds) *Women and Poverty in Britain, in the 1990s*, Hemel Hempstead: Harvester Wheatsheaf.

Labour Research (1988) 'Are Europe's unions united?'

Lewis, J. (1984) *Women in England 1870–1950*, Hemel Hempstead: Harvester Wheatsheaf.

Lewis, J. and Piachaud, D. (1992) 'Women and Poverty in the Twentieth Century', in C. Glendinning and J. Millar (eds) *Women and Poverty in Britain, the 1990s*, Hemel Hempstead: Harvester Wheatsheaf.

Lonsdale, S. (1992) 'Patterns of Paid Work', in C. Glendinning and J. Millar (eds) *Women and Poverty* in Britain, in the 1990s, Hemel Hempstead: Harvester Wheatsheaf.

Lovering, J. (1990) 'On Economic Restructuring, Spatial Change and Labour Market Segmentation in Britain in the 1980s', in *Work, Employment and Society: A Decade of Change*, London: British Sociological Association.

Martin, J. and Roberts, C. (1984) *Women and Employment: A Lifetime Perspective*, London: HMSO.

Meehan, E. (1987) 'Women's Equality and the European Community', in Ashton and Whitting (eds) 'Feminist Theory and Practical Policies', Occasional Paper 29, School for Advanced Urban Studies.

Meehan, E. and Whitting, G. (1989) 'Gender and Public Policy: European law and British Equal Opportunity Policies', Special issue of *Policy and Politics*, 17 (4).

Metcalf, H. and Leighton, P. (1989) *The Under-utilisation of Women in the Labour Market*, IMS Report No. 172.

Meulders, D. (1989) 'Employment', paper given at a Conference on Evaluation of Community Policy on Equal Opportunities, Toledo, April.

Millar, J. (1989) 'Employment for Disadvantaged Groups: Single Parents', paper given at a Conference on Evaluation of Community Policy on Equal Opportunities, Toledo, April.

Mitter, S. (1986) 'Industrial Restructuring and Manufacturing Homework: Immigrant Women in the UK Clothing Industry', *Capital and Class*, 27, pp. 37–80.

Moss, P. (1988) *Consolidated Report of the European Childcare Network*, Brussels: Commission for the European Communities.

Moss, P. (1989) 'Childcare and Employment', paper given to the Annual Conference of the Social Policy Association, University of Bath.

Moss, P. and Brannen, J. (1987) 'Fathers and Employment', in C. Lewis and M. O'Brien (eds) *Reassessing Fatherhood*, London: Sage.

Myrdal, A. and Klein, V. (1956) *Women's Two Roles*, London: Routledge & Kegan Paul.

Nielsen, R. and Szyszczak, E. (1991) *The Social dimension of the European Community*, Copenhagen: Handelshojskolens Forlag.

O'Higgins, M. (1988) 'Horizon 1992 and the Guarantee of a Minimum Income', paper given to a European Seminar CRESGE/EEC, Tilques, October.

O'Higgins, M. and Jenkins, S. (1989) 'Poverty in Europe', paper presented at EUROSTAT Seminar on Poverty Statistics, Nordwijk-an-Zee, Netherlands, October.

Oppenheimer, V. (1970) *The Female Labor Force in the United States: Demographic and Economic Factors Governing its Growth and Composition*. Greenwood Press.

Organisation for Economic Cooperation and Development (1985) *The Integration of Women into the Economy*, Paris: OECD.

Phizaclea, A. (1983) *One Way Ticket*, London: Routledge & Kegan Paul.

Pollert, A. (1988) 'The "Flexible Firm": Fixation or Fact', *Work, Employment and Society*, 2 (3), pp. 281–316.

Prondzynski, I. (1989) 'The Social Situation and Employment of Women in the European Community', in *Policy and Politics*, 17 (4).

Rapoport, R. and Moss, P. (1990) 'Men and Women as Equals at Work', Thomas Coram Research Unit Occasional Paper No. 11, London: TCRU.

Siltanen, J. (1990) 'Social Change and the Measurement of Occupational Segregation by Sex: An Assessment of the Sex Ratio Index', *Work, Employment and Society*, 4, pp. 1–29.

Roll, J. (1992) *Lone Parent Families in the European Community*, London: European Family and Social Policy Unit.

Room, G., Lawson, R. and Laczko, F. (1989) 'New Poverty in the European Community', *Policy and Politics*, April.

Sivanandan, A. (1988) 'The New Racism' *New Society*, 4 November.

Standing, G. (1986) 'Meshing Flexibility with Security: An Answer to British Unemployment', *International Labour Review*, 125 (1), p. 63.

Sutton, K. (1989) 'Equal Pay: Getting It Right for Women', *Low Pay Review, 1987*.

Szyszcak, E. (1989) 'The Future of Women's Rights: The Role of Community Law', in *Year Book of Social Policy 1986/7*, London: Longman.

Walby, S. (1986) *Patriarchy at Work*, Cambridge: Polity Press.

Westwood, S. and Bhachu, P. (eds) (1988) *Enterprising Women*, London: Routledge.

Whitting, G. (1988) 'Women and Poverty in Europe: Experience and Action from the 2nd EC Programme to Combat Poverty', paper to the European Network of Women's Tribunal, November, Brussels.

Whitting, G. and Quinn, J. (1989) 'Women and Work: Preparing for an independent Future', *Policy and Politics*, 17 (4).

Whitting, J. (1990) 'Women and 1992: Opportunity or Disaster?' *Social Policy Review, 1989–90*, pp. 214–27.

III

Women and Child Care

Introduction

MARY KEMBER

One of the most significant changes in many Western societies in the past 30 years has been the expectation that women will spend much of their adult lives in the workforce (either through choice or economic necessity). Whether or not women have been positively *encouraged* to participate in the workforce by government policy decisions has been determined by the political stance of governments in individual countries. One of the clearest messages of encouragement to women to participate in the workforce on equal terms with men is through positive policies on child care provision. Elsewhere in Europe there are examples of well-thought out and well-developed child care policies (particularly in the Scandinavian countries); in the UK child care has, until very recently (1996), rarely appeared on the government's agenda. In the late 1980s, child care provision in this country ranked amongst the worst in Europe and there is a lot of catching up to do (Phillips and Moss, 1989). Local authority places have actually dropped over a ten-year period. In 1991, almost two-fifths of working mothers with children under 5 used unpaid family and friends to care for their children (Central Statistical Office, 1994). Child care provision in the UK is sparse, inconsistent and patchy: 'Unlike most of its EC partners, the UK has no national policy, but merely a jumble of fragmented, inconsistent and often poor-quality services, developed on an ad hoc basis' (Cohen and Fraser, 1991).

Julia Brannen and Peter Moss, in the excerpt reproduced here, give a brief overview of post-war government policy on child care: successive governments have adopted a 'hands-off' attitude. The 'woman as carer / man as breadwinner' model of household has been explicitly supported and perpetuated by a string of governments, not only by lack of child care but by other familistic policies (Borchorst, 1990). Only when there appeared to be a threat of an acute labour shortage in the late 1980s because of the availability of fewer school-leavers, was child care put on the agenda, but then, as during two World Wars (Summerfield, 1984), child care seemed merely to have a place as a means of regulating the flow of female labour. With the onset of recession in the late 1980s, child care disappeared as a matter for debate as quickly as it had arrived.

Lack of child care has regularly been quoted by women themselves as the main reason for their non-participation in the workforce (Martin and Roberts, 1984). In the excerpt reproduced here, Sophie Bowlby demonstrates how women's job opportunities are often constrained by the location of available child care. While it is impossible to estimate the financial costs of mothering precisely (Joshi, 1992), women never make up for the earnings they lose through being out of the labour market during their child-bearing and rearing years. Subsequent part-time working, returning to work at a lower grade and loss of pension rights all contribute to substantial financial disadvantage. Men, meanwhile, are likely to maintain their wages throughout the same period.

The cost to the country of losing women's talents and training because they give up work to look after children has been estimated as extremely high: one of the driving factors for many private child care initiatives in Britain in the late 1980s was that companies wanted to hold on to employees in whom they had invested so much training and expense. There is also a substantial gain for government revenues to be made from women's employment through taxation (Cohen and Fraser, 1991). Yet blind to the implications of its own lack of provision, the government recently made much of the expense to the country of paying social security to lone mothers who do not go out to work (White Paper, 1991). That they eventually recognised that lack of child care might explain why many lone mothers do not enter paid work was indicated in the 1993 autumn budget, when an allowance for child care costs was reintroduced into the means-testing formula for Family Credit.

The other element so often overlooked in debates about child care is, ironically, that of the needs of the child. Unlike many other European countries, in the UK there has never been any great sense of the importance of child care in the socialising and educat-

ing of a child – indeed the legacy of Bowlby's 'maternal deprivation' theories (Bowlby, 1953) has been hard to shift. In contrast, in
France, for example, there was a belief very early on in the century
that very young children actually *benefited* from socialising in day
care with other children, and, linked with the concept of preventa-
tive medical care, child care was accepted as an important part of
the child's development. Despite the fact that there is research
which suggests that children who have experienced pre-school
child care are more likely to socialise better, do better at school,
etc. (Thomas Coram Childcare Project, 1990), child care is not seen
as a children's issue in this country. Significantly, the Children's
Act of 1989 only specified local authorities' duty to provide care
for children 'in need'. Yet it has been estimated that half of
the children under 5 who are currently living in poverty (1.25
million) could be brought out of this hardship if child care were
provided which allowed their mothers to work (Cohen and Fraser,
1991).

However, even if the argument is accepted that child care is good
for both mothers and children, there remains the question as to the
means by which care should be provided. Conservative governments of the last decade have repeatedly made it plain that they
view child care arrangements as a matter for parents, with provision being a matter for the market to dictate:

Women make their own arrangements now and they can carry
on doing so. (Margaret Thatcher, 1990)

If you have to work you do and if you have to find child care
you find it. When I say 'have' I mean if you really want to.
(Angela Rumbold, 1991, in Cohen and Fraser, 1991)

If we go down the route of universal child care provision, the
sums are enormous. We shall have to look at employers to see
what help they can give. (John Patten, 1990)

Clearly market forces are partially responding to increased effective demand. Places in local authority nurseries and playgroups
have substantially declined over the decade of the 1980s while
places in private nurseries, playgroups and childminders increased
(Central Statistical Office, 1994). Yet child care left up to the
market is likely to be patchy and unlikely to respond to all parents'

needs or to meet the requirements of children with special needs. Private child care also tends to fluctuate according to the economic climate: companies preoccupied with making staff redundant no longer consider child care to be on the agenda. In 1990, a personnel executive of a defence company stated child care 'wasn't considered appropriate under the circumstances [of recession]' and a child care consultant stated that her efforts to get more child care initiatives off the ground were failing because of companies' financial uncertainties (*Personnel Today*, 11.9.90). Coats (1993) cites how a Confederation of British Industry memo stated that since the 'demographic time-bomb' had been defused members need no longer recognise equal opportunities.

But how might a publicly funded system of child care be funded? The excerpt from Coote, Hewitt and Harman discusses the various options that a government could consider in funding a comprehensive child care service, bearing in mind public expenditure constraints. While tax concessions to those using child care or child care credits can help with the costs (demand subsidies), they do little to help with a more fundamental problem – that of the shortage of facilities. Government could help either by providing services themselves or by helping others to fund them (supply subsidies). Employers themselves could rightly be expected to contribute as they stand to benefit from women's expertise. Other possibilities include consortia of local authorities, businesses and private child care companies; or local authority 'planning gain' schemes whereby they give permission for private development in exchange for help with child care facilities; or the creation of a small local tax on businesses which would be available to local authorities to spend on child care facilities. Cohen and Fraser (1991) argue strongly that it is up to government to take the lead responsibility for a national child care policy.

While there are signs, in the mid 1990s, that some parts of the British Conservative government are starting to accept that some form of government intervention will have to occur, in the form of tax concessions both to users and employers or in the form of vouchers to be exchanged for care, there are still powerful voices from the New Right who argue that women should not have children if they do not want to look after them, as does Patricia Morgan in the excerpt reproduced here. On the political Left, and in Europe, debate continues as to how to bridge the family/employment divide most effectively and find a new discourse that includes men as well as women, and tries to unlock them from the gendered and separate parts of parenting.

In the short term at least, UK women are likely to have to continue to trade motherhood against employment. It is possible that the European Equal Opportunities programme may push the issue of child care on to the agenda of UK government of whatever colour. Perhaps moral outrage by the New Right at so called 'home-alone' children and great concern about single mothers 'draining treasury coffers' will lead to political consensus on this issue. One thing is certain, without a *policy*, child care provision will remain patchy and unreliable and quality will go largely unmonitored.

Government Policy

JULIA BRANNEN AND PETER MOSS

Policies which might provide some support for employed mothers or fathers have met a mixture of indifference and hostility from successive post-war governments. The tone was set in 1945. During the war, faced by a chronic labour shortage, rapid expansion of nurseries took place to encourage mothers into the labour force, where their work was desperately needed. Immediately the war ended, government urged women with young children to stay at home and began a rapid reduction in nursery provision. In 1986, there were only 29,000 places in public day nurseries, slightly less than one place for every 100 children under 5 – in 1945 there had been 62,780 places. Moreover, the limited places that have been available in these publicly funded child care services have become essentially a social work resource, for the use of families with major problems, rather than a service for the general run of employed parents (Moss, 1990). The only other intervention on child care services for employed parents by government was similarly negative: between 1984 and 1990, government has taxed most parents using nurseries which are subsidized by their employer.

The one measure of support to be introduced by a post-war government has been maternity leave. Even this one policy has been reluctantly and only partially conceded. The measure, introduced in 1976, is not really leave as such. In a proper maternity leave scheme, women maintain their status as employees while absent from work due to pregnancy and childbirth. Instead, under British legislation women have their contracts terminated with a guarantee of reinstatement in similar work, though not

From Julia Brannen and Peter Moss (1991) *Managing Mothers*, London: Unwin Hyman, pp. 29–31.

necessarily in their previous job, and are not entitled to non-statutory benefits, such as bonuses, during their absence. Moreover, the qualifying conditions imposed are so restrictive – women having to have worked for at least two years for the same employer – that many pregnant employed women, nearly a half according to one study (Daniel, 1980), are not eligible. Benefit payments are only available for 18 of the 40 weeks 'leave' period, and for two-thirds of this time only at a low flat-rate level.

The measure was limited from its inception, and since then it has been made if anything more restrictive, rather than being improved. No further leave entitlements for employed parents have been introduced. Indeed, the present UK government has opposed a draft Directive, put forward by the European Commission in 1983, that would have required all Member States of the Community to provide parental leave and leave for family reasons and set minimum standards for these two types of leave.

Government policy, or lack of it, since 1945 has been justified by several arguments. The post-war rundown of nurseries was heralded by a Ministry of Health Circular (221/45) which articulated an ideology about motherhood and child care that has been dominant in the post-war period:

> The Ministers concerned accept the view of medical and other authority that, in the interests of the health and development of the child no less than for the benefit of the mother, the proper place for a child under two is at home with his mother. They are also of the opinion that under normal peacetime conditions, the right policy to pursue would be positively to discourage mothers of children under two from going out to work.

Over 20 years later, another Government Circular (on 'Day Care for Children under 5'; Ministry of Health 37/68) reiterated the view 'that wherever possible the younger pre-school child should be at home with the mother... because early and prolonged separation from the mother is detrimental to the child'.

More recently, another line of argument has been used to justify non-intervention. Government, it is argued, has no direct role to play in making provision to support employed parents and their children; if parents wish to go out to work, then they must deal with the consequences, either by themselves or in cooperation with their employers. This argument (with others) was being used in the mid 1980s to justify blocking the European Commission's proposal on Parental Leave, and for not providing public funds for child care services.

> The Government considers that the most appropriate way of dealing with the issues covered by the draft [European Commission] Directive [on Parental Leave] is through voluntary negotiations between employers and employees. (Select Committee of the European Communities, 1985, p. 2)

> Day care will continue to be primarily a matter of private arrangement between parents and private and voluntary resources except where there are special needs. (John Patten, Parliamentary Under-Secretary of State at the DHSS, Hansard, 18.2.1985, col. 397)

This policy stance reflects a number of themes in the thinking of the post-1979 Conservative government – reducing, rather than increasing, 'dependency' on the state; reducing legislative demands and constraints imposed on employers, and not adding new ones, as a means of improving economic competitiveness and performance; and viewing children and child care as in general private issues, except in certain areas with long-established social involvement (compulsory schooling and health services) and in cases of extreme need (dire poverty, abuse).

Government policy in the mid 1980s was based not on an explicit objection to mothers with young children being employed, but on the view that 'parents' were free to choose whether they went out to work, and that if they did it was up to parents and employers to cope with the consequences. Provisions for working parents should be left to the operation of market forces, either through parents' paying for private child care services, or through employers' providing child care (either directly or indirectly through financial support) and other types of support for employees with children (for example, through employment adaptations) where labour shortages and similar considerations made it in the employer's interests to do so. Government therefore 'recognis(ed) that there is a range of measures which can be of help in reconciling career and family responsibilities', but limited its role to 'commending to employers the advice on these matters contained in the Equal Opportunities Commission's Code of Practice' (Central Office of Information, 1987, p. 3).

Locational Issues in Child Care Provision

SOPHIE BOWLBY

The impact of the location of child care on its accessibility to working parents is linked closely to the time–space budgets of those parents. These will clearly be affected by: the location of work and hours of work; the location and hours of the child care facility; the transport available to the parent(s); and the period during which a child needs minding. The hours a child needs minding differ for pre-school and school-age children with the latter needing extended hours of care during the school holidays but relatively short hours during school terms (assuming that a major part of the parent(s) work hours coincide with the school hours).

Some research on women's time–space budgets and child care has been done. In what follows I will outline some of the main points to emerge from existing research in relation to different forms of child care for pre-school children and point to areas where further research is needed.

A useful illustration of the combined impact of child care location, hours of operation and transport on women's access to work is provided by a study of women's access to job locations in Reading by Pickup (1983). He used data on job locations and job hours for women in the town and detailed data on travel times by different forms of transport. With these data he was able to develop a simulation model of women's access to job locations, assuming different domestic and child care constraints. This model showed that the time required for mothers' journeys to day nursery or school before and after work substantially reduced the number of

From Sophie Bowlby, 'Women, Work and the Family: Control and Constraints', *Geography* (1990), pp. 22–5.

accessible job locations. For example, for women living in a northern suburb of Reading who were without domestic constraints
about 90 job locations were accessible to women travelling by car,
about 70 for those travelling by bus and about 5 to those travelling
on foot. For women taking children to and collecting them from
the local day nursery before and after work the comparable figures
are 25, 18 and 0; for those taking school-age children to and from
the local school the figures are 20, 6 and 0. Changing the school
hours increased the number of job locations accessible to 21, 15
and 0, thus nearly tripling the number of job locations accessible by
bus. This example suggests that the location of child care facilities
can have more than a trivial effect on women's access to paid work.
It also shows how important for such access is the time at which
school or child care is available. Thus, improving the access of
women with children to work depends not only on the provision
of child care, but the provision of child care at appropriate locations and times. Otherwise the time–space constraints created by
transporting children to care or to school limit women's job choice
to locations close to the care location.

That the job choice of women with children who do succeed in
working is spatially constrained is shown by the more strongly
local pattern of such women's employment compared to men's
and to that of women without children. For example, Tivers, in a
study of the constraints on women with young children in the
London Borough of Merton, found that of the 77 (19 per cent)
of her 400 respondents who did paid work outside the home only 6
(8 per cent of the 77) worked in Central London compared to 40
per cent who worked there before the birth of their children and
to 36 per cent of all respondents' husbands. A further 37 women (9
per cent of the total) did paid work at home (Tivers, 1985; 1988).

Such limitation of women's job locations to areas near home or
near child care decreases women's access to well-paid jobs or to
jobs with good career prospects. It follows that it also diminishes
the supply of women's labour to such jobs and hence restricts
employers' choice of employees. Better paid jobs tend to be
found in town centres or in large peripheral industrial or office
areas (Pickup, 1983). However, this does not necessarily mean that
child care facilities should be located in these areas. Many women
want child care facilities to be located near their homes. This is a
particularly attractive option for women without access to a car
since travelling with a small baby or child and the paraphernalia

of clothes, toys and nappies which may also need transporting is both tiring and slow. A woman can travel to better work opportunities more easily after leaving her child at the nursery or with the carer.

Despite the attractions to many women of child care located near home, an alternative being advocated at the moment by the government is child care provided by employers in workplace-based nurseries. Indeed, some large employers who have a high proportion of women employees are starting to provide such nurseries – for example, the Midland Bank. Although this option may involve a longer journey with the child than care near home, it is also an option with locational advantages – for example, the possibility of visiting the child during a meal break or of being at hand in case of illness, as well as the obvious advantage of making only one journey. However, for workplace child care to be attractive economically to the employer a reasonably large number of employees must use the service. This means that such facilities will only be provided by large employers or by a group of employers located near one another. Town centres with many large offices or large industrial estates offer suitable locations for such cooperative provision.

If workplace-based care becomes the only or the major form of provision, however, parents working for small firms or in less central locations are likely to become disadvantaged. Workers in such firms are often already disadvantaged in terms of pay or job security and thus workplace-based care could add to the polarisation between 'core' workers and 'peripheral' workers. Furthermore, unless workplace nurseries are widely available parents will be tied to particular employers while their children are small. Another shortcoming of the workplace nursery is that by definition it only caters to those in work, yet child care is needed also by many women in order to undertake training for work.

A longer term, yet potentially very significant, drawback of child care provided by employers is that it is likely to be withdrawn once the labour shortage it was designed to meet is over. For example in the 1950s employers in East Kilbride provided nurseries in order to attract married women at a time of labour shortage. Once the shortage was over the nurseries were closed down despite continued demand from employees (Lewis and Foord, 1984). A further important issue remains the price of such care. At present the taxation of subsidised child care provided by the employer as a 'perk' and the absence of any tax allowance on child care costs means that such workplace care can only be afforded by dual-income, well-paid employees and not by those on lower incomes.

Clearly there is considerable need for further research on the implications of alternative forms and locations of childcare for women's access to paid work. Such research will need to be sensitive to the different types of socio-economic and built environment in which the care is to be provided. The potential role of local authorities or other public agencies as providers or facilitators of provision should also be considered.

Two other forms of care that are used by many parents today are the childminder – caring for two to three children in her home (I use 'her' since it is a job almost invariably done by women) or the nanny, 'au pair', or 'mother's help' caring for the child in the parents' home. In 1985–6 there were some 66,415 registered childminders in the UK and an estimated 30,000 nannies/au pairs/mother's helps (Cohen, 1988). Martin and Roberts (1984) found that 16 per cent of working women with pre-school children who made some arrangement for child care used childminders, 4 per cent used someone whom they employed to work in their own home and 8 per cent used some form of nursery care.

Childminders, unlike nurseries, offer a relatively cheap form of child care. A survey in 1986 by the National Childminders Association (NCMA) found the rates being charged were 50p–£1.00 per hour. By the same token, childminding is a poorly paid job, often involving long hours. The NCMA survey found 55 per cent of childminders worked 40 hours or more per week and their *gross* income with 3 full-time children was only £81 per week. Ironically, many women become childminders because they are constrained to work at home by their own children's need for care. From the parent's point of view, use of a childminder ought to provide a flexible, locationally and temporally convenient form of care which can be used by the parents of very young children. However, whether this is in fact the case is unclear. Basic knowledge of urban social geography suggests that at present the home locations of potential childminders and of parents with children to mind will rarely coincide closely, since they are likely to come from different social groups. At present there is very little research on the problems parents and childminders face in 'matching' their requirements, and on the difficulties parents have in both transporting children to minders and travelling to work or on any difficulties that 'live-out' nannies and mother's helps face in getting to their work.

Social Support for Families

ANNA COOTE, HARRIET HARMAN AND PATRICIA HEWITT

Child care

There are several reasons why a public policy intervention is needed in child care provision.

First, public intervention and investment in child care is justified on precisely the same grounds as public intervention and investment in education. Few would suggest leaving the education of the over-fives to parents; it is inconceivable that any Minister would say in relation to schooling that 'the state should only step in if the mother's life has collapsed'. But child care for the under fives is also education – education in the years when a child's intellectual and emotional development is faster than it will ever be again. Studies both in this country and in the USA have demonstrated the benefits of educational provision for the under-fives.

Changes in employment patterns are a second, and important, reason for public intervention in child care. As fewer women, and virtually no men, are willing or able to be full-time parents for five years or longer, then more small children will need alternative child care provision. Without it, some will be inadequately cared for, their future abilities damaged, and a growing number of school-age children will be left to fend for themselves after school and in the holidays. The social and economic costs of such neglect are very

From Anna Coote, Harriet Harman and Patricia Hewitt (1990) *The Family Way*, IPPR, pp. 39–42.

substantial. Furthermore, the *nature* of the child care provision that is needed is affected by parental employment. Our first objective could be met by educational provision in school hours and terms, provided parents were available for the rest of the time; with a majority of parents of the under-fives working full-or part-time, that will not be enough.

The third reason for public investment in child care is the promotion of more equal opportunities for women in employment. As we argued above, the expectation that women will do most of the caring (for elderly dependants as well as for children) severely restricts their employment prospects. The losses for individual women are substantial: but so are the costs to employers and to the economy as a whole. Proper child care provision – including policies which make it easier for women, and also men, to *combine* family responsibilities with employment which makes full use of their abilities – is therefore justified by the needs of the economy, as well as the interests of individual women.

We now look briefly at the child care policies of the Conservative and Labour Parties and suggest some of the directions which an effective child care programme would follow.

In 1972, as Secretary of State for Education, Mrs Thatcher announced her aim of a nursery or child care place for 50 per cent of 3-year-olds and 90 per cent of 4-year-olds. This target has not been reached. The abolition of income tax on workplace nursery places in the 1990 Budget was estimated to affect no more than 3,000 working mothers. Opposition amendments to the Finance Bill, which would have extended tax relief to other forms of employer-assisted child care, were defeated by the government.

The Labour Party's policy is to provide nursery education for every 3 and 4 year old whose parent wants it, together with the extension of children's centres, playgroups and other community-based facilities for younger children, and out-of- school and holiday facilities for those of school age.

Local authorities would be the focus for a comprehensive network of child care provided free of charge to parents. It is, however, improbable that comprehensive, nationwide provision could be put in place within five or perhaps even ten years. The potential demand is enormous: the 1980 Women in Employment survey found that, amongst employed mothers who make arrangements for the care of pre-school children, only 30 per cent paid for the care and only 6 per cent used a local authority nursery or school place; where school-age children are involved, only 10 per cent paid. The majority relied on their husband, a grandparent or other relative. The costs are substantial and will compete with other pressing claims on public expenditure. (Estimates made in 1985 suggested an overall gross cost of just under £3 billion, equivalent to £4 billion in today's prices.) The trained staff are not available and local authority and other community-based child care facilities will be competing for staff with the growing market, particularly in the South-East, for private nannies commanding considerably higher salaries than the public sector can offer.

A child care 'partnership' between parents, local employers and community groups will be central to solving the funding problem. But a partnership of providers also recognises that uniform provision for the care of young children is not possible (at least in the short to medium term) and may not be desirable. Young children have different needs; parents have different views of what is best for their children and different needs for care which will fit their own working arrangements. Other family members, childminders, nannies, playgroups, local authority-run children's centres and nurseries, nursery classes in schools, private nurseries and workplace nurseries all have a part to play in creating a comprehensive network of child care provision.

Furthermore, it is essential to recognise that many mothers (and a few fathers) prefer to work shorter hours while their children are young and would not opt to work full-time even if affordable child care were available. But the part-time facilities currently available (for instance in playgroups, or part-time places in nursery classes) usually offer hours which are too short or otherwise unsuited to the needs of a working parent. New child care facilities need to include those designed to offer part-time places, with a range of hours available to suit parents' and children's different needs.

There are several options open to any government seeking to fund a substantial expansion of child care facilities, but facing public expenditure constraints. First, it must be borne in mind that increased support for child care increases the number of mothers in employment – who, in turn, pay income tax and National Insurance contributions, thus reducing the net cost to the Exchequer of public investment in child care. Where new jobs are created in child care, and those are filled by people currently receiving unemployment benefit or income support, further savings will be made.

Second, it is reasonable to expect employers themselves to contribute to child care provision: as a growing number of firms recognise, policies which enable women to remain in their job (or return to it reasonably soon) after the birth of a child substantially reduce the company's training and recruitment costs. A few employers have invested substantially in child care, either by establishing workplace nurseries or by 'buying in' places at private nurseries. Others, particularly in the financial sector, have created 'career breaks' which enable women to remain at home longer with their young children without jeopardising their return to employment. Some have experimented with 'child care vouchers' (operated by Luncheon Vouchers) which do not attract tax relief, although they are exempt from National Insurance contributions.

Most enterprises, however, have not yet made any investment in child care. One possibility which deserves further consideration is the creation of a small local tax on businesses (possibly integrated with the Uniform Business Rate or revived business rates) which would be available to local authorities to spend on child care facilities. Such a tax could either be at the discretion of the local authority (on the model of the old 'penny rate') or uniform throughout the country. A company which was already investing in child care, through subsidised nursery places, 'child care vouchers' or in some other way, could have its contribution offset against its child care tax liability.

A third possibility, successfully used already by some local authorities, lies in 'planning gain'. Planning approval for a new office, shopping, housing or entertainment development may be made conditional on the provision of a site and building for a new nursery or children's centre, which could then be staffed and run by the local council, or by the development company itself (with, of course, qualified staff). In this way, capital costs (and even some revenue costs) can be met by the private sector. In a variation on the theme, a council may make planning permission for a private nursery dependent on a proportion of places being made available, at a reduced or no charge, to children nominated by the local authority itself.

A fourth possibility is the creation of 'consortia' of local authorities, businesses and private child care companies to establish and operate child care facilities. A local authority might, for instance, make available premises in a school with a falling roll or which had been closed; the child care company could operate the nursery, with a proportion of the places available free of charge to the council; and local businesses could subsidies places for children of their employees. (There would still, of course, be a cost to the local authority in such a case, since it would lose the capital it would otherwise have obtained from selling the premises.) All kinds of variations are possible: the point is simply to illustrate what part- nership might mean in practice.

Fifth, there is the question of charges to parents for public as well as private child care. For many policy-makers, particularly on the Left, the goal remains provision free of charge. But for most working parents, the problem is not simply the *cost* of child care, it is finding any satisfactory child care at all. Of course, unemployed or low-paid families cannot afford to pay for child care. While it is true, however, that most working parents do *not* pay directly for child care at present, most pay indirectly – through the wages (and promotion prospects) lost when the mother gives up her job or works part-time. Clearly, if publicly provided child care is to be free of charge, then fewer places will be provided than if some charge were made. Although charges should not be made for provision within the public education system (and are indeed prohibited by law), part of the costs of other provision should be met through charges (with appropriate exemptions or a sliding scale to reflect the needs of poorer families).

These funding options (and others could be added) deal essen- tially with the problem of *supply* – creating enough child care places to meet the rapidly growing demand. An alternative is to direct funding towards *demand* – in other words to give financial support to parents, leaving them to pay for the child care they choose in the private, public or community sector.

Tax relief for child care expenses – the classic demand- side subsidy – would be enormously popular with those working mothers who now pay for child care. Because the costs are both substantial and open-ended, the Treasury has, so far successfully, resisted it.

Quite apart from the cost, tax relief on child care expenses would give the greatest help to parents paying higher rate tax and with the largest child care expenses. It would give the least help to those with low child care expenses and incomes too low to take advan- tage of the full relief. And it would give nothing to those with incomes below the tax threshold, who need help most. It would, therefore, be a regressive use of public revenue. Evidence from the

USA, where some tax relief is already available on child care expenses, suggests that it has widened the gap between the quality of child care for well-off families and that for poor children.

An alternative form of help is to offer parents a 'child care credit' which could either take the form of tax relief (up to a limit and only at the standard rate of income tax) for those paying tax and a cash payment for non-taxpayers, or more simply a cash payment for all. The payment could be tied to the use of approved child care facilities, in which case it would help to raise standards; if it were not, it would in effect be an addition to Child Benefit. It could go to working parents (increasing the incentive for mothers to take employment) or to all parents (recognising that costs are also involved in full-time mothering).

If a child care credit were made available for children aged between 6 months and 3 years, together with those 3-and 4- year-olds for whom no educational provision is made, some 2.5 million children might qualify. (A child care credit could, of course, be extended to parents of older children in recognition of the need for after-school and holiday care, raising the total considerably.) The approximate gross cost would be £130 million per annum. for every £1 a week in credit, or £650 million per annum for a credit of £5 a week. (This would be equivalent to tax relief at the standard rate on £1,040 a year of child care expenses.) The net cost would, however, be lower depending on the number of mothers who took up employment as a result: it has been estimated that the net cost of a child care grant of £25 a week to employed mothers would be of the order of £300 million per annum.

The strongest argument in favour of some form of child care benefit is that it gives some help to *every* family, leaving parents to choose between whatever facilities, public or private, are available in their community. It recognises that some local authorities, for whatever reason, will not ensure that child care places are available for all the children in their area whose parents want it. Credits spent on publicly provided child care facilities would, of courses, increase the local council's revenue. The difference between using public funds for a benefit to parents, and using it for direct grants to local councils, playgroups and other organisations would be that parents themselves might have more choice over the provision they used.

The argument against a child care credit is that it fails to tackle the real problem – which is the *supply* of child care places. Giving parents more money, even if it is tied to the use of a child care place, does not by itself create any additional playgroups, children's centres or nurseries. If the money were in fact linked to child care expenditure, then local councils, playgroups, community groups and private organisations would presumably respond by expanding provision – in which case it might be more effective, and involve less administration, to give the money directly to the council. If, however, the benefit were *not* linked to the use of child care, then much of it might not in fact be spent on child care.

Difficult public expenditure choices will confront the next government. The first priority should be the expansion of nursery education for 3-and 4-year-olds. The costs involved will be substantial, well over £1 billion a year in current prices. But such a sum could not all be spent immediately, even if it could be made available. The commitment for the first two or three years will be significantly smaller. Some additional funding, on a far smaller scale, will also be needed to help local authorities monitor the quality of child care more effectively; strong quality control measures will be essential. In general, the demand for child care will not diminish in the foreseeable future and is likely to increase. More detailed consideration needs to be given to a range of options for funding more and better provision.

Families in Dreamland

PATRICIA MORGAN

Making daddies into mummies?

What the activists are not willing to admit is that the 'equality program' has failed when it comes to changing people's fundamental *attitudes*. For example, although Swedish parental leave is neutral with respect to sex, it is overwhelmingly mothers who have taken advantage of it. In 1974, parliament allowed either parent to take the paid leave (in addition to the father's ten days fully paid time off at childbirth). In 1979, changes in family law explicitly said that spouses should share breadwinning, housework and child care. By 1983 there were widely publicised 'working parties' to study and engineer men's role change. In 1987, the father's eligibility for leave was no longer dependent upon the mother's work record.

But men's take up has stayed at 27 per cent of fathers. Only 4 per cent of all fathers take an equal amount of leave to mothers and only 14 per cent of those who take any leave at all. Sharing leave has its inconveniences since both spouses have to keep leaving and returning to the workforce. Leave taking is often interpreted by employers, superiors and colleagues as signifying low commitment to work. Couples clearly feel more secure developing one principal occupation (even if, alone, it cannot provide enough to live on), than having two more insubstantial jobs. The higher the father's income, the less leave he takes, while men with women who earn more both absolutely and relatively are more likely to take leave (Haas, 1991).

From Patricia Morgan (1992) *Families in Dreamland: Challenging the New Consensus for State Childcare*, London Social Affairs Unit, pp. 13–18.

However, if there are obviously strong economic reasons for these choices, it may say little about the preferences of the couples involved. Statistical tests to find out which factors had the strongest independent effects on whether fathers took leave, reveal the overwhelming importance of attitudes. Three-quarters of fathers and two-thirds of women still believe that men should be more responsible for breadwinning than mothers and almost equally they also believe that success at work is more important for men. Women's attitudes to work in the child-rearing years have remained different from those of men. As was also found in the former Soviet Union, men are more likely to want to improve their prospects for advancement, independence and opportunities to take initiatives. Women are more interested in the proximity of their job to home and convenient working hours (Lepidus, 1982). Those pushing for equality have found it hard to 'understand' why women are taking on poorly paid jobs, for example as cleaners, clerks or sales ladies, instead of 'demanding training for better jobs' and blame the 'unequal division of tasks in the home and the shortage of day care places' (Lewis, 1982) and have advocated more flexible opening and closing times for nurseries, with 'night care' (Broberg and Hwang, 1991).

But the evidence points to the fact that mothers are *unwilling* to put their children into municipal care even when it is freely available. They may utilise places on offer to work 'long' part-time hours, but many have not been prepared to 'have their children in day care for ten hours a day'. Working-class mothers are particularly likely to consider home care to be ideal. Those not allotted a day care place tend to elect to 'wait' at home until one is vacant, while middle-class parents are more likely to make private arrangements.

Refusing to change

There is acute frustration among Swedish equality planners at the tenacity of sexual preference and differentiation (Lewis, 1982). This has proved more resilient than the family structure itself in the face of an onslaught from just about every technique of persuasion open to modern educators. Videos presented the problem of girls 'in conflict between their sexuality and their fantasy images of themselves as glamour girls or secure housewives'. Saturation techniques, experimental teaching aids and special teachers have been used for particular schools or age groups, with children continually exposed to 'unconventional' role models and traditional norms and roles incessantly condemned and mocked. Parents were bombarded with similar material as the media blasted away at 'parasitic mothers'. Has there been a change, asked one 800-page report on special intensive projects to 'remodel sex roles' by 'restructuring' girls and boys aptitudes and preferences? 'Yes, there has been. *Every* girl now thinks in terms of a job. This *is* progress. They want children, but they don't pin their hopes on marriage. They don't intend to be housewives for some future husband. But there has been no change in their vocational choices' (Johannsson, 1982). Even in 'model schools' where pupils were inundated with sex-role instruction there was 'a difference in attitudes' between the sexes 'but in their choices, no' (ibid.).

Even the most ardent equality activists have been forced to admit that the evident desire of mothers 'to monopolise child-care' is related to 'social–psychological' barriers that 'we might expect . . . - *will take generations*' to dismantle (Haas, 1991); and this after the most concerted attempt in history to engineer the freedom of women from childbearing responsibilities.

New sexes for Europe

This failure has not deterred the European Commission, in collaboration with the British Equal Opportunities Commission, from considering plans for the wholesale transformation of European families – in reply to the European Community's call for action to achieve equality between men and women in access to employment, vocational training, advancement and pay. Reports to it describe the habits and beliefs of 'asymmetrical' or complementary families (i.e. ones where there is a division of labour) as obstructions to the Euro-utopia of labour equality (Moss, 1988; 1991). There is concern that Britain is among those nations where employment rates for women with children under 5 are around a third, most of whom are employed for less than 30 hours a week and horror at the way in which fathers maintain their earnings when they have children, or even try to increase them through longer hours or promotion – leaving many mothers financially dependent upon men.

The commonplace emerges as insidious and bizarre as it is related how 'In two-parent households, women carry a disproportionate share of family responsibilities, especially concerned with children and their care'. Men, on the other hand, appear irresponsible, uninvolved, or only want to know about 'the more enjoyable, "cleaner" and less demanding aspects, such as play'; everywhere putting their interests before those of women (Moss, 1988, pp. 23–5, 190). Moreover:

> In many marriages, wives are still expected to provide, and often do provide, support services to their husbands which benefit them in many ways, including their employment. Some of these services are practical – including cooking, washing and ironing clothes; others are emotional – providing encouragement, showing sympathy and support.

A negative and pervasive ideology is held to propagate the view that:

> the 'good' mother should not be employed until her children reach a certain age, and then possibly only on a part-time basis. This is usually based on the belief that young children should be cared for at home by their mothers... For those who hold this view, the main role of the 'good' father is to support his family financially through employment.
>
> Such views can influence women's employment once they have children, they can provide pressures to stop work. (Ibid., pp. 26, 27; 1991)

If almost four out of five people opt for this traditional pattern, the task of combating it means concerted and urgent action, with policies which are sufficiently comprehensive to 'break into this vicious circle and change the present relationship between childcare, gender and inequality of employment' (Moss, 1988, p. 28). To this end, member states and the Community must play a leading role in initiating and supporting an immense, coordinated European programme, directed from a European centre, specifically concerned with child care, employment and equal opportunities. The centre would consist of a coordinating office and several regional sub-offices, each of which would specialise in a particular broad area – initially child care services; employment adaptations and changing the role of fathers.

In turn, to create 'a new climate of opinion' means that 'governments, political parties, employers, trades unions, services and their workers, and not least, the media, with their enormous influence and ability to create role models', must be encouraged to join in an immense exercise in re-education (ibid., p. 192). Experts are even to issue a guide to good practice for the instruction of fathers. The mother's career advancement must provide the criteria of responsible fatherhood. The nurseries will provide an excellent opportunity to pre-empt any harm that families do when, at present 'By the time they enter primary school, many children have already formed a clear view of the roles of men and women in society' (Cohen, n.d., p. 69). The goal is then a comprehensive service of publicly provided facilities, with a giant apparatus of functionaries to provide support, supervision, management and development for child care services.

Conclusions

What are we to make of this ambitious plan? Any careful observer of the Swedish example can only wonder whether more than minimum standards will ever be achieved, since the Eurocrats themselves have no more idea than their Swedish forerunners where the resources, particularly in the terms of personnel, to operate such facilities, can be found.

On the other hand, a quicker fix to put mothers to work is widely urged, involving tax allowances for child care and contract compliance (to make employers provide workplace crèches) together with a heavier financial squeeze on one-earner families through the complete abolition of the marriage allowance. Thus the prospect is of further impoverishment of families and deterioration in the care of young children born to increasingly pressurised parents and placed in makeshift institutions – at a time when child-rearing is already being pushed to the margins of parents' available time, energy and resources, and when the failure to provide properly for this may have serious consequences for us all.

Throughout the history of policies on the family, there has been a disturbing tendency for groups and individuals, whose views are far from those of the majority of families, excessively to influence policies which shape the lives of everyone else. It has now been given tremendous scope by the advent of unelected, unaccountable authorities in Europe. These minorities consider insufficiently, if at all, the wishes and views of most people. In turn, ordinary people are regarded as infinitely pliable, so that they can be remodelled, against their inclinations, in any desired form. There is no inkling that change may not occur, or that, if it does, it may not be in the direction desired, or that it might have unwelcome consequences. Unfortunately, the failure to learn from other societies' *actual* experiences, as much as the impetus to further engineering, is helped along by fantasies of what these should be – but never were.

Bibliography to Section III

Armstrong, H. (1989) *The Early Years: Consultation Document on Education and Child Care for the Under-Fives, London: Labour Party.*

Borchorst, A. (1990) 'Political Motherhood and Childcare Policies', in C. Ungerson (ed.) *Gender and Caring*, Hemel Hempstead: Harvester Wheatsheaf.

Bowlby, J. (1953) *Childcare and the Growth of Love*, Harmondsworth: Penguin.

Broberg, A. and Hwang, C.P. (1991) 'Day Care for Young Children in Sweden', in E.C. Melhuish and P. Moss, Day Care for Young Children: International Perspectives, London: Tavistock/Routledge.

Carlson, A. (1988) 'Having Children, Helping Children. Part 1, What to do', *Public Opinion*, March–April.

Central Office of Information (1987) *Policies for the Advancement of Women in Britain*, London: COI.

Central Statistical Office (1994) *Social Trends 24*, London: HMSO.

Child Health and Education study (1987) Osborn and Millbank.

The Children Act 1989: Guidance and Regulation (1991). Vol. 2. Family Support, Day Care and Educational Provision for Young Children, London: HMSO.

Coats, M. (1993) 'Women's Education. A Cause for Concern?', *Adults Learning*, November, pp. 60–3.

Cohen, B. (1988) *Caring for Children: Services and Policies for Childcare and Equal Opportunities in the United Kingdom*, London: Commission of the European Communities, Report for the European Commission's Childcare Network.

Cohen, B. and Fraser, N. (1991) *Childcare in a Modern Welfare System*, London: Institute for Public Policy Research.

Daniel, W.W. (1980) *Maternity Rights: The Experience of Women*, London: Policy Studies Institute.

Department of Social Security (1990) *Children Come First*, CMND 1263, London: HMSO.

Haas, L. (1991) 'Equal Parenthood and Social Policy: Lessons from a Study of Parental Leave in Sweden', in J.S. Hyde and M.J. Essex (eds) *Parental Leave and Child Care*, Temple University Press.

Hoem, J.M. (1990) 'Social Policy and Recent Fertility Change in Sweden', *Population and Development Review*, December.

Johannsson, E. (1982), quoted in H. Lewis, *Sweden's Right to be Human*, London; Allison & Busby, p. 125.

Joshi, H. (1992) 'The Cost of Caring', in C. Glendinning and J. Millar (eds) *Women and Poverty in Britain. The 1990s*. Hemel Hempstead: Harvester Wheatsheaf.

Lamb, M.E. and Levine, J.A. (1983) 'The Swedish Parental Insurance Policy: An Experiment in Social Engineering', in A. Sagi and M.E. Lamb (eds) *Fatherhood and Family Policy*, Lawrence Erlbaum Assoc.

Lepidus, G.W. (ed.) (1982) *Women, Work and the Family in the Soviet Union*.

Lewis, H. (1982) *Sweden's Right to be Human*, London: Allison & Busby.

Lewis, J., and Foord, J. (1984) 'New Towns and New Gender Relations in Old Industrial Regions: Women's Employment in Peterlee and East Kilbride', *Built Environment*, 10, pp. 42–52.

Marsh, A. and McKay, S. (1993) 'Families, Work and the Use of Child-care', *Employment Gazette*, August, pp. 361–70.

Martin, J. and Roberts, C. (1984) *Women and Employment: A Lifetime Perspective*, London: HMSO, Department of Employment, Office of Population Censuses and Surveys.

Melhuish, E.C. and Moss, P. (eds) (1991) *Day Care for Young Children: International Perspectives*, London: Tavistock/Routledge.

Metcalf, H. and Leighton, P. (1989) *The Under-Utilisation of Women in the Labour Market*, IMS Report No. 172, Institute of Manpower Studies, September.

Moss, P. (1990) 'Daycare for Young Children in the United Kingdom', in E. Melhuish and P. Moss (eds) *Day Care for Young Children: International Perspectives*, London: Tavistock/Routledge.

Moss, P. (1988) *Childcare and Equality of Opportunity: Consolidated Report to the European Commission*.

Phillips, A. and Moss, P. (1989) *Who Cares for Europe's Children?*, Luxembourg: OOPEC.

Pickup, L. (1983) 'Travel Issues in Women's Job Choice: An Activity Based Approach', unpublished Ph.D. thesis, Reading University: Department of Geography.

Simpson, R. (1986) 'The Cost of Childcare Services', in *Children and Equal Opportunities: Some Policy Perspectives*, London: Equal Opportunities Commission HMSO.

Summerfield, P. (1984) *Women Workers in the Second World War*, Beckenham: Croom Helm.

Tivers, J. (1985) *Women Attached: the Daily Lives of Women with Young Children*, London: Croom Helm.

Tivers, J. (1988) 'Women with Young Children: Constraints on Activities in the Urban Environment', in J. Little, L. Peake and P. Richardson (eds) *Women in Cities: Gender and the Urban Environment*, London: Macmillan, pp. 84–97.

IV

Lone Mothers

Introduction

MARY KEMBER

In the first edition of this book, there was no separate section on 'lone mothers'. Lone mothers are currently, however, at the centre of much political thought. On the left, the poverty by which so many lone mothers are entrapped is seen as a problem in itself, while on the right, lone mothers are seen as the source of other problems – juvenile delinquency, social disorder, and so on. Indeed, much of the current backlash against feminism stems from the fact that women have shown that they *can* survive without men – however straitened their circumstances – and indeed in many cases have deliberately chosen this way to live.

Isolating lone mothers is not intended to problematise them: from a social policy point of view, the issue of lone motherhood highlights the dilemmas for all mothers as to where their primary income should come from. For women with dependants, whether married or not, the three main potential sources of income include the state, the labour market and the man with whom they are living. In the first edition of this book, the problem as to how women derive an income was outlined as being one of whether they should be treated fundamentally as mothers or primarily as workers, by social policy. The dilemma is widened by the possibility, now outlined by the Child Support Act, of women having a claim to income from men with whom they have had some form of sexual relationship – whether in marriage or not.

Why has the situation become so much more complex for social policy? Lone parenthood has become a feature of most Western societies over the past decade (Roll, 1992a). In the UK lone mothers now form one in ten of all mothers. Over the decade 1981–91, the number of divorces rose by 10 per cent, while the rate of marriage continued to decline. At the same time, the percentage of live births outside marriage doubled to a figure of almost one in three births in 1992 (Central Statistical Office, 1994). In 1991, there were calculated to be 1.3 million lone-parent families in Great Britain, containing 2.2 million dependent children: one in five or six of all dependent children lived in a lone-parent household. That the shape of the family has changed over the last 30 years, then, is indisputable.

Political focus on the family tends to be highly controversial and emotive. The Conservative Party has long claimed the moral ground – calling themselves the 'party of the family'. The traditional family has been aligned with morality in society and the lone-parent family with moral decay. Ministers have variously blamed lone mothers for adolescent crime, for the poor performance of their children at school, for exacerbating the homelessness problem. At the Conservative Party Conference in October 1993, Michael Howard announced that the government was studying proposals to cap benefits to single parents with more than one child (*The Independent*, 6.10.93), while George Young, Housing Minister, supported by Peter Lilley, Social Security Minister, proposed that young unmarried mothers should be housed in hostels or with their parents rather than being given council housing (ibid., 8.10.93). Behind the rhetoric was the belief that lone parents, by their dependency on the state, should not 'undermine' the attempts of traditional two-parent families to be self-supporting.

The moral indignation expressed by government ministers is also to be found in the writings of Charles Murray, an American social scientist who has been deeply influential in Great Britain since the late 1980s, particularly on Conservative politicians. Murray upholds marriage as the 'natural' relationship in which to have children – with the traditional role of breadwinner allocated to the father. The target of his criticism is specifically households where children are brought up without fathers and without the mother being married at the time of their birth. These he defines as part of the new 'underclass': they are not just the 'poor', but the 'undeserving', 'unrespectable', 'feckless' poor whose values 'contaminate the life of entire neighbourhoods' (Murray, 1990). A similar message comes out of readings from the right-wing IEA Health and Welfare Unit (Dennis and Erdos, 1992; Davies, 1993) where mother-led families are blamed for spawning 'serious pathologies', marijuana use in children, depressive effects, lower academic achievement. Indeed, this is believed not only to be the case in lone-parent households, but in any household where the mother works, where there is any attempt at 'equal roles' between the sexes: 'maternal employment has shown up consistently as a link to higher delinquency and juvenile crime' (Davies, 1993, p. 46). Healthy, well-balanced children, he concludes, will only emerge from households where the father plays a strong, traditionally dominant role and where the mother is a housewife.

Throughout the 1980s the Conservative Party adopted a stance whereby families were not an area to be 'interfered' with by governments and public policy – that somehow family life was a bastion against the world. A government whose policy was built on a belief 'that individuals and families were no longer taking responsibility for themselves' (Millar, 1993), who wanted to move away from 'a dependency culture' – combined with a determination to cut public expenditure drastically – would inevitably sooner or later come to regard lone mothers as a 'problem'. By the late 1980s, more lone mothers than ever before were receiving benefits, and a declining number were going out to work: 41 per cent in 1988–90 compared to 49 per cent in 1979–81 (Burghes, 1993).

While recession was clearly not helping women to find suitable paid employment, the main policy direction on the left was to focus on ways of helping lone mothers get back into the workplace as the most likely route out of poverty. The 1990 policy document by the trade union funded Institute for Public Policy Research advocated the 'view that women as well as men should be expected to earn their own living and share in the financial support of their children' (Coote *et al.*, p. 56), albeit with provision to support women until their youngest child was at least five, to provide appropriate child care facilities, training programmes and increased Child Benefit payments. Joan Brown (1989), however, points out that there are more than material considerations involved in many lone-mothers' decisions not to go out to work: many lone mothers want to avoid having to leave their children for hours on end at a stage in their lives when they are probably having to deal with varying emotional conflicts and changes in circumstances. There may well be a desire to compensate in this way for the lack of a parent (Burghes, 1993). Yet there is no doubt that greater concessions on the part of employers towards allowing leave with pay in times of child sickness, in allowing women more paid leave in the first year of their child's life – as occurs as a matter of course in Sweden, for example

– would go some way towards relieving a mother's anxiety at the prospect of spending many hours at work.

But whether to encourage more women back into the workplace or whether to support increasing numbers of lone mothers with social security benefits posed a conflict of values for the UK government in the 1980s and 1990s. Holding fast to traditional views of a mother's place being at home with her children, they argued that surely it could not then be right for government policy to *encourage* her to leave her children with a carer in order to go out to work. That more UK women than ever before were participating in the workforce was really only acceptable because they worked, on the whole, in part-time jobs which allowed their primary role, still, to be as unpaid carer within the family. For lone mothers this was no solution – going out to work, once they had paid for child care and lost pound for pound of what they earned against their benefit payment, gave them no more money than state benefits. The loss of travel and child care allowances in the arrangements for Family Credit as a result of the social security reforms of 1988 meant it was even more disadvantageous for lone mothers to go out to work (although child care allowances were reinstated in 1993).

It was not surprising then that the focus of attention became the 'absent' fathers. In 1989, only three out of ten lone mothers were receiving maintenance payments (Bradshaw and Millar, 1991). The Joseph Rowntree Foundation in a report in 1993 calculated that less than 10 per cent of lone-mothers' income came from maintenance payments. The chapter by Jane Millar included here outlines the main content of the resulting 1991 Child Support Act and its implications. Not only could the government reduce public expenditure but, in switching financial focus back on to the father, they could be seen to be upholding traditional gender roles. Despite the fact that the family might no longer physically exist together, the male would still carry financial responsibility and the female bear the caring responsibility for the children (in most cases). The new Child Support Agency would have the function of tracing absent fathers and collecting maintenance payments worked out to a given formula. At the same time, as Millar (1992) points out, the Child Support Act can be seen to be yet another example of social policy upholding the traditional idea of the 'family' – despite the various family structures that now exist in our society.

Additional controversy has resulted from the forcing of lone mothers to name absent fathers with the threat of withholding benefits if they do not do so: threats of violence and ill-effects on children in such relationships have not sufficiently been taken into account (Monk and Slipman, 1991). Indeed, the first year of work by the Child Support Agency saw increasing disquiet about the Agency and its work. For all this effort, it should be noted that most lone *mothers* currently on state support do not actually benefit from any settlement from maintenance, should this be extracted from absent partners – unless they receive a sufficient amount to carry them above benefit levels. The only gainer is the Treasury.

The UK, of course, is not alone in its policy debates over lone mothers. The chapter by John Baker compares the situation and status of lone mothers in France and in the UK. Lone mothers in France are relatively well off: it seems that this is because they are helped by family policies directed at *all* mothers, rather than targeted by anti-poverty measures alone, as in this country. As Baker says, in France family policy is popular and is regarded as an investment, rather than as a 'consumption expense' as is the case in the UK. Where family policy and employment policy address the particular problems of women as mothers – by such things as attractive family benefits, child care provision and good maternity provision – *lone* mothers will almost inevitably be helped.

The full impact of the legislation of the early 1990s remains to be seen. Yet women's poverty in lone parenthood is unlikely to be seriously addressed until policy decisions are taken regarding the inequality women experience both through the marriage relationship and through child-rearing.

State, Family and Personal Responsibility: The Changing Balance for Lone Mothers in the UK

JANE MILLAR

Introduction

In the UK there are about one and a quarter million lone-parent families, making up 19 per cent of all families with children. The numbers of lone parents have almost doubled since the early 1970s and this increase is part of wider patterns of change in family structure. These include, for example, the rise in extra- marital births (now accounting for over a quarter of all births), the increase in cohabitation (half of women have cohabited prior to marriage), the rise in divorce (one in three marriages currently contracted will end in divorce), and the extent of remarriage and cohabitation after divorce (about a quarter of all marriages are second marriages for one or both partners). Kiernan and Wicks (1990) suggest that by the year 2000 it may be that as few as half of all children in Britain will have spent all their lives in a conventional two-parent family with both their natural parents.

These changing family structures present something of a challenge for social policy, especially in relation to the issue of state financial support for families. The British post-war social security system was founded on three important assumptions: full employment, male breadwinners and stable families. Thus the main form of family support is male wages, which the state will replace under certain conditions (for example, in the case of involuntary unemployment,

From a seminar on 'Gender and Family Change in Industrialised Countries', International Union for the Scientific Study of Population, Rome, January 1992, in K.O. Mason and A.M. Jensen (eds) *Gender and Family Change in Industrialised Countries*, IUSSP/Oxford University Press (forthcoming).

sickness, disability and death). The state will also supplement male wages with Child Benefit for all families, and more recently with means-tested benefits for families with low wages. Otherwise, the financial arrangements of families are considered to be essentially private. This has two particular consequences. First, decisions about how families allocate and spend their money are seen as the responsibility of the family and not the business of the state. Secondly, because male wages are perceived as the main element of family support, decisions about whether or not the woman should work outside the home are also seen as private family decisions.

But separation and divorce, and unmarried motherhood, do not fit easily into this model. The financial arrangements of the 'family' are not private because the state becomes involved in deciding the allocation of resources between the two new households: the lone parent and the children on the one side; and the absent parent, usually the father, on the other side. The state must also take responsibility for enforcing the financial arrangements made and, if the absent parent is unwilling or unable to pay, must either replace his contribution or expect the lone mother to support herself and her children through employment. Thus the mother's decisions about employment are no longer simply private but are influenced, or even determined, by state policy.

The rising numbers of lone-parent families therefore raise fundamental issues about the balance between family, state and individual financial responsibilities; and about the roles of men and women as parents and as workers. The 1991 Child Support Act, implemented from 1993, represents an attempt to change this balance by introducing new mechanisms for setting and enforcing maintenance payments for children. It is similar to the 'child support' schemes recently introduced in some other countries, notably parts of the USA (Kahn and Kamerman, 1988; Garfinkel and Wong, 1990) and Australia (Harrison *et al.*, 1990; 1991). This chapter examines these policy developments in the UK and their implications for separated couples and their children. The first section provides the background, describing recent trends in lone parenthood and the financial circumstances of lone parents in the UK. The second section looks at the context in which recent policy has been developed. The third section looks at the provisions of the Child Support Act in more detail, and the final section concludes by considering some of the wider implications for family and gender roles.

Background

In 1974 the Finer Committee on One-Parent Families (Finer, 1974) reported, in two large volumes, on the circumstances of lone parents in the UK. The committee had been set up in response to concerns about the increasing numbers of lone parents, who were very often reliant upon state benefits and at risk of poverty. In the early 1970s there were about half a million lone-parent families. Today that number has more than doubled and lone parents are once again the subject of policy concern. The reasons are similar.

First, there has been a significant rise in the numbers of lone-parent families. Table 1 shows the increase in the numbers of lone-parent families since the early 1970s, when the 1969 Divorce Reform Act came into operation. This made divorce much more widely available and led to a substantial increase in the number of divorcing couples. Between 1971 and 1990 the number of divorced and separated women with children rose from 290,000 to 650,000; the number of single mothers rose from 90,000 to 390,000. The numbers of lone fathers have also increased (from 70,000 to 185,000) but they remain very much in the minority, at about 10 per cent of all lone parents. Thus most lone parents are women and just over half are women who are divorced or separated from their

Table 1   *Numbers of lone-parent families, Great Britain 1971 and 1990*

	1971	1989
Single mothers	90,000	390,000
Divorced/separated	290,000	650,000
Widowed mothers	120,000	75,000
All mothers	500,000	1,115,000
Lone fathers	70,000	110,000
Lone parents	570,000	1,225,000
As a proportion of all families with children	8%	19%

Source: Haskey (1993), figure 2.

former husbands. Black families are slightly more likely than white families to be headed by a lone parent (18 per cent and 15 per cent respectively in 1988) with particularly high rates of lone parent-hood (about half of all families) among West Indian families (Haskey, 1991).

Many other countries have also seen significant increases in the number and proportion of lone-parent families, again mainly as a consequence of marital breakdown (Ermisch, 1990). It is difficult to get estimates for the number of lone-parent families which compare different countries on exactly the same basis because different countries define and count lone parents in different ways (Roll, 1992b). However, Table 2 shows some recent estimates for the proportion of lone-parent families in other countries. The UK has a relatively high proportion of families headed by a lone parent in relation to other European Community countries (at about 17 per cent compared with an EC average of about 10 per cent), but many other countries have at least as many, or more, lone-parent families as the UK.

Table 2   *Proportion of families headed by a lone parent, various countries, late 1980s (percentages)*

European Community Countries	
The UK	17
Denmark	15
France, Germany	11–13
Belgium, Luxemburg, Ireland	
Portugal, The Netherlands	9–11
Greece, Spain, Italy	5–6
OECD Countries	
USA	21
Sweden	15
Australia, Austria, Canada	
Finland	13

Note: refers to families with children aged under 18.
Sources: European Community from Roll (1992b); OECD from OECD (1993).

The increase in the numbers of lone parents would not, by itself, necessarily give rise to policy concern. However, alongside the increase in overall numbers there has been a substantial rise in both the number and proportion of lone parents in receipt of state benefits, especially social assistance benefits (Supplementary Benefit, or as it is now known, Income Support). In 1979 there were about 310,000 lone mothers on Supplementary Benefit, equivalent to about 45 per cent of all lone mothers. By 1989 this had risen to about 740,000 lone mothers on Income Support, or about 72 per cent of the total (Department of Social Security, 1991). In all about 30 per cent of people of working age receiving income support are lone parents, and over 60 per cent of the children living in families on Income Support live in lone-parent families.

The main reason for the increased reliance on state benefits has been a fall in employment rates, especially in full-time employment. In the late 1970s just about half (47 per cent) of lone mothers were employed, 22 per cent full time and 24 per cent part-time. By the late 1980s less than two-fifths (39 per cent) of lone mothers were employed, 17 per cent full time and 22 per cent part time (OPCS, 1990). Lone mothers are now less likely to be employed than married mothers, of whom 56 per cent are employed (18 per cent full-time and 38 per cent part-time).

Falling employment and increased reliance on state benefits have in turn meant that the incomes of lone mothers have fallen, both relatively (compared with other families) and absolutely (compared with prices). In 1979 lone parents had incomes which were on average equivalent to about 57 per cent of the incomes of couples with two children, but by 1989 this had fallen to about 40 per cent. Over the same period the average incomes of lone parents rose by less than the Retail Price Index (Department of Employment, 1980; 1990; see also Roll, 1988). Thus lone mothers are increasingly at risk of poverty, as shown in both official statistics (Department of Social Security, 1993) and independent research studies (Bradshaw and Millar, 1991; Frayman, 1991). According to the official statistics the proportion of lone parents with disposable incomes of less than half of the average (taking into account family size) rose from 19 to 60 per cent between 1979 and 1990–1.

In recent years, therefore, the number of lone parents in the UK has been increasing, their reliance on state benefits has been rising and their employment rates have been falling. Poverty has increased and most lone parents live on incomes substantially lower than the average for other families with children. However, during this time policy for lone parents has been, as Bradshaw (1989) puts it, 'in the doldrums'. The Finer Committee recommendations were not taken up and such policy developments as there have been have consisted of fairly minor modifications to existing benefits rather than any fundamental review (Millar, 1989).

Changing policy

In the late 1980s, however, lone parents came under more detailed scrutiny from the government. The social security system as a whole had been reviewed in the mid 1980s and legislation introduced in 1986. Lone parents were not particularly targeted in that review although they were, of course, affected by the changes introduced (Millar, 1992). After that review was completed, policy attention turned specifically towards lone parents. One of the most important reasons for this was financial. As described above the numbers of lone parents on Income Support had been rising rapidly throughout the 1980s and so therefore had the costs – in real terms social security spending on lone parents increased three-fold between 1981 and 1988 (Department of Social Security, 1990). The control of public expenditure was a key economic objective for Conservative governments in the 1980s and so these rising costs were bound to cause concern.

However, although the pressure for policy change may have been primarily financial, it was ideological factors which largely determined the direction of the policy response. These ideological factors included a number of related threads, tied in various ways to ideas and ideals about the 'family' and family obligations. First, there was the longstanding and generalised concern that lone parenthood *per se* is bad for both the families themselves and for society in general, and the state, therefore, should seek to discourage the formation of such families, or at the very least not encourage them. This is a view which, despite the lack of evidence to support it, has gained even more ground recently with a series of speeches from government ministers – including Peter Lilley as Secretary of State at the Department of Social Security – critical of lone parents. Dennis and Erdos (1992) and Dennis (1993) have gained significant publicity for their argument that 'families without fatherhood' are destroying communities and society.

Secondly, one of the central tenets of Conservative social policy in the 1980s was that the state had become too supportive, providing too much welfare, and this meant that individuals and families were no longer taking responsibility for themselves. This, it was argued, meant that a 'culture of dependency' had grown up in which people had lost the motivation to help themselves and instead relied on the state to meet all their needs. Separated, or unmarried, parents provided two prime examples of this abdication of personal responsibility. On the one hand there is the father, walking away from his family responsibilities and expecting the state to carry the cost. On the other hand there is the lone mother, increasingly relying on the state to provide an income. Receipt of benefits, or 'dependency' as such receipt was pejoratively termed, was thus increasingly defined as a matter of personal choice rather than external constraint.

These ideas are linked in the concept of the 'underclass' as it was developed in the US (most influentially for British social policy by Murray, 1984; 1990). According to these accounts the underclass is mainly composed of unemployed men and single mothers, who have no incentive to work or to marry, and no motivation either to support their families or to help themselves out of dependency on the state. They are thus excluded from the labour market and excluded from the values of society as a whole (Smith, 1992). The US debate has had very strong racial overtones that are largely lacking in the UK context (Morris, 1994) but, that aside, these sorts of ideas have been influential in policy, especially towards unemployed people. Unemployment has been increasingly defined as a problem of unemployed people not wanting to work rather than a problem of lack of jobs, and this has led to a very harsh benefit regime for unemployed people in the 1980s, with cuts in benefit and restrictions on benefit entitlement (Atkinson and Mickelwright, 1989; McLaughlin, 1992).

However, for lone parents – especially lone mothers – the solution to the 'culture of dependency' is not so straightforward. This is because there is considerable ambiguity over the way in which the 'personal obligations and duties' of lone mothers should be defined. On the one hand, because they are mothers, their primary role and responsibility is defined as being the care of their children. This means that they should not necessarily be expected to work outside the home and indeed current policy does not require lone parents to work if they have dependent children under 16 years of age. On the other hand, however, many mothers are now employed and nearly all the recent, and predicted future, employment growth has been among women (NEDO, 1989). The question of mothers and employment thus raises some difficult issues for Conservative values and the situation of lone mothers brings these very clearly into focus (Brown, 1989). Should lone mothers be expected, or even compelled, to reduce their 'benefit dependency' through employment? Or should they, as mothers, be expected to stay at home and care for their children? Are they, as Lewis (1988) has put it, mothers or workers?

Directly confronting the issue of whether lone mothers should or should not be expected to take paid work therefore raises much wider issues about the state's role in relation to women's employment. If lone mothers were to be required to work outside the home the state would almost certainly have to make much more provision for child care, or accept that children might not be properly cared for while their mothers were at work. Providing, or subsidising, such child care would not only be expensive but would also raise the issue of the child care demands of married mothers. In comparison with other EC countries the UK has very low levels of child care provision (Moss, 1990) and, as employment rates of married mothers have risen, there has been increasing pressure on the government to reconsider child care policy (Cohen and Fraser, 1992). This has so far largely been resisted but if child care were to be provided for lone mothers this would undoubtedly raise the pressure from employed married mothers for more help with their pressing child care problems. Thus the current policy – that the state is neutral with regard to employment among lone mothers, neither encouraging nor discouraging paid work (National Audit Office, 1990) – is important in maintaining the notion that for mothers paid employment is a private choice and the needs that arise out of it, such as the need for child care, are not the responsibility of the state.

But if lone mothers cannot be rescued from benefit dependency by their own employment, then what other alternatives are there? Fortunately for the government a potential solution to this dilemma can be found by turning to the 'personal obligations and duties' of the absent parent, which is usually the father. Here the obligations and duties can apparently be much more easily and unambiguously defined: 'parenthood is for life... Legislation cannot make irresponsible parents responsible. But it can and must ensure that absent fathers pay maintenance for their children' (Margaret Thatcher, reported in *The Independent*, 19.7.90). The role of fathers is to support their families financially through employment, and so enforcing this obligation for separated couples would seem to provide the required alternative to either open-ended state financial support or to a positive employment policy for lone mothers. Enforcing maintenance obligations thus has the potential to kill as many as three birds with one stone – it increases the 'responsibility' of the absent father (who would no longer simply be able to walk away from his financial obligations to his family); it reduces the 'dependency' of the lone mother on the state (if Child Support can replace Income Support); and it saves the state money. Policy-makers therefore started to look towards the issue of maintenance and this led to the 1991 Child Support Act.

The 1991 Child Support Act

In theory children are already entitled to financial support from both parents following family breakdown. In practice many children in lone-parent families receive little or no financial support from their absent parent. Table 3, drawn from a recent national survey of lone-parent families, shows that only about three in ten of the families were receiving maintenance. Separated and divorced families were more likely to receive maintenance than those who had never been married. For those receiving maintenance the payments contributed, on average, about a fifth of net income. For all lone parents maintenance contributed only about 7 per cent of total net income.

Table 3   *Receipt of maintenance among lone mothers, UK 1989*

	Proportion in receipt	(base)
All lone parents	29%	(1420)
– divorced	40%	(622)
– separated	32%	(279)
– single	14%	(519)

Source: Bradshaw and Millar (1991), table 7.1.

Prior to the introduction of the Child Support Act the courts had responsibility for setting and enforcing maintenance obligations. The White Paper introducing the Child Support proposals (Department of Social Security, 1990; para 1.5) identified a number of problems with these existing procedures:

- discretionary decisions and hence inconsistent and inequitable treatment;

- the levels of maintenance awarded are often low;
- there is no automatic review of awards;
- many awards are not paid or not paid regularly;
- the system takes too long; and
- requires considerable effort of the part of the lone parent to pursue maintenance.

The Child Support Act aims to solve these problems by establishing an agency to take responsibility for setting and enforcing maintenance payments for children; and by determining levels of maintenance according to a fixed formula. Thus the Act has shifted child maintenance away from a system of judicial discretion to a system of administrative procedures, with the aim of producing 'consistent and predictable results' and enabling 'maintenance to be decided in a fair and reasonable way' (Department of Social Security 1990b, para 2.1). However, it should be noted that only child maintenance is included in this, all other financial matters (e.g. property settlements) are left to the courts; as are all issues of child custody and access.

Alongside the Agency and the formula the Act also introduced a major change to the eligibility criteria for claiming Income Support and Family Credit. This relates to the hours of paid work that are allowed for each benefit. Prior to 1992 the dividing line between these two benefits was set at 24 hours – only those working for less than 24 hours could claim income support while those working for 24 or more hours (and with low wages) could claim Family Credit. Now the cross-over point comes at 16 hours, so anyone working 16 hours or more per week cannot claim Income Support but may be able to claim Family Credit. At first sight this might seem a little out of place in this legislation, given that the main concern is with child maintenance. In fact it is an integral part of the philosophy behind the Act because the aim of these rules is to encourage more part-time work among lone mothers. As we have seen part-time work is relatively uncommon among lone mothers, although for married mothers it is more common than full-time work. Part-time work is expanding and has the advantage of reducing the need for child care but, for lone mothers, it has the serious disadvantage of not providing an adequate income. Part-time earnings tend to be low and cannot provide lone mothers with enough money to support themselves and their children (Bradshaw and Millar, 1991). The Child Support Act aims to get round this by encouraging lone mothers to work part-time and to supplement their earnings with Child Support and with in-work benefits such as Family Credit. So, instead of relying on one source of income (earnings or benefits or maintenance) total income can be made up as a 'package' of all three. The rules are intended to encourage this – any Child Support received by lone mothers on Income Support is deducted from their benefit, so there is no financial gain from Child Support for those receiving Income Support. But, for those who take jobs and claim Family Credit, the first £15 of any Child Support received is ignored. (The subsequent announcement in the 1993 budget of a 'child care disregard' for Family Credit also relates to this policy objective.) The three parts of the Act – the Agency, the formula, and the changed benefit rules – all work together to encourage more *private* as opposed to *public* financial support for lone parents.

When the Act went through parliament there were two issues in particular that caused the most controversy. The first concerns the point mentioned above that lone mothers on Income Support gain nothing financially from any child maintenance collected. About three-quarters of lone parents are on Income Support, so unless they can get off Income Support benefits and into employment they will be no better off financially, no matter how much Child Support is collected. Thus it was argued that these proposals would increase rather than reduce family poverty, because second families could be struggling to make Child Support payments which do not even financially benefit the first families (Millar, 1992). Secondly, the Act requires all lone parents who claim means-tested benefits (Income Support, Family Credit, Housing Benefits) to register with the Agency and to comply by giving details of the absent parent. Those who refuse to do so will in effect be fined by having their Income Support personal allowance reduced unless they have 'good cause' not to name the absent parent. The government have been reluctant to define 'good cause' but have indicated that this includes rape, incest and fear of violence. Critics have argued that this measure penalises lone mothers and allows violent partners to escape making payments.

These two features of the legislation lead some commentators to suggest that the White Paper that introduced these changes should have been called 'Treasury Comes First' rather than 'Children Come First', since it seems that saving money was the main policy objective. This view is strongly reinforced by the fact that registration with the Child Support Agency will be compulsory for benefit recipients but only voluntary for other separating couples. But alongside this drive to reduce public expenditure the Child Support Act also reflects a particular response to changing family structures and gender roles.

Family structure and gender roles

The UK is not alone in either the problems with the 'old' maintenance system or in the proposed solutions. Studies in other countries (for example USA, Australia, Canada, Ireland, France) find the same sorts of difficulties – low and variable awards, irregular or non-existent payments – and so maintenance rarely contributes much to the incomes of lone-parent families (Griffiths *et al.*, 1986; Millar, 1989; Maclean, 1990; Millar *et al.*, 1992). In a recent review of child support measures in the OECD countries, Garfinkel and Wong (1990, p. 112) conclude that there has been a movement towards 'standardisation and administrative enforcement across countries' and that many countries are looking at ways to strengthen and enforce the financial obligations of noncustodial parents. Thus Britain is far from alone in responding to the increasing numbers of lone- parent families by trying to ensure more private as opposed to public support. However, as a response to changing family structures, the measures introduced in the UK seem to be aimed at *containing* change rather than *adapting* to it. There are several aspects to this.

First, what these proposals do is to try to reproduce traditional family and gender relationships after couples have separated. The separated family is treated almost as if the relationship had not broken down at all. Thus the men are to fulfil their traditional role as financial provider and the women are to fulfil their traditional role as mother. These days the acceptable role for mothers includes some part-time work, so lone mothers are also to have improved access to part-time employment. In a way the government is trying to 'turn back the clock' and make policy on the assumption that the traditional gender division of labour within the family can continue even when other aspects of the family, such as marriage, have begun to disappear.

For lone mothers there are likely to be a number of negative consequences of this fixation on traditional gender roles. In the first place, the women's ability to improve their incomes much above basic levels will be very limited. The income 'package' of part-time (low-paid) work, Child Support and means- tested benefits creates a very long 'poverty trap' since increases in either earnings or Child Support will simply mean reductions in benefit so that total income changes very little. Furthermore, if lone mothers do try to achieve this package they will continue to be financially dependent on their former partners, and their incomes will to some extent depend on the circumstances and choices that he makes. The child maintenance is not guaranteed by the state (as it is in some countries) and so the women will continue to be dependent on the willingness and ability of the men to pay. Finally, the focus on part-time work means that the question of state responsibility for child care can continue to be side-stepped. Lack of child care is the largest single barrier to employment for lone mothers and nothing in these proposals is going to increase child care provision. Thus it could be argued that lone mothers will suffer the disadvantages of marriage – the double burden of paid and unpaid work, the financial dependency on men, the responsibility for arranging child care – but with none of the advantages.

Secondly, the child support proposals centre on reinforcing the financial obligation of the 'natural' or 'biological' parents. Fathers (and mothers) remain responsible for 'their' children, no matter what happens. So, for example, if a man remarries his maintenance bill will be reassessed if he has children with his second wife but not if she already has children for whom he becomes a stepfather. About a million children live in stepfamilies (Kiernan and Wicks, 1990) but these measures imply that step-parents are not financially responsible for their stepchildren, who always remain the financial responsibility of their 'natural' parents. Given current patterns of marriage and remarriage the outcome of the strict application of this principle would be that money would have to pass between and through several households. Even a fairly simple example – two divorced people each with children who marry and have more children – produces quite a complicated set of financial obligations across a number of households.

In addition, all children do not have two 'natural' parents – 'family formation can be as diverse as assisted reproduction, surrogacy, substitute parents, serial marriage or cohabitation and single parenthood, as well as the normal [sic] situation of blood parents married to each other' (Craven-Griffiths, 1991, p. 326). Such families are difficult to fit into the current provisions and will tend to remain so in the future.

Thirdly, the provisions are based on the principle that the obligations of natural parents are absolutely unconditional. As the opening words of the White Paper setting out the changes put it:

> Every child has a right to care from his or her parents. Parents generally have a legal and moral obligation to care for their children until the children are old enough to look after themselves. The parents of a child may separate. In some instances the parents may not have lived together as a family at all. Although events may change the relationship between the parents – for example, when they divorce – those events *cannot in any way* change their responsibilities towards their children. (Foreword to *Children Come First*, DSS, 1990b, emphasis added)

But, as the response to this legislation has shown, not everyone agrees that there is such an unconditional responsibility. Clearly, many men do not think so and have been very active in their opposition to the Act, and indeed instrumental in having changes made to the formula since the Act was introduced (Social Security Committee, 1993). Criticisms of the Act from pressure groups such as 'Families Need Fathers' (and the many other groups that have been formed to oppose the legislation) have focused on issues such as the retrospective nature of the Act (i.e. that previous 'clean break' arrangements can be overturned); the failure to recognise adequately the needs of second families; the failure to take account of the costs of being an absent parent (costs to visit children, etc.); the introduction of higher payments without any phasing in period; the way in which the formula includes an amount of money for the lone parent (intended to reflect her role as carer of the child but perceived by many as spouse maintenance). In addition, the way in which the Act was implemented – apparently focusing on extracting higher payments from those already paying rather than on enforcing payments among non-payers – has led to criticisms of inequity and injustice (ibid.).

The groups representing absent parents have given much less attention to the issues of principle raised by the Act, which is not surprising given that they have sought to stress their 'responsibility' towards their children. However, the issue of contact with children has been stressed and it has been argued that, if fathers are not allowed access to their children, they should not have to pay child maintenance. Burgoyne and Millar (1994), on the basis of in-depth interviews with a small group of absent fathers, argue that the obligation to maintain children is not seen as an unconditional obligation but rather depends on a number of factors including the men's views of their own, and their former partner's, situations. If former partners had remarried then very often the view was taken that maintenance obligations should be reduced or even cancelled, and evidence from the 1990 *British Social Attitudes Survey* found the population in general ambivalent about this. Half (51 per cent) of the respondents said maintenance payments should continue if the woman remarried, 13 per cent said they should stop, and 33 per cent that it would depend on the new husband's income (Kiernan, 1992). The absolutely unconditional obligation that underpins the White Paper does not seem to command widespread support.

From the point of view of the women there are also many reasons why some will be reluctant to receive maintenance. For some there is a fear of violence and Bradshaw and Millar (1991) found that violence was reported by 20 per cent of the lone mothers as a factor in the breakdown of their relationship. Others might have had no substantive relationship with the child's father. Others might want the relationship to end completely and not want to be financially dependent on their former partners. Others might be trying to maintain a relationship between the father and the children and fear that this would be more difficult if financial matters were introduced. Among lone mothers on Income Support both the women and the men might consider that there is little point in the man having to make payments which reduce his income quite substantially, while doing nothing to increase hers or that of the children. The lone mothers interviewed in depth by Clarke *et al.* (1993) were thus rather uncertain about the value of the Act to them in practice:

> There was a marked contrast between the lone mothers' beliefs about the principles underpinning fathers' continuing financial obligations to their families, and the realities surrounding such payments...[there was] a profound ambivalence surrounding the receipt of maintenance by these lone mothers. On the one hand, they felt that fathers did have a continuing obligation to

make a financial contribution to their children. But on the other hand, the giving of that support enmeshed them in the very same patterns of obligation and control from which they had tried to escape in the course of rebuilding their lives as single parents.

The response of the government to these sorts of points has been that it is right to enforce Child Support because the obligation to support children *is* unconditional and that neither the mother nor the father has the right to abrogate this responsibility, either for themselves or for the other person. Thus the mother cannot refuse to cooperate in finding the father and the father cannot refuse to pay. But in practice enforcing a particular definition of family responsibilities requires at least some degree of acceptance that the definition is fair or just (Finch, 1990), and it is by no means clear that these Child Support provisions will be seen in this way – indeed quite the reverse seems be the case.

Finally, these measures do little or nothing to tackle the under-lying issues of gender inequality that are apparent in the break-down of marriage. When couples separate the extent to which the costs of caring for children fall on women and not on men becomes very clear. The women's access to employment is limited and so current income tends to be low, making it difficult for them to support themselves. Their future income security is reduced because they lose access to the pension entitlements derived from their partners. The distribution of property, including pension rights, after divorce does not fully take into account the unpaid contribu-tion of women's work to the marriage. The Child Support scheme focuses mainly on the direct costs of children, attempting to share these more equally between the mother and the father. The indirect costs are partially recognised in that the maintenance bill includes an assessment for the 'mother as carer', but this relates to the caring costs incurred after separation and does not compensate for the costs incurred during marriage.

Allocating the direct and indirect costs of children between the mother, the father and the state raises many difficult issues. The Child Support approach analysed here for the UK and also adopted, in broadly similar ways, by several other countries in what have been called the 'liberal' welfare state regimes (Esping-Andersen, 1990) provides one response to these issues. An alter-native approach can be seen in the 'advanced maintenance schemes' adopted in many of the 'social democratic' welfare regimes, notably

Sweden. The key features of this approach are that it provides an assured child-support benefit, payable to all lone parents regardless of income or employment status, and recouped by the state from the absent parent. In Sweden, the children receive a payment set at 40 per cent of the officially determined basic needs of a child and the absent parents pay a standardised amount (Kamerman and Kahn, 1983; Garfinkel and Wong, 1990). Thus advanced maintenance payments seem to 'provide something of a bridge between the private and the public systems of income support, providing the custodial parent with guaranteed support without entirely undermining the obligation of the absent parent to provide support' (Millar, 1989, p. 150).

As Joshi (1987, p. 131) has written:

> The price a man pays for parenthood is generally being expected to support his children and their mother. The price a woman pays is that of continuing economic handicap and an increased risk of poverty. One of the many advantages of being male is that it is easier to opt out of the obligation to maintain than it is to opt out of the unwritten obligation to care.

Whether measures such as these are enough to prevent men from 'opting out' remains to be seen. But also legislation such as this arguably starts in the wrong place – in order to reduce inequalities *after* marriage (or relationship) breakdown we also need to find ways to reduce inequalities between women and men *within* marriage. Women and children will continue to be poor as lone-parent families until women in general are able to achieve a more substantial degree of equality and independence.

The Relative Prosperity of French One-parent Families

JOHN BAKER

One-parent families appear to be better off in France than in Britain, both absolutely and relatively. The first is, of course, to be expected, given the generally poorer living standards of the British compared at least with the original six members of the European Community. The French may be on average some 50 per cent better off, according to Gross National Product per head. The relative prosperity may be more interesting, given that in other respects French income may be less equally divided than the British (CERC, 1979), despite ragged recent moves towards greater equality (Kessler and Masson, 1985).

However, before coming on to the greater relative prosperity of French one-parent families, there are clearly qualifications to make. French one-parent families are still disadvantaged over money, housing, day care, social isolation and other signs of deprivation. Their children are more likely than others to have to repeat years in school, and one-parent families – widows excepted – are much less likely to be owner-occupiers (Le Gall and Martin, 1987; Rallu, 1982). They are particularly likely to have to move house once or several times (Boudoul and Faur, 1987; Taffin, 1987). A minority of one-parent families may be markedly worse off than in Britain, because of the different social security systems. In Britain, Income Support is comprehensive and fairly easy to claim. It is a safety net which allows few people – and certainly few one-parent families – to fall to even lower standards of living. French social security may

From John Baker, 'Family Policy as an Anti-poverty Measure in M. Hardey and G. Crow (eds), *LoneParenthood: Coping with Constraints and Making Opportunities,* Hemel Hempstead: Harvester Wheatsheaf, pp. 114–25.

provide better benefits to most claimants, but it does not have the same safety net function. Where it does, 'constituting the dossier' can be long and complex, leaving people, including one-parent families resorting to it, with little or nothing – apart from discretionary payments, loans or charity – for short or long periods. Aide Sociale – the safety net – is residual and has largely disappeared except as a means of paying medical bills for the indigent. For those who receive it, it is local, a loan, subject to family means tests, discretionary and a contribution only towards food, or even bread alone (Verdier, 1984). There is a more generous Allocation de Parent Isolé (One-Parent Benefit) but it affects only some 7 per cent of one-parent families. None the less, most French one-parent families seem to be better off than their British counterparts.

A major survey in 1978 compared the incomes and other features of different types of family in France (Villac, 1984). The national average income per 'consumption unit' in households was given an index of 100. The unit of consumption is a crude attempt to standardise living standards across different sizes and types of household. The first adult counts as 1, a second or a child over 14 counts as 0.7, and other children as 0.5. The index of the standard of living per consumption unit in two- parent families varied, by age of the 'head', from 89 to 95. Lone-father households generally had higher-than-average standards of living, ranging from 97 to 109. Lone-mother households ranged from 68 to 89. Sixty-eight is a low score, but it was for separated women, a small group often in a temporary predicament. The figure for the largest group of one-parent families, those headed by a divorced mother, was 79. For other types of one-parent family the index varied between 75 and 89. Interestingly the highest score, 89, was for single mothers. This was exactly the same as that for two-parent households with a 'head' aged under 30, probably the group with which they would most naturally be compared.

Since these figures were collected there has been a considerable relaunch of family policy. In 1981 family benefits were substantially increased, then allowed to slide back again somewhat, but some were then increased again (Laroque, 1985; Liaisons Sociales, 1989; 1990). The gap between all families and the rest of the population must have closed, some one-parent families benefiting especially from the extra help given to mothers of young children.

There can be no precise calculation of comparable British figures. There is no series of figures with 'equivalence scales', with two exceptions. Historically, many British sources have compared household incomes with Supplementary Benefit scales for families of different compositions. This precludes any international comparison and the 'equivalence' for children is low compared with the French calculations. Even these figures are no longer published. There are now figures which purport to show how one-parent families compare with others, but the source contains no details of how 'equivalence' is calculated (Department of Social Security, 1990a). There are also figures for gross and net incomes of one-parent households and how these compare with other types of household, but these are of very limited use without equivalence calculations, given how different one-parent families are in size and composition from other sorts of household.

However, such data as do exist render unbelievable the idea that many British one-parent families enjoy even the two-thirds average income that was the lowest figure for France, let alone the four-fifths enjoyed by the biggest group. Taking, first, Supplementary Benefit scales (now Income Support), at the time of the Family Finances Survey (Knight, 1981; Millar, 1989), over half of all one-parent families living on their own had incomes within 10 per cent either way of Supplementary Benefit scales. Only three in a hundred had incomes 40 per cent or more above. Eekelaar and Maclean's sample (1986) were marginally more prosperous, but only 8 per cent enjoyed what they called an 'average family' standard of living. The large and growing gap between social security incomes and earnings has been copiously documented, for example in Walker and Walker (1987). The scale rate on social security for single parents in 1978, for example, was only 18 per cent of average male earnings – a gap so enormous that additions for children and housing costs could never have remotely closed it. For a single person under 24 the figure in 1989 was 10 per cent (Department of Social Security, 1989). Using the new DSS equivalence scales (whatever they may mean), a quarter of single parents had less than half average incomes after housing had been paid for, and half less than 60 per cent. Only one in six had an average income or more (ibid.). British one-parent families are clearly less well off.

A comparison of social security entitlements is interesting. Social security is the principal or exclusive income of most British one-parent families. In France the Allocation de Parent Isolé is one of the few 'safety net' benefits. In theory all pregnant women or sole parents should have their income brought up to this level if it would otherwise be below. Despite the fact that it is considerably higher than Income Support, only some 7 per cent of French one-parent families receive it. Table 1 shows the figures for July 1990.

Table 1   *Social security support in Britain and France (in £ Sterling)*[1]

	Allocation de Parent Isolé[2]	Income Support (exclusive of housing costs)
Pregnant woman (18–24)	55.44	28.80
Parent (over 18) with one child under 11	74.16	60.50
Parent (over 18) with 2 children under 11	94.11	72.85

Notes
1 £1 = 12.63F – the purchasing parity equivalent calculated by CERC (1979). The market exchange rate is approximately £1 = 10F, which would make the difference seem greater.
2 French benefit rates, July 1990.

Another area of comparison is the effects of divorce. According to a 1980 survey of divorced women in France, only a minority (38 per cent) felt that their standard of living had fallen. Nearly as many (31 per cent) felt that they were better off. Eekelaar and Maclean (1986) have looked at the effects of divorce on British women. They talk of 'exceptional adversity' suffered by lone parents following a divorce, with four out of five of those who had not found a new partner being below their poverty line. The questions posed were not the same; none the less, there is a stark contrast.

The last area of comparison is poverty studies. Again there can be no exact comparisons. The French have no tradition of poverty studies compared with the British and use different tests in the few studies that have been done. Franco-British research has found one-parent families in France only slightly more likely to be in 'poverty' as they defined it than two-parent ones, but much more so in Britain (Mitton and Willmott, 1983; Smeeding *et al.*, 1990). Hauser and Fischer, analysing 1979 data for Britain, reported 31 per cent of the smallest one-parent families and 56 per cent of the largest as having less than half average net incomes. Figures for France in 1975 quoted by O'Higgins (1987) indicate 23 per cent of French one-parent families as having less than half average incomes. Again, the methodologies are not strictly comparable, but the differences between the situations of one-parent families in France and Britain are very large.

The French 'poverty studies' that have been done are little more than exploratory (Debonneuil, 1978; Pascaud and Simenon, 1987). One-parent families do not feature strongly. British studies do not appear to bear out the French suggestion that only a few one-parent families are among the poorest 5 per cent of the population.

Why are French one-parent families better off?

Three main sources of income go to one-parent families: maintenance from ex-partners, social security and wages. The role of all three is debated in both countries, but in Britain the first seems to get priority political attention and the last the least.

The relatively better position of French one-parent families is the result of better maintenance only to the extent that the money paid benefits the mother rather than, as in Britain, being deducted from social security income. That happens in France only to Allocation de Parent Isolé claimants. Maintenance is nevertheless only a modest additional contribution to the incomes of one-parent families – worth about 13 per cent of their income, according to Roll (1989). The figure is not higher for two reasons: court orders are frugal and payment is incomplete. The sums awarded by the court vary widely, but the commonest sum for 1980 was £50 per month from husband to wife as an adjustment of income, and rather less for the support of a single child (Meulders-Klein and Eekelaar, 1988). However, only 35 per cent of these orders are paid fully and promptly, and 13 per cent are never paid at all. There may be scope in both countries for boosting payments from fathers to one-parent families, but clearly this difference cannot contribute much to an explanation of the differences between Britain and France. However, the French, who now have a system of 'advance payments', have encountered similar difficulties in getting more money out of fathers as may be anticipated in Britain. Defaulters are difficult to trace, have little money or produce good reasons for not paying; not all mothers want to pursue the matter, and small, erratic civil debts are not easy to collect.

French social security benefits and tax benefits are not particularly generous to lone parents either. Several benefits and

concessions are aimed at encouraging people to have more children, targeting families of three or more. For example, the Allocation Parentale d'Education pays up to £211 per month to mothers
who give up work to have a third child, and there is a guaranteed
minimum income for such families. Even the standard Child Benefit starts only with the second child – although they get £47 per
month – and more still is paid for third and subsequent children
and older ones. The tax system also privileges large families by
dividing taxable income by a formula (*le quotient familial*) which
reflects family size, and gives an extra 'point' to one-parent
families. Hence large – or, better still, large and prosperous –
one-parent families may do well, but there are very few such
families. Most one-parent families are small and of modest
means. Other benefits, however, may be of more use – the Allocation au Jeune Enfant (Young Child Benefit) and the Allocation
Logement (Housing Benefit).

The Allocation au Jeune Enfant is a regular payment of £68 per
month for nine months around the birth of a baby, but extended
until the baby is 3 for families of below-average income. This often
dovetails with employment law and pre- schooling to enable a
mother to keep a job. The housing allowance is too complex to
give even meaningful illustrative figures. It is aimed not only
at helping particular sorts of households but at financing
house building and improvements, but some one-parent families
benefit.

Eighty per cent of French lone parents work, nearly all of them
full-time. It is this, combined with supporting and complementary
legal social security and maintenance provision, that explains their
comparative prosperity. Moreover, the jobs performed by lone
mothers are 'normal' ones rather than the marginal, semi-casual
ones – with appropriate wages and conditions – which most British
lone parents do. The occupational distribution of French single
mothers is much the same as for other working women. For example, 22 per cent of divorcees are in manual work, compared with 20
per cent of all women; 30 per cent are in office work (31 per cent);
5.3 per cent are senior staff (5.9 per cent) (Villac, 1984). French
women tend to be bunched in two types of work – routine manual
and routine non-manual – but to a lesser extent than in Britain.
Fifty-eight per cent of workers on the minimum wage are women,
compared with 42 per cent men – a significant difference, but
probably less than would be found on a British definition of low

pay. Further, gender differences in pay are falling in France but growing again in Britain (Benveniste and Lollivier, 1988).

The reason for this rate of employment is a highly developed system of day care and pre-schooling. Pre-schooling is practically universal for children of 3 or over – 94 per cent go to school, the balance being almost entirely in rural areas where the number of one-parent families is negligible. Over a third of 2-year-olds attend a nursery school. Taking children under 3, 11 per cent are in school, 5 per cent in officially approved subsidised crèches, 8 per cent with 'official' childminders – only slightly over half are with their mother full-time.

There are good grounds for assuming that 'official' provision of substitute day care for a quarter of babies covers most one-parent families where the mother seeks to work, though this does not mean that there are not particular difficulties in some cases. Anecdotally and informally one hears many stories of how hard it is to get a nursery place and about the pleading, wheedling and cajoling necessary to find one, but most of them seem to have happy endings – something turns up or has been found rather than a job offer lost. However, this pressure could be successful only in the context of a policy to encourage day care.

There are immediate and longer-term reasons for the availability of day care. The immediate reason is often the role of the Family Benefit Funds (Caisses des Allocations Familiales). Family Benefits are administered on a local basis, albeit within a tight national framework. The local committee – consisting of employers, trade unionists, elected representatives of users and Family Association representatives – has discretion on how to spend a proportion of the contributions they collect from employers on services for children and families. This gives a local source of funds which may be spent on day care facilities. As important as direct Caisse provision are joint projects. Pressure from the Caisses and their affiliate bodies results in services provided and/or funded jointly by the Caisses, employers, local authorities and voluntary bodies. Places in these nurseries or crèches may take need into account. One-parent families benefit as a by product of services intended to help all families, all children, and working mothers.

Policies for combining day care and work would, of course, be useless without work opportunities. There are special provisions in France to help the employment of women, and mothers in particular, which are of special benefit to one-parent families. Jobs must be kept open for mothers for two years. This, of course, bridges the period from advanced pregnancy until the age of the baby at which nursery places are generally available. It is also the period for which the Allocation au Jeune Enfant is paid. Mothers do not have to give up their place in the job market. In addition, parents have an absolute right in large organisations and a qualified one in small ones to have unpaid holidays or to go part-time for up to two years. This again keeps mothers – and especially single mothers – in jobs. Also of considerable help is the public sector. The state is an enormous employer. The public sector tries to lead society in matters of social attitudes, and this includes provision for parents. Most employees, including senior ones, are women. A substantial proportion of women 'at risk' of becoming single parents are found there: others gravitate towards it. There are modest wage supplements to parents working for the state (Fournier, 1989). By contrast, British public sector employment is more gender-segregated than other employment.

Why does France have a stronger family policy?

French one-parent families appear to be better off than Britain's as an indirect and probably unintended result of policies aimed at helping women, children and families generally. The main driving force behind those policies appears to be the wish to increase the birth rate, by reducing the difficulties working mothers have in rearing children.

Historically, the reasons for the French wanting an increased population were economic, military and religious (Baker, 1986). Economically, France has always been portrayed as capable of supporting a larger population than it possesses. There has always been spare agricultural land, and until the 1970s there was never a national unemployment problem – both of which are linked in popular attitudes (if not in economic theory) with desirable population size. Military reasons (the ability to recruit soldiers) led even the arch anti- interventionist Napoleon to offer to take over the entire support of every seventh son born to a couple, provided he joined the army. The military reasons for population policy probably reached a peak in the interwar period and became irrelevant only with nuclear weapons. Catholic enthusiasm for large families does not always produce a family policy, but in France it did, and even today many attitudes to children seem to be secularised versions of religious beliefs. All these factors operated in the opposite direction in Britain. A high population relative to land and cyclical unemployment gave credibility to the theories of Malthus. Militarily, threats to Britain's naval supremacy meant that having a large population to feed was the threat. The Protestant religion has emphasised discipline in procreation.

Today, these differences have become largely irrelevant, although the traditions have acquired their own momentum. One is left with contemporary economic and political arguments. French economists and most British ones who have studied the question argue that in most circumstances the best long-term policy for rising standards of living is modest, steady population growth (Sauvy, 1969; Simon, 1983). In France the indicator used is that couples ought on average to have 2.4 children. This spreads the burden of the elderly. It keeps demand buoyant. Perhaps most important in the eyes of French economists, it provides a supply of new entrants to the labour force without which the existing pattern of economic activity will stagnate. Family policy is not something to be financed if resources permit. In Britain social policy is regarded as a consumption expense. In France it is regarded as an investment. Expenditure on it preceded the French economic boom and is seen as one of its causes.

The second argument is political. In France, family policy is popular. For example, only 4 per cent of the population in 1982 thought family benefits were too generous, two out of five thought benefits were too low, and nearly three-quarters wanted mothers of large families paid a wage (Bastide *et al.*, 1982).

The popularity of family benefits may be for traditional reasons, but there are other factors. Family provisions are on a scale that makes them of real help. The sums involved are such that even middle-and upper-class parents feel they have an interest in them. Most French people, like British people, have been, are, or intend to be parents They identify with provisions that help them. Family policy mitigates the crash in the standards of living that would otherwise occur when children arrive, with all the expense involved plus, possibly, loss of a wage. French academics appear amazed that in Britain the state is happy to see children reared during an economic trough in their parents' life cycle. Ordinary people seem amazed that the British public are not concerned about the drop in income that occurs when they become parents. Finally, there is the electoral support of women. French feminism is an ill-documented area, but impressionistically there is less 'American-style' feminism with its ambivalence and at times hostility to the family, and there appears to be a much more deeply structured concern about women's rights, including social policy to enable them both to take paid work and to have children.

The policy relevance

Kamerman and Kahn (1988a) identify four main types of policy response to one-parent families – an anti-poverty strategy (Britain), a categorical strategy (Norway), a universal young child strategy (France, Hungary, Austria, Germany, Finland) and a family policy and labour-market strategy (Sweden). They note, of course, that while poverty is a common problem for one-parent families, economic issues are not the only ones. It could be held, for example, that mothers ought not to take paid work but instead provide full-time care and love, at least for young children. Their own preference seems, however, to favour mothers retaining contact with the world of work, lest (among other things) they have problems when child-rearing is over. Hence packages which combine work provision with other measures appear to appeal most.

This author would disagree with Kamerman and Kahn's classification of France, in that they appear to underemphasise the labour-market aspect of French policy. It could be more precisely labelled universal young child and labour-market policy. It appears, from the comparison with Britain at least, to be far more successful on the economic front than the anti-poverty strategy adopted here. The question, then, is: might such a strategy win support in Britain?

The 'demographic time bomb' – the decline in the working population compared with the old, and a predicted shortage of labour – appears to have been discovered in Britain very recently. French commentaries on other countries have highlighted this feature of Britain's future for about 20 years, and the French's own policy of modestly increasing the birth rate for themselves has had the avoidance of this as an objective for much longer (Laroque, 1985). An ageing population can be a vicious circle, for a short-term response to it may be to stimulate the employment of married women. Unless that is combined with day care policies, the birth rate may fall again.

Day care policies are necessary not only to enable mothers to work but to enable workers to have children. When Norman Fowler and others, reviewing social security arrangements in 1984 and 1985, panicked about the demography of pensions provision, their solution was to cut pensions. It should have been to improve day care. The links between the two are not often made and the fault lies, ultimately, with academics. British demographers and social policy students do not often talk to each other, let alone to politicians. Since the issues are not politically obvious, there will not be a public debate before there is an intellectual one.

The second lesson from France is a political one. French family policy has a broad base. It appeals to all women, all parents and would-be parents, and all income ranges. Broad-based alliances are being sought in Britain, but lobbies have historically tended to be more narrowly based – defending the interests of the poor, or one-parent families, for example. The broad base would appear to be the more promising strategy. With the 'demographic time bomb' it could now include business, which in France has always backed a strong family policy.

Bibliography to Section IV

Atkinson, A.B. and Mickelwright, J, (1989) 'Turning the Screw: Benefits for the Unemployed, 1978–1988', in A.B. Atkinson, *Poverty and Social Security*, Brighton: Harvester Wheatsheaf.

Baker, J. (1986) 'Comparing National Priorities: Family and Population Policy in Britain and France', *Journal of Social Policy*, 15(4), pp. 421–42.

Bastide, H., Girard, A. and Roussel, L. (1982) 'Une enquète d'opinion sur la conjoncture démographique', *Population*, 37 pp. 904–20.

Benveniste, C. and Lollivier, S. (1988) 'Les écarts de salaire entre les hommes et les femmes continuent à se réduire', *Economie et Statistique*, 210, pp. 3–9.

Boudoul, J. and Faur, J.P. (1987) 'Trente ans de migration intérieure', in *Données Sociales*, Paris: Institut National de la Statistique et des Etudes Economiques.

Bradshaw, J. (1989) *Policy in the Doldrums*, London: Family Policy Studies Centre.

Bradshaw, J. and Millar, J. (1991) *Lone-parent Families in the UK*, London: HMSO.

Brown, J.C. (1988) *In Search of a Policy: The Rationale for Social Security Provision for One Parent Families*, London: National Council for One Parent Families.

Brown, J.C. (1989) *Why don't they go out to work? Mothers on benefit*, Social Security Advisory Committee Research Paper 2, London: HMSO.

Burghes, L. (1993) *One Parent Families: Policy Options for the 1990s*, London: Family Policy Studies Centre.

Burgoyne, C. and Millar, J. (1994) 'Child Support: The Views of Separated Fathers', *Policy and Politics*.

Central Statistical Office (1994) *Social Trends 24*, London: HMSO.

Centre d'Etude des Revenus et des Couts (CERC) (1979) *Rapport sur les Revenus des Français*, Paris: Editions Albatros.

Clarke, K., Craig, G. and Glendinning, C. (1993) *Children Come First? The Child Support Act and Lone Parent Families*, Manchester: The Children's Society/NSPCC/NCH/Save the Children/Barnado's.

Cohen, B. and Fraser, N. (1992) *Childcare in a Modern Welfare State*, London: Institute for Public Policy Research.

Comitato Italiano por lo studio de problemi della populazione (1982) 'Economic and Social Features of Households in the Member States of the EC', EUROSTAT, Brussels: EC.

Coote, A., Harman, H. and Hewitt, P. (1990) *The Family Way*, Social Policy Paper No. 1, London: Institute for Public Policy Research.

Craven-Griffiths, J. (1991) 'New Families for Old: Have the Statutes Caught Up with Reality?', *Family Law*, August, pp. 326–30.

Davies, J., Berger, B. and Carlson, A. (1993) *The Family: Is It Just Another Lifestyle Choice?*, London: IEA Health and Welfare Unit.

Debonneuil, M. (1978) 'Les familles pauvres d'une ville moyenne', *Economie et Statistique*.

Dennis, N. (1993) *Rising Crime and the Dismembered Family*, London: Institute of Economic Affairs.

Dennis, N. and Erdos, G. (1992) *Families without Fatherhood*, London: Institute for Public Policy Research.

Department of Employment (1980) *Family Expenditure Survey 1979*, London: HMSO.

Department of Employment (1990) *Family Expenditure Survey 1989*, London: HMSO.

Department of Social Security (1989) *Social Security Statistics 1988*, London: HMSO.

Department of Social Security (1990a) *Social Security Statistics 1989*, London: HMSO.

Department of Social Security (1990b) *Children Come First*, Cmnd 1263, London: HMSO.

Department of Social Security (1991) *Social Security Statistics 1990*, London: HMSO.

Department of Social Security (1993) *Households Below Average Income: 1979–1990/91* London: HMSO.

Eekelaar, J. and Maclean, M. (1986) *Maintenance after Divorce*, Oxford: Clarendon Press.

Ermisch, J. (1990) 'Demographic Aspects of the Growing Number of Lone-parent Families', in E. Duskin (ed.) *Lone-parent Families: The Economic Challenge*, Paris: OECD.

Esping-Anderson, G. (1990) *The Three Worlds of Welfare Capitalism*, Oxford: Polity Press.

Finch, J. (1990) *Family Obligations and Social Change*, Oxford: Polity Press.

Finer, M. (1974) *Report of the Committee on One Parent Families*, London: HMSO.

Fournier, J.V. (1989) 'Traitement de fonctionnaires en 1988', *Economie et Statistique*, 129, pp. 11–29.

Frayman, H. (1991) *Breadline Britain in the 1990s*, London: Domino Films/LWT.

Garfinkel, I. and Wong, P. (1990) 'Child Support and Public Policy', in E. Duskin (ed.), *Lone-parent Families: The Economic Challenge*, Paris: OECD.

Griffiths, B., Cooper, S. and McVicar, N. (1986) *Overseas Countries' Maintenance Provisions*, Canberra, Australia: Department of Social Security.

Harrison, M., Snider, G. and Merlo, R. (1990) *Who Pays for the Children?*, Melbourne: Australian Institute of family Studies.

Harrison, M., Snider, G., Merlo, R. and Lucchesi, V. (1991) *Paying for the Children*, Melbourne: Australian Institute of Family Studies

Haskey, J. (1991) 'Estimated Numbers and Demographic Characteristics of One-parent Families in Great Britain', *Population Trends*, 65, pp. 35–49.

Haskey, J. (1993) 'Trends in the Number of One-parent Families in Britain', *Population Trends*, 67, pp. 26–33.

Joshi, H. (1987) 'The Cost of Caring', in C. Glendinning, and J. Millar (eds) *Women and Poverty in Britain*, Brighton: Harvester Wheatsheaf.

Kamerman, S. and Kahn, A.J. (1983) 'Income Transfers and Mother-only Families in Eight Countries', *Social Service Review*, 57, pp. 448–64.

Kamerman, S. and Kahn, A.J. (1988a) *Mothers Alone*, Dover, Mass.: Auburn House.

Kamerman, S. and Kahn, A.J. (1988b) *Child Support*, New York: Sage.

Kessler, D. and Masson, A. (1985) 'What are the Distributional Consequences of the Socialist Government Policy in France?', *Journal of Social Policy*, 14 (3), pp. 403–18.

Kiernan, K. (1992) 'Men and Women at Work and at Home', in R. Jowell (ed.) *British Social Attitudes: The Ninth Report*, London: Social and Community Planning Research.

Kiernan, K. and Wicks, M. (1990) *Family Change and Future Policy*, London: Family Policies Studies Centre.

Knight, I. (1981) *Family Finances*, London: OPCS.

Laroque, P. (1985) *La politique familiale en France depuis 1945*, Paris: Documentation Française.

Le Gall, D. and Martin, C. (1987) *Les familles monoparentales*, Paris: ESF.

Lewis, J. (1988) 'Lone-parent Families: Politics and Economics', *Journal of Social Policy*, 18 (4), pp. 595–600.

Liaisons Sociales (1989) *Mémo social*, Paris: Liaisons Sociales.

Liaisons Sociales (1990) *Barrière sociale périodique*, Paris: Liaisons Sociales.

McLaughlin, E. (1992) *Understanding Unemployment*, London: Routledge.

Maclean, M. (1990) 'Lone-parent Families: Family Law and Income Transfers', in E. Duskin (ed.) *Lone-parent Families: The Economic Challenge*, Paris: OECD.

Meulders-Klein, M. and Eekelaar, J. (eds) (1988) *Family, State and Individual Economic Security*, Brussels: Story Scientia.

Millar, J. (1989) *Poverty and the Lone-parent Family: The Challenge to Social Policy*, Aldershot: Gower.

Millar, J. (1992) 'Lone Mothers and Poverty', in C. Glendinning and J. Millar (eds) *Women and Poverty: The 1990s*, Hemel Hempstead: Harvester Wheatsheaf.

Millar, J. and Whiteford, P. (1993) 'Child Support and Lone-parent Families: Policies in Australia and the UK', *Policy and Politics* 21(1), pp. 59–72.

Millar, J., Leeper, S. and Davies, C. (1992) *Lone Parents, Poverty and Public Policy in Ireland: A Comparative Study*, Dublin: Combat Poverty Agency.

Mitton, R. and Willmott, R. (1983) *Unemployment, Poverty and Social Policy in Europe*, London: Bedford Square Press.

Monk, S. and Slipman, S. (1991) *Making Maintenance Pay*, London: NCOPF.

Morris, L. (1994) *Dangerous Classes: The Underclass and Social Citizenship*, London: Routledge.

Moss, P. (1990) *Childcare in the European Community*, Brussels: European Commission Child Care Network

Murray, C. (1984) *Losing Ground*, New York: Basic Books.

Murray, C. (1990) *The Emerging British Underclass*, London: Institute for Economic Affairs.

National Audit Office (1990) *Department of Social Security: Support for Lone-Parent Families* London: HMSO.

National Economic Development Office (1989) *Defusing the Demographic Time-Bomb* London: NEDO.

Office of Population Censuses and Surveys (1990) *General Household Survey 1988*, London: HMSO.

Organisation for Economic Cooperation and Development (1993) *Breadwinners or Carers? Lone Mothers and Employment*, Paris: OECD.

Pascaud, E. and Simenon, B. (1987) 'Pauvreté et précarité', *Données Sociales*, Paris: Institut National de la Statistique et des Etudes Economiques.

Rallu, J.L. (1982b) 'Les enfants des familles monoparentales', *Population*, 37(1), pp. 51–74.

Roll, J. (1988) *Family fortunes: Parents' Incomes in the 1980s*, London: Family Policy Studies Centre.

Roll, J. (1989) *Lone Parent Families in the European Community*, London: Family Policy Studies Centre.

Roll, J. (1992a) *Lone Parent Families in the European Community*, London: European Family and Social Policy Unit.

Roll, J. (1992b) *Lone-parent Families in the European Community: The 1992 Report*, London: Family Policy Studies Centre.

Sauvy, A. (1969) *General Theory of Population*, London: Weidenfeld & Nicolson.

Simon, J.L. (1983) 'The Present Value of Population Growth in the Western world', *Population Studies*, 37(1), pp. 5–21.

Smeeding, T.M., O'Higgins, M. and Rainwater, L. (1990) *Poverty, Inequality and Income Distribution in Comparative Perspectives*, Hemel Hempstead: Harvester Wheatsheaf.

Smith, D. (1992) (ed.) *Understanding the Underclass*, London: Policy Studies Institute.

Social Security Committee (1993) *The Operation of the Child Support Act*, London: HMSO.

Taffin, C. (1987) 'La mobilité résidentialle entre 1979 et 1984', in *Données Sociales*, Paris: Institut National de la Statistique et des Etudes Economiques.

Verdier, P. (1984) *Mémento d'Aide Sociale*, Paris: ESF.

Villac, M. (1984) 'Les familles monoparentales', in *Données Sociales*, Institut National de la Statistique et des Etudes Economiques.

Walker, A. and Walker, C. (eds) (1987) *The Growing Divide: A Social Audit 1979–1987*, London: Child Poverty Action Group.

V

Women and Housing and Planning Policy

Introduction

CLARE UNGERSON

Access to housing, the adequacy of that accommodation and the conditions under which it is occupied are of universal and central interest, irrespective of age, sex, race, disability, class and income group. Clearly, though, men and women can make differential claims to access to housing – in many societies women have great difficulty in forming separate households from their parents unless they are creating a second household in conjunction with a male partner, or in forming separate households from their long-term male partners unless they are accompanied by children (Watson with Austerberry, 1986; Watson, 1988). Similarly, differential income resources between men and women (Glendinning and Millar, 1992) mean that in housing markets where housing is accessed through purchase or payment of profit-rents, unsubsidised by the state, women are at a considerable disadvantage compared to men. Thus, in the area of women and housing, there is an important (although relatively underdeveloped) stream of literature that looks at the gendered determinants of housing access (for example, Munro and Smith, 1989). The chapter by Hilary Graham excerpted here describes the particular problems that women heads of household encounter in gaining access to decent housing in Britain, and the way in which, even if they manage to find some form of shelter, often through being defined as 'homeless', they then find themselves living in totally inappropriate temporary forms of housing, or living in heavy concentrations in particularly unattractive parts of cities, on 'sink' local authority estates.

It is important to note that there are two issues contained within the general topic of 'access'. The first issue concerns the question of the basic ability to form a separate household at all, while the second issue is concerned with the quality of accommodation and its location. Women's material conditions, and the way in which allocation systems of subsidised housing operate, will largely determine whether they have the financial and legal resources to form separate households (Ungerson, 1994). This is a question of opportunity, and such opportunities are strictly limited. At the same time there are questions of choice, however constrained. If one is adequately housed, but nevertheless living with people one dislikes, or who are violent, then there are obvious reasons for choosing to leave. But if the only alternative accommodation available is an overcrowded women's refuge in which one might expect to live for at least a year, or the sixteenth floor of a tower block tenement, then an apparent 'choice' may well seem like no choice at all. In other words, women may have legal rights to housing (though heavily constrained), but these rights are available only within a housing system and housing market which allocates them accommodation of such low quality as to render those rights inoperable for a great many individual women, particularly those who are mothers who will also need to consider the best interests of their children. It is the particular lot of many women to be forced to make trade-offs between intolerable relationships within adequate accommodation on the one hand, and rather better relationships within quite awful accommodation on the other.

However, it would be disingenuous to suggest that all women are completely trapped in dreadful relationships due to their highly restricted opportunities to move elsewhere. It appears to be the case that, particularly in the decade of the 1980s, women have been opting for divorce, and that, for these women, the housing consequences of their decisions to end bad relationships have been of secondary importance relative to their desire to distance themselves from their men. In 1992, the United Kingdom had the highest divorce rate in the European Union, and more than two and a half times as many divorces were granted to women as men in England, Wales and Northern Ireland. Men were granted divorce largely on the grounds of their wives' adultery, but the overwhelming reason for women suing for divorce was their husbands' 'unreasonable behaviour' (Central Statistical Office, 1995). The household and housing consequences of these decisions are considerable. For example, the proportion of all households who were lone parents doubled from 5.8 to 10.6 per cent between 1981 and

1993 (ibid.). In calculations based on the divorce rate of the previous decade, 1971–81, it was estimated that divorce alone accounted for the formation of an additional 80,000 households per year (Holmans, Nandy, Brown, 1987). But many of these divorced women will have moved into very bad housing, or at the very least, moved into less desirable accommodation. Between 1982 and 1993 the number of homeless households (the huge majority of which would have been headed by women) living in temporary accommodation rose from 10.5 thousand households to 58.4 thousand (Central Statistical Office, 1995). Rose Gilroy (1994), using data from McCarthy and Simpson (1991), demonstrates that although women with custody of their children are much more likely than 'non-custodial fathers' to retain the marital home immediately after divorce, they are much less likely to remain in it in the long term than 'custodial fathers'. This is because women find the expense of paying for and maintaining the one time marital home far more difficult than men.

Thus it is certainly arguable that a sea-change is taking place in housing demand that is part and parcel of the great social changes that constitute the rapid rise in lone parenting and divorce. Women are bringing bad relationships with men to an end, or refusing to enter them in the first place, and finding their separate – often extremely inadequate – housing solutions. It is these kinds of social trends that persuade men on the right of politics, who think within a rationalist and behaviourist framework that links human behaviour and desires with penalties and rewards, that an effective way in which to reduce lone parenting is to use legislation to limit lone parents' access to housing. In a House of Commons debate on proposed changes to the homelessness legislation which restrict its application, a backbench Conservative MP expressed a commonly held view when he asked the Minister, Sir George Young: 'Does my right honourable Friend agree that the Housing (Homeless Persons) Act 1977 . . . was the origin, both in time and in cause, of an unparalleled explosion in illegitimacy and the breakdown of family life in this country?' (Julian Brazier MP, 18 July 1994, Parliamentary Debates, 1993/4).

It is preposterous to explain changes in family and household structure using one factor alone. Cross-national data indicates that trends of rapid increase in divorce and lone parenting are common to all EU countries, particularly those of Northern Europe (Kiernan and Wicks, 1990). Given variations in housing policy across these nations, there are clearly deep and complicated forces at work, and it is quite wrong to lay these trends at housing policy's door. In the face of features of marital breakdown common to so many developed societies, any policy attempt to force marriages to stay together, or reluctant women to marry reluctant men, is bound to fail; and, given the fact that violence against women is largely domestic violence (Dobash and Dobash, 1979), it is positively dangerous to use the minutiae of housing legislation to restrict the housing opportunities of women without men. What must be argued for is a housing system which is sensitive to and responds to wider social change rather than a system that attempts to impose its own restrictive values.

'Home' for women, though, is something of a mixed blessing. It is the place where women have to provide very considerable amounts of unpaid work (Kiernan, 1992) and where they are most under threat of personal violence. Yet at the same time, as Jane Darke argues, home is a place where women can take pride in household tasks satisfactorily completed, and where women can feel safe and private. As she says: 'Women value their homes in a particular way. Our feelings are a mixture of affection, reciprocated towards the home as a nurturing environment, and resentment at the demands of the home' (Darke, 1994, p. 11). 'Home' is also the place where individuals and households can demonstrate their identity. Through choice of room arrangements, house extensions, add-on conservatories, front doors, furniture and furnishings, women and men can impose their own sense of themselves on their immediate built environment.

Nevertheless, the housing stock we inhabit in the Western world is predominantly one designed and built by previous generations and so there are also limits to the ways in which we can change our dwellings. An important stream of literature written largely by feminist architects has outlined the ways in which, historically, speculative builders or professional architects working in the public sector have, over the last century and more, operated with clear views about gender relations, and have built houses and designed public spaces that reflect those views. The article reproduced here by Ruth Madigan and Moira Munro is part of that literature and there are others whose work on the built environment is similarly informed by a gendered perspective (Matrix, 1984; Boys, 1989; Roberts, 1991).

It is also important to bear in mind that a 'home' cannot be treated in isolation, separated from its location. As much of the literature on housing has demonstrated, written as a great deal of it is by geographers, the place where one lives is both a crucial determinant and expression of prevailing social and economic relations (McDowell, 1983; Mackenzie, 1989). Thus urban planning in the twentieth century, with its sharp division between urban centres in which manufacturing, administration, commerce and entertainment take place, and suburbs, where residential living, education and child care take place, has echoed the public–private dichotomy, largely arising out of industrialisation, between 'men's space' and 'women's space' (Davidoff, 1995). This in turn has restricted women's economic opportunities and physical mobility, and has tended to create public spaces where women on their own are uneasy (Valentine, 1992) – the city centre at night with its odd mix of conviviality and masculinised threat (Wilson, 1991; Hey, 1986), the quiet suburb with its curtained windows and social and family life turned inwards away from the street, the messy lifts and long badly lit walkways of graffiti-ridden tower blocks situated on the edge of major cities. While the advent of the motor car is changing these sharp spatial divisions a little by encouraging suburban shopping and entertainment centres, the accessibility of these newly developed public spaces is confined to those with private cars – and cars are more often used and managed by men than by women.

If women are frightened of moving out of the home into the neighbourhood, then the only option for them is to stay trapped within the confines of the private domain. But there are ways of using policy which can both make cities safer in reality and render women's perception of danger less paralysing. The article excerpted here by Sylvia Trench and her colleagues considers the way in which safe transport schemes can be used to alleviate some of the problems of women's physical mobility. In the original article, not wholly reproduced here, they also consider how urban planning policies should be used to construct a greater mix of use within city centres such that women workers, many of whom are working very early or late shifts as cleaners and shop assistants, feel safely overlooked by residents who live in the centre. More short-term proposals, such as locating bus stops near centres of activity, eliminating pedestrian subways, and providing specialist, supervised, women's car parks, would also increase women's perceptions of their personal safety.

The long-term question remains as to how far women can create their own environment which reflects their own desires. The utopian dreams of communal living and shared housework of the early American feminists (Hayden, 1981) and their British imitators (Pearson, 1988) seem a far cry from the cramped box-like houses currently being built for single family owner-occupation in Britain today. It may be, of course, that the increasing divorce rate indicates that women are taking another route towards making their own space: instead of trying to alter the built environment they are taking a radical hammer to marriage and choosing to live without men (at least on a permanent basis). This tendency is neatly encapsulated by the American novelist Marge Piercy whose novel, *The Longings of Women*, is about three women with housing problems. All of them end up without men, although one has a male lover whom she keeps at bay. At the end of the story, Leila, an academic in the middle of a divorce from a philandering husband, and increasingly involved in finding housing for homeless women, ruminates about her new house:

> She had realised she did not care whether Zak liked it; he was not going to live here. The same was true of her son, now engaged to Ikuko. It was a priority for Leila to have a house she could afford by herself, one she could heat, hold on to. In spite of her accountant's paean to mortages and deductible interest, she would pay off this mortgage as rapidly as she could. There was nothing in the world like dealing with the homeless to make a woman engage in financial planning...She had also bought the house for the yard...the neighbour's maple had just begun to blush, speckles of red and orange on the green of the wide leaves. She shouldn't sit here. Why not? Aside from her duties at school, she was on no one's schedule but her own. (Piercy, 1994, pp. 531–2)

Finding a Home

HILARY GRAHAM

This chapter begins by reviewing the recent changes in housing policy, as a backcloth against which to set women's experiences of trying to find decent accommodation for themselves and their children. The central sections of the chapter examine different dimensions of housing inequality among women with children. The sections look in turn at women's access to housing, the increase in homelessness among families with children and the role of council housing in accommodating mothers who cannot buy themselves out of this residual housing sector. The chapter concludes by considering some of the evidence which links poor health among mothers and their children to the poor housing in which they live.

Housing policy

From 1945 to the early 1970s, Britain followed a 'twin-track' housing policy. It was a policy in which both owner-occupied (private) and council-rented (public) housing was encouraged. While the public sector was designed to accommodate a broad cross-section of the population, it was recognised that it had a particular role to play in the provision of social housing, housing for people who were disadvantaged in the commercial market. New houses were built by local authorities and new town corporations, while owner-occupation increased through a combination of rising real incomes, tax relief on mortgage interest and the expansion of credit facilities. The result was a significant growth in both council-

From Hilary Graham, *Hardship and Health in Women's Lives* (1993), Hemel Hempstead: Harvester Wheatsheaf, pp. 55–71.

rented housing and owner-occupation and a decline in privately rented accommodation through the 1950s, 1960s and 1970s (Hills and Mullings, 1990). By the late 1970s, over half (55 per cent) of Britain's homes were owner-occupied, with nearly a third (32 per cent) rented from local authorities and new towns.

The twin-track framework, however, was giving way. Through the late 1970s and 1980s, housing policy was shunted onto a single track through the stimulation of home ownership and the withdrawal of support for council housing (Ginsberg, 1992). Owner-occupation was encouraged by maintaining tax relief on mortgage interest which, by the end of the 1980s, represented three-quarters of total public expenditure on housing, including housing benefit (Hills and Mullings, 1990). Owner-occupation was also supported through increasing the opportunities for council house tenants to buy their homes at discounted prices, enshrined in the Right to Buy measures of the 1980 Housing Act. The homes lost to the council sector have been predominantly houses with gardens on suburban estates. Because most of the tenants on these estates are white, the effect of Right to Buy measures has been to widen racial inequalities in housing (Ginsberg, 1992).

Under the single-track policy of the 1980s and 1990s, the social housing function of local authorities has been shed. Over the last decade, housing associations have been encouraged to take on this role, but in the context of declining capital investment in housing (Hills and Mullings, 1990). The number of new housing association homes completed each year has fallen across the last decade, at a time when fewer new council homes have been built. The number of new homes built by local authorities and new towns fell from 146,000 a year in the mid-1970s, to less than 19,000 by the end of the 1980s, a fall of nearly 90 per cent (ibid.). At the same time, local authority rents rose substantially in real terms and, as a result, tenants found themselves spending a larger proportion of their income on their rent.

The changes in housing policy and provision have occurred against a backdrop of wider social and economic change. Patterns of family life in Britain are diversifying. Recent decades have also witnessed a large-scale restructuring of employment in Britain, with declining job opportunities in the old industrial areas and conurbations. These factors have combined to widen inequalities in women's access to decent housing for themselves and their children. Specifically, they are affecting women's access to tenured housing and are increasing the number of mothers caring for children in temporary accommodation. Council housing is increasingly becoming a residual sector for those who do not have the money to buy into owner-occupation.

These interlocking aspects of housing inequality are explored in turn in the sections below.

Access to housing

Today two-thirds (66 per cent) of homes in Britain are owner-occupied (Office of Population Censuses and Surveys, 1991a). The growth in owner-occupation reflects the long-term trend away from the private-rented sector. It also reflects the transfer of dwellings out of the council sector since 1980.

Access to the owner-occupied sector depends on income. It is those on higher incomes who take out mortgages and exercise the Right to Buy their council homes (Hills and Mullings, 1990). Through the 1980s and 1990s, an increasing number of homebuyers have faced problems meeting the costs of their mortgage repayments. In 1979, around 8,000 homeowners were more than six months in arrears on their repayments. By the middle of 1991, the figure was over 150,000, nearly 20 times higher. By mid-1992, 300,000 households were at least six months in arrears. The increase in arrears has gone hand in hand with a sharp rise in the number of repossessions. In 1979, 2,500 properties were taken into possession, by 1991, the figure was over 75,000 (Coles, 1990; Skellington, 1993).

While an increasing number of households are being forced out of owner-occupation, there has been a sharp reduction in the supply of rented accommodation. Through the 1980s, the number of homes for rent fell by over a million (Raynsford, 1989). London has been particularly hard hit by the increasing shortage of rented accommodation (Greve, 1991). As the supply of homes for renting has fallen, so council-house waiting lists have lengthened and the number of households accepted as homeless by local authorities has increased. Between 1978 and 1990, the number of officially recognised homeless households in England trebled to 150,000 (Hills and Mullings, 1990; Central Statistical Office, 1992).

Officially homeless households are those defined as homeless according to the 1977 Housing (Homeless Persons) Act (now Part

III of the 1985 Housing Act). Local authorities are obliged to rehouse people who are, or are likely to be, without accommodation and who have a 'priority need'. People in priority need include pregnant women, households with children and those who are vulnerable because of old age, mental illness or physical disability. Women escaping domestic violence do not have a statutory right to accommodation, and women without children who leave home because of domestic violence are not normally accepted as a priority group within the terms of Part III of the 1985 Housing Act (Sexty, 1990).

Because most single and childless people are excluded from the rehousing provisions of the 1985 Housing Act, official statistics significantly underestimate the scale of homelessness in Britain. It is, as Nick Raynsford (1989) observes, a chilling reminder of the inadequacy of housing statistics that most of those sleeping rough do not feature in the official homelessness figures.

The growth in official and unofficial homelessness has been identified as part of a wider 'access crisis', in which increasing numbers of people are finding it impossible to gain access to the formal housing market (Kleinman and Whitehead, 1988). Significant among those affected by this access crisis are mothers searching for decent housing in which to build a home for their children. Housing problems are often particularly acute for disabled women, who rely heavily on the public sector for housing that supports independent living (see 'Living in council housing') (J. Morris, 1990). Young mothers, disabled and non-disabled, are also facing increasing problems in finding a place to live. In one study of mothers aged under 20, nearly half were living with parents or relatives after the birth of their babies and not in independent households of their own. Four in ten were living in overcrowded conditions (a density of one or more persons per room), a proportion four times higher than the national average (Simms and Smith, 1986). Not surprisingly, housing was identified by the mothers as a significant cause of the depression and anxiety that many experienced (Simms and Smith).

> I hate living in this flat. I can't stand it, but I can't get a council flat ... So at the moment we're waiting because the council might be compulsorily purchasing the building, so, crossed fingers, we might actually end up being council tenants ... Well, it's the room really, 'cos Benjamin shares the bedroom with us. Also,

as you can see, there's not a bit of privacy, you know, you can't switch off from Benjamin at all, you know. He can't be in a separate part, he's there all the time. You can't turn the telly on too loud because it might wake him up or whatever. But, I mean we manage reasonably well, y'know. I only lose me cool every now and then [laughs] apart from that we sort of work it out okay. (Fulop, 1992, p. 188)

Like young mothers trying to set up homes, black and white women trying to leave relationships face particular housing problems. Relationship breakdown often involves a change in housing circumstances for one or both partners, and is a significant cause of rent and mortgage arrears and homelessness (Kemp, 1989). Women's homelessness is linked, particularly, to the experience of violence in domestic relationships.

I left my husband. I had a flat in Putney. I left him because he started to become violent...I'd been with him about ten years, married for about four. Finally, I couldn't stand any more so I left him...not only am I pregnant now, but I haven't got a job. So I moved in with my sister. And my sister couldn't put up with me; she only has a two-bedroom flat. She's got two children of her own. There was her and her boyfriend, she was pregnant again, and she had my mum living with her. So it was a great strain to live with my sister. Well, in the end I went along to Lewisham Council. Lewisham said they weren't taking any responsibility, that I should be under Wandsworth. So I've been in bed and breakfast now a year. (Miller, 1990, p. 38)

As the account above suggests, the accommodation changes that follow separation and divorce typically involve moving downmarket, into poorer housing (Bradshaw and Millar, 1991). Living with relatives and living in crisis accommodation are woven into the housing experiences of many lone mothers.

Friends who have known me for a long time say that I started at the top and have worked my way down! I didn't want to be dependent on him [ex-husband] and it was agreed that the house would be sold. I got half the sum and an extra sum which paid for most of this house. I have moved from one of the 'better' neighbourhoods of Birmingham to one of the poorer areas. I see it as the price I pay for independence. (Crow and Hardey, 1991, p. 55)

Restricted access to the housing market is linked to restricted access to good quality housing in materially advantaged neighbourhoods. The patterns found among lone mothers and black mothers (groups which are not, of course, mutually exclusive) illustrate how social divisions are meshed into the housing circumstances of Britain's families. Census data suggest that one-parent families are overrepresented in the metropolitan authorities: in Greater London, Greater Manchester and Merseyside, and underrepresented in the suburban and rural areas of Britain (Haskey, 1991). Within the metropolitan areas, one-parent families are concentrated in the inner city cores, areas that have been hardest hit by the movement of jobs and people out of Britain's major conurbations. The highest concentrations of one-parent families are found in the London boroughs, including Lambeth, Hackney and Hammersmith (Haskey, 1991).

A similar spatial patterning is evident among black families. The conurbations, and Greater London in particular, have provided the major areas of residence for Britain's black minority populations. While 9 per cent of the white population live in Greater London, the General Household Survey suggests that 44 per cent of the Indian population of Britain do so. Three in five (60 per cent) African–Caribbean people live in Greater London. Of the other conurbations, the West Midlands and West Yorkshire are also significant areas of black settlement, particularly for people from Pakistan and Bangladesh (Office of Population Censuses and Surveys, 1991). Within these conurbations, analyses of the census data suggest that black families are underrepresented in neighbourhoods which are materially advantaged: in suburban and rural neighbourhoods with high levels of employment, owner-occupation and car-ownership. They are overrepresented in poorer urban areas, with high rates of unemployment and low car-ownership (Robinson, 1989).

We live in this dump because I couldn't find nothing else. It's very difficult to find places to rent with children. Most landlords just don't want to know and those that do charge more for places they couldn't let to other people. They take advantage because they know that you couldn't find another place. So I'm in no position to stick up for myself and complain about the damp and the smell from the drain. (Crow and Hardey, 1991, pp. 59–60)

The disadvantages that black families, and black and white mothers caring for children alone, face in the housing market are reflected in the patterns of homelessness in Britain. These patterns are the focus of the next section.

Homeless families

Reflecting the priority categories laid down in the 1977 Housing Act, the vast majority of those accepted by local authorities as homeless and found accommodation are pregnant women and families with children (Central Statistical Office, 1992). Figure 1 indicates that, in 1990, 78 per cent of the homeless households who were found accommodation by local authorities fell into one of these two categories.

An increasing proportion of expectant mothers and parents with children who are recognised as officially homeless are being placed in temporary accommodation. Temporary accommodation

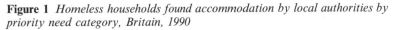

Figure 1 *Homeless households found accommodation by local authorities by priority need category, Britain, 1990*

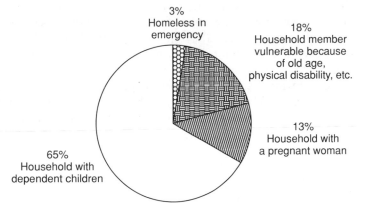

Note: Households for whom local authorities accepted responsibility to secure accommodation under the Housing Act 1985 which defines 'priority need'. Data for Wales include some households given advice and assistance only.
Source: Central Statistical Office (1992), derived from table 8.12.

includes bed and breakfast hotels, short-life tenancies, women's refuges and hostels.

> I was here [in the hotel] before the baby was born, two weeks before. I was so frightened, so alone. I had no transport, nothing. I sat here and cried my eyes out the whole night, I felt so alone. Then, later when I went into labour, I didn't even know I was in labour, I just waited and then went to the hospital and said I was terrified. I came back five days after the birth, and the first few days were terrible, you want to show off, you know, but you haven't got the space, the organisation, you're just ashamed of where you are and that you haven't got a home for your child. (Bonnerjea and Lawton, 1987, pp. 38–9)

The evidence suggests that the majority of households in temporary accommodation are households with children, and a large proportion are headed by lone mothers. In a recent Department of Environment study of 1,000 households in temporary accommodation, 40 per cent were single-parent households (Thomas and Niner, 1989). Mothers can expect to spend 33 weeks in temporary accommodation before being rehoused.

> When I first went into bed and breakfast, they stuck me up 72 stairs with a baby and a buggy and shopping. I was in a tiny little room which wasn't even six foot by eight foot. After many months of complaining...they moved me right downstairs into the basement. It wasn't too bad, apart from people chucking dirty, soiled nappies into the basement. Every morning when I opened my window, I've got a dirty nappy looking at me. The kitchens are atrocious, absolutely filthy downstairs, so that I can't cook in that sort of condition. I used to buy food from takeaways and things like that, but my son got ill. He went into bed and breakfast when he was about four months old; he's now about fourteen months old. I've got so many problems with him. Because he's not on a proper diet, he still wakes up of a night time, he very rarely sleeps. Now he's walking but he's still very, very small for his age. (Miller, 1990, p. 39)

'Race' is also deeply structured into the patterns of official and unofficial homelessness in Britain. A survey in Brent found that the number of African–Caribbean people who were officially accepted as homeless was three times that of white people (Bonnerjea and Lawton, 1987). There is also evidence that black families are offered temporary accommodation inferior to that offered to white families and spend longer in it (Ginsberg, 1992). As the latest group of newcomers to Britain, Bangladeshi families have suffered disproportionately from the squeeze on public sector housing and the restrictions on recourse to public funds imposed by immigration legislation (Miller, 1990). Evidence presented to the House of Commons Home Affairs Committee (1986) on Bangladeshi families suggested that 90 per cent of those classified as homeless in Tower Hamlets in the mid-1980s were Bangladeshi, and they made up over 80 per cent of the homeless families placed in bed and breakfast accommodation.

Temporary accommodation often means substandard accommodation. A government survey reported that about half of the properties housing homeless people were below an acceptable standard (Thomas and Niner, 1989). The report also found that over three-quarters (76 per cent) of local authority hostels and over 90 per cent of hotels were substandard or poor based on such measures as overcrowding, amenities and means of escape in case of fire.

> My family came to England in 1975 or '76. My dad was here, we came to join him [from Bangladesh]...I was living with my mother, and I got pregnant with my first child. It's a very small flat, near Victoria. When she was born, I had to go to the Homeless because there was no room for me. When I first went there, I went straight from the hospital. They put me in the first hotel and it was terrible; really like an attic; the window was broken...There were plenty of cockroaches. I was terrified of them. I used to be out most of the day, I used to come home just to sleep. When I used to go into the room I used to think, this is a prison. I used to cry to myself. I think people living in a hotel long-term probably go mental. I find it myself, and I'm a very capable woman. (Miller, 1990, pp. 79–80, 81)

Living in council housing

Public sector housing is increasingly becoming a residual housing sector, occupied by households without the income to buy a home of their own. Rather than accommodating a broad social mix, as intended in the twin-track policies of the post-war decades, council accommodation houses those who are struggling against disadvantage. Council tenants live on the margins of the labour market. Over 60 per cent of the heads of council households are economically inactive and, among those in paid work, incomes are less than 60 per cent of the average for all economically active heads of households (Office of Population Censuses and Surveys, 1991). Council homes are increasingly female-headed homes. While one-quarter (25 per cent) of all households in Britain are female-headed, over 40 per cent of council-rented households have a female head.

It is older women living alone and lone mothers who predominate among these female-headed households. As Figure 2 indicates, lone-parent households are concentrated in the rented sector while two-parent households are concentrated in the owner-occupied sector. Within the rented sector, it is council accommodation that provides homes for the majority (54 per cent) of Britain's one-parent families. The role of public housing was underlined in the

Figure 2 *Housing tenure of lone-parent families and other families with dependent children, Britain, 1988–9*

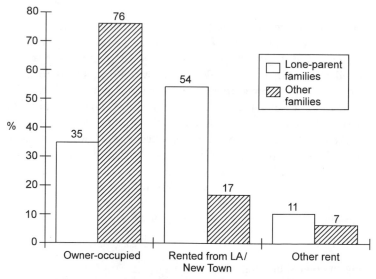

Note: Dependent children are persons under 16 or aged 16 to 18 and in full-time education, in the family unit and living in the household.
Source: Office of Population Censuses and Surveys (1991), derived from table 2.41.

Bradshaw and Millar study of 1400 lone parents. Reflecting the class differences in marriage breakdown and single motherhood, more lone parents came from local authority housing. Becoming a lone parent was associated with a change of address for the major- · ity (58 per cent) of their respondents and most of those who moved house, passed through or were eventually housed by local authorities (Bradshaw and Millar, 1991).

The patterns mapped out in Figure 2 match those found among parents caring for non-disabled children. Families with a disabled child, however, are less likely to be owner-occupiers than other families with children. In the late 1980s, 76 per cent of two-parent families were owner-occupiers: the evidence from the OPCS surveys of disability suggest that the proportion of homeowners among two-parent families with a disabled child was under 60 per cent. Similarly, the national evidence on lone mothers suggests that 54 per cent rent from the local authority: among lone parents caring for disabled children, the proportion is 77 per cent (Smyth and Robus, 1989). These patterns of housing tenure are summarised in Figure 3.

Figure 3 *Housing tenure of households with a disabled child, Britain, 1985*

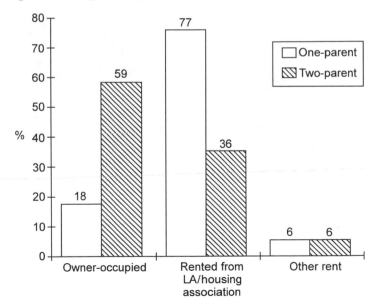

Source: Smyth and Robus (1989), derived from table 2.5.

Council housing is the sector in which most disabled adults live (J. Morris, 1990). As Morris notes, this is partly because of their generally lower incomes. It is also because most housing which is purpose-built or adapted for disabled people is owned by local authorities. Among disabled parents, too, the evidence suggests that the public sector is a much more important source of housing than it is among non-disabled parents. Data from the OPCS surveys of disability, reproduced in Figure 4, relate to the housing tenure of disabled parents who are householders. It is likely, therefore, to reflect the tenure patterns among fathers rather than mothers in two-parent households and mothers rather than fathers in one-parent households. It indicates that, compared to the general population of married and cohabiting parents, disabled parents who head a two-parent household are much more likely to be council tenants (42 per cent compared with 17 per cent among two-parent families as a whole). Among disabled lone parents, over seven in ten (73 per cent) are council tenants compared with five in ten (54 per cent) of lone parents in general (see Figures 2 and 4).

Figure 4 *Housing tenure of disabled adults who are householders in households with children, Britain, 1985*

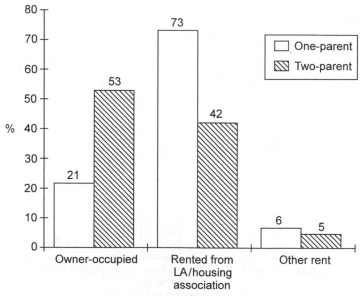

Source: Martin and White (1988), derived from table 2.14.

Public sector housing reflects the divisions of 'race' as well as those of class, gender and disability. Local authorities provide homes for a large proportion of African–Caribbean families, Data from the General Household Survey suggest that African–Caribbean households are significantly more likely to rent their accommodation from local authorities (42 per cent) than white households (25 per cent), Pakistani and Bangladeshi households (17 per cent) or Indian households (8 per cent) (Office of Population Censuses and Surveys, 1991). A complex of factors are woven into these different patterns, including the preference of many Asian families to own the homes they live in. However, housing preferences are not the only influences at work. Studies have recorded how the allocation procedures governing access to public sector housing have discriminated, directly and indirectly, against African–Caribbean and Asian households.

One major study highlighted the formal procedures which restrict the access of Black applicants seeking council housing. The criteria relating to length of residence, the disqualification of owner-occupiers and the rejection of applications from joint families worked against Asian applicants particularly, while the less favourable treatment of unmarried cohabiting couples was a major obstacle for African–Caribbean applicants. The study also highlighted the informal working practices which meant that applicants were 'matched' to properties and areas on the basis of their 'race', gender and class characteristics (Henderson and Karn, 1987).

While Henderson and Karn's research was conducted in the 1970s, their conclusions have been confirmed by more recent studies. A study of council housing in the London boroughs of Wandsworth and Southwark pointed to longer waiting periods among black women than among white women. The study also found that white women were more likely to live in semi-detached and terraced housing, while black women were more likely to live in flats, and on the upper floors of high-rise blocks (Rao, 1990). These differences were reflected in the patterns of council housing among women with children. For example, among the white women with three or more children in the study, 65 per cent were living in one-bedroomed flats or maisonettes; the proportion among black and minority ethnic women was 90 per cent.

I don't think it's just chance that there are so many black families in this block, the council puts us here. Lots of them are lone parents too. I don't think it's good to put us all together like this because the block gets a bad reputation and just because we are alone with our kids doesn't mean we all get on. But I do have some good mates round here. (Crow and Hardey, 1991, p. 62)

Poor housing and poor health

A house provides the physical context in which domestic relationships are built and lived out. It is the place in which women experience what it is to be a mother and have responsibilities for the health of children. As the accounts included in this chapter illustrate, women recognise that the physical environment of the home affects how they feel about themselves and their lives. They recognise, too, that poor and poorly designed housing spells danger for their children (Mayall, 1986). It brings with it hazards which mean that children must be constantly restrained and mothers must be constantly vigilant.

> The flat's too restricted – he's no room to play and he loves climbing. And if there was a fire, how would we get out? It worries me terribly. My Nan was in a fire, she was very badly burned. I try to keep him out of the kitchen while I'm cooking, because he can reach up to things. But if I shut him out, I can't see what he's up to.

> He's too confined. He's not getting enough exercise. It'll be worse when he's older. I won't be able to let him run around outside because it's a rough area, and the people – it's like any council estate. The windows are very bad. They're low down and they've got loose handles – he'll soon be able to open them. He can reach up to them now. I have to keep the windows shut – it's a problem in these small rooms. It gets very hot. I have to watch him, all the time. Keep telling him – it's wrong, mustn't do that. (Mayall, 1986, pp. 60–1)

The relationship between poor housing and poor health was underlined in a recent study of households with children in Glasgow, Edinburgh and London (Hunt *et al.*, 1988). Reflecting the design of the study, a large proportion of the parents and children lived in low-income households where there was no one in employment. It was typically the mother rather than the father who was interviewed about their health and the health of children in the household, while the presence and severity of dampness and mould was assessed by surveyors. The survey pointed to a gradient of physical ill-health with the proportion of adults reporting a range of symptoms, including nausea, coughs, blocked nose and high blood pressure, increasing in line with the levels of damp and mould in the home (Hunt *et al.*, 1988).

A similar gradient in children's health also emerged. Children in homes with high damp and mould scores were reported to have higher rates of respiratory and gastrointestinal symptoms, aches and pains, and fever than children in dry and mould-free homes (Platt *et al.*, 1989). For example, the proportion of children with headaches rose from 12 per cent of those in damp-free homes to 30 per cent of those in homes judged to be very damp (Hunt *et al.*, 1988). The association between damp and mouldy housing and a child's poor health status has been confirmed in other studies (Strachan, 1988).

Poor housing conditions were not only associated with symptoms of physical ill-health. The survey found a similarly strong association with mothers' and children's emotional well-being. Mothers living in households assessed to be damp and mouldy were more likely to report such symptoms as tiredness, 'bad nerves', headaches and feeling low. Mothers living in homes that they assessed to be cold, noisy and in poor repair also reported more emotional distress than those living without these problems (Hunt, 1990). Children growing up in homes which were damp were more likely to be described by their mothers as irritable, tired and with a poor appetite. They were also more likely to be described as unhappy.

Other studies have confirmed the links between poor housing and emotional distress among women. For example, a study of 800 families in Waltham Forest found that mothers with pre-school children living in council-rented accommodation were more likely to be depressed than mothers in owner-occupied accommodation (Richman *et al.*, 1982). This study, like others, pointed to higher rates of depression among mothers living in flats above ground level and in tower blocks (Littlewood and Tinker, 1981).

> It's the house. It just gets on my nerves. We can't get another one until they pull it down. It's damp, we've no hot water, no bath and the toilet's outside. It's just this place.

It's too cramped. There's five of us in one bedroom at the moment. He has to sleep in his carry cot as I don't have enough room to put his proper cot up. (Simms and Smith, 1986, pp. 70, 62)

The links between housing difficulties and emotional distress figured strongly in Brown and Harris' research into the social origins of depression among white women. On the basis of information collected from over 700 women, they identified a set of difficulties and experiences which provoked depression. Difficulties were only included if they were markedly unpleasant, were long term (of at least two years' duration) and involved problems other than health. Housing was the major long-term difficulty faced by women. For half the women with difficulties, their problems were related to their housing: severe overcrowding, lack of amenities, noise and insecurity of tenure. The researchers concluded that major housing problems 'are highly associated with chronic psychiatric conditions' and that such difficulties 'play a definite aetiological role in depression' (Brown and Harris, 1978, pp.199, 276).

...there's no door to the bedroom, there's no privacy whatsoever and consequently 'cos there's no door there you can't put him down like most people do at 9 o'clock in his own little room. You try putting him down and he just screams his head off. Midnight it was last night and it has been for about the last week...also, when I'm on nights most of the week I know I have to get up for him in the morning, but on Fridays his dad gets up and gets him breakfast and I should by rights be able to sleep through but it's impossible. (Fulop, 1992, p. 187)

Poor housing in materially deprived neighbourhoods provides the setting in which an increasing number of women are working to bring up their children.

Gender, House and 'Home': Social Meanings and Domestic Architecture in Britain

RUTH MADIGAN AND MOIRA MUNRO

Recent work has argued that analysis based on the household obscures the fact that women and men experience housing differently in at least four respects. First, women predominate in some low-income household types (particularly single parents and single elderly) and further, even in ostensibly similar household forms (e.g. as single people), women's weak labour market position means that they do not inevitably enjoy equal access to housing transacted in the market (Watson and Austerberry, 1986). Similarly, there may be sufficient discrepancies of power within two-adult households to imply the existence of significant differences over the enjoyment of the benefits of owner-occupation. Work on the feminisation of poverty has shown that women may be kept poor even within relatively affluent households (Glendinning and Millar, 1987). Hence, it would be expected that many women will benefit less, either as households or compared to their partners, both from the potential for wealth accumulation from housing and also the enhanced access to capital markets that are argued to derive from owner-occupation.

Second, there are good grounds for believing that the home occupies a greater centrality in the lives of women as compared with men, as a result of women's domestic role. Although the precise division of labour has changed over time there is ample evidence to show that women still take on the major burden of domestic labour and the responsibility for child care (Cowan, 1983; Green et al., 1990). It seems likely that this will affect their

From Ruth Madigan and Moira Munro, 'Gender, House and "Home": Social Meanings and Domestic Architecture in Britain', *Journal of Architectural and Planning Research*, 8, (2) (1991), pp.117–27.

evaluation of a house, both as a practical place in which to work and also as a vehicle for personal expression.

Third, housing consumption is likely to have a different salience for men and women at the symbolic level. We have argued in a longer paper (Madigan, Munro and Smith, 1990) that the meanings of housing consumption coalesce around at least three themes: the display of wealth and status: the organisation of family life; and the quest for safety, security and well-being in the broadest sense, all of which should be analysed in a gender-differentiated framework. It is true that a crude equation of women = domestic sphere, men = public sphere does not describe the way in which people actually live, but it remains a strong current in the ideology of family and home in spite of the fact that women are increasingly active in the labour market. Similarly men have, now as always, an emotional and practical investment in home life, both as a place of comfort and retreat and also as an outward symbol of status and achievement. Just because both sexes attach positive meanings to the concept of home (Pahl, 1984; Saunders, 1990) does not mean that they seek the same ideal solutions or that they evaluate their own reality in the same way. In our culture the concept of 'home' embraces amongst other things ideas of security, affection and comfort which are almost bound to evoke favourable responses (Franklin, 1986). This does not preclude the possibility that at times our homes are cramped, stifling, oppressive or even dangerous.

Fourth, a fast-growing area of research has investigated the impact of housing on men and women as mediated by urban structure: the division of the city into strictly segregated residential and employment zones (Fava, 1980). By the early twentieth century suburbia had come to represent the ideal of family life in both Britain and the USA: 'individual domesticity and group monitored respectability' (Thompson, 1982, p.8). Thompson further argued that the growth of the suburbs in Britain at the turn of the twentieth century with its increasing segregation of home and work, created a protected, semi-rural environment for wives and children. The enclosure of the private household behind the formality of the public facade encapsulated the dimensions of bourgeois family ideology, with its strict demarcation of public and private, masculine and feminine.

Feminist writers (such as Hayden, 1980; Saegart, 1980; McDowell, 1983) have raised questions about the implications of housing developments which segregate residential and non-residential space to such a degree that women are trapped in the domestic environment of the suburb. This becomes an obstacle to combining paid employment with domestic responsibilities, it marginalises non-family households, it inhibits women from participating in adult non-family activities and it gives substance to an ideology of domesticity (Fava, 1980).

There is some evidence that the traditional role of the suburbs may be changing as women have increased their participation in the labour market and some households seek housing closer to the city to reduce the costs of commuting and improve access to public transport, day nurseries and other services (Wekerle, 1984; Little, Peake and Richardson, 1988). Conversely, suburbs themselves are changing, so that an increasing number of jobs, especially service jobs, are located in suburban areas (van Vliet (ed.), 1988). It is apparent that women do not all share the same demands and needs and that no single environment, either suburban or urban, will provide an unambiguously best living environment (Egar *et al.*, 1988, Fava, 1988; Saegart, 1988).

Our aim in this chapter is to explore a further dimension of gender inequality in housing, which has received rather less attention to date, namely that which is structured in and reflected by the physical form of housing. Our purpose is to expose the assumptions about the use of domestic space and the sharing of domestic labour that are embodied in the internal and external design of housing and the way this is responding to changing economic and social conditions.

An immediate problem in attempting to discuss physical design and its impact on women is the tendency to present women in very conventional roles: mothers with prams facing flights of stairs, housewives with young children negotiating busy roads, elderly women with heavy shopping bags and a long walk to the bus. All these are important but they serve to confirm rather than question women's subordination and lack of influence. We believe it is important to locate these criticisms in the context of an analysis of the structural inequalities and ideologies which shape women's experience (Matrix, 1984). Without this there is a danger that, instead of a radical critique, these criticisms will be subsumed under traditional understandings of women as mothers, carers and housewives. It is that old problem. If we discuss kitchen design on the assumption that women are the main users, are we recognising the inequality of domestic labour or reinforcing stereotypes of women in the kitchen?

At the very least we need to be sure that physical design does not trap people in existing roles even if we recognise that physical design cannot in itself change social relations.

Before considering some of the practical limitations of contemporary housing design we wish to identify some of the intentions and assumptions implicit in that design, and to look at the role of design in housing production.

The role of design professionals

It is commonly assumed that the most important input into the design of housing emanates from architects. Though architects by profession have the opportunity to articulate their design intentions, a closer analysis of the housing production process quickly reveals that architects do not have control over the finished product. It is therefore important to have some understanding of the part they play in housing production and the interaction of architectural design with other factors which impinge on housing design. It is immediately apparent that architects have very different roles in the public and the private sector.

In the public sector architects have played a key role in the design process. In the 1930–40s and again in 1960–70s they were encouraged to adopt experimental technologies in response to a housing crisis (Ball, 1974), and to design on a scale which expressed the municipal grandeur of their local authority clients rather than the more homely aspirations of the potential occupants. The scale of comprehensive redevelopment undertaken in the public sector gave opportunity for specifically architectural innovation. In particular, the radical philosophy of the Modern movement appeared to offer new solutions for cheap mass-produced, high density housing. The sparsity of the design and the readiness to experiment with new technologies appealed to housing authorities under pressure to produce quick solutions (Dunleavy, 1981; Rodger, 1989). Because housing in the public sector has been viewed as a form of social engineering, a means of dealing with social problems, architects at this time were also encouraged to build in to their designs a range of dubiously grounded academic theories of neighbourhood and community (Bacon, 1986).

In recent years popular–public debate about housing design in Britain has taken the form of an attack on Modernism and its architects, who are held responsible for the shortcomings of low-income housing built in the 1960s and 1970s for the public rented sector. These estates have been criticised for their hard, inhuman environment, for difficulties of access, poor facilities for children and a lack of safety from assault. The segregation of roads and pedestrians often means long walks down unsupervised, poorly lit pathways, stairways and access balconies. Women, in particular, feel vulnerable at night and resentful by day, negotiating these difficult routes with heavy bags, prams or small children. Children's play is not visible from the windows and the complex levels and entrance ways encourage dangerous activities (Jacobs, 1961; Coleman, 1985).

By contrast, architects play a surprisingly minor role in the design of housing for volume (i.e. large-scale, speculative) builders in the private sector, which accounted for a full 84 per cent of housebuilding in Britain in 1987 (Central Statistical Office, 1989). Private sector architects have operated within a very conservative design philosophy and they have a relatively low status within the profit maximising regime of the volume builders. In a rare series of articles on 'Volume Housing', Davison (1987) underlines the market constraints on architects operating in the field of private housing. The role of the architect in designing mass housing is, he shows, first, to maximise the number of dwellings on a site, and second, to enhance the external appearance in order to improve marketability. It is only in the new high density urban housing developments in which he sees opportunities for architectural innovation. As Leopold and Bishop (1983) point out, the volume builders look to standardisation as a means of minimising design costs and technical difficulties and to assess development possibilities quickly when land becomes available (Booth, 1982). Private builders 'believe they must cater to the buyers' wish for privacy, for a degree of exclusiveness and for cars parked within the curtilage' (Leopold and Bishop, 1983. p. 240). These minimum requirements tend to produce a suburban solution of a range of standard models subtly differentiated according to price and style (Booth, 1982). Styling rather than design is important from a marketing point of view (Lawrence, 1985).

Within this remit a range of styles has emerged, each redolent with social meanings. Typically, it is the outside of the house, particularly the front of the house which maintains a special symbolic significance and which receives most attention. Ravetz (1989) has argued that the concern with external appearances is part of the masculine world of class differentials (reflected as much in Victorian housing as in present day estate agents' displays), whereas the women's view from the interior is largely unacknowledged. The styling tends to be nostalgic (apart from a brief flirtation with Scandinavian modern in the 1960s) (Oliver *et al.*, 1981). There is a search for consoling images, images which conjure up ideas of community, stability and social order (Forty and Moss, 1980). As Forty and Moss indicate, the pseudo-vernacular (and that may mean that rustic imagery of the country cottage or the cosiness of the nineteenth-century courtyard) is popular both as a marketing device and as a political strategy. Builders find it easier to overcome any opposition to new developments from planners and residents if their designs are in tune with, or a variant of the local surroundings. Even in the public sector where Modernism now appears to have been abandoned, quite explicit revivals are currently evident, illustrated for example in the resurgence of the art-nouveau style of Charles Rennie Mackintosh in Glasgow, or neo-Georgian designs in Liverpool.

In this chapter we would like to concentrate on the evolution of design in the private sector, looking at the sort of volume-built speculative housing which most people live in, rather than the one-off architect design. This is partly because building in the public sector now represents such a small proportion of total housebuilding, but also because we believe it is here in the speculative housing sector that popular tastes are molded. The retreat from comprehensive redevelopment, the decline in public investment and widespread dissatisfaction with the products of Modernism have brought about a convergence between the commercial products of the private mass market and the designer products produced by architects. As an architectural movement Postmodernism has made a virtue of the eclecticism which has always been a feature of the market-oriented speculative builder (Jencks, 1977). In order to understand something of the symbolic meanings attributed to contemporary housing design it is, therefore, appropriate to look at the evolution of the volume-built house and how this relates to ideologies of family, class and gender.

The historic evolution of mass housing

Architectural historians have demonstrated how a single dominant house form, the terraced house in England (Muthesius, 1982) and the tenement in Scotland (Worsdall, 1989), was constantly reinterpreted to reflect the increasing differentiation of the class structure in the late nineteenth century. Historical referents (for example classical, gothic or regency) were deployed as status symbols to provide a subtle differentiation between classes.

Matrix (1984) argue that the design of the Victorian (late nineteenth century) 'gentleman's town house' reflected the internal hierarchy of the bourgeois family with the public masculine domain at the front of the house and the private feminine domain confined to the rear. The artisan household enjoyed lower space standards than the middle classes, but maintained the same distinctions between front and back, public and private, masculine and feminine. Lawrence (1987) discusses the concentration of family life in the back room, the kitchen, in small working-class terraced houses. Worsdall (1979) comments on the way in which in Scottish tenements even quite modest households reserved a parlour for 'best', virtually unused while the family lived at the back in the kitchen. As Lawrence (1985) notes, this reveals the fundamental difference in approach by designers who viewed the home in a utilitarian and functional light and the occupants, who imbued the internal space with (differentiated) symbolic meanings. It is the front of the house which displays the socio-economic status of the household, while the back has a more utilitarian design, often in cheaper materials, which reflects the demands of domestic labour (wash houses, bin shelters, trades entrance, etc.). Children, particularly young children, remain confined to the back regions and the female sphere.

For the poorer working class the public masculine domain was likely to be outside in the street and the pubs. Muthesius (1982) suggests that the more respectable and status conscious the household, the greater the differentiation between front and back, the public sphere of the street and the parlour and the private sphere of the kitchen, the yard and the back lane. Hence during the Victorian period, the ideal of the bourgeois family became crystallised not merely as the norm of social propriety for the middle classes, but also increasingly for the working classes. It was a model which relied centrally on female domesticity.

Inter-war housing in Britain has generally been understood as a scaled down version of the Victorian model, retaining the parlour at the front and the domestic private sphere at the back. Thus, the so-called living-room was preserved for best while living continued in the back room. Burnett (1978) has argued that there was a convergence of housing types in the twentieth century as the size of middle-class housing declined and the space standards for working-class housing grew. The Tudor Walters Report of 1918 set space standards for working-class housing which were in some ways more generous than present day standards (Powell, 1974). In response to working-class representation, however, Tudor Walters retained the parlour house as the basic model, despite arguments from officials that keeping one room for formal use only represented a waste of space. The parlour still held social and symbolic significance which respectable working people wished to defend.

For the middle classes the decline of servants, smaller families, the introduction of improved domestic technologies, the rise of owner-occupation and the aesthetic impact of the 'Garden City Movement' produced important revisions in housing styles in the 1920s and 1930s (Burnett, 1978; McKean, 1987; Oliver *et al.*, 1981) including a more rustic styling which characterised the semi-detached house and the cottage flat (four flats in a building which looks like a pair of semi-detached dwellings). As an architectural movement Modernism, although popular with the avant-garde in the 1930s, had a rather limited impact on the design of speculative housing in this period (Gould, 1977). In the private sector at least it tended to provide just one more style to add to the existing menu. The flat-roofed, metal-windowed, white walled houses which came to epitomise Modernism took their place as a minority taste along-side the far more numerous examples of rustic cottages and Tudor semi-detached houses.

The parlour house with its connotations of public and private, front and back, masculine and feminine remained the deminant house form until the 1950s. But from then on the volume built estate house was increasingly designed around one single living room (Hole and Attenburrow, 1966). Since post-war kitchens were typically a small work area rather than a social space this left the household with only one public area.

To some extent this change in design can be explained in relation to commercial pressures. Building plots have become smaller as land prices have risen. The spread of owner-occupation and the need, therefore, to sell housing to lower income households has produced further pressure on space standards and profits. At the same time, the Modern aesthetic which values a sense of light and space produced a less cluttered look which gained ground in pop-ular taste. The new house type is a compromise between declining overall space standards and the desire to achieve a sense of spaciousness by providing one relatively large room which runs the full length of the site.

We wish to explore some of the practical implications, but also the symbolic meanings attached to the demise of the parlour house. How does the change in design relate to changes in family ideology and gender relations? Despite a growth in the number of adult households, the design of houses is still framed in terms of the nuclear family, although some assumptions here have changed. The ideal of family organisation no longer conforms to the hierarchical model of the nineteenth century, but is presented as a democratic grouping centred on marriage as a partnership between two equals (Parsons, 1949, Fletcher, 1973; Mount, 1982). This is directly reflected in the provision of undifferentiated, common space presumed to be jointly used by the new democratic couples and their children. Despite this ideological shift the division of labour remains intact. Women's role may have changed but it is not allowed in this idealised model to challenge the differentiation between the sexes. Indeed the 1950s saw a very powerful reassertion of familial values and a restatement of femininity as the role model for women (Birmingham Feminist History Group, 1979; Wilson, 1980; Heron 1985). The post-war period also saw a growth in consumerist ideology in which the home featured as the major focus of consumption and women as major consumers (Tomlinson, 1990). Indeed the whole post-war expansion in home-ownership and suburban development can be seen as part of a deliberate (and according to Rees and Lambert, 1985, state-aided) strategy for creating the consumer markets which fuelled the post-war economic boom (Harvey, 1973; Castells, 1977; Duncan, 1981).

Fox draws on parallel American experience to make links between post-war social and economic changes in family relations and the houses that families live in:

Most prominent as instrument, symbol and artifact of the new suburban culture was the detached single family suburban house on its grassy plot. The house styles favored by postwar suburbanites evolved in conjunction with day-to-day activities of the isolated structure family. The differences from the typical business-class suburban house of the 1920s were considerable, and very revealing of the cultural changes under way ... All traces of the nineteenth century 'parlor' for formal entertaining disappeared... The new suburban house style emphasized both family unity and individuality. By the on-set of adolescence at the latest, all children required a room of their own... Rooms for interacting with visitors and non-resident relations... could disappear as the locus of activity shifted to eating and recreational activity rooms suitable only for family members. (Fox, 1986, pp. 65–6)

Certainly these design changes have not always been welcomed. Attfield (1989) suggests that the new fashion in design was often resisted by the initial occupants. This is particularly true for those being compulsorily rehoused by local authorities who had a restricted choice of house and virtually no influence over design decisions. The families who moved into Modern post-war housing in British New Towns often ignored, and in the eyes of contemporary architects sabotaged, the design by covering picture windows with lace curtains, camouflaging clean lines with frills and flounces and heavily patterned furnishings. In the new, more open-plan, living rooms they arranged furniture to recreate the cosy parlour of their parents' home. Conversely, as the style achieved popularity, many occupants of the small inter-war parlour house have created a more open plan effect by demolishing the intervening wall to create a variant on the modern contemporary design.

As Scoffman (1984) notes, when planners designed estates which in the interests of safety aimed to segregate pedestrians and road traffic, they frequently created layouts which contravened basic social conventions regarding the meaning of front and back. Vehicle access and parking organised to the rear of the house meant that visitors arriving by car entered the house through the back garden, past the bins and directly into the kitchen rather than using the correct pedestrian-only access to the front door. Ironically, in view of the safety considerations, children also played at the back of the houses, attracted by the hard surfaces of the vehicle access routes and the focus of domestic activity to the rear. The front thus remained pristine and formal but the planners' objectives were defeated.

It is important to remind ourselves that most households live in housing built for a different generation with different patterns of use in mind. New housing should therefore be flexible, able to accommodate different household types and different future sets of demands. It was with this in mind that the last major government report on housing (Parker Morris, 1961), which though it set high space standards for public sector housing until the 1970s, none the less abandoned attempts to detail patterns of domestic life as earlier reports had done (Tudor Walters, 1918; Dudley, 1944) and settled instead for general guidelines. This is partly because it was a period in which flats rather than houses were being constructed in the public sector and partly a response to the growing belief that undesignated spaces gave greater flexibility in use. This may be true in flats where rooms are less differentiated, but houses in Britain where the rooms upstairs generally provide the same floor space as those downstairs are by convention very clearly designated; upstairs are private bedrooms, downstairs is daytime public space (Lawrence, 1987). In a small house with an open plan ground floor this may have the effect of reducing ways in which space can be used.

Gender differentiation and housing design

It has been suggested that the abolition of the front parlour and its replacement with the through lounge-dining room may at some level reflect the new 'democratic' family ideology (see Watson, 1986); but what implications does it have for the privacy of household members? There is inevitably something of a gulf between the ideal and the reality for most people. Fox (1986) speaks of twin goals of 'family unity and individuality' but the latter is hard to express in a small house where private space is severely limited (Cooper Marcus and Sarkissian, 1986). How are non-family households served by contemporary housing design? A single public room implies a degree of communality which may not exist in family households, let alone in other household groups (Allan and Crow, 1989).

Having only one public room implies that this space, the most heavily used in the house, is permanently on display. There can be no 'back region' (Saunders and Williams, 1988) restricted to household members and intimates only. Most people have, in any case, abandoned the maintenance of a room kept mainly for show to outsiders. To what extent does this reinforce the message of consumerism that every aspect of life is open to scrutiny and commercialisation? Is the other face of the labour saving home a demand for higher standards and a house which is not just clean but tasteful, in a way which changes according to commercially sponsored fashion every few years, expanding the skill and the time to be expended on consumption (Cowan, 1976)? It has been shown that despite great advances in domestic technology, women's work in the home has not been greatly reduced, being directed towards ever higher standards of cleanliness (Hardyment, 1988). Women clearly bear the brunt of the work involved in maintaining this consumerist ideal (Lloyd, 1981; Bose, 1982).

Contemporary design also raises questions about the assumptions made in relation to domestic labour and the likely impact of design on domestic labour. The modern kitchen, often designed as a starkly functional workspace, may segregate the housewife cook from the social centre of the house. But does it assume one single user (reduced space standards often imply that it is very small)? Is the technological kitchen designed to give the impression that modern housework can be done effortlessly, at the flick of a switch? It can surely be no accident that the fitted kitchen emerged in a period of increased demand for women's paid labour and effectively reinforced the view that domestic labour can be combined with paid employment outside the home, without any significant threat to a gender-based division of labour (McKenzie and Rose, 1983; Boys, 1984, p.27). We are now seeing a move away from the overly high-tech hard surface kitchen towards a more folksy, wood panelled image. Even refrigerators are disguised to look like antique cupboards rather than the metallic boxes they really are (what could be more post-modern?). In the more spacious house this may signify the reinstatement of the kitchen as a social space. For others the new style is just that, a fashion without any special utility.

Perhaps the biggest change in the post-war period has been the revolution in the status of children. More and more children have rooms of their own, often elaborately equipped as study bedrooms with TV, computers and so on, even in quite modest households, while adults continue to share bedrooms and public space. Better equipped households have a study or workroom for men, but women rarely have space of their own. Privacy is typically considered in terms of the segregation of adults and children. But where do adults go for privacy from each other? As Katherine Whitehorn put it: 'Women have real difficulty in knowing what if anything is their own exact territory. In one sense a woman controls the whole house, but in another she may feel she owns nothing personally but her side of the wardrobe' (Whitehorn, 1987).

Safer Cities for Women

SYLVIA TRENCH, TANER OC AND STEVEN TIESDELL

This chapter is based on the findings of the Home Office Safer Cities Projects and a series of interactive meetings organised by the authors at the University of Nottingham, bringing together women's groups and planning officers. The first objective was to make those responsible for transport and land-use planning aware of how seriously women's use of town centres and access to work and leisure was affected by the fear of attack. The second objective was to explore with women's groups their response to some of the planning remedies that are being proposed to make the environment less conducive to crime or to insulate women from their effects.

Surveys (Atkins, 1989) in a number of UK cities establish that around two-thirds of women are afraid to go out at night alone and significant numbers will not use public transport, and are worried about city centre car parks. In Nottingham 45 per cent of all the women who did use the city centre after dark felt either 'very' or 'fairly' unsafe (Nottingham Safer Cities Project, 1990) Women were also found to be taking a variety of measures to reduce perceived risks: avoiding walking alone at night, only going out if a safe return had been arranged in advance, avoiding unsafe areas like subways and back streets and avoiding waiting at bus stops. In Bradford, a survey found that as many as 59 per cent of women avoided using any form of public transport at night (Local Transport Today, 1990). A comprehensive picture of the extent of fear of crime over the whole country can be found in Table 1, which

From Sylvia Trench, Taner Oc and Steven Tiesdell, 'Safer Cities for Women: Perceived Risks and Planning Measures', *Town Planning Review*, 63 (3) (1992).

summarises a wide range of local and national surveys covering reported fear of crime.

Table 1 *Fear of crime: summary of surveys*

Location	Date	Finding
London	1984–5	56 per cent of women felt 'very unsafe' or 'not very safe' walking alone at night: 22 per cent never travelled after dark.
Islington	1985	73 per cent of women and 27 per cent of men felt worried about going out alone at night.
Manchester	1987	63 per cent of women never walked home alone at night.
Birmingham	1987	69 per cent (both sexes) deterred from visiting city centre at night.
Southampton	1986	59 per cent of women felt unsafe walking after dark: over 90 locations identified as unsafe by respondents.
Lewisham	1985	53 per cent of respondents felt unsafe going out at night on one estate: 79 per cent on another.
Croydon	1986	'Almost two-thirds' of respondents did not feel safe walking alone after dark: 'over half' in another location.
Swansea	1986	Half the respondents felt unsafe when walking about estate after dark.
Wellingborough	1986	58 per cent felt they would be victims of violent street robbery: 54 per cent felt they would be assaulted in the street: 60 per cent of women thought they would be sexually assaulted.
Great Britain	1987	40 per cent of respondents feared going out at night: 59 per cent of retired persons; 64 per cent of women.
England and Wales	1984	31 per cent of respondents felt 'fairly unsafe' or 'very unsafe' walking alone after dark.

Source: Compiled from various sources by Atkins, 1989, p. 8.

   This chapter singles out women, not because they are exclusively the victims of attacks in cities, but because they are especially vulnerable. Statistics for attacks do not always bear out this assertion, but there are reasons for this: first, many kinds of harassment and anti-social behaviour do not get reported to the police; and secondly, if fear leads to a reluctance to go out alone at night, then very few women are, so to speak, available for attack. Women's fears have sometimes been dismissed as an irrational response to irresponsible media reporting, but it could be argued that the irrationality is in the crimes themselves (Platt, 1991) and in the pressure on women to curtail their movements and adapt their behaviour to avoid 'dangerous' places. Perceived fear itself imposes a significant psychological cost and seriously inhibits the behaviour of a large number of women.

As city centres are perceived to be dangerous, they are either deserted or given over to gangs of revellers and drunkards after dark. This not only denies large numbers of men and even greater numbers of women the use of their city centre at night, but it also has a significant economic and employment cost. The Nottingham Safer Cities project estimated that this could be in the order of £24 million per annum and over 600 jobs in a city like Nottingham.

Planning policies should be examined to see how they affect these problems even though the potential of physical changes to improve this situation is limited to what are termed 'opportunistic' crimes – those crimes committed by the rational criminal who weighs up the opportunity for gain against the cost of being observed, physically prevented or caught. Even in these cases where the effects are limited, there are many instances of robberies and assaults in relatively well-lit and public places. It should also be recognised that changes in the built environment involve balancing other costs against safety benefits. For example, there may be a choice between a longer, safer route or a shorter unsafe route, especially at night: the trade-off is between travel time and safety. Clearly the built environment alone will not stop those who are determined on criminal activity, nor will it reduce crimes like violence in the home or fraud which are not related to the environment.

This point has to be forcefully acknowledged in any discussion of crimes against women. More women experience violent attacks within the home than out of it. Many women's groups were at pains to emphasise the unreality of the planners' concept of the home as a safe haven from a hostile world. In fact it is often quite difficult to structure discussions on safety issues outside the home if these are seen as a way of diverting attention from the problems of domestic violence, rather than a professional attempt to examine policies within the planners' area of potential influence.

Design can only create the preconditions for a safer environment: it is a poor substitute for changing the conduct of the offending individual. The Comedia Report (1991) argues that young men in Britain 'get drunk' in pubs and look threatening, whereas young men and women on the Continent 'socialise' at bars and cafes, very seldom becoming drunk and disorderly. Shared use of city centre facilities by both sexes creates a safer environment. It is, in part, different behaviour patterns which makes the centres of most European cities comparatively safe for women, even at night. It is not clear how these can be changed in Britain, nor does it seem that planners could contribute much to this side of the problems. Nevertheless, in so far as some planning policies can affect either actual crime or perceptions of safety, planners have a responsibility to explore what contribution they could make.

New policies

There is no national policy on planning for safety in the United Kingdom, but there are now a number of interesting local initiatives. The authors think it is time that some of these were systematically evaluated and that the views of women affected were actively sought and incorporated in an overall evaluation. It is the aim of this article to contribute to this process.

Local initiatives have originated from two main sources: first, from the local authorities, mainly in London and most notably the Greater London Council – abolished in 1985 – which established specialist women's committees and provided finances for a number of interesting developments in the field of transport and housing: second, from the government's 'Safer Cities Programme' – part of its 1988 'Action for Cities Initiative' designed to promote economic and social regeneration in the inner cities. In this programme, crime and the fear of crime were seen as major problems contributing to the population decline, loss of business and weakening of community spirit in problem urban areas. Creating 'safer cities where economic enterprise and community life can flourish' is one of the three main objectives of the Safer Cities Programme. The Home Office is now supporting projects in twenty towns, cities and London Boroughs, chosen because they have high crime rates together with other economic problems. Projects have been funded in the following: Birmingham, Bradford, Bristol, Coventry, Derby, Hartlepool, Hull, Hammersmith and Fulham, Islington, Leicester, Lewisham, Middlesbrough, Nottingham, Rochdale, Salford, Sunderland, Tower Hamlets, Wandsworth, Wirral and Wolverhampton (Home Office Crime Prevention Unit, 1992).

There are three main strategies for dealing with the kind of fears under discussion. The first, tackling directly the root causes of crime, is outside the remit of this chapter. The other two strategies which do concern planners are segregation, and general environmental improvements. Segregation involves separate protected provision of services reserved partly or solely for women: this is a strategy which leaves the environment as dangerous as it ever was but exempts women from the consequences. In its effects it is like the 'fortress approach' to more general threats to safety, for example, the development of walled estates with guards for the wealthy. These are already common in the USA and gaining popularity in Europe. Measures which improve the environment for all are usually more expensive but they provide benefits for other vulnerable groups and yield other kinds of benefits besides improvements in safety.

The rest of this chapter will look in more detail at some of the remedies suggested for places identified in discussions as particularly dangerous. The places most often mentioned as causing concern were lonely bus stops, unstaffed stations, pedestrian subways, multistorey car parks, badly lit quiet streets, and dark corners and hiding places on housing estates.

Women's safe transport schemes

There are a number of suggestions for dealing with each of these problems individually, but there is one general way of bypassing all the above problems that is being adopted by a number of local authorities or voluntary groups: namely, segregated safer women's transport schemes.

Segregated women's transport schemes

The first scheme, established in Bristol in 1988 after a 23 per cent increase in reported rapes and other violent attacks, is a good example of this type of service. It provides a door-to-door evening lift service for women who cannot afford or who do not feel able to use other forms of transport at night. It uses volunteer drivers and runs two vehicles, both adapted for wheelchairs. In its first year of operation its 200 members made over 4,000 trips. Unfortunately, the limited number of vehicles and drivers has meant that they have had to limit use of the service, giving priority to women on low incomes, black and ethnic minority women, disabled, elderly and young women and those with a particular fear of violence. The 'Homerunner' service in Bradford, started in October 1989, targets similar groups to those in Bristol, with the addition of female shift workers and those wishing to attend evening classes. It was set up as a door-to-door service for women only, operating three mini-buses between 6 p.m. and 11 p.m. Monday to Saturday. Users pay a 90 pence flat fare which covers about one-third of the costs, with the deficit being covered by a £45,000 per annum subsidy from Bradford Safer City Project and the West Yorkshire Passenger Transport Authority. The service has carried between 300 and 400 passengers a week, coming predominantly from households without a car. Research shows that 60 per cent of journeys are to and from work and around 60 per cent of the leisure trips would not have been made without the service. Employers have shown interest in the service for night-time travel by their female employ-ees, and offers of sponsorship are being investigated. Other Safer Cities transport schemes are running in Brighton, Stockwell, Hammersmith and Fulham. Two more schemes along the lines of the Homerunner scheme are currently planned for Manchester and Preston.

Safe transport schemes clearly meet a genuine need. At the moment a few projects operate over relatively small areas, and those that operate them cannot satisfy even a fraction of the potential demand. There is little doubt that those who use them are very conscious of significant benefits despite the fact that they usually need to be booked well in advance. There is a strong argument for all local authorities to consider supporting such schemes on the same basis as they support community buses for low revenue routes in rural areas, so that some safe transport scheme is available in all areas.

The big question for those concerned with women's mobility is, however, whether to go for the expansion of such schemes as the main way of dealing with the general problem of safety across the whole spectrum of public transport services for all women. This would appear to have two big dangers. First, it perpetuates the notion that women must operate under some kind of curfew and thus may actually contribute to increasing women's fear of crime, discouraging even more women from using public transport. This in turn leads to the second danger that if such services were run on a scale to make a significant impact on transport for all women, the numbers of people using public transport at night would fall to even lower levels and increase the financial pressures for economies in staffing.

When this issue was discussed in the women's transport workshop there was general agreement that safer women's transport schemes should continue to be supported, since their numbers were so far away from levels which could threaten public transport and cause these longer-term drawbacks. In the short term, they provided a lifeline to the very vulnerable women who used them and in cases where women had been intimidated into not going out at all, they got them back into the city centres and were the first stage in changing their attitudes to going out and about.

Cars and taxis

Two other forms of protected travel exist independently of local authority intervention and funding – private cars and taxis. However, as Ohlenschlager (1990) has noted, it is well known that women have less access to cars than men – even if they live in a car-owning household they are half as likely as a man to hold a valid driving licence, and often do not get the use of the family car. Where they do use cars, two problems were frequently raised – having to leave the security of the car for help in the case of breakdown on lonely roads, and using multi-storey car parks, especially at night. The Nottingham University seminar felt strongly that the tax increase on car phones in the 1991 budget was particularly undesirable in view of their importance to lone women drivers, and if anything it should be easier rather than more difficult for women to have them in their cars.

Research has shown that taxi use among women even in the low-income groups is increasing and provides a safety net for women without cars (Trench and Lister, 1991). However, some women have had bad experiences of taxi drivers and there was clearly some anxiety about all taxis, especially about using the so-called 'mini-cabs' in the London area. Clearly the proposals currently under discussion to extend licensing to all forms of private hire throughout the country would receive wide support. Two developments were welcomed by our workshops: the 'Lady Cab' service, a franchise operating five companies in London and run for and by women, and the Hackney voluntary code for taxis designed by the women's committee of Hackney Borough Council.

Safer public transport

The alternative to segregated services is to put money and effort into measures which improve public transport so that women can feel safe and comfortable travelling on ordinary services. The good news is that the kind of measures involved – increased staffing at stations, conductors on evening buses, hail and ride minibus services penetrating housing estates and taking all passengers very close to their homes – provide other kinds of benefits as well as improving safety, and assist other groups beside those worried about attacks. The bad news is that this involves much more expensive provision in a sector that is already underfunded and under pressure, and even if the money were to be found there would still not be a public system that is as secure as a door-to-door service for female passengers. One problem for public transport is that the traditional layout of housing estates with peripheral main roads round the edge and smaller access roads to the houses makes it harder both physically and financially for convenient bus services to penetrate the housing areas and take people close to their homes. The expansion of minibus services is clearly a helpful development.

Not all the measures are expensive. Moving bus stops nearer to shops or petrol stations where there is some evening activity, is a simple measure. Changing evening bus services to hail and ride on less densely-used routes has been successfully tried in Stockport. This development allows women and other bus users to choose where they intercept their bus. It has not required any special financing apart from some expenditure on publicity – in fact the new service generated extra travel. On some stations London Transport is offering passengers the opportunity to wait in the well-lit station entrance where there is a ticket collector, going to the deserted platforms only when the train is announced. Tyne and Wear Metro runs shorter trains in the evening to concentrate their passengers and thus reducing the need to travel in empty compartments. Women wanted the fact that radio contact points on stations existed to be more widely publicised, and some asked for the wider availability of telephone help lines. A version of safe women's transport that provided an emergency call-out for someone stranded in a threatening situation was suggested, though such facilities might well be abused by hoaxers and vandals. Some women said they wanted transport operators to show the public which side they were on. For example, while posters warning about pickpockets made it publicly plain that this activity was considered wrong, London Transport did not issue similar warnings to women about gropers.

Bibliography to Section V

Allan, G. and Crow, G. (eds) (1989) *Home and Family: Creating the Domestic Sphere*, Basingstoke: Macmillan.

Atkins, S.T. (1989) *Critical Paths: Designing for Secure Travel*, London: Design Council.

Attfield, J. (1989) 'Inside Pram-town: A Case Study of Harlow House Interiors, 1951–1961', in J. Attfield and P. Kirkham (eds) *A View from the Interior*, London: Women's Press.

Attfield, J. and Kirkham, P. (eds) (1989) *A View from the Interior*, London: Women's Press.

Bacon, C. (1986) 'The Rise and Fall of Deck Access Housing', Department of Town and Regional Planning, Working Paper 64, University of Sheffield.

Ball, M. (1974) 'British Housing Policy and the House Building Industry', *Capital and Class*, 4, pp. 478–99.

Birmingham Feminist History Group (1979) 'Feminism or Femininity in the Nineteen-fifties?', *Feminist Review*, 3, pp. 48–65.

Bonnerjea, L. and Lawton, J. (1987) *Homelessness in Brent*, London: Policy Studies Institute.

Booth, P. (1982) 'Housing as a Product: Design Guidance and Resident Satisfaction in the Private Sector', *Built Environment*, 8, pp. 20–4.

Bose, C. (1982) 'Technology and Changes in the Division of Labour in the American Home', in Whitelegg, E. *et al.* (eds) *The Changing Experience of Women*, Oxford: Martin Robertson in association with the Open University.

Boys, J. (1984) 'Is There a Feminist Analysis of Architecture?', *Built Environment*, 10 (1), pp. 25–34.

Boys, J. (1989) 'From Alcatraz to the OK Corral: Images of Class and Gender', in Attfield, J. and Kirkham, P. (eds) *A View from the Interior*, London: Women's Press.

Bradshaw, J. and Millar, J. (1991) *Lone Parent Families in the UK*, London: Department of Social Security, Research Report No. 6, London: HMSO.

Brown, G. and Harris, T. (1978) *The Social Origins of Depression*, London: Tavistock.

Burnett, J. (1978) *A Social History of Housing, 1815–1970*, Newton Abbot: David & Charles.

Castells, M. (1977) *The Urban Question: A Marxist Approach*, London: Edward Arnold.

Central Statistical Office (1989) *Social Trends 19*, London: HMSO.

Central Statistical Office (1992) *Social Trends 22*, London: HMSO.

Central Statistical Office (1995) *Social Trends 25*, London: HMSO.

Coleman, A. (1985) *Utopia on Trial: Vision and Reality in Planned Housing*, London: H. Shipman.

Coles, A. (1990) 'Mortgage Possessions and Money Advice – Building Society Views', *Housing Review*, 39 (14), pp. 88–90.

Comedia Report (1991) *Out of Hours: A Study of Economic, Social and Cultural Life in Twelve Town Centres in the UK: summary report,* London: Comedia in association with the Calouste Gulbenkian Foundation.

Cooper Marcus, C. and Sarkissian, W. (1986) *Housing as if People Mattered: Site Design Guidelines for Medium-density Family Housing*, Berkeley: University of California Press.

Cowan, R.S. (1976) 'The "Industrial Revolution" in the Home: Household Technology and Social Change in the Twentieth Century', *Technology and Culture*, 17, pp. 1–23.

Cowan, R.S. (1983) *More Work for Mother: The Ironies of Household Technology from the Open Hearth to the Microwave*, New York: Basic Books.

Crow, G. and Hardey, M. (1991) 'The Housing Strategies of Lone Parents', in G. Crow and M. Hardey (eds), *Lone Parenthood*, London: Harvester Wheatsheaf.

Darke, J. (1994) 'Women and the Meaning of Home', in R. Gilroy and R. Woods (eds) *Housing Women*, London: Routledge.

Davidoff, L. (1995) *Worlds Between: Historical Perspectives on Gender and Class*, Cambridge: Polity Press.

Davison, I. (1987) 'Volume Housing (1, 2 and 3) *Architects' Journal*, 2 September, 186(35): pp. 63–7; 9 September 186 (36): pp. 59–65; 186(37): pp. 61–5.

Dobash, R.E. and Dobash, R. (1979) *Violence against Wives: A Case against the Patriarchy*, New York: Free Press.

Dudley, W.H.E. (1944) *Design of Dwellings*, Ministry of Housing, London: HMSO.

Duncan, N.G. (1981) 'Home Ownership and Social Theory', in J.S. Duncan (ed.) *Housing and Identity: Cross-cultural Perspectives*, London: Croom Helm.

Dunleavy, P., (1981) *The Politics of Mass Housing in Britain, 1945–1975: A Study of Corporate Power and Professional Influence in the Welfare State*, Oxford: Clarendon Press.

Egar, R., Sarkissian, W., Male, D. and Hartmann, L. (1988) 'Coping with the Suburban Nightmare: Developing Community Supports in Australia', in Vliet, Van W. *Women, Housing and the Community*, Aldershot: Avebury.

Fava, S.F. (1980) 'Women's Place in the New Suburbia', in G.R. Wekerle, R. Peterson and D. Morley (eds) *New Space for Women*, Boulder, Col.: Westview Press, pp. 129–49.

Fletcher, R. (1973) *The Family and Marriage in Britain: An Analysis and Moral Assessment*, Harmondsworth: Penguin Books.

Forty, A. and Moss, H. (1980) 'A Housing Style for Troubled Consumers: The Success of the Pseudo-vernacular', *Architectural Review*, 167, pp. 73–8.

Fox, K. (1986) *Metropolitan America: Urban Life and Urban Policy in the United States, 1940–1980*, Jackson: University Press of Mississippi.

Franklin, A.S. (1986) 'Owner-occupation, Privatism and Ontological Security: A Critical Reformulation', Working Paper 62, Bristol: School for Advanced Urban Studies, University of Bristol.

Fulop, N.S. (1992) *'Gender, Parenthood and Health: A Study of Mothers' and Fathers' Experiences of Health and Illness'*, Ph.D. thesis, Institute of Education, University of London.

Gilroy, R. (1994) 'Women and Owner Occupation in Britain: First the Prince, Then the Palace?', in R. Gilroy and R. Woods (eds) *Housing Women*, London: Routledge.

Gilroy, R. and Woods, R. (eds) (1994) *Housing Women*, London: Routledge.

Ginsberg, N. (1992) 'Racism and Housing: Concepts and Reality', in P. Braham, A. Rattansi and R. Skellington (eds) *Racism and Anti-racism: Inequalities, Opportunities and Policies*, London: Sage.

Glendinning, C. and Millar, J. (eds) (1987) *Women and Poverty in Britain*, Hemel Hempstead: Harvester Wheatsheaf.

Glendinning, C. and Millar, J. (eds) (1992) *Women and Poverty in Britain: the 1990's*, Hemel Hempstead: Harvester Wheatsheaf.

Gould, J. (1977) *Modern Houses in Britain, 1919–1939*, London: Society of Architectural Historians of Great Britain.

Green, E. Hebron, S. and Woodward, D. (1990) *Women's Leisure, What Leisure?* London: Macmillan.

Greve, J. (1991) *Homelessness in Britain*, London: Joseph Rowntree Foundation.

Hardyment, C. (1988) *From Mangle to Microwave: The Mechanization of the Household*, Cambridge: Polity Press.

Harvey, D. (1973) *Social Justice and the City*, London: Edward Arnold.

Haskey, J. (1991) 'Lone Parenthood and Demographic Change', in M. Hardey and G. Crow (eds) *Lone Parenthood*, London: Harvester Wheatsheaf.

Hayden, D. (1980) 'What Would a Non-sexist City be Like? Speculations on Housing, Urban Design and Human Work', *Signs* 5, pp. 170–87.

Hayden, D. (1981) *The Grand Domestic Revolution: A History of Feminist Designs for American Homes, Neighborhoods, and Cities*, Cambridge, Mass.: Mit Press.

Henderson, J. and Karn, V. (1987) *Race, Class and State Housing: Inequality in the Allocation of Public Housing in Britain*, Aldershot: Gower.

Heron, L. (ed.) (1985) *Truth, Dare or Promise: Girls Growing Up in the Fifties*, London: Virago.

Hey, V. (1986) *Patriarchy and Pub Culture*, London: Tavistock.

Hills, J. and Mullings, B. (1990) 'Housing: A Decent Home for All at a Price within their Means?', in J. Hills (ed) *The State of Welfare: The Welfare State in Britain since 1974*, Oxford: Clarendon Press.

Hole, W.V. and Attenburrow, J.J. (1966) *Houses and People: A Review of User Studies at the Building Research Station*, London: HMSO.

Holmans, A.E., Nandy, S., Brown, A.C. (1987) 'Household Formation, Dissolution and Housing Tenure: A Longitudinal Perspective', in Central Statistical Office *Social Trends 17*, London: HMSO.

Home Office Crime Prevention Unit (1992) *Safer Cities: Progress Report 1990/91*, London: Home Office.

House of Commons Home Affairs Committee (1986) *Bangladeshis in Britain*, Session 1986–7, vol. 1, London: HMSO.

Hunt, S.M., Martin, C.J., Platt, S., Lewis, C. and Morris, G. (1988) *Damp Housing, Mould Growth and Health Status*, Edinburgh: Research Unit in Health and Behavioural Change, University of Edinburgh.

Hunt, S.M. (1990) 'Emotional Distress and Bad Housing', *Health and Hygiene*, 11, pp. 72–9.

Jacobs, J. (1961) *The Death and Life of Great American cities*, New York: Vintage Books.

Jencks, C.A. (1977) *The Language of Post-modern Architecture*, London: Academy Editions.

Kemp, P. (1989) 'The Housing Question', in D.T. Herbert, and D.M. Smith (eds) *Social Problems and the City*, Oxford: Oxford University Press.

Kiernan, K. (1992) 'Men and Women at Work and at Home', in R. Jowell, L. Brook, G. Prior and B. Taylor (eds) *British Social Attitudes: The 9th Report*, Aldershot: Gower.

Kiernan, K. and Wicks, M. (1990) *Family Change and Future Policy*, York: Joseph Rowntree Memorial Trust in association with the Family Policy Studies Centre.

Kleinman, M. and Whitehead, C.M.E. (1988) 'The Prospects for Private Renting in the 1990's', in Kemp P. (ed) *The Private Provision of Rented Housing*, Aldershot: Gower.

Lawrence, R.J. (1985) 'Survey 6: Urban History, Housing and Politics in Britain', *Environment and Planning D: Society and Space*, 3, pp. 323–36.

Lawrence, R.J. (1987) *Housing, Dwellings and Homes: Design Theory, Research and Practice*, Chichester: John Wiley.

Leopold, E. and Bishop, D. (1983) 'Design Philosophy and Practice in Speculative House-building' (Part 1 and Part 2), *Construction Management and Economics*, 1, pp. 119–44, 233–68.

Little, J., Peake, L. and Richardson, P. (eds) (1988) *Women in Cities*, London: Macmillan.

Littlewood, J. and Tinker, A. (1981) *Families in Flats*, London: HMSO for the Department of Environment.

Lloyd, B. (1981) 'Women, Home and Status', in J.S. Duncan (ed.) *Housing and Identity: cross-cultural perspectives*, London: Croom Helm.

Local Transport Today (1990) 'Easing Women's Travel Fears: A Suitable Case for Special Treatment?' *Local Transport Today*, 17 October, p. 3.

McCarthy, P. and Simpson, B. (1991) *Issues in Post-divorce Housing: Family Policy or Housing Policy?*, Aldershot: Avebury.

McDowell, L. (1983) 'Towards an Understanding of the Gender Divisions of Urban Space', *Environment and Planning D: Society and Space*, 1, pp. 59–72.

McKean, C. (1987) *The Scottish Thirties*, Edinburgh: Scottish Academic Press.

Mackenzie, S. (1989) 'Women in the City', in R. Peet and N. Thrift (eds) *New Models in Geography: The Political-economy Perspective*, London: Unwin Hyman.

Mackenzie, S. and Rose, D. (1983) 'Industrial Change: The Domestic Economy and Home Life', in Anderson, J., Duncan, S. and Hudson, R. (eds) *Redundant Spaces in Cities and Regions*, London: Academic Press.

Madigan, R., Munro, M. and Smith, S.J. (1990) 'Gender and the Meaning of the Home', *International Journal of Urban and Regional Research*, 14, pp. 625–47.

Martin, J. and White, A. (1988) *The Financial Circumstances of Disabled Adults Living in Private Households*, OPCS Surveys of Disability in Great Britain, Report 1, London: HMSO.

Matrix (1984) *Making Space: Women and the Man Made Environment*, London: Pluto Press.

Mayall, B. (1986) *Keeping Children Healthy*, London: Allen & Unwin.

Miller, M. (1990) *Bed and Breakfast: Women and Homelessness Today*, London: Women's Press.

Morris, J. (1990) *Our Homes, Our Rights: Housing, Independent Living and Physically Disabled People*, London: Shelter.

Mount, F. (1982) *The Subversive Family: An Alternative History of Love and Marriage*, London: Jonathan Cape.

Munro, M. and Smith, S.J. (1989) 'Gender and Housing: Broadening the Debate', *Housing Studies*, 4 (1), pp. 3–17.

Muthesius, S. (1982) *The English Terraced House*, London: Yale University Press.

Nottingham Safer Cities Project (1990) *Community Safety – Nottingham City Centre: Report of the Steering Group*, Nottingham: Nottingham Safer Cities Project.

Office of Population Censuses and Surveys (1991) *General Household Survey 1989*, London: HMSO.

Ohlenschlager, S. (1990) 'Women also travel', in S. Trench and T. Oc (eds) *Current Issues in Planning*, Aldershot: Gower.

Oliver, P., Davis, I. and Bentley, I. (1981) *Dunroamin: The Suburban Semi and its Enemies*, London: Barrie & Jenkins, 1981.

Pahl, R.E. (1984) *Divisions of Labour*, Oxford: Blackwell, 1984.

Parker Morris (1961) *Homes for Today and Tomorrow*, Ministry of Housing and Local Government, London: HMSO.

Parsons, T. (1949) *The Family: Essays in Sociological Theory – Pure and Applied*, Glencoe, Ill.: Free Press.

Pearson, L.F. (1988) *The Architectural and Social History of Cooperative Living*, London: Macmillan.

Piercy, M. (1994) *The Longings of Women*, London: Michael Joseph (Penguin Books, 1995).

Platt, S. (1991) 'Crime without Reason', *New Statesman and Society*, 17 May, p. 7.

Platt, S.D., Martin, C.J., Hunt, S.M. and Lewis, C.W. (1989) 'Damp Housing, Mould Growth and Symptomatic Health State', *British Medical Journal*, 298., pp. 1673–8.

Powell, C. (1974) 'Fifty Years of Progress: The Influence of the Tudor Walters Report on British Public Authority Housing', *Built Environment*, October, pp. 532–5.

Rao, N. (1990) *Black Women in Public Sector Housing*, London: Commission of Racial Equality.

Ravetz, A. (1989) 'A View from the Interior', in J. Attfield and P. Kirkham (eds) *A View from the Interior: Feminism, Women and Design*, London: Women's Press.

Raynsford, N. (1989) 'Housing', in M. McCarthy (ed) *The New Politics of Welfare*, London: Macmillan.

Rees, G. and Lambert, J. (1985) *Cities in Crisis: The Political Economy of Urban Development in Post-war Britain*, London: Edward Arnold.

Richman, N., Stevenson, J, and Graham, P. (1982) *Preschool to School: A Behavioural Study*, London: Academic Press.

Roberts, M. (1991) *Living in a Man-made World: Gender Assumptions in Modern Housing Design*, London: Routledge.

Robinson, V. (1989) 'Economic Restructuring, the Urban Crisis and Britain's Black Population', in D.T. Herbert and D.M. Smith (eds) *Social Problems and the City* Oxford: Oxford University Press.

Rodger, R. (ed) (1989) *Scottish Housing in the Twentieth Century*, Leicester: Leicester University Press.

Saegert, S. (1980) 'Masculine Cities and Feminine Suburbs: Polarized Ideas, Contradictory realities' *Signs*, pp. 96–112.

Saegert, S. (1988) 'The androgynous city: from critique to practice', in W. Van Vliet (ed) Women, Housing and the Community, Aldershot: Avebury.

Saunders, P. (1990) *A nation of home owners*, London: Unwin Hyman.

Saunders, P. and Williams, P. (1988) 'The constitution of the home: towards a research agenda', *Housing Studies*, 3, pp. 81–93.

Scoffman, E.R. (1984) *The Shape of British Housing*, London: Longmans.

Sexty, C. (1990) *Women Losing Out: Access to Housing in Britain Today*, London: Shelter.

Simms, M. and Smith, C. (1986) *Teenage Mothers and their Partners*, London: Research Report No. 15, London: HMSO.

Skellington, R. (1993) 'Homelessness', in R. Dallos and E. McLaughlin (eds) *Social Problems and the Family*, London: Sage.

Smyth, M. And Robus, N. (1989) *The Financial Circumstances of Families with Disabled Children Living in Private Households*, OPCS Surveys of Disability in Great Britain, Report 5, London: HMSO.

Strachan, D.P. (1988) 'Damp Housing and Childhood Asthma: Validation of Reporting Symptoms', *British Medical Journal*, 297, pp. 1223–6.

Thomas, A. and Niner, P. (1989) *Living in Temporary Accommodation: A Study of Homeless People*, London: HMSO.

Tomlinson, A. (ed.) (1990) *Consumption, Identity, and Style: Marketing, Meanings, and the Packaging of Pleasure*, London: Routledge.

Thompson, F.M.L. (ed) (1982) *The Rise of Suburbia*, Leicester: Leicester University Press.

Trench, S. and Lister, A. (1991) '*A Survey of Taxi and Private Car Use in Nottinghamshire*', Institute of Planning Studies Working Paper No. 2, Nottingham: University of Nottingham.

Tudor Walters (1918) *To Consider Questions of Building Construction in Connection with the Provision of Dwellings for the Working Classes in England and Wales, and Scotland*, London: HMSO.

Ungerson, C. (1994) 'Housing: Need, Equity, Ownership and the Economy', in V. George, and S. Miller (eds) *Social Policy Towards 2000: Squaring the Welfare Circle*, London: Routledge.

Valentine, G. (1992) 'Images of Danger: Women's Sources of Information about the Spatial Distribution of Male Violence', *Area*, 24 (1), pp. 22–9.

Van Vliet, W. (ed.) (1988) *Women, Housing and the Community*, Aldershot: Avebury.

Watson, S. (1986) 'Women and Housing, or Feminist Housing Analysis', *Housing Studies*, 1, pp. 1–10.

Watson, S. with Austerberry, H. (1986) *Housing and Homelessness: a Feminist Perspective*, London: Routledge & Kegan Paul.

Wekerle, G.R. (1984) 'A Woman's Place is in the City', *Antipode*, 16 (3).

Whitehorn, K. (1987) 'What's Ours Is Really Mine', *The Observer*, 4 October, London.

Wilson, E. (1980) *Only Halfway to Paradise: Women in Postwar Britain, 1945–1968*, London: Tavistock.

Wilson, E. (1991) *The Sphinx in the City: Urban Life, the Control of Disorder, and Women*, London: Virago.

Worsdall, F. (1979) *The Tenement: A Way of Life*, Edinburgh: Chambers.

Worsdall, F. (1989) *The Glasgow Tenement: a Way of Life: a Social, Historical and Architectural Study*, Glasgow: Drew.

VI

Women and Education

Introduction

MARY KEMBER

The academic achievement of girls relative to boys over the past two decades is indisputable. Girls have overtaken boys both in terms of GCSE and of A-level passes: in 1990–1 29 per cent of girls left school with at least one A-level compared to 25 per cent of boys; 16 per cent of girls to 12 per cent of boys left school with five GCSEs (Central Statistical Office, 1994). Participation at higher levels of education has also substantially increased: in Further Education, almost three-fifths of all students are now female compared with two-fifths twenty years ago; in Higher Education, the number of women students has more than doubled, bringing the numbers almost to parity with men.

Yet in spite of this success, it appears that girls' experience of education is still very different from that of boys. In 1990–1, at GCSE Grades A–C, boys still outperformed girls in Mathematics, Chemistry, Physics and Geography, while girls outperformed boys at English, French, History and Biology. In Further and Higher Education, there remained higher numbers of men in Mathematics, Physical Sciences and Engineering while women substantially predominated in Languages and the Creative Arts. Choice of subjects at undergraduate level – with the exceptions of Medicine and Dentistry – seems as gender-bound as ever.

Nominally, the 1988 Education Reform Act legislated for equality. Boys and girls were to study the same subjects under the new curriculum – there would be no sending boys off to the workshop while girls were sent to the domestic science block. But would providing the same curriculum for everyone regardless of gender and race guarantee 'equality'? Many educationalists argued that it would not: indeed, early critics of the new curriculum argued that it

233

promoted a framework of knowledge that was white, Anglo-Saxon and male. As a result, it was *more* likely that minorities would be marginalised and gender divisions perpetuated:

> Despite the 'golden opportunities' found in the possibility of all girls studying science and technology and all boys taking modern languages, the prevailing message of the National Curriculum could be just the reverse of encouraging social equality. Indeed it could confirm girls' sense of themselves as second class citizens in a world where female subjects such as domestic science and child care are not compulsory and hence low status, where the spheres in which boys excel and the teachers are predominantly male have high status... Is the National Curriculum not transmitting male definitions of what constitutes educational knowledge? (Arnot, 1989)

As studies have demonstrated in the past (Byrne, 1978), the hidden curriculum is as significant in education as the taught syllabus. The chapter by Michelle Stanworth is kept in this second edition as a reminder as to how the experience of schooling can be very different for boys and girls, in terms of teachers' attitudes and expectations and as a result of the socialisation processes of the school. These factors can have far-reaching effects on pupils' future lives but cannot be legislated for. A survey carried out by HMI between 1990 and 1991 into Equal Opportunities provision in a few selected schools, pointed out amongst its findings: 'Many schools assume that an egalitarian framework is sufficient as a policy for equal opportunities. This survey suggests that classroom management, a curriculum policy, counselling and guidance, all need to be developed and reviewed in the light of continuing monitoring and evaluation of a range of outcomes.'

While the job market remains segregated and government fails to address issues of reconciling employment and family responsibilities, girls will find that despite a so-called 'equal' curriculum they remain in a disadvantaged position outside the school. Class and race will undoubtedly interweave with gender to keep the most disadvantaged women in the worst position. With a veneer of 'equality', those who fail will be blamed individually without structural disadvantage being taken into account: a national hidden curriculum is particularly insidious.

A similar hidden agenda lies beneath women's greater participation in Higher Education. Access to Higher Education has been widened in recent years and, encouraged by government policies to return to employment, many women want to improve their skills and job prospects by acquiring higher qualifications. Many want to compensate for an alienating educational experience that did little other than land them in traditional dead-end jobs when they were young. At the same time, increasing numbers of women, left with sole responsibility for households, desperately need to increase their earning power, and seek means of improving their prospects through further training and education. Statistics are encouraging: in 1979, male students over 25 outnumbered female students of a similar age group by almost 2:1 in the case of full-time students and almost 3:1 in the case of part-time students; in 1990 numbers of female students came close to numbers of male students of this age group in both categories. In the case of first degree courses, women of this age now outnumber men, although numbers of male post-graduate students remain higher than female (Department for Education, 1993). Yet Liz Sperling, in the article from which the excerpt here is taken, says women still have more arduous hurdles to overcome than do men before they can enter Higher Education. While Access courses are undoubtedly enabling many women to gain entry to institutions previously out of bounds to them (Ryle and Stuart (1994) point out that there is as yet no comprehensive statistical information about the gender profile of Access students), policies of admission do not necessarily recognise their non-traditional qualifications or their prior experience as valid.

Once in Higher Education, mature women students' experience is often very different from that of male students. Many cannot use study facilities because they need to rush home after formal classes to collect children from school. Others miss classes because of family illnesses and domestic crises. At the same time, many lose confidence through missing studies and doubt their abilities to catch up – possibly compounded by unsympathetic partners who undermine their efforts. On top of this, many mature women students have severe financial problems. A non-gendered experience of Higher Education must, then, extend further than making access more equal.

Inevitably the gender agenda in education has radically altered in recent years: education in Britain is in a period of turmoil. Conservative government policies have introduced a new education ethos, turning schools into market-places, students into clients, head teachers into accountants and governors into hirers-and-firers. Power has been taken away from local authorities and schools have been given local management and responsibility for funding, governors have been given increased responsibilities and power has been directed into the hands of parents. But as Rosemary Deem notes from her own research, parent-governors, who were more likely than other governors to be women, were often silent in meetings and side-lined, or appealed to only in matters seen to affect them directly. Deem suggests that financial experts are likely to dominate governing bodies, and, as a result, there is little reason for optimism in terms of equal opportunities: governors giving priority to budgets are unlikely to give a high profile to equal opportunities when employing or promoting staff.

Miriam David, in the excerpt reproduced here, looks at how the educational reforms have impacted particularly on *women* as parent-consumers. If parents are to be given more power then they must feel they are in a position to use this responsibly. But while educational reforms of the 1980s have assumed a continuation of the traditional family form, the *actual* shape of the family has been moving in different directions, with a large percentage of families headed by lone mothers, an increasing number of women in paid employment and women themselves returning to Further and Higher Education as mature students. So while in *theory* women have more say in what goes on in their children's schools, the practice may be very different. Potential for conflict in women's roles is enormous – whether as mother/governor, governor/employee, teacher/parent or mother/student. Women's lives threaten to become even more complex and burdensome than they already are. At the same time, it will be highly detrimental to women's interests if they do *not* become involved.

Policy changes are happening in education almost overnight, and, writing in 1995, no one is really sure what will happen next. A clash of ideologies is already apparent throughout the education system: that of equality issues versus the strategies of the market-place. Yet at a time when education funding is so closely linked to numbers of students, when the labour market is demanding more trained women and when educational institutions are looking to broaden their appeal, women *may* be well placed, if only they are given the *means* by which to use these opportunities. In the same way, if women can get their hands on the power that is nominally theirs to take in school and college management, it could be an opportunity for real influence. More local collaboration amongst teachers and between teachers and parents, as well as school-based policy-making, could result in equal opportunities strategies and initiatives taking place to the benefit of all women.

'Just Three Quiet Girls'

MICHELLE STANWORTH

Initial impressions of pupils: 'Just three quiet girls'

In the early weeks of the academic year, teachers are faced with the arduous task of getting to know not just one, but several, groups of pupils; it is not surprising that it takes a while for the name and face of every pupil to be clearly linked in teachers' minds. What is remarkable is that the pupils who were mentioned by teachers as being difficult to place were, without exception, girls.

Interviewer: What were your first impressions of Emma?

Male teacher: Nothing really. I can only remember first impressions of a few who stood out right away; Adrian, of course; and Philip; and David Levick; and Marion, too, because among the girls she was the earliest to say something in class. In fact, it was quite a time before I could tell some of the girls apart.

Interviewer: Who was that?

Teacher: Well, Angie, and her friends Leonore and Helen. They seemed rather silent at first, and they were friends, I think, and there was was no way – that's how it seemed at the time – of telling one from the other. In fact, they are very different in appearance, I can see that now. One's fair and one's dark, for a start. But at the beginning they were just three quiet girls.

Interviewer: What were your first impressions of Lucy?

Female teacher: I didn't start teaching that class until a bit later, by which time my mind was dulled. Although I had seen them once

From Michelle Stanworth (1983) *Gender and Schooling: a Study of Sexual Divisions in the Classroom*, London: Hutchinson.

a week, she hadn't made any impression on me at all. I didn't know which one she was. She was one of the people who it took me longest to cotton on to her name. She was one I got mixed up, actually, with Sharon, who was equally quiet and somewhat the same build. Now they're quite different, I realise, but at the time I was never quite sure which one it was.

Interviewer: So Lucy was very slow to make any impression at all, then?

Teacher: Well, a positive impression, yes. I won't say she made a negative impression, but . . . well, you see the trouble is that that group had got more girls in it, which makes a difference. The other group had a lot of foreigners, and within a day or two I knew Belinda, who was the only foreign girl. And Dennis had curly hair and Tony had straight hair, so they were well fixed in. In fact, in that group there were only Lyn and Judith who took me a few days to get straightened out, and the rest I knew straight away. Whereas in this group, there were only seven boys and about ten girls, I suppose.

Interviewer: So you found it easiest to learn the names of the boys, did you?

Teacher: Yes, that's it.

As these quotations suggest, the anonymity of girls is due in part to their reticence. The girl who is mentioned as speaking out early is instantly 'fixed' by her teacher; she has, among the girls, a sort of rarity value. However, this cannot entirely explain the greater readiness with which teachers identify boys, for the few male pupils who were reported by their teachers to be exceptionally quiet in class were, nevertheless, clearly remembered. Teachers' slowness at identifying girls has strong implications for the comfort and involvement of female pupils for, as we shall see later on, pupils take it as a sign of approval if teachers know names right away.

Advice and expectation

Teachers were asked what advice they would give to particular pupils if they were considering abandoning A-levels either in order to get married, or to take a job. Many of the teachers refused to accept that marriage might imply an interruption of studies; as one woman exclaimed (perhaps drawing on her own experience in combining marriage and academic work), 'I don't know why you think marriage is such a disruptive activity!' For the rest of the teachers, the advice offered was often cautionary, and female pupils were warned against giving up A-levels as often as males – although, as the first passage below indicates, some men were worried that to advise a girl against early marriage might be taken as a slur on her character.

Male teacher: Don't do it. I would say, 'Don't do it.' Don't get me wrong, she could certainly cope with marriage, she wouldn't be an inept housekeeper or a child-beater or anything like that. But if she could get her qualifications before she took all that on, I'd say stay.

Male teacher: If Sheila's getting married meant giving up her chance of getting A-levels, I'd say it would be disastrous.

Male teacher: I'd probably tell Howard the story of my life, how easy it was to get married and how difficult it was to get back. I would remind him of the disadvantages.

Female teacher: I think I'd say that nowadays, in her age group, half the marriages will end in divorce by the time they're 30. And although she may have got a boyfriend whom she feels she's going to love for life, you don't know what's going to happen. I've told some of them in the past, that your husband may die (because accidents do happen!) and you'll have to support the family, and if you don't have two A-levels it is much harder to start again.

Largely because of the steadier academic record of their female pupils, teacher were less likely to dissuade boys than girls from giving up A-levels to take a job; only one teacher made the point that it might be more risky for girls in general to abandon their studies than for boys:

Female teacher: I think I would say no ... The type of jobs girls get offered are rather different from the ones boys get offered. It's likely to be a job lacking in prospects; and it's also quite a lot harder for girls to come back to academic study than it is for men.

The most important point to emerge from this section of the interviews is that teachers tended to find the questions much less credible for their male pupils than for their female ones. When asked about their male pupils, teachers commented that it was very unlikely the boy would contemplate leaving college for employment (in one-third of the cases) or for marriage (in one-half).

Male teacher: To take a job? Now? I don't think that's even con-
ceivable. It's like having Alastair McMaster (a teacher noted for being very untrendy) announce he was off to join a rock group.
Female teacher: I'd be amazed. I can't imagine Ted thinking of marriage. He's definitely still got the schoolboy atmosphere. I don't think he'd have the kind of maturity to cope with a girl at this stage.
Male teacher: Well, it wouldn't arise, would it? Boys don't usually give up their studies when they get married, that's what girls are more inclined to do.

No equivalent comments were passed about girls. It appears that while teachers are equally concerned that girls and boys should avoid a disruption of study due to marriage, and more concerned to prevent the girls abandoning their studies for employment, teachers *expect* such disruptions more often from girls than from boys. In other words, teachers feel at least as strongly that girls should complete their A-levels compared with boys; but they combine this with a lower expectation that girls will actually do so.

Looking to the future

Teachers were asked to predict what each of their pupils might be doing two years, and five years, from the time of the interview. Boys – even those in danger of failing their examinations – were seen in jobs involving considerable responsibility and authority, the most frequent predictions being for civil service or management careers. One boy, for example, of whom his teacher had earlier said, 'His essays are bald, childlike and undeveloped; his statements are simple and naive', was expected to rise to head office:

Female teacher: I suppose he might be quite good at summing things up. I don't know quite whether local government or civil service, but I can't just see him pushing paper around. I can see him writing reports on things. Perhaps an information officer, or sales planning, or something like that; something in head office.

Marriage cropped up in teachers' predictions of boys' future only once, in the case of a pupil who was academically very weak, but in whom his teachers recognised exceptional personal qualities; they described him as having 'a warm streak, almost Mediterranean', and 'the gift of communication' (a reference to his sympathetic manner in face-to-face encounters, for he was reported not to speak in class). He alone among the boys is defined more in terms of his personality than his ability, and it may be no accident that he is the *only* boy for whom the future anticipated by his teachers includes marriage and parenthood.

Male teacher: I wonder if he's the kind of boy who will marry fairly young, once he's sure of his sexual self as it were.

Female teacher: I see him having a frightfully happy girlfriend who's terribly fond of him. So long as she's not ambitious, I think they'll be very happy. He would be a super father. I think children would adore having him for a father, thought I'm not immediately sure what he'd be doing to support his family.

By contrast, the occupations suggested for girls seldom ranged beyond the stereotype of secretary, nurse or teacher. These predictions do not match either the girls' academic standing or their own aspirations. For instance, the girl who is envisaged as a secretary in the following quotation is thought to be fully capable of getting a university degree, and is herself considering a career in law.

Female teacher: I can imagine her being a very competent, if somewhat detached, secretary. She looks neat and tidy, her work's neat and tidy, she's perfectly prompt at arriving. And she moves around with an air of knowing what she doing. She doesn't drift.

Interviewer: Why would she be a *detached* secretary?

Teacher: I can't imagine her falling for her boss at all! Or getting in a flap.

Interviewer: What about in five years' time?

Teacher: Well, I can see her having a family, and having them jolly well organised. They'll get up at the right time and go to school at the right time, wearing the right clothes. Meals will be ready when her husband gets home. She'll handle it jolly well.

Another girl, who intends to qualify as a professional psychologist, is predicted, in five years' time, to be at home with the children:

Female teacher: I don't know what she got in mind, but I can imagine her being a nurse. She's got a very responsible attitude to life. I don't know if nursing would be the best thing for her, but something like that, something which is demanding.

Interviewer: What about being a doctor, say?

Teacher: I don't think she has quite enough academic capacity for that, but she might go into teaching. A caring kind of vocation, that's what I see her in.

Interviewer: What about in five years' time?

Teacher: Obviously married. She's the sort of girl who could very easily be married in five years' time.

Interviewer: Would she be working then, do you think?

Teacher: She might. But she's the sort of girl, I think, to stay at home with the children. She's a caring person, as I said.

Remarks such as this indicate an implicit assumption that girls' capacities for efficiency and initiative will be channelled into nurturant or subordinate occupations (and, of course, into child care and housework) rather than into other, less traditional spheres.

Marriage and parenthood figure prominently in teachers' visions of the futures of their *female* pupils: teachers volunteered that two-thirds of the girls would be married in the near future. The prediction of marriage was applied not only to girls whose academic record was unremarkable as here:

Male teacher: She is the sort of girl who might up and get married all of a sudden and kick over the traces.

Interviewer: You mean she might abandon her A-levels?

Teacher: I'm not saying she would, but I wouldn't be surprised.

Interviewer: What do you imagine her doing in five years' time?

Teacher: Definitely married.

but also to girls who were considered to have outstanding academic capacity:

Male teacher: Well, I'd be surprised if she wasn't married.

Interviewer: Is she the sort of person you would expect to marry young?

Teacher: Well, not necessarily marry young, but let's see ... 16, 17, 18, 19 years old ... somewhere along the line, certainly. I can't see what she'd be doing apart from that.

In only one instance when teachers anticipated the future was the possibility of early marriage viewed regretfully, as a potential interruption to a girl's development:

Male teacher: I should like to see her doing some kind of higher education, and I wonder whether something in the HND line might be more suitable than a degree course.

Interviewer: Because it's slightly more practical?

Teacher: Yes. This is pure supposition, but it does seem to me that there is a practical vein in her. She successfully holds down a job in one of the chain stores. I can see her making a very great success of management, retail management, because I would have thought she would be very skilled at dealing with people. And though she's a little unsure of herself still, there is a vein of sureness in her. She wouldn't be taken aback by awkward situations, for instance.

Interviewer: What about in five years' time?

Teacher: Quite possibly early marriage, which I think would be a pity. Not because I'm against the institution of marriage, but because I think that an early marriage would prevent her from fully realising her potential.

Apart from the reaction to marriage, the preceding quotation is atypical of teachers' comments about their female pupils in other respects. First, it is the only prediction in which a management post was suggested for a girl. Second, the fact that a possible career was specified by a male teacher is itself unusual; in two-thirds of male teachers' discussions of female pupils, the girl could not be envisaged in any occupation once her education was complete. In some cases, it is almost as if the working lives of women are a mystery to men:

Male teacher: She would be competent enough to do a course at a university or polytechnic, though not necessarily the most academic course.

Interviewer: What sort of a course might suit her then?

Teacher: I can't say. I don't really know about jobs for girls.

Male teacher: She will probably go on to Further or Higher Education. You'd know better than I what a young girl with an independent sort of mind might be doing in five years' time!

The type of futures teachers anticipate for girls seem to be related to classroom interaction in two important ways. First, teachers' views of 'women's work', and their emphasis upon the centrality of family in women's lives, are likely to make high achievement at A-level seem less urgent for girls than for boys. To the extent that teachers underestimate the ambitions of their female pupils, they will be reluctant to make girls prime candidates for attention in the classroom. Second – and more pertinent to this study – it seems likely that the current dynamic of classroom interaction does nothing to undermine stereotypical views of appropriate spheres for women and men. The reports gathered here from both teachers and pupils indicate that (whatever girls may be like outside) they are in the classroom quieter, more diffident and less openly competitive than their male classmates. No matter how conscientious and capable female pupils are, they are perceived by their teachers to lack the authoritative manner and the assertiveness which many teachers seem to believe to be prerequisites of 'masculine' occupations.

This interpretation seems to be the best way of accounting for a curious anomaly in the teachers' predictions. One girl who is ranked as the top performer in both her main subjects, and who wants a career in the diplomatic service, is envisaged by her teacher as the 'personal assistant to somebody rather important'. In contrast, the girl with the poorest academic record is one of only two girls to be suggested for a job that is not in the traditional feminine mould. The comments made about these two pupils are reproduced below; they indicate that teachers attach a great significance to assertiveness in classroom situations.

Interviewer: And can you think ahead to five years' time, what Clare might be doing in five years' time?

Female teacher: I could possibly see her as a kind of committee-type person. She's not a forceful public speaker, you see. She says something rather quietly, and it's absolutely right. The people next to her take it in, but it doesn't have any impact if you see what I mean. I can imagine her as the personal assistant to somebody rather important, dealing with things very competently, and arranging things very competently, and giving ideas backwards and forwards and dealing with individual callers face to face. She's good at face-to-face things, or in small groups, rather than in large groups.

Interviewer: What about Alison in five years' time?

Female teacher: She could have a professional job of some sort, I think. I can imagine her in publicity or almost anything. She's got a strong presence, and she definitely makes an impression. She's pretty downright and forthright and forthcoming in her opinions. In fact, she is a very good stimulus in the group, though she does make some of the pupils feel a bit antagonistic.

It is, apparently, only when a girl's behaviour in class sharply contradicts the retiring feminine stereotype (a contradiction that may produce antagonism from classmates) that teachers are likely to imagine her in a career at odds with highly traditional expectations.

A Gender Agenda

MIRIAM DAVID

Education reforms and family change

The 'education reforms' developed throughout the 1980s do not seem to have taken account of family changes especially in women's role as mothers. Rather they have assumed a continuing traditional family form of two parents, with clear gender differentiation, albeit only alluded to implicitly and not explicitly.

Thus, policy changes in parents' role in education decision-making towards being consumers allowing both for more choices of type of school – between state and private school – and parental involvement in governing bodies as financial and business managers are built upon a traditional family notion. Apart from the limited evidence provided by Edwards *et al.* (1989) about choice of school, it is not clear how changes towards more consumerism will affect different types of family. However, Elliot *et al.* (1981) in a very small-scale study showed that mothers and fathers had a rather different balance of criteria for choice of schooling, especially between 'process' – a child's happiness – and 'product' – a child's likely achievements. On balance, mothers tended to favour 'process' and 'product', together with 'proximity'. Similarly, Fox (1985) and Johnson (1987) found that mothers and fathers had different reasons for choosing private (and state) education, especially differentiated for sons and daughters. Other studies of school choice, however, such as Stillman and Maychell (1986), have taken a more traditional and conventional approach, ignoring differences in family form.

From Miriam David, 'A Gender Agenda: Women and Family in the New ERA?', *British Journal of Sociology of Education*, 12(4), (1991), pp. 441–5.

In a situation where over a quarter of parents choosing schools are lone mothers this might have a considerable effect on whether or not parents do effectively demand to raise educational standards. Thus, the assumption built into the policy change that parents will demand higher educational standards through the market-place may not have uniform results, in a situation of a diversity of families with differential needs and demands. Where lone-mother families are financially pressured, they may not have the resources to consider a wide and comprehensive range of factors about school choice. They may have to rely or depend upon the nearest or proximate school.

As regards involvement in wider school decision-making, particularly as parent representatives on school governing bodies Deem (1986) and Brehony and Deem (1989) have collected some evidence from small scale surveys to suggest that 'women parent – governors', or rather 'mother – governors', have more difficulties in articulating their views than the 'father – governors' or businessmen representatives on governing bodies. These difficulties may have to do with the kinds of women who have become involved as parent governors. It appears that they tend to lack the skills that the male governors, whether fathers or not, have in terms of business and financial acumen. However, they have also experienced conflict over loyalty to their own child and the representative role on the governing body less clearly articulated by other governors. Similarly, many of the 'mother–governors' not only had conflicts over commitments to child or school, but also as teachers or parents – the wearing of 'two hats' syndrome. What is evident is that women's roles as parents have become much more complex, not only involved in the public sphere as mothers making choices of school, but also as governors or involved in an individual child's schooling and/or 'workers', especially involved in education. Yet none of this has had an appreciable effect on the development of public policies for parents of schoolchildren.

Women's changing public involvements

Women's lives as mothers of schoolchildren have become even more complex and varied than the above trends would indicate, and yet these have not had an impact on education reforms. At the same time as changing family and employment patterns, there have also been changing trends in women's involvement in further and higher education, especially as mature women and even as mothers of dependent children (Edwards, 1991). Part of the explanation for these developments may be the changing structure of households, and the balance between the dependency population and the labour force. Indeed, these shifts in demographic trends have led some commentators to suggest that there is a 'demographic time bomb' at work, whereby there will be an insufficiently large labour force to cater for the needs of the elderly population in particular, but also for dependent children. As a result of these gloomy prognostications, women have increasingly been drawn into both the labour force and the education system as a prelude to paid employment, to provide for the 'dependency population'.

It is clearly the case that there are trends towards more single households, especially though not exclusively of elderly people. As noted in *Social Trends 21* (Central Statistical Office, 1991, p. 36) this trend to a quarter of all households containing only one person has been caused by an increase in the numbers of elderly people and young people who live alone. Moreover, the trends are also of more childless women, more smaller families and, where families are formed, over a quarter are of children born illegitimately.

> Most women have children, though families are on average becoming smaller... The percentage of women who had a child at all increased steadily from about 80 per cent of those born in 1920 up to a peak of 90 per cent of women born in 1945. For women born more recently the likelihood of remaining childless has increased and it is estimated that 17 per cent of women born in 1955 will not have any children. Corresponding to the upward trend in the proportion of women remaining childless, the proportion of women projected to have two or more children now looks likely to fall. It is assumed that the proportion of women remaining childless will level off, so that just over 80 per cent of women born in 1975 and later years are projected to have at least one child. (Ibid., p. 42)

The percentage of births outside marriage has risen steeply, so that by 1989 it has reached 27 per cent of all births (ibid., p. 43). However, the vast majority of these births are registered in the name of both not only one parent. It is predicted that the dependency population, by the year 2025, of those children under 15 years old and the elderly over 65 will be the same, at 30 per cent each (ibid., 1989, p. 23). In 1985, dependent children were 30 per cent of the population, whilst the dependent elderly were only 23 per cent A large proportion of the elderly are themselves women. Expectations are that women will have to be involved in paid employment to help care for the growing dependency populations.

Thus, in the 1990s, the lives of women as mothers again will change appreciably. First, more such women will be involved outside the private household and family in the public world either of paid employment or of education (albeit, possibly private education). Secondly, the proportion of traditional families will continue to decrease, to be replaced by lone or 'single' parent/mother households. These latter type of families are increasingly being created by 'choice' – through the decision not to marry – rather than 'force', through marital breakdown. What impact these 'family choices' will have on parents' educational decision-making for their own children is difficult to ponder. However, choices not to marry but to cohabit, or at least coparent, may have implications for choice of type of school and parental involvement in a range of educational decisions as well as care. It is not yet clear, though, what kinds of parents, from amongst those choosing single parenthood status, are making these kinds of choices – whether they are more proportionately from amongst the middle or the working classes.

It is nevertheless clear that increasing proportions of women are choosing to enter Further and Higher Education as a route to increased work opportunities. They are, indeed, encouraged to do so by a range of governmental public policies over the last decade. Many of these women are mature students and, given the known evidence about the average age of childbirth, are likely already to be mothers. However, there is little substantial evidence to indicate the exact proportion of mothers. The number of students who enrolled on Further Education courses in the United Kingdom began to increase between 1980/1 and 1988/9. Female students accounted for the vast majority – over four-fifths of this increase (ibid., 1991, p. 55). They were mainly part-time, since the proportion of full-time students remained the same.

Between 1980/1 and 1988/9 there was an increase in students in full-time higher education of 20 per cent (ibid., p. 57). This increase took place almost entirely in polytechnics and colleges rather than the universities. A large proportion of that increase was accounted for by female students: in 1980/1, they were 41 per cent of the total: by 1987/8, they were 46 per cént. The women students were, too, disproportionately involved in particular subjects being 80 per cent of all full-time students on education degrees (and only 13 per cent on engineering and technology courses) and, therefore, directly preparing to be teachers.

The changes in part-time higher education have, perhaps, been even more dramatic than in full-time Higher Education. Between 1970/1 and 1988/9, the numbers of places in part-time Higher Education more than doubled. By 1988/9, women accounted for 40 per cent of the places, compared to 14 per cent in 1970/1. Of those women, 75 per cent were mature and over 25 years old. As noted in *Social Trends 21* (Central Statistical Office 1991, p. 58): 'The increase in the number of mature women students was greater than for men regardless of the institution or academic level of study, or whether the course was full or part-time. In 1988 men accounted for 56 per cent of mature students compared to 66 per cent in 1981.' Thus, by the end of the 1980s, women's lives as parents were becoming increasingly complex, juggling family obligations, and responsibilities for child care and education, with the demands of not only parental involvement, but also forms of paid employment or Further and Higher Education.

Many of the original arguments for women's paid employment or involvement in education as teachers were their being able to juggle family responsibilities with the demands of paid employment (David, 1980). However, new arguments, more germane to education, have often now replaced these more instrumental views. Involvement, as adults, in education is a means of ensuring their own children's better educational prospects. This argument has built upon the 'liberal' notion of parent education in the 1960s and 1970s towards women's more regular and routine involvement in education as a means to enhance their children's educational achievements.

These arguments, important though they may be for children's long-term educational progress, are only tangential to the general arguments for educational reform in the 1980s. Nevertheless, they have led to women's greater public involvement in a range of educational activities in and on behalf of their children: from parental involvement in schooling to parental involvement in a range of educational decisions, including as parent governors, to education as a form of, or prelude to, paid employment.

Conclusions

In conclusion, over the last two or three decades women's lives as mothers in families have become increasingly complex and public – as mothers themselves, especially as 'lone' mothers, as 'workers' in paid employment, especially as teachers, and as students. The 'education reforms' of the 1980s have not addressed these massive changes in family life, especially in gender relationships. Yet they have provided the occasion for mothers' greater involvement in the educational decision-making processes, given the fact that they have expected *parental* involvement to improve educational standards.

It can, therefore, be asked whether or not these educational policy changes will make women's greater public involvement in decision-making more 'democratic'. There is, indeed, substantial evidence to suggest that women as mothers are now, perforce, more involved in educational decision-making at all levels – in making choices of school, in parental involvement, as 'women parent–governors', as teachers, as mature women students. Given the fact that over a quarter of all families are currently lone-mother or single-mother families this must mean that, for many families, women are now shouldering a hugely increased set of responsibilities. Similarly, in two-parent households, women as mothers are more heavily implicated than the past policies would require: being 'involved' in choice of school, in balloting about type of school and governing representation.

Although the language of the public policy agenda of 'education reform' has the ring of democracy, it seems to be the case that women's lives as mothers have not, in the event, become democratic. Rather, many women as mothers have had to shoulder greater responsibilities, not only for child care and schooling, but also as consumers and through involvement in the processes of education decision-making. Given the diversity of family life and parental socio-economic circumstances, these obligations are likely to continue to fall disproportionately. Women as mothers will in all likelihood be expected to care for and be involved in the regular and daily schooling of their children, whilst at the same time being involved in extra-curricular activities as parents, such as school governors, and also in forms of paid employment, as teachers. They may also be involved, whilst bringing up children, in the education process itself, on the assumption that education can bring about improvement not only in their own lives but also those of their children.

However, given a more market-oriented education system, with less state intervention to iron out differences in family circumstances, the effects will probably be increasingly complex, with yet more highly gender-differentiated education and labour markets. Differences between children not only on the basis of parents' socio-economic circumstances but also of parents' gender are likely to have an impact upon their future lives. Thus, the class and gender structure of opportunities, given a more complex pattern of family and working lives, will be more difficult to characterise.

Since democracy has not been the hallmark of the agenda of education reforms of the 1980s, despite the language of parent power and participation, it may not have that effect on the lives of gendered participants in education in the 1990s. Rather, for some families, the responsibilities and obligations of involvement in education are likely to be more burdensome, whereas for others there will be more opportunities for improved life chances. Just what that complex mix will entail in social class terms is not easy to adduce. However, many women are choosing, and are likely to continue to choose, to rear and educate their children alone, although not necessarily in conditions of their own choosing. Although gender is, in fact, on the public policy agenda, it is not likely to be resolved in ways which make women's lives as parents more equal. Rather, the effects of education reforms, in a situation of increasing family and parental diversity, will produce a variety of educational experiences and not necessarily more democratic forms. Differences between mothers' and fathers' lives as parents of schoolchildren may be accentuated, not made more equal. Gender on the education reform agenda is not, in fact, about equal forms of parent power or democracy.

The New School Governing Bodies – Are Gender and Race on the Agenda?

ROSEMARY DEEM

The 1988 Education Reform Act

This Act is not entirely consistent with the provisions of the 1986 Act, which adds support to the view that the idea of a Reform Act was cobbled together during the 1987 General Election to attempt to deal with perceived parental concern about the workings of the education system, prior to subsequent privatisation (Chitty and Lawson, 1988). The Act may be seen as an attempt to 'do something' about education which is more motivated by political ideology than anything else. The sheer number of changes required, the speed of their implementation, and the drastic shortage of teachers and resources seem to suggest a strategy which is either doomed to failure or will lead to the end of a state education system as a major provider of schooling (Flude and Hammer, 1989). The main features of the Act which are relevant to school governors are the National Curriculum, open enrolment, local management of schools, the possibility of opting out and the policy on charging for education (a fuller account of the Act may be found in Maclure, 1988). The Reform Act takes much further two strands of educational control – the enhancing of the power of the Secretary of State, even though some of this is in conjunction with other bodies like the National Curriculum Council – and the increase in consumer power over teachers and LEAs, or 'educational producers', as it is becoming fashionable to call them.

A major feature of the bill was its rapid pace of progress. The proposals were first set out in the Queen's Speech of June 1987,

From Rosemary Deem, 'The New School Governing Bodies – Are Gender and Race on the Agenda?', *Gender and Education*, 1(3) (1989), pp. 250–7.

discussion papers were issued in the school holidays of 1987 and views sought by the early autumn. The short time allowed for consultation on the bill itself merely prepared the way for what was to follow, although the consultation time scale attracted a good deal of adverse comment from both sides of the political fence, as did many aspects of the bill itself. Indeed, giving people little time to implement changes in schools seems to be part of the critique of education implied by the Act – education always moves slowly, unlike industry, so it must be made to hurry up – with little thought given to exactly how all the necessary work would get done or its impact when it got done hurriedly. There is scant scope or encouragement for governors to work cooperatively and collabora-tively in conjunction with governing bodies in other schools. The bill itself made rapid progress through both Houses during the autumn of 1987 and early 1988, receiving the royal assent at the end of July 1988.

Many of the innovations in the 1988 Act can only work with the help or at least the tacit consent of governors. Governors play a key role in making the initial decision of balloting parents on whether to apply to the Secretary of State to opt out of local authority control. Indeed some parent governors may have stood for election with just this purpose in mind. Governors will have the responsibility of ensuring that their school's curriculum and assess-ment arrangements conform to the national curriculum. They will have to work out a way of coping with open admissions policy – which could become a significant problem if their schools are either under or oversubscribed. The complex arrangements for charging for educational activities as set out in a DES circular in January 1989 have had to be turned into a workable policy by governors and heads. The whole Local Management of Schools (LMS) policy, once LEAs have worked out their formula funding arrangements and had these approved by the Secretary of State, will stand or fall by the ability and capacity of governors to cope with the heavy responsibilities it will impose on them, including not only managing school finances but also effective hiring and firing of staff. Given that most women already have at least a dual role in employment and in the home, for those who are also school governors, we can be sure that they will hardly have time left to breathe! The Act will enable all secondary schools and primary schools with more than 200 pupils to have full responsibility for managing their own schools and budgets. This will include staffing, resources, heating, lighting and cleaning, although LEAs will retain control over school transport, advisory services and administering pay, tax and pensions.

The notion of LMS has been welcomed by many schools and governing bodies, but the responsibilities it implies are very considerable ones to give to a governing body of untrained volunteers doing the task unpaid and in their spare time. Some people have interpreted LMS as being mainly about finance. This in itself is problematic for women. Although schoolgirls are showing increasing enthusiasm and aptitude for mathematics, this is a very recent trend and many adult women lack confidence in their ability to handle finance in the public domain. Indeed in our case study governing bodies, although there are a few women involved, places on finance subcommittees are largely being filled by male governors. But the actual implications of LMS go far beyond finance. Coopers and Lybrands' Report for the Department of Education and Science on LMS (Coopers and Lybrand, 1988) makes this point strongly: 'The changes require a new culture and philosophy of the organisation of education at the school level. They are more than purely financial' (ibid., p. 5). Similar messages are loud and clear in the other innovations of the 1988 Act. Reshaping governing bodies is ostensibly supposed to be about transferring power from producers to consumers and about making schools more 'effective'. But is this notion of producers and consumers a helpful one? Will it exclude some categories of people from being governors? Will it help schools to provide high quality teaching and learning as well as a non-sexist, non-racist education for all their pupils? When the consumer (as in the food industry) is believed to be female (the housewife), she is often blamed for the shortcomings of the producer (eggs, cheese, precooked foods). Yet when the producer is a teacher (the majority of whom are female) it is she or he who is blamed for the shortcomings of the service rather than the consumer, who in the educational instance can do no wrong. Much of course hinges on which educational consumers are seen to be hailed by the legislation.

Consumer power – which consumers?

Underlying the last ten years of discussion and debate about the role of governors has been a desire to increase the participation and involvement of parents and employers (educational consumers), and to a lesser extent other lay members of the community, in the running of schools. But who are the consumers of schooling? The most obvious are pupils but this is not what the 1986 and 1988 Acts imply. Indeed the 1986 Act specifically prohibits pupil governors. Consumers are instead seen to be parents, employers and rate-payers. Nor are the changes in the composition of school governing bodies just straightforwardly about making the running of schools more democratic, a desirable aim in itself. There is a view present in the underlying philosophy of the legislation which pays lip service to parental and community choice and involvement, but which also contains a hidden agenda about the future private funding of education. Making people other than teachers and LEAs respon-sible for running schools is one important step towards this process of privatisation. Local management of schools, with budgetary control level, will be a further major plank in the transfer of power from the producers of education to the consumers.

There are only really two out of the five possible categories of governor who would count as consumers – elected parent gover-nors and coopted governors. The others, teacher governors, heads where they choose to be governors (there is an option to simply attend governors' meetings) and LEA nominees, are seen to be representing either teachers or the LEA, on the side of the produ-cers. In practice this distinction is difficult to sustain – some LEA governors are business people indistinguishable from the business people who are coopted and some parent governors are teachers, just as some teacher governors are also parents. What the distinc-tion between consumers and producers reflects, however, is not so much reality as an ideological construction. Producers are left wing, lazy, idealistic advocates of profligate spending, whilst con-sumers are right wing, sensible, hard-working people who value traditional educational methods and the three Rs. Why else would there have been so much fuss by the DES when it discovered that some parent governors were teachers (Judd, 1988; Hadfield, 1989), to the extent of commissioning the NFER to undertake an immedi-ate study of the exact number? My sense too is that women are invoked in the ideological construction of parent governors, since to do otherwise would be to lose sight of one of the central Thatcherite beliefs, that women are at the centre of the family and child care (David and New, 1985). Furthermore, within the sphere of the household it is acceptable to call women consumers, but they are to an extent excluded from the ideological construction of coopted governors, since women are not 'supposed' to be part of the higher levels of the labour market and rarely figure as major employers, although many women are involved in voluntary work in the community.

Only one of the governing bodies in the study has more female than male governors. Women are most numerous in primary school governing boards. The secondary schools are much more male-dominated. Women are most likely to become members of governing bodies as teacher or parent governors. Over half the teacher governors in the project are women (here the type of school does not seem to make much difference) and a large minority of the parent governors are women (there are most in primary schools). Black and Asian women and men are more likely to be LEA or parent governors than teacher or coopted governors, although some schools have used coopted places as a way of increasing or getting ethnic minority membership. There is very low representation across all the 15 bodies of black and Asian women, regardless of categories. Coopted governors are overwhelmingly white males, which has much to do with the emphasis being put on coopting high-status business people. Where women are coopted, they are usually either accountants (accountancy has a high proportion of women compared to many professions), or else they have jobs in the voluntary sector, are involved in a community organisation or are primary headteachers of feeder schools. The great majority of all governors (250 in all 15 schools) in our study are male and middle class. One-third of the 250 are women and 7 per cent are black or Asian. The middle-class dominance is consistent with the national survey of the recomposition of governing bodies, which also comments on the low national representation of ethnic minority groups. The absence of working-class and black people is not surprising. Not everyone is attracted by the thought of spending all their spare time at meetings, visiting schools and reading DES circulars – whatever their gender or ethnic group membership – whilst many working-class people are still suspicious of going into school at all. A similar pattern of class and gender distribution to that in our study has been found in the Leverhulme study of parent governors based at Exeter University (Anon., 1988). Some 57 per cent of parent governors in that study were female, although only two-thirds of coopted governors in 23 schools were male. Of course, sometimes the social composition of governors reflects the social composition of the school's pupils, but where the intake is mainly working class or has a high proportion of students from ethnic minority groups, this appears almost never to be the case.

Politicisation and school governing bodies

The political or other nature of school governing bodies has long been argued about, perhaps particularly because party political nominations have for several decades dominated school governing bodies in many areas, despite Kogan's argument that the intention of the 1944 Act was that no single group should occupy a dominant position in the running of the state education system. Indeed Kogan *et al.*'s (1984) own study found that the political culture of the LEA itself was a fairly crucial variable in determining whether or not governing bodies were party politicised. Since party politics in this country is heavily male dominated, this aspect of politicisation has marginalised many women and the typical style of party politicised governing bodies prior to 1988 was one in which there were often long meetings (and pre-meetings), sometimes discussing trivial issues like the colour of the school jumper, for long periods of time, rigid chairing, very formal conduct of meetings (which can be inhibiting to someone not used to it) and a heavily bureaucratic air in which women (usually LEA employees) clerked the meetings and men ran them. Of course, as the Kogan study (1984) points out, not all governing bodies were heavily party political or bureaucratised and overformal. Indeed some female governors seem, if Sallis's (1988) account is typical, to have enjoyed more positive experiences.

There is, however, an important distinction to be made between governing bodies as political animals, which they undoubtedly are, since they are clearly involved in the exercise of power over schools and those governing bodies whose meat and drink is party politics and who decide everything in terms of which party governors represent (for example when choosing a chairperson or determining who will sit on an interview panel). Of course, in the present climate both party political views and other ideological and philosophical stances on education are easily drawn in, since the recent educational legislation is so clearly political in nature. But parent governors have emerged as a group who particularly dislike the notion that governing bodies are political. The Leverhulme study

(Exeter Society, 1987) found that parent governors were very concerned about party politics surfacing in governor meetings, something they did not regard as appropriate. Sallis, equally concerned
about any such trend, feels that it is unlikely that school governing
bodies will become politicised and has commented thus: 'My
impression from visiting many schools is that the majority of
school parents are frightened of politics in school affairs and very
suspicious of anyone who introduces party issues' (Sallis, 1988, p.
173). Since many women are parent governors, it is possible that
this is a view particularly held by women, something which a later
stage of the research will seek to address.

The concern of parent governors about 'political' governors is,
however, worthy of a little unpacking. There are good reasons why
some parents and the governor pressure groups feel as they do. Past
research on parent governors has indicated that political governors
do not necessarily behave in an exemplary manner on governing
bodies and may alienate other governors, especially parents (Exeter
Society, 1987), by élitist attitudes, the way meetings are conducted
and by suggesting to them that mere parents are too insignificant to
be of much use. Several parents in the Exeter project complained of
being patronised or 'fobbed off' on issues they felt were deserving
of more detailed attention. Parents in the same Leverhulme study
also made complaints about cooptions being rushed through so
that new governors hardly understood what was happening (Exeter
Society, 1987). In our own research it is clear that in some schools
the election of a chairperson was little more than a ritual, with new
governors playing little part in it, since unlike previous governors
of the school (usually those from the LEA) they did not know any
of the actors. This was not true of all our research governing bodies
– 5 out of 15 did elect parent governors as their chairs and 3 have
women chairs – but in several instances new governors of any
category were at a disadvantage. In a body made up of a mix of
old and new members some of this is probably inevitable, however.

The dynamics of school governing bodies

Although it is clearly an intention of the new legislation that
consumer governors should take over from producer governors,
so far our study suggests that headteachers and LEA governors are
still firmly in control in most governing bodies, although some

parent governors are beginning to gain confidence (especially the male ones). During the Spring Term of 1989, our governing bodies, in common with most others in England and Wales, have been discussing how they will implement a school policy on charging for educational activities, following a DES circular on the subject issued in January 1989. Most vocal in this debate have been LEA governors, who perhaps understand better than other governors how this particular aspect of the Education Reform Act has come about. Parent governors, who might be expected to express the most concern about the impact, on educational visits, of only being able to ask for voluntary contributions, have not been noticeably vocal on this point. School governing bodies have also been discussing Local Management of Schools (LMS) recently – here coopted governors have been more active since many of them have business and finance expertise – but again many parent governors have been hanging back. This could present problems in the future, since as I have indicated earlier, LMS is not just about finance and managing budgets but about the whole philosophy and organisation of schooling. If LMS is dominated by those who see only the financial aspects as important, it bodes ill for the survival of any equal opportunities initiatives or other innovations in schools, unless these are seen as cost effective. It seems unlikely that really money conscious governors will want to use equal opportunities criteria in employing new or promoting existing staff.

There is a tendency in some governing bodies in our study to treat parent governors differently, appealing to them only on particular issues and apparently not expecting them to contribute on other matters; this is especially marked where there are female and black or Asian parent governors. It is difficult to decide whether parent governors are deliberately treated differently or whether it is a function of their relatively inexperienced status and lack of confidence. Not all parent governors are marginalised. Those with educational expertise (in the areas where our governing bodies are located there are two universities and two HE Colleges, so teachers are not the only source of educational expertise amongst parent governors) are taken seriously, as are those who have high status jobs. But parent governors without any obvious educational, financial or management expertise do tend to get sidelined, whether consciously or not. Gender and ethnicity are significant factors in this process too. For example in one inner-city school, where there are three male, Muslim parent governors (many of the pupils are

Muslims) it is rare for the three to speak except on issues to do with the Mosque and sex education. But the other white governors sometimes say, 'What do our parent governors think?', although they rarely wait for the answer. This might be interpreted as a genuine attempt to gain participation or it might be construed as having racist undertones. In general black and Asian governors have a hard struggle and are amongst the quietest governors in our study, although there is one very politicised governing body where the black governors are much more vociferous; however, this is very much the exception. In other governing bodies black governors are in a minority and do not always get the support they need either from other governors or from the education authority to do their job well. So, for instance, in one primary school an Asian governors asked at a meeting if the handbook for governors had been translated into Urdu. Failing a response from anyone else, the clerk said no and offered him first a leaflet in Urdu about how elections for parent governors were being organised (presumably to get there in the first place, he'd already passed that stage) and then a booklet in Urdu about choosing a child's secondary school place. The clerk concerned was clearly trying to be helpful and it was not her fault that the authority had not at that time considered getting a wider variety of information translated into minority languages. But it would not be surprising if the governor concerned did not feel more marginalised than ever by the situation. The rest of the mostly white governors sat without comment through this dialogue.

In other schools in the study, especially primary schools, most of the silent governors are women parent governors, who appear to feel that they should only voice opinions on things that are of legitimate concern to them, such as passing on parental views about classes who are constantly taught only by supply teachers. When we have completed our questionnaire study and carried out more interviews we will perhaps be in a better position to understand why some governors are much quieter and less participative than others. At the moment it is not always easy to understand why some quiet governors, who appear capable of making a fuller contribution, apparently lack the confidence to do so. To be in a governors' meeting and never speak seems almost to be a contradiction. On the other hand there are also a number of overconfident, mostly, but not exclusively, male governors who are more than capable of dominating every discussion whether they have any useful information to offer or not. On the whole, when quiet women do contribute, they are much better at sticking to the point than men. Women also appear to be more tolerant of others in discussions than are men, listening to what is being said rather than waiting impatiently to get in on the debate when not speaking themselves.

Only three of the 15 governing bodies in the study are chaired by women and only one board has an Asian chair. The smoothest and most effective chairing of meetings, at this early stage in the lives of the governing bodies, comes generally from those who have learnt their chairing skills through local authority politics, although this situation may change as the new 'business' governors begin to find their feet. Given the middle- class background of most of the governors in our study, it is likely that there are many more governors, including women and blacks or Asians, who are capable of chairing a governing body than have actually put themselves forward. Those women who do get to chair governing bodies do not always have an easy time of it. In one school, the female chair was unsuccessfully opposed in her election by a male LEA nominee who is also a councillor. He and another male governor do their best to make her life difficult, to the extent of whispering to themselves and others what they think should be happening, correcting her grasp of committee procedure and constantly suggesting courses of action which differ from what she has suggested. This behaviour is quite overtly sexist; nothing of the same kind occurs in the governing body meetings chaired by men, even if the men themselves are not always well versed in the skills of chairing meetings. In experienced male chairs seem to get a lot of positive help and support from other governors. They are not a threat to patriarchal power in the way that even experienced female chairs are seen to be.

Other issues to do with racism and sexism typically arise in one of three ways. First, this happens when discussing teachers' capacity to discipline their pupils; questions are often raised about the ability of 'young girls' [*sic*] to control classes containing disruptive children. Secondly, sexism and racism may arise in relation to the kind of pupils (and by implication the kind of parents) the school contains. The latter may include derogatory references to 'working mothers' and 'inadequate' mothers (fathers are more rarely blamed) who are seen to be responsible for the bad behaviour of unruly pupils. There may also be oblique references to pupils' membership of ethnic minority groups; 'these children need more teachers' or 'these children require more support and resources' or 'what can you expect of these children'. Such comments are almost unknown in middle-class white schools and though they are probably not consciously intended to be racist, it is hard to avoid this as one interpretation, even though genuine concern and care may underlie some of such statements. A third way in which sexism arises is in the nature of the interactions between governing body clerks and the governors themselves. Most of those clerking meetings, whether they are employed by the LEA or by the school (the two LEAs have different systems for clerking meetings) are women and there is sometimes considerable sexism in the way they are treated. They are sometimes blamed for things which are nothing to do with them; they are also often ignored altogether, rather like an invisible servant who does her job, but is not really 'seen' and may not speak unless spoken to first. On the few occasions when men have clerked meetings, they have been of evident high status (e.g. Education Officers) as well as being male, and have been treated with considerable deference, something rarely extended to female clerks.

Governors, especially since the reforming of governing bodies, are under pressure to attend not only the termly formal meetings but also many extra meetings, either of the whole governing body or of subgroups dealing with things like finance, pupil matters and school visits. When extra meetings are suggested at one female chair's governing body, some governors pointedly say things like 'Well that time is fine for the ladies who look after the house but not for busy men like me'. Similar comments are sometimes made when it is suggested that several rather than one governor should try to visit the school at the same time, implying that whilst this is fine for women (by implication, their work is seen to be less important and therefore easier to rearrange in order to come into school), it will be difficult to arrange for male governors. In general, meeting times at all the governing bodies are scarcely chosen for their ability to blend in with domestic commitments; for example the most popular times for formal meetings are either around 4–5 p.m. or 7 p.m., which are the usual times for children to come home from school or for households to eat their evening meals. The 'typical' governor is thus perceived to be one who has no domestic commitments, whose 'wife' is ready with a warming meal once the long meeting is over and who has enough spare time to read the endless papers which school governors these days have constantly to devour. Spare time, as studies of women and leisure have shown, is not something which many women have vast amounts of (Deem, 1986; Talbot and Wimbush, 1989). Given this situation it is amazing how many women do manage to find the time to be governors (a third of our sample of 250, for example). There have been instances in our research on governing bodies of female governors resigning because of the pressure of domestic commitments and the difficulty of arranging childcare for meetings whose duration may vary from an hour to five or six hours. From what we have seen so far in our research it is not enough for women and black governors to be on governing bodies, they also need support and help if they are to undertake the task fully and in ways which are not bureaucratic and formalistic.

Can the Barriers be Breached? Mature Women's Access to Higher Education

LIZ SPERLING

The barriers unveiled

Admissions: A-level and access

The first barrier that women have to face within Higher Education is the admissions process. The fact that the majority of students on Access courses are women but that fewer mature women than mature men students enter Higher Education indicates either that the admission process filters out women applicants, and/or women are not applying for places in Higher Education after taking Access and Access-level courses. Despite the apparent willingness of Higher Education to widen access to non-standard entrants, the validity of alternative entry qualifications has not been accepted by many admissions tutors. Statistics show that the number of entrants to universities (the more traditional sector of higher education) with qualifications other than A-levels and BTEC has increased from 1,324 in 1983 to 2,016 in 1987. Although this may demonstrate a small change in attitude by Higher Education admissions officers and tutors regarding non-standard entry, and consequently mature women students, it is difficult to say whether attitudes have changed in relation to A-level *measures* of academic progress. Indeed, Access courses were originally developed as an alternative route to Higher Education for people whom it was considered were not served well by the A-level system designed for 18-year-olds (Percy and Powell, 1980; Sanders, 1989). This suggests that alternative entry qualifications are expected to be

From: Liz Sperling, 'Can the Barriers be Breached? Mature Women's Access to Higher Education', *Gender and Education*, 3(2) (1991), pp. 200–4.

analogous to A-levels in order to guide admissions tutors on the suitability of non-traditional applicants for undergraduate study.

There is a danger that recent trends in Access provision will lead to Access courses becoming not just an alternative to the A-level route into higher education, but a parallel prerequisite for entry, thus becoming a further barrier for mature women to overcome. With a plethora of often innovative Access courses available throughout the nation, the 'kitemark' of the national validation system, administered by the Council for National Academic Awards (CNAA), may well be necessary as a means of ensuring academic standards. Indeed, it looks as though such validation is welcomed, with some reservations, by Access course providers. However, it would appear that, eventually, unless Access qualifications carry the CNAA 'kitemark', they will not be recognised by admissions officers and tutors or, indeed, employers. The Steering Committee's statement that 'the development of Access Courses and their recognition will not preclude nor detract from the use of other less formalised routes into higher education' seems particularly hollow when later in the same document it is suggested that the need for a national validation system of Access Courses will 'increase institutions' and public confidence in such Access Courses' (CNAA, 1989). In other words, students are, sooner or later, going to have to produce evidence of 'valid' Access study in order to prove eligibility for higher education. Mature women students are likely to be at a disadvantage if such a situation does occur. For example, courses that have to be completed either in terms of hours of attendance and/or examination results do not account for the often erratic study patterns that women have to adopt as a result of their family and domestic circumstances. An extra year of studying prior to gaining a place in higher education may make all the difference between progression or dropping out of the education system. The decision to drop out or progress may be more acute for mature women students if they have to retake courses that were not completed due to circumstances beyond their control. Again, such arguments could well be propounded for mature male students. However, special concern must be afforded mature women students in this respect. Many such students, who often wish to enter Higher Education in order to improve their job prospects after a period out of the workforce, will actually lack accepted marketable skills that mature male students have often acquired through their public occupations. Thus, women actually have to 'make up' for the time spent in domestic and/or other low status occupations and often cannot afford time spent taking and retaking entry courses.

Whether in the last analysis the access debate and concern with admissions to Higher Education is relevant is open to speculation. The debate has concentrated on the need to widen access in order to fill the gap left by the fall in the traditional intake. Despite fears of the effect of demographic change on Higher Education applications, it is mainly the birth rate of the 'working classes' that has diminished and which will continue to do so until the mid-1990s. The number of middle-class 18-year-olds, the traditional clientele of Higher Education, has remained steady (Smithers and Robinson, 1989). Thus, Higher Education's traditional clientele has not altered to any great extent. Furthermore, the subject areas in which mature students concentrate are far from suffering from a shortage of applicants. Therefore, rather than relinquish the misguided belief in A-levels being a measure of future attainment in Higher Education, it will be possible to continue selection of applicants on the basis of set standards arising from long-standing, 'safe' ideals. Indeed, the 1989–90 Higher Education admission figures, whereby admissions tutors accommodated an average 6 per cent increase in admissions by drawing mainly on traditional A-level applicants, indicate that non-standard entry may now be of less importance than was originally forecast.

The myth of domesticity and the admission process

The structural–qualifications admissions barriers to womens' greater access to Higher Education are exacerbated by the less tangible policies that arise from the dominant ethos of Higher Education. The history of Higher Education, its perceived purpose as being the training ground for young people to reach the upper echelons of business, industry and commerce, and the Civil Service, precludes the high participation of mature women, who are then further excluded from such prestigious occupation. Of course, this is integral to the debate about what should be the purpose of Higher Education. When Higher Education is defined in terms of self-developed and the pursuit of knowledge, academics, as well as women themselves, often perceive mature women as being incapable of study at degree level. A circular argument for such an idea exists for this view: 'women's' work is not on the whole intellectually challenging, thus they do not need an education that stimulates their intellectual capacities. As a result, women are seen as being intellectually incapable rather than being seen as the casualties of patriarchal socialisation. Moreover, the myth of women as being unreliable and uncommitted students due to their domestic responsibilities may prejudice the decisions of admissions tutors in an increasingly competitive and pressurised Higher Education system.

In the present climate, where Higher Education is looking increasingly to industry and business to contribute in terms of curriculum content and outlet (as well as in terms of finance), a further danger exists that women will be excluded from this entry route, via work-related and employer-sponsored courses, either because of their concentration in the lower echelons of the workforce or because they are not in paid employment. (It is yet to be seen whether the predicted skills shortage will counteract such a pessimistic outlook. However, the history of women's wage labour and the relationship between their private–domestic responsibilities and public activities would suggest that the women who are now being urged to re-enter the workforce will be concentrated predominantly in part-time, low-status-jobs). As with the intellectual barriers to mature women's greater participation in Higher Education, the male gatekeepers to the institutions tend to devalue the experiences, skills and abilities of women and thus justify the exclusion of mature women students. However, women who return to study after some time out of the education system often achieve great success in academic subjects, including those taken at degree level despite the logistical difficulties that they have to cope with. Thus, womens' 'deficiencies' can no longer be used as an excuse by Higher Education for not showing a higher participation rate of mature women students. The difficulty lies in persuading admissions officers and tutors, as well as women themselves, that this is the case.

Curriculum and assessment: course structures

The structural barriers that mature women students have to overcome in order to enter and persevere with study at degree level include the logistical problems involved in meeting domestic and family commitments alongside meeting study requirements. The present structure of courses is usually designed for young people who have little responsibility outside their own study. Thus, classes, seminars and lectures, as well as examinations, are often scheduled for 9–9.30 a.m. and as late as 5–5.30 in the evening. For women with young children such timetabling is a disincentive to study. Women students are frequently not resident on campus and have to travel to the institution, often by public transport, as well as having to travel to and from children's schools before and after their contact hours at the college/university. Moreover, womens' other domestic commitments have to be fitted to their study time-table, a situation that most mature male students do not have to cope with. Smithers and Griffin, in their survey of students who entered university under the Joint Matriculation Board mature students' scheme, showed 'there was quite often a difference between men and women (here). Men frequently said that they stayed on at university to study because it was difficult to do so at home with the children, women said they could not use the study facilities because they had to be at home for the children' (Smithers and Griffin, 1986). Although individual tutors may be sympathetic to this plight and will allow parents to come into lectures and classes late and/or leave early, women in this situation are at a disadvantage both in terms of information lost and related psycho-logical factors. Women who consistently have to lose contact time may always feel that they have 'lost out' and are lagging behind their peers.

In addition to the possibility of 'lost time' due to unfavourable class and lecture times, the often erratic study patterns of mature women students may further involve loss of study time that can sever aspirations of completing, or even starting, higher education courses. For many mature women three year's full-time study is often too large a commitment to make for reasons that are fre-quently beyond their control. Moreover, without the the provision of adequate credit transfer facilities, a family move may terminate women's study. More common disclocations in study can occur through such things as children's or other relatives' illness and other domestic/private crises with which women have to deal. It is easy for people with academic experience and confidence to say that such women can 'catch up' on what they have missed as a result of such incidences. For the women themselves this may not be such a simple exercise. To begin with, their other commitments often do not allow time for the 'extra' work necessary to catch up. Moreover, as recent entrants to the formal education system, fall-ing behind in their studies may cause a crisis of confidence that is difficult for mature women students to overcome, even if under-standing tutors help to assuage any fear of failure which may arise as a result of this. Solutions to such problems are difficult within the present structure of higher education. However, anticipation of such difficulties might well enable more sympathetic structures to be introduced that would accommodate the often erratic study patterns of mature women students.

Examination assessment

One thing that many potential non-standard entry mature students have in common is that they have been labelled 'failures' as a result of their past educational experiences. As well as sapping students' confidence generally, such a stigma precipitates a fear of examina-tion and formal assessment that may possibly prevent mature students from returning to study or from progressing to Higher Education from the more informal environment of adult and Further Education. Although mature students who embark on 'traditional' courses do as well, if not better, than 'conventional' students in formal assessments, it must be recognised that exam-inations are not the best method of assessment that is now avail-able. Indeed, in my own research into Open Colleges as routes into Higher Education for mature women, 72 per cent of respondents to a questionnaire about their educational experiences, both in com-pulsory education and as adult returners, cited less formal 'friendly' assessment and teaching methods as a reason for choosing Open Colleges as their reintroduction to study. Apart from the examina-tion context itself, revision may be marred for mature women students by the intrusion of outside responsibilities and commit-ments, and examination timetables may not fit into their schedule. The task of taking children to school and travelling to college before an examination, arranging after-school child care for after-noon examinations and the worry that this entails about the relia-bility and suitability of the care chosen, all serve to deflect concentration from the subject at stake. However, assessed course-work may well absorb such problems as occur during the study period, being done at more leisure and allowing greater scope to articulate the knowledge that a student has gained throughout a course.

Access and Assets: the Experience of Mature Mother Students in Higher Education

ROSALIND EDWARDS

Gender and experience

The women talked about their experiences in the public world, of paid work in, for example, the health service, personal social services, and adult education, as being regarded as useful by themselves and lecturers when it came to feeding into seminar discussions and writing essays. On the other hand, their private world experiences as mothers bringing up children and running homes were rarely valued.

Helen, a white working-class woman, spoke of the feeling that family life experiences were somehow inferior even where they might have been relevant. *'We felt that by bringing in sort of our home, er, life, what was going on, we would be sort of demeaning the conversation that was going on about a particular problem or Freud's theory or something like that.'*

Where women did use their experiences of family life they frequently had an awareness that this was not really permissible. However, those who did talk about personal areas often did so in order to challenge knowledge that was being put forward. Alexandra, another white working-class woman, declared:

> I would challenge things. My experience of being married, of trying to raise a family, of expecting my husband to play an equal part in it, er, would give me an insight into what the other people are saying, so I'd use that. Areas of like bringing up kids and so on.

From Rosalind Edwards, 'Access and Assets: the Experience of Mature Mother Students in Higher Education', *Journal of Access Studies* (1990), pp. 191–4.

(Would you just use your experience to make a point but not actually talk about yourself personally?)

Oh no. I talk about myself personally, yeah, yes. I'd make the point if somebody said – well, I would explain it... I think it's no good just saying I don't agree with you. You've got to say why and what is it in your experience that makes you disagree with what they've said.

Some of the women accepted the view that bringing up children, in particular, was not a 'valuable asset'. Victoria, who came from a working-class background and still felt she was working class despite living in a middle-class area, said she rarely used any examples of her mothering experience when she was discussing issues. *'I don't like to ever harp on about having children, not because, um, I'm ashamed of it or anything, but I don't actually think people want to hear about – you know... I don't think people would want to know about that.'*

Others, like Alexandra, fought against this rendering as invisible of their experiences within the family. Jackie, a white working-class woman who now had what she described as 'middle-class aspirations', mentioned a particular seminar session that had annoyed her.

I mean [the lecturer] today was, he was talking about when he was a boy, 'I used to carry the coal on a Sunday, hot coal on a shovel from the back room to the front room, and the whole family would go into the front room and listen to "Two-Way Family Favourites"'? And I thought well yeah, I can remember listening to that as well and that's on at lunchtime. And I said to him, 'but your mother was in the kitchen', and he said, 'yeah, yeah, she was, she was', you know, 'yeah, she was in the kitchen'. And I thought it's this damn invisible woman again isn't it. The family go into the front room. It's not the family because – and, and the more I think about it the more invisible women seem to be.

Stella, a white middle-class women, felt that acknowledgment of the mothering side of her was difficult for lecturers and others because it was often seen as incompatible with being able to do academic work.

One thing sticks in my mind that one particular person that I knew quite well and, er, when he taught me for the first time I happened to go along to his room when he was marking one of my essays and he said, 'this is really good, you write really well', and he sounded so surprised! And I said, 'what did you expect then?' So I think maybe sometimes people, if you are a mother people define you as that and they don't really consider that you can do anything else! And that wasn't because he's a particularly insensitive person or whatever. But I do remember the note of surprise and I've never forgiven him for that!

The sense of mothering and mothers being devalued by the educational institutions was reinforced in various practical ways. A lack of freely available child care provision and administrative arrangements (for instance, non-availability of timetable details until they started the academic term left them unable to make child care arrangements in advance), that many of the women saw as taking no account of their domestic responsibilities, made them feel they were not really considered by the institution in the way that students without such responsibilities were, particularly the conventional 18-year-olds. One of the institutions the women attended did not allow them to bring their children on site and where this applied it was mentioned by nearly all of them. This caused not just practical inconvenience but went against what many of the women felt was an integral part of their mothering – that their children should know and be able to picture where they were. Anna, a black women, summed up the feelings expressed by many of the women,

It's terrible. 'Cos sometimes there are a lot of, um, Baker days and things like that, holidays or – I mean it wasn't too bad because sometimes the childminder had them all day, but sometimes she couldn't. I would take them there just to go and get a book from the library, something like that, and you had to leave them by the door if you haven't got a pass... But I would love to take them there like, you know, maybe one of the days I'm off, just to walk into the library and walk round, but you can't do that.

(Why do you feel like you want to do that?)

'Cos I say I'm going to poly. They only hear me say that, they don't know where I'm going. So I like to show them this is where

mummy comes when I leave you at the childminder's or whatsoever. But I would like to take them in there a few times so they
could actually get used to this place that I'm going to, you know.

Again there was the impression that the institution was shutting
out a part of them which was important, to themselves at least, and
which meant they had certain responsibilities.

However, in addition to the sense that mothering and family life
were not valid experiences upon which to draw, there were other
reasons why not all the women would have wished to talk about
these even if encouraged to do so. The idea of the privacy of family
life was mentioned by some of the women. Wendy, a white working-class woman explained,

Sort of low wages and that, you know, I've used my experiences.
I've got a lot of them concerning that, you know, [laughs] and
that sort of thing. But it depends, I will draw the line. I won't
sort of, you know, let out sort of things that – you know, I've
got things that I want to keep private and I wouldn't sort of
bring them out in that sort of situation.

Two of the women who had been in violent relationships said
these were experiences they would not wish to share with others in
a seminar situation, even if relevant to the topic under discussion.
A few of the black women additionally voiced a fear of any
revelations rebounding on themselves. Maureen, who described
herself as black and working class, commented,

My personal experiences I expect is my private experience, you
know. My private affair as they say, you know. And then you
tend to think that even if you sit down and you speak to, um, the
group about it, you know, you just have this idea that, you
know, they're trying to suss you out, you know. And I think,
you know, it's like taking a part of you away.

There was also an awareness on the part of many of the women
that if they talked about family problems this could be construed as
'making excuses' for themselves. The overall feeling was that
mothers should not really be studying at a Higher Education
institution at all, and that any problems that resulted from their
being there would 'tarnish' all mothers.

The ethos of the institution overall, combined with a realisation that a particular set of experiences which formed an important part of their identity were not really *de rigueur*, obviously reinforced this sense of being deviants within a system of which Robinson has said 'The norms of our higher education policies and higher education system are the norms of the bachelor boy student' (1980, p.4).

Bibliography to Section VI

Anon. (1988) 'Governor Power Entices More to Stand', *Education*, 23 December, p. 600.

Arnot, M. (1989) 'Crisis or Challenge: Equal Opportunities and the National Curriculum', *NUT Education Review*, 3(2), pp. 6–13.

Brehony, K., and Deem, R. (1989) 'Changing for Free Education: An Exploration of a Debate in School Governing Bodies', *Journal of Education Policy*, 5, pp. 333–47.

Byrne, E.M. (1978) *Women and Education*, London: Tavistock.

Central Statistical Office (1989) *Social Trends 19*, London: HMSO.

Central Statistical Office (1991) *Social Trends 21*, London: HMSO.

Central Statistical Office (1994) *Social Trends 24*, London: HMSO.

Chitty, C. and Lawson, D. (1988) *The National Curriculum*, London: Bedford Way Papers.

CNAA (1989) *Access Courses to Higher Education: A Framework of National Arrangements for Recognition* London: Council for National Academic Awards.

Coopers and Lybrand (1988) *Local Management of Schools*, London: HMSO.

David, M.E. (1980) *The State, the Family and Education*, London: Routledge & Kegan Paul.

David, M. and New, C. (1985) *For the Sake of the Children*

Deem, R. (1986) *All Work and No Play*, Milton Keynes: Open University Press.

Department of Education and Science (1993) *Higher Education Statistics for the United Kingdom*, London: DES/HMSO.

Edwards, A., Fitz, J. and Whitty, G. (1989) *The State and Private Education: An Evaluation of the Assisted Places Scheme*, Basingstoke: Falmer Press.

Edwards, R. (1991) 'Degrees of Difference: Mature Women Students in Higher Education', unpublished Ph.D. dissertation, South Bank Polytechnic, London.

Elliot, J. *et al.* (1981) *School Accountability*, London: Grant McIntyre.

Exeter Society for Curriculum Studies Research Group (1987) *Parents as School Governors: interim report*, University of Exeter.

Flude, M. and Hammer, M. (1989) *The 1988 Education Act* Barcombe: Falmer Press.

Fox, I. (1985) *Private Schools and Public Issues: The Parents' Views* London: Macmillan.

The Guardian (1989) 'Fee Shake-up Boosts Intake of Students', 23 September.

Hadfield, G. (1989) 'Teachers "exploiting parent power laws"', *Sunday Times*, 22 January.

Hills, N. (1981) 'Britain', in J. Lovenduski and J. Hills (eds) *The Politics of the Second Electorate*, London: Routledge & Kegan Paul.

Johnson, D. (1987) *Private Schools and State Schools: two systems or one?*, Milton Keynes: Open University Press.

Judd, J. (1988) 'Parents Robbed of School Power', *The Observer*, 23 October.

Kogan, M., Johnson, D., Packwood, T. and Whittaker, T. (eds) (1984) *School Governing Bodies*, London: Heinemann.

Maclure, S. (1988) *Education Reformed: A Guide to the 1988 Education Act*, London: Hodder & Stoughton.

Percy, K. and Lucas, S. (1980) *The Open College and Alternatives*, Lancaster: University of Lancaster.

Robinson, E. (1980) 'Course Design and Structure', in Equal Opportunities Commission, *Equal Opportunities in Higher Education*, report of an EOC/SRHE conference held at Manchester Polytechnic, 6–7 March.

Ryle, M. and Stuart, M. (1994) 'An Access Curriculum for Women? A Case Study', *Journal of Access Studies*, 9, pp. 79–90.

Sallis, J. (1988) *Schools, Parents and Governors*, London: Routledge.

Sanders, C. (1989) 'No Access', *New Statesman and Society*, 17 March, pp. 18–19.

Sheridan, L. (1992) 'Women Returners to Further Education: Employment and Gender Relations in the Home', *Gender and Education*, 4(3), pp. 213–28.

Smithers, A. and Griffin (1986) 'Mature Students and University: Entry, Experience and Outcomes', *Studies in Higher Education*, 11(3), pp. 257–68.

Smithers, A. and Robinson, P. (1989) *Increasing Participation in Higher Education*, London: BP Educational Service.

Sperling, L. (1989) 'Barriers to women participating in Higher Education', Departmental Paper No. 23, Department of Politics and Contemporary History, University of Salford.

Stillman, A. and Maychell, K. (1986) *Choosing Schools: Parents LEAS and the 1980 Education Act*, Windsor: NFER Nelson.

Talbot, M. and Wimbush, E. (eds) (1989) *Relative Freedoms*, Milton Keynes: Open University Press.

Times Higher Education Supplement (1989) 'Fees Promise Way for 6000 More Students', 22 September.

Universities' Central Council on Admissions (UCCA) *Statistical Supplement to the Annual Report*, Cheltenham: UCCA, table 5.

VII

Women and Health Care

Introduction

CLARE UNGERSON

It was a primary objective of the second wave of feminism, which began in the early 1970s, that women should wrest control over their bodies from men. One of the major ways identified by the women's movement in which men exerted that control was Western medical care: the medical profession, it was claimed, had masculinised the healing professions and medicalised women's natural functions at the major milestones of puberty, childbirth and menopause. Publications such as those by Ehrenreich and English (1973), which argued that the persecution of witches by male priests in the medieval and renaissance periods had been the equivalent of a healers' holocaust, and by the Boston Women's Health Collective (1976) which presented a critique of the medicalisation of women's reproductive capacity and offered advice as to how women should organise their own care, were much discussed in women's groups meeting in Britain in the 1970s. North American in origin, this literature was rapidly followed by writers in Britain looking particularly at the medicalisation and masculinisation of childbirth (for example, Donnison, 1977; Oakley, 1979; 1980; 1984) and at relations between women and their doctors (for example, Roberts, 1981; 1985).

From those beginnings, the literature on women and health care has expanded enormously both in Britain and worldwide, such that it would be quite impossible within the scope of a reader of this kind to do justice to that literature's depth and complexity. Moreover, much of that work is written within the framework of medical sociology, and while this analysis often has policy implications and always has a policy context, the implicit claim made by much of it is that the relationships outlined between, for example, medical men and female patients, are common to all countries and cultures where Western medicine prevails. A reader, such as this one, on women and *social policy* should direct its attention specifically to the policy context within which the relationship between women and health care is played out. In Britain that context is a National Health Service, funded by taxation and free at the point of consumption, subject to the planning and implementation decisions made by hierarchies of administrators, professionals and paraprofessionals. Two of the readings selected here are designed to direct attention to issues which have entered the policy arena in Britain, and will remain on the political agenda for the foreseeable future.

The extract from the House of Commons Select Committee on Health indicates that policy can – and has – shifted to take account of the feminist critique of the medicalisation of childbirth. The committee recommended that women should be able to make their own informed decision as to whether to give birth at home or in hospital. The language in which the committee's work is framed is clearly highly critical of the medical profession and comes directly from the women's movement, referring, in its commentary, to a 'women's right to choose' and a 'medical model of the management of childbirth'. Moreover, the Select Committee report has had further policy implications as a result of the later broad brush acceptance of its main recommendations by the Department of Health (1992; 1994). The fact that the recommendations of the Select Committee have moved into general policy directives could be taken as one of the very few social policy victories which British second wave feminism has managed to win. The process by which these changes have come about has taken two decades and been hard fought, and it is not clear – until the necessary historical research has been undertaken – as to how it has happened. A medical profession which, starting from a very low base 20 years ago, now has one in four general practitioners and hospital medical staff who are women may have helped a little (Department of Health, 1991). But it should also be noted that, in the more senior and powerful positions, only about 15 per cent of all consultants are women, and when one senior female obstetrician radically liberalised her management of childbirth she was suspended from work, although, after a bitter battle through the courts, eventually reinstated (Savage, 1986). Whatever the reasons – and they are clearly very complicated – the intentions for change are in place and come directly from central government. It now remains for a conservative profession to implement them, for health authorities to fund the necessary midwifery and health visiting services, and for women who wish to give birth at home to insist on so doing.

The second excerpt, on private hospital care, is here because it demonstrates why women particularly are attracted by private hospital care as it has developed in Britain during the 1980s (Higgins, 1988; Calnan *et al.*, 1993). There is an interesting paradox about private health care: that is that women, who are poorer than men, and much less likely than men to be covered by private health insurance funded or subsidised by their employers, are also likely to be larger consumers of private health care than men. This is partially, because, as Rose Wiles points out, there are aspects of women's lives, particularly constraints on their time imposed by their caring work at home, which mean that they prefer to use health services which they can fit round their own schedules and time needs, rather than use services that are allocated on some other, more collectively organised, set of principles. However, it is also important to note that women in Britain are more likely than British men to use private health care because this system of care has gone in for 'niche-marketing' in areas of health and disease particularly applicable to women (Foster, 1995). Three of these important niches – along with drug dependency and alcoholism which are not necessarily gender related – are abortion, infertility treatment and hysterectomies – which clearly are (Higgins, 1988). The published data on abortion in Britain indicates just how important private provision in this area is: in 1992, of the 172,000 abortions in total in that year, 54 per cent were carried out in the private sector, and a further 15 per cent had been purchased from the private sector by the NHS (OPCS, 1995).

It is interesting to speculate as to why these three procedures – abortion, hysterectomies and infertility treatment – which have been so effectively colonised by the private sector in health care, all have in common women's reproductive capacity and its management. It is certainly arguable that a male dominated medical profession is somewhat careless of women's needs and fails, within a publicly funded system, to give them proper priority. It is also undeniable that for both abortion and infertility treatment there are ethical and religious issues embedded within them (Overall, 1987; Holmes and Purdy, 1992; Kelley *et al.*, 1993). From these ethical issues follows a view that, in these cases, 'need' is not professionally and medically straightforward; collective responsibility and provision should not necessarily be automatic and so such procedures should be given low priority. Typically, the National Health Service uses waiting time to sort priorities, and the race against time, particularly for abortion, but also for infertility treatment, is absolutely of the essence. Hysterectomies also have a relationship to time. They are often classified as 'elective' in the sense that they bring to an end symptoms, such as pain, anaemia and nuisance, which some medical practitioners, and some women, may think are bearable and which will, with luck and patience, disappear in the long run with the onset of the menopause. But for many women, the prospect of waiting until called for this major procedure, and lack of control as to when both the operation and the ensuing lengthy convalescence will occur, is enough to drive them into the more than willing arms of the private sector. Thus rights to a procedure within a publicly funded system can be fundamentally diluted to the point of disappearance by the manipulation of time: and women's reproductive capacity is particularly vulnerable to time's passing. Only a private sector, allocating resources according to ability to pay, is able – and eager – to bypass the time constraints built into a public, rationed, system.

Whatever distaste feminists committed to equality may feel for the extension of private health care in Britain and the way in which it will inevitably lead to further divisions between women, the 'special relationship' between well-resourced women and private health care is likely to continue. Equally, it is possible that National Health Service provision, under new administrative and financing regimes which have set up an 'internal market', will begin to ape the more desirable aspects of private provision (Salter, 1995). That is certainly one of the intentions of the new financial structures. If the newly established Hospital Trusts, in competition with each other for public sector business, recognise the 'women's market' as a lucrative source of trade, then it would be foolish of them to ignore the special wishes of women, particularly their desire for more consultants' time and for greater privacy. The ultimate arbiter in this situation is resource. If the NHS internal market equips its purchasers – namely, fundholding general practitioners and district health authorities – with adequate funding for the effective demand of women-friendly services then, in theory and all other things being equal, it is possible that the quality of the service delivered to all women via the National Health Service will improve.

The third excerpt, by Jennifer Strickler, presents some of the debate among feminists concerning the development of the 'new' reproductive technologies, in particular, *in vitro* fertilisation. The feminist literature on these technologies is deeply split. On the one hand, socialist feminists argue for a health care system that underwrites all women's rights to reproduce including those without partners, disabled women and those in lesbian relationships (Doyal, 1987; Feldman, 1987). On the other hand, radical feminists argue that the methods by which these rights can be implemented are essentially masculine, demeaning and damaging to all women, and subscribe to a cult of femininity and female identity achieved through motherhood (Arditti *et al.*, 1984; Corea, 1984; Duelli-Klein, 1989; Spallone and Steinberg, 1987; Spallone, 1989). Both positions accept that these techniques are essentially invasive of women's bodies, and that they raise, in a very acute form, the issue of control over women's bodies which is so central to second wave feminism. But the question remains as to whether these techniques render to women more or less control over their bodies.

The policy implications of these technological developments and the feminist debates surrounding them are manifold. The radical feminist critique of masculine science implemented by 'gynecidal' obstetricians raises questions as to how far public money should be spent on the research and development of reproductive technologies and how far a public health care system should be dominated by professionally driven scientific enquiry. The socialist feminist critique raises questions about the way in which a public system of health care is rationed in such a way that it develops divisions between women whereby only the 'conventional' woman in a 'conventional' relationship is able to claim a public service.

Maternity Services

HOUSE OF COMMONS SELECT COMMITTEE ON HEALTH

25.   The emphatic conviction that birth in a consultant obstetric unit provided the surest guarantee of a healthy baby has led to the current situation where 98 per cent of women in this country now give birth in NHS hospitals, of which about 4 per cent in 1989 were in GP units and the rest in consultant obstetric units. Assessments of the benefits of this development differ. Perhaps the most radical view is presented by Mrs Marjorie Tew, to whom we have earlier referred, a medical statistician and author of *Safer Childbirth? A Critical History of Maternity Care* (1990) whose analysis of the statistics relating to the safety of different places of birth provides what she herself describes as 'revolutionary conclusions'. She says:

> First of all there is the obvious evidence that since 1950 mortality rates have gone down a lot. At the same time hospitalisation rates have gone up and everybody fell into the trap of making a causal connection between these two serial time trends. When you carry out the first statistical test to see whether there is likely to be a causal connection, you find that the causal connection, if any, is in the opposite direction. We found that the years when hospitalisation increased most were the years when perinatal mortality declined least. There is a strong negative correlation between these figures.

In her analysis which she provided to the Committee in a written memorandum she alleges that the policy of directing all confinements

---

From House of Commons Health Committee Second Report (1992) *Maternity Services*, House of Commons, Session 1991–2, vol. I, London: HMSO.

into hospitals was driven more by the territorial imperatives of the Royal College of Gynaecologists (RCOG) than by a disinterested analysis of the evidence. While her views provoke strong reactions, they are not dismissed as without foundation. Professor Eva Alberman, an epidemiologist and Adviser to the Social Services Committee in 1979–80 and subsequently, said of her work: 'She has really made us think very hard about assumptions that I had made pretty readily', and when pressed to give a view on whether Mrs Tew's work proved conclusively that consultant unit or other births were safer, she declined to come down on either side.

26.   Other witnesses take a stronger view than Professor Alberman, though few follow Marjorie Tew so far as to assert that the negative correlation between year to year decreases in the perinatal mortality (PNM) rates and increases in the level of hospitalisation implies that hospital birth is more dangerous than home birth. The most recent and convincing work in this area, and work which has, as far as we are aware, not been substantially challenged, is that by Rona Campbell of Queen's University, Belfast and Alison Macfarlane of the National Perinatal Epidemiology Unit at Oxford. While they said of Mrs Tew's work that they were 'not convinced that she has taken adequate account of the selection factors involved when drawing her conclusions', in the memorandum which they submitted to the Committee summarising their work, they remark that:

> The statistical association between the increase in the proportion of hospital deliveries and the fall in the crude perinatal mortality rate seems unlikely to be explained by a cause and effect relation

and, most importantly, they state unequivocally that:

> There is no evidence to support the claim that the safest policy is for all women to give birth in hospital, or the policy of closing small obstetric units on grounds of safety.

27.   These views were endorsed by the Royal College of Midwives (RCM), by the Association of Radical Midwives, by the Maternity Alliance, by the National Childbirth Trust, by the Association for Community-Based Maternity Care, and by the Association for Improvements in Maternity Services, among many others from whom we heard both formal, and informal evidence.

In an editorial in *The Lancet* in 1986 it was acknowledged that 'in the light of the accumulated British evidence, neither the lack of safety of birth at home nor the greater safety of birth in hospital had been proved, a judgement contrary to established medical claims'.

28.   The position was disputed by a number of witnesses who maintain that hospitals are the safest place to give birth. At its most unsophisticated this was attempted by the officials from the Department of Health who simply presented the statistics for PNM rates and the level of hospital deliveries in 1955 and 1989. They made no attempt to justify this crude and now thoroughly discredited approach to the evidence, but Dr Walford went on to maintain, without new evidence, that 'the safest place, as far as we [the Government] can ascertain, to have a baby is in hospital with full facilities'. Dr Walford also stated that the Department had 'no indication that that advice, were we to seek it again, from the professional bodies would be different.' The Department clearly has not heard the views of midwives and epidemiologists on this subject. Nor have they taken account of the statement of Mr Duncan Nichol, Chairman of the NHS Management Executive, to the Public Accounts Committee, that 'there is no statistical evidence to show whether GP Maternity Units are less safe than those in District General Hospitals'. The RCOG gives some support for Dr Walford's belief in that they have said 'labour remains a potentially dangerous time and delivery in hospital is the only safe option'. However they have also said 'there is no conclusive evidence that hospital delivery is safer than home'.

29.   In the course of a prolonged series of exchanges between the Minister for Health and her officials and the Committee on this subject, the Department stuck to its position that women should be encouraged to give birth in hospital for reasons of safety. This position was reiterated as recently as 22 November 1991 in an answer to a parliamentary question which stated

the Department's policy remains that, as unforeseen circumstances can occur in any birth, every mother should be *encouraged* to have her baby in a maternity unit where emergency facilities are readily available.

However, when the Minister of Health returned to give evidence to the Committee at the final session of this inquiry on 16 January, we detected a shift of emphasis. She acknowledged, without reservation, that there was no reliable statistical evidence which established the superior safety of birth in consultant obstetric units as against home births and those in GP units, stating that

> there is no overwhelming... unequivocal evidence, about the relative merits of different settings [for delivery] and some of the evidence is conflicting.

30.   Despite this change of emphasis, the Minister continued that although

> there is no clear, overwhelming evidence on that front... that has to lie alongside commonsense and, indeed, professional judgements about what is the safest way for a woman to give birth.

32.   While the report of the Social Services Committee in 1980 still stands as a landmark in the battle to reduce unnecessary deaths among babies, this inquiry has led us to acknowledge that it has been used, too often, as an excuse for pushing the delivery of maternity care in a direction which goes against the grain of many women's wishes. The views that prevailed more than a decade ago now need objective reassessment. We believe that the debate about place of birth, and the triumph of the hospital-centred argument, have led to the imposition of a whole philosophy of maternity care which has tended to regard all pregnancies as potential disasters, and to impose a medical model for their management which has had adverse consequences in the whole way in which we think about maternity care.

Women and Private Medicine

ROSE WILES

Introduction

The private market in health care in Britain expanded rapidly during the 1970s and 1980s, with growth in the numbers taking out private health insurance (Higgins, 1988), new building of for-profit hospitals (Davies, 1987) and the development of specialist services in areas such as psychiatry, alcohol treatment and health screening (Timmins, 1985). It has often been argued that these significant changes arose out of the rapid growth in occupational health policies being offered primarily to male white-collar workers. These were designed essentially to recruit and retain the workers and to enable them to return to the workforce as quickly as possible after episodes of illness. However, while this expansion may have occurred as a result of the growth in insurance programmes available to men, it appears that women have been the main users of private sector facilities (Horne 1984; Nicholl *et al.*, 1989). In part this is because much of the expansion that has taken place in the private sector has been in areas that have particular significance for women and in which the NHS has provided an inadequate service for women's needs, such as residential long-stay homes, fertility clinics and abortion services (Clarke *et al.*, 1983). This does not explain why women should comprise a greater proportion of the patient population in the private acute hospital sector than men (Nicholl *et al.*, 1989).

Many studies have shown that women experience more ill health and make more use of health services than men (Reid and Wor-

From Rose Wiles, 'Women and Private Medicine', *Sociology of Health and Illness*, 15 (1) (1993), pp. 68–84.

mald, 1982; Roberts, 1990). However, it appears that higher usage is even more marked in the private sector. Two national surveys of private hospitals in 1981 and 1986 showed that, even when termination of pregnancy was excluded from the calculations, women were still greater users than men, and the difference was more pronounced than in the NHS (Williams *et al.*, 1985; Nicholl *et al.*, 1989).

While there is a considerable literature on the experiences of women in the statutory health care services, there is little that has examined the experiences of women within the private sector. The aims of this article are, first, to examine the extent to which women choose to 'go private' because it offers specific benefits not offered in the NHS and, second, to identify whether these are specific to women and different from the benefits that men may feel they acquire. This chapter focuses on the advantages or benefits respondents felt that they gained by going private. This is not to argue that there are no disadvantages associated with private health care, but this was not a focus of the study. The sample had chosen to go private because it would offer them specific benefits and the aim of this study was to discover what these were. The broader issue of satisfaction was pursued in the research but will not be a focus of this chapter.

Method

The data were collected as part of a large-scale study designed to examine why patients opt for treatment in private hospitals rather than using the NHS, carried out in the Wessex Region between January and June 1991. The methods of data collection were twofold. First, a postal survey was carried out among patients in eight private hospitals and among pay bed patients in three NHS hospitals. Second, a 10 per cent sub-sample of respondents was interviewed at home after their discharge from hospital.

These data indicate that the typical private patient in this region is similar to that identified in other studies in terms of sex, class and age range (Nicholl *et al.*, 1989). In particular it appears that middle-class, middle-aged women are the highest users of in-patient services in this region. Of the 60 people interviewed, 58 per cent (35) of these were female and 42 per cent (25) male. The age and class range of the interview sample reflected the questionnaire sample: 63 per cent (38) were in the 25–50 age group and 82 per cent (49) were in social classes I and II.

Respondents were asked in the questionnaire why they decided to go private for their in-patient care. The three reasons most frequently cited were 'to avoid NHS waiting lists', 'to make use of private health insurance' and to enjoy the 'better surroundings of private hospitals'. The interviews provided scope for discovering more details about patients' reasons for going private. The main reasons given in the interviews were generally the same as those most frequently recorded on the questionnaires, that is to avoid waiting lists and to make use of health insurance. In addition, people mentioned the ability to choose a date when they could be admitted, the privacy of having a private room with en suite bathroom and the 'better care' they felt they received in private hospitals. There appeared to be no differences between male and female interviewees in the reporting of these reasons.

Details of the method of payment and types of health insurance policies held were obtained at the interviews. Thirty people (50 per cent) had company insurance which was either a perk or subsidised by their employers, 27 (45 per cent) had their own private insurance and three people were not insured and paid for their treatment themselves. Of those with company insurance 17 were female and 13 male, of those with their own insurance 16 were female and 11 male, and of those paying for their treatment themselves, two were female and one male. There appeared to be no differences between the two policy types in the reasons given for going private. Unsurprisingly, those paying for themselves did differ in that their primary motivation was speed and they expressed greater concern over cost.

While there appeared to be no differences between male and female interviewees in the reasons given for going private, distinct differences emerged about why these reasons were viewed as important and the advantages they felt they had gained. For many of the men, the advantages were important primarily on a practical level: minimal disruption to their working or leisure activities would be caused by their hospital stay. In addition, the possession (in all but one case) of private health insurance, together with the lack of waiting and the perceived better care, made the choice to go private a rational response that a person would, in the words of one respondent, 'be mad not to take'. For many of the women, too, these reasons were significant. However, in addition many of them identified four other factors. Again, the policy type did not appear to affect the primacy given to these. These reasons were: first, factors related to women's role as 'carers' which were identified by 16 women (46 per cent of the female sample) of whom seven had their own insurance, seven had company insurance and two had no insurance; second, to have their health needs met in a way that they are not in the NHS, which was identified by 20 women (57 per cent) of whom seven had their own insurance and 13 had company insurance; third, to retain an element of dignity and modesty, which was identified by 18 women (51 per cent) of whom ten had their own insurance and eight had company insurance, and, fourth, to maintain control over their health care, which was identified by seven women (20 per cent) of whom three had their own insurance and four had company insurance. These reasons were not mutually exclusive.

Women as carers

In our society it is women who tend to do the 'looking after' or caring for or about other people. This is not to say that men do not 'care' for significant others in their lives. Rather it is to assert that the physical act of caring and looking after others, whether inside or outside the family unit, is generally carried out by women (Finch and Groves, 1983). Furthermore, women who live alone are less likely to enjoy the benefits of the social support found amongst lone men (Burgoyne *et al.*, 1987).

Women who have primary responsibility for 'looking after' family members inevitably experience difficulties when they become ill and need looking after themselves. Not only are they likely to experience anxieties about who will look after dependants if they have to be absent from home for any period but also about who will look after them if they are incapacitated. A similar problem arises for women who live alone. Although they may not have to look after others, they have no one to 'care' for them. These points were raised by 16 women (46 per cent), but only one man, and emerged as factors which encouraged women to opt to go private rather than use the NHS. The private sector was viewed by these women as offering them advantages that were not available within the NHS. On a practical level, having a choice over the admission date and the length of period in hospital meant that anxieties about dependants and their own care could be alleviated. In addition, on an emotional level, being 'cared for' (in a way they felt they would not be in the NHS) was seen as especially important because it was something that they felt they did not usually get, either because it was they who did the caring or because they lived alone.

The private sector allows the patient a degree of choice of admission dates which can be altered without causing long delays in treatment. This flexibility and choice of dates enables women to make arrangements for alternative care for dependants. Such a facility is not normally available with the NHS, when admission dates may be sent at short notice and cancellations may mean a long wait before a further appointment. For some women, finding alternative care for their children while they are in hospital is a source of great anxiety. Women who live a long way from kin, who are single parents, who have husbands who spend long periods away from home or whose husbands cannot take time off work are all likely to experience difficulty. This is especially so when no choice of dates is given or when appointments are cancelled at short notice. Probably even greater difficulty occurs for those women who have to find alternative carers for disabled or elderly dependants. Seven of the women interviewed noted that the choice of dates that would enable them to make alternative arrangements for dependants was an important reason for going private. The following excerpt from an interview illustrates the primacy of this reason for some women:

Q: Can you tell me why you decided to go private this time?
A: Because I have an elderly mother which necessitated my having my operation done at a time when she could be cared for, because I knew I would be off my feet and unable to move around. That was the only reason.
Q: Did you tell your GP that you wanted to go private?
A: Yes, he knew why I was doing it because he's also my mother's GP, he knew therefore that there was no way round the situation. If I'd been put on a waiting list, even if they had been fairly cooperative, I couldn't have arranged when I would have been admitted. I have to be dependent on my sister, who is a school teacher, being available to look after my mother and therefore school holidays was my only available time.

While a choice over admission dates as a primary reason for going private was not exclusive to women, the reasons why such a choice was important, was. Five men reported that having a choice over admission dates was a primary reason for going private. For four of them it was important primarily so that they could arrange their work commitments, and two women noted this too. However, no man faced the problem of making alternative arrangements for dependants. Arrangements concerning employment, while necessary, are often not crucial in the way that arrangements concerning dependants can be.

The better care that the women felt they would receive in the private sector was also viewed as an important factor in their decision to go private. In comparison with NHS hospitals, private hospitals are smaller, have lower levels of occupancy, and have patients who, in the majority of cases, are admitted for elective surgery rather than for acute conditions. As a result, patients typically receive more nursing time than they would in the NHS. In addition, many private hospitals often have 'ward hostesses' who cater to patients' personal needs thus freeing nurses to concentrate on nursing rather than domestic duties. The level of attention from consultants also tends to be greater in private hospitals.

The reasons for seeing standards of care as an important reason for going private were again related to women's social situation. 'Better attention' was not seen as important just because it would enable patients to have a more pleasant hospital stay, but because it offered benefits specific to their social situation. For some women with families (seven in this group), better attention was equated with faster recovery, which was seen as important in enabling them to return more quickly to their domestic and familial responsibilities. Again, this factor was not mentioned by men in relation to dependants. Better attention was viewed as especially important where women had young children or children who were at important stages in their lives and in need of support:

> In my particular state at that time it was wonderfully helpful because my husband was living and working in America, my son was at Edinburgh as a student, my daughter was taking her A-levels in June, you know, I really needed to be fit as quickly as I could because I needed to be there, at home with her and I really appreciated the immediacy of the service and the quality.

Nine women in the study lived alone and for eight of them the high level of attention they received in private hospitals was important, more for emotional than practical reasons. On the practical side, some women felt that they were able to choose how long their stay would be in a private hospital. Where women lived alone with no one to look after them this was seen as a crucial choice. However, the benefits that going private offered to such women in emotional terms emerged as even more beneficial. The women who lived alone included elderly widowed people and young single women. These women had no family or close friends living locally, and they noted that the high level of attention given by nurses helped them to feel less lonely than they might have done and made up for their lack of visitors. In addition, the attention was welcomed by such women who, in general, rarely had anyone to look after them:

> I felt like royalty almost... You get waited on hand and foot and have a private room and your own television and everything and when you live on your own it makes a change for someone to look after you. Just to be able to rest is really important in my circumstances. If you go into an NHS hospital, into a ward, there's quite a lot of hustle and you might come out feeling worse because of that and then you have to go home and cope on your own. I felt I wanted to stay there a bit longer, because once you get home you even have to get up and get a cup of tea for yourself.

Only two of the male interviewees lived alone and only one of these reported 'better care' as an important reason for going private. The man who reported this was divorced and lived alone with little social support. However, he is in the minority, both in this sample and in wider society, in having low levels of social support. For men, 'better care' may be a reason for going private but this is unlikely to be related to their familial responsibilities (except in terms of income), or for the novelty of being 'looked after'.

Women's health needs

With the rise of 'consumerism' in the NHS there has been a number of surveys evaluating people's satisfaction with services. One of the overwhelming findings has been that dissatisfaction is focused primarily on the interpersonal behaviour of doctors within the clinical encounter (Stewart, 1984; Speedling and Rose, 1985; Calnan and Williams, 1991). Studies focusing on women have reached the same conclusion (Roberts, 1985). It is within the hospital, rather than the primary health care setting, that these dissatisfactions are most marked. Patients commonly complain of feeling on a 'conveyor belt' in hospital, both as out-patients and in-patients. They complain that they rarely see the same doctor twice and that during consultations doctors seldom give the amount of information they desire or seek regarding their condition. Gail Young has noted that the interpersonal behaviour most desired by patients of their doctors is precisely the opposite of that encouraged by the 'hospital subculture' (Young, 1981).

The poor interpersonal behaviour of hospital doctors is experienced more negatively, and possibly more frequently, by women than men for several reasons. First, the conditions that women commonly present for are ones that require the greatest use of interpersonal skills on the part of doctors. Women tend to present with unspecific complaints more commonly than men (Roberts 1985), and are more likely than men to present with illnesses that may be social in origin and related to the frustration experienced in their social roles or their stage in the life-cycle (Barrett and Roberts, 1978). Secondly, women, in general, want to discuss their condition or the feelings engendered by it more than men (Roberts, 1985). Thirdly, the sexism inherent in medical culture may mean that doctors behave more negatively to female than male patients. There is some evidence that doctors' ideal patient is male rather than female (Roberts, 1985) and that the conditions that women frequently present for are not taken seriously (Lennane and Lennane, 1973). If this is the case, it seems likely that women's experience of doctors in terms of their interpersonal skills is more negative than that of men.

The improved relationship with doctors that was obtainable by going private was identified as one of the great benefits. In general, private patients are seen by consultants (rather than junior doctors) and the same consultant is seen throughout an entire course of treatment. In addition, consultants' behaviour with their private patients is often different from that which an NHS patient could expect: private patients are visited more frequently (in our research private patients were visited daily and sometimes twice a day to check on progress); they are given more time with their consultants; they are treated more informally; they are encouraged to ask any questions or seek information regarding their condition from the consultant and they are given the consultant's home 'phone number which they are invited to ring if they have any concerns or any questions they want to ask. In short, the relationship between patient and consultant tends to be more informal, friendly and egalitarian than in the public sector. Reasons why this different attitude exists do not necessarily lie entirely with consultants. Certainly the principles of the market have some part to play: consultants are doubtless aware that payment for treatment means patients expect a first-class service and failure to provide this may mean a lack of 'customers' and consequently a lack of income. In addition, the less rushed atmosphere in the private sector and the absence of emergencies may enable them to provide this in a way that they cannot in the public sector. However, the element of payment also encourages patients to behave differently. A number of interviewees in the study noted that they expected and demanded more from their consultants because they were paying for their treatment, albeit in most cases indirectly through insurance.

The importance of the improved relationship with doctors in the private sector was noted far more frequently by the women than the men in this study. This indicates the importance women place on the behaviour of clinicians. It may also indicate that women 'demanded' this type of treatment from their doctors more often than men. A total of 20 women (57 per cent), compared with three men, reported the attitude and behaviour of doctors in the private sector was a primary benefit of, if not a reason for, going private.

Nearly half of the sample of women was in the 41–60 years age group. Women in this age group, particularly those not in paid employment, are high users of medical services and tend to express more anxieties about their health and to present with unspecific complaints or illnesses that may relate to their social roles, or lack of them, at this stage in their life-cycle (Barrett and Roberts, 1978). Nine of the 15 middle-aged women in the sample were not in full-time paid employment. These women were high users of GP services, consulting an average of seven times a year, compared with the women in full-time paid employment and the men in the study who, on average, consulted their GPs less than three times a year. Doctors often do not take seriously women's complaints when they are high users of their services, categorising them as 'neurotic' (Lennane and Lennane, 1973; Barrett and Roberts, 1978). There was evidence that when they were referred to consultants in the

NHS some of these women felt that their conditions were not taken seriously. In all, seven women reported experiences of not being 'taken seriously' by doctors:

> My mother had just died from ovarian cancer and I was worried because I thought I might have the same thing and it was decided that I should see this consultant and he was terribly intimidating. He just gave me no time at all, just swept in and swept out. He pronounced, and I can remember his words as he deposited me on the ground, 'Madam, you have a very quiet pelvis' was what he said as he swept out.

> I had an experience when I had writer's cramp, my hand just seized up and I couldn't write. I saw one doctor after another and in the end I gave up because it wasn't getting anywhere and they weren't taking me seriously... They just thought I was a hysterical woman.

These women wanted not just to be taken seriously but also to have the opportunity to discuss their conditions and have their anxieties about their health allayed. In addition, a further 13 women reported that the greater attention from doctors was a primary reason for going private:

> My prime reason for paying was to have lots of time with this man... I thought: no, I'm going to have a bit more time to really talk to somebody and to get some sort of follow-up.

The expectation that going private would enable the women to have the attention that they required from their consultants was realised in many cases:

> When I went to see Mr R he looked at my knee and said 'Right, we'll have it X-rayed' and then you look at the X-ray and discuss it. You know what's going on. They don't treat you as an idiot.

> He was very nice, very pleasant. He spoke to me, but there again he had the time – instead of having five minutes per patient he had half an hour... I felt more at ease, I think, because he had more time for me and I suppose I had more chance to say what was bothering me. I thought he was more approachable than

perhaps he would be on the NHS. I've seen the same chap with my daughter on the NHS and he was very short, very brisk.

Thus, for these women going private meant that they could get the sort of treatment that they wanted from their consultants. They were given, or encouraged to seek, the information and reassurance that they needed. Furthermore, they had their health concerns taken seriously in a way that they felt did not happen in the NHS, even though the consultants that they saw privately may have been the same ones that they would have seen as NHS patients.

Only three men reported that the greater information or reassurance they received from consultants was a primary reason for, or benefit of, going private. Two of these three men were divorced and these were the only men in the study who lived alone.

Privacy, dignity and modesty

The privacy, dignity and modesty available in the private sector emerged as reasons for women choosing to go private or benefits that women felt they gained by going private. A total of 18 women (51 per cent) reported these factors as important, to some degree, in their decision to seek private treatment. Eight men (40 per cent) reported privacy as an important factor but their reasons differed from those given by the women. For the men, privacy was noted as important, in most cases, in that it offered them 'peace and quiet'. For the women there were four ways that privacy, dignity and modesty were seen as important. First, the use of single rooms in the private sector enabled patients to control how much other patients knew about them, their feelings and their condition. This is not usually possible in the NHS where the majority of patients are in wards of at least four beds with the only privacy available being a thin curtain around the bed. Secondly, the en suite bathrooms in private hospital rooms eliminated the necessity of sharing the same toilet as others, which many patients viewed as distasteful. Thirdly, privacy and the absence of medical and nursing students in private hospitals encouraged some people to feel that they could maintain an element of dignity which was not possible in the NHS. Finally, a number of patients felt that privacy enabled them to retain some modesty concerning their bodies and their bodily functions.

Willcocks *et al.* (1987, p. 5) note that privacy, which they conceptualise as being 'the potential for both concealing and revealing certain information about oneself' is seriously threatened in institutional settings. Certainly this is true within hospitals, at a time when heightened feelings of vulnerability may occur. Being able to control information about oneself is greatly increased in private hospitals because of the privacy a single room offers. Nine women noted that they did not want other people to see them in pain or that they wanted to control the amount of information people had about them, particularly if they felt distressed. The following responses were typical:

> Well, with that sort of problem [infertility], it's better than being in a ward with lots of people . . . it's probably better to keep it anonymous.

> I don't like people to see me upset and I found that very distressing [in the NHS] because I needed to cry but I had to bury my head in the pillow and the people in the next bed could hear what the doctor was saying.

No men said that they wanted privacy so that people would not see them in pain or know how they were feeling.

Having a private bathroom was also viewed as an important benefit. Twelve women reported an acute distaste at having to share toilets in NHS hospitals. They felt that sharing toilets with others was something that was 'not nice' or 'not hygienic'. Some women felt that the toilets in NHS hospitals were 'dirty' but more than this there was a feeling that sharing toilets with strangers, who may have different standards of cleanliness from themselves, was distasteful.

Only one man in the study noted the importance of en suite facilities in his decision to go private. The reasons why this was more important for women than men probably stems from their greater involvement with cleaning and housework and the greater emphasis on personal hygiene in their socialisation.

Ten women noted that they were treated with more dignity in the private sector than the NHS. Again the privacy afforded in a single room meant that other patients did not overhear intimate discussions of their condition or care. Additionally, the absence of medical and nursing students meant that people did not feel that they were 'on show' as 'exhibits' as some people felt in the NHS. Again, only two men mentioned this.

The reason most frequently cited by women regarding this topic was to maintain some modesty over their body and bodily functions. One of the central lessons of socialisation that girls learn is that to be socially acceptable they must dress and behave with modesty and not 'flaunt' their bodies and their sexuality (Smith, 1990). The same behaviour is not taught to, or expected from, boys from whom a certain brashness regarding their body, bodily functions and sexuality is tolerated and even expected. Evidence of the classic 'double standard' is widespread: the communal baths of male sporting activities, of which there is no equivalent in female sports, and the communal nature of male urinals as opposed to the privacy of women's toilets are two such examples.

On admission to hospital, patients have to allow their bodies to be seen and touched by strangers and their bodies and bodily functions become, to some extent, public property. In the NHS far less modesty regarding bodies is possible than in the private sector. In the NHS rooms, bathrooms and toilets are shared and wards are often mixed sex. Given women's greater socialised modesty than men's it would seem likely that they would experience more embarrassment regarding their bodies in NHS hospitals than men:

> I don't like the thought of having to sort of cock your leg out of bed and show the world everything you've got... I didn't want to be wandering around on a ward with men wandering around as well.

This contrasts with the following description from a male interviewee regarding a stay in an NHS hospital, which clearly indicates the differences that exist for men and women in relation to their bodies:

> I had a good time in there with the young nurses. They used to have to wash my back in the bath and things like that. And I just used to lie on the bed in my boxer shorts and to wander round the ward like that, because it was comfortable and the sister said 'Mr W I really think you should put some more clothes on' and I used to laugh and the nurses used to say 'Oh no we like him like that.'

A futher factor encouraging women to opt for the private sector is the perceived greater use of male nursing staff in the NHS. One interviewee noted her mother's acute embarrassment at being nursed by a male nurse following a mastectomy. Such feelings may be widespread and relate to the 'taboos' regarding men caring for women's intimate health needs (Ungerson, 1987). However, this was not mentioned as a reason for, or benefit of, women going private among this sample.

Control over treatment

The experience of illness is often one of fear resulting from feelings of loss of control over one's body. This is particularly so with illnesses that are potentially life-threatening, such as cancer, or chronic conditions, such as back pain (Fallowfield and Clark, 1991). People with such conditions commonly feel that their bodies are being taken over by illness and that they are being carried towards a future over which they have little control (Martin, 1990). One way to regain feelings of control over one's body is to gain knowledge about what is happening and why, and to participate, at some level, in the treatment. By doing this patients can feel less like victims and more like positive actors in the fight against their illness (Kfir and Slevin, 1991). In addition to the psychological benefits, patient participation in medical treatment can be of advantage in finding the most appropriate and effective forms of treatment. There is some evidence of moves towards greater patient participation in treatment in the public sector. However, progress is slow and the growth of self-help groups and alternative therapies which aim to give patients greater control over their condition / treatment demonstrate the failure of the statutory sector to provide this. The potential for patient participation is far greater in the private sector where the element of payment gives patients greater power.

Only a minority of the women in the interview sample (seven) noted the importance of being 'in control' of their treatment in some way as a factor influencing their decision to go private. One of the reasons may have been that the majority of women, in common with most private patient populations, were admitted for elective routine surgery. Such conditions are generally specific, operable and in many cases visible (for example, hernias and varicose veins) and do not, in general, lead to the strong feelings of lack of control that chronic or more serious conditions do. All the women who noted the importance of being 'in control' were admitted for conditions that were not visible and were potentially dangerous, such as gynaecological operations where there was the threat or fear of cervical cancer, or conditions that were chronic and incurable, such as severe back pain. However, while only a minority of women in this study noted the importance of being 'in control' of their treatment, those who did stressed the importance of this very strongly and noted their inability to achieve this in the NHS. The importance of feeling 'in control' in the face of illness was articulated quite clearly by these women:

> I'm not keen on putting myself 100 per cent in the hands of the medical profession. I'm not very good at that. I like to be in control.

> I get very nervous when I'm not in control when I'm ill.

The women noted that, as private patients, they were able to maintain control by negotiating the sort of treatment that they had in a way that was not possible in the NHS. They were able to talk to their consultant about the form their treatment would take and their own perspectives on their condition and treatment were discussed. This was viewed as particularly valid when people had chronic health problems which involved pain control: rather than being prescribed medication patients were consulted about the sort of treatment they wanted and the efficacy of particular drugs. The following quotation is from a woman who had experienced long-term back problems which caused her severe pain:

> It's a two-way thing. I can offer up suggestions to my consultant, he can say no to some of my suggestions, I can say no to some of his. We work together. The same with the nurses, particularly on the drug situation. And I've been able to say 'I'm only having Dr N anaesthetising me' he's the only one I trust ... Pain makes you feel very vulnerable and out of control so it's important to me to feel in control of my treatment.

Interestingly, no men reported feeling a need to be 'in control' as a reason for going private.

Conclusion

At the beginning of this chapter two questions were posed: first, whether the benefits of going private for women are benefits that are not available in the NHS and, second, whether men and women feel they acquire different benefits from the private sector. The factors that the women in this study identified as reasons for, or advantages of, going private centre around three issues: the ability to choose admission dates; the availability of 'better' care/attention; and the opportunity for privacy. For many women in the sample, these conditions were not currently being met by the NHS to their satisfaction. This is particularly true of the ability to choose admission dates and the opportunity for privacy. The availability of 'better' care and/or attention in the private sector is a more debatable point. The lack of regulation in the private sector coupled with the high levels of satisfaction reported in some NHS consumer surveys may indicate a greater equality between the two sectors than some private patients believe (Halpern, 1985). However, private hospitals do, in general, provide the patient with more care and/or attention (through access to more professional time) and allow for greater participation in treatment than the NHS and this is what 'better' meant to the people in this study. This 'better' care occurs in the private sector because of the element of payment which both encourages patients to demand more and encourages nurses and consultants to view patients' needs and wants as central. Such practices may be less likely in the NHS, given the lack of power that can be wielded by patients, the greater numbers of patients and the pressures of time and money.

However, while some of the advantages of going private identified by the women are not, at present, available within the NHS, the question arises as to whether they could be in the future. The Government's White Paper *Working for Patients* focuses on some of the issues identified by the women in this study. In terms of choosing admission dates it notes the need for change in the NHS from a system in which people 'may have little if any choice over the time or place at which treatment is given' and where 'admission to hospital is sometimes too impersonal and inflexible'. The need for improvements in care is also acknowledged in the White Paper which notes the importance of providing a service which 'considers patients as people' (Department of Health 1989, p. 6). In addition, the need for medical audit to assess the quality of medical care in the NHS is noted (ibid., 1989, p. 39). The *Citizen's Charter* document goes further in relation to some of the issues identified by the women in this study. It argues that patients have a right to expect 'involvement, as far as is practical, in their own care and treatment' and 'control, with a right to give or withhold consent to medical treatment'. It also tackles the problem of lack of privacy in the NHS and states that patients have the right to expect 'respect at all times for privacy, dignity, religious and cultural beliefs' (John Major, 1991, p. 10).

The second issue is whether the reasons for, or perceived benefits of, going private for women are different from those of men's. While the men and women in this study gave similar primary reasons for going private, a closer examination showed clear sex differences. Obviously these differences were not uniform: some men and women reported the same reasons. In general, the reasons given followed a division by sex.

For the men in the study the most common reason for going private was to allow for minimum disruption to their employment. Thus, the ability to choose admission dates, the availability of 'better' care and the opportunity for privacy were all important in that they allowed the planning of work schedules, encouraged a fast recovery, and enabled work to be carried out in hospital without interruption. While a number of the women in the study were in paid employment, work was not given the same priority. For the women, choice of admission date and 'better' care were important to enable planning and to aid a quick recovery, not to minimise disruption at work but, rather, or more importantly, to minimise disruption at home. This difference is a result, and a reflection, of the differing sex roles of men and women. While a large proportion of women remain in paid employment through most of their lives and make a large or even equal contribution to the family income, the sex role ideology of man as provider and woman as carer persists. Where women live in families, whether in paid employment or not, they have primary responsibility for child care and domestic work.

'Better' care emerged as an important reason for the women choosing to go private because of their greater inclination to discuss their condition and participate in their treatment than men and the advantages gained by being 'looked after'. In terms of discussion of condition and participation in treatment, the men appeared to have great trust in their doctors and felt no need to discover more about their condition or discuss treatment to any great degree. In part this may be due to the fact that interest and responsibility for health is primarily a woman's concern. In terms of being 'looked after', the men did not report this as an important reason for, or benefit of, going private. Again, this may relate to women's social roles where being 'looked after' is a novel situation.

Privacy emerged as a reason for, or benefit of, going private in a different way for the women than for the men. For the women in this study, the desire for privacy was related to maintaining modesty and dignity. Again, reasons for this are likely to be related to women's socialisation.

This research has demonstrated that while the broad reasons for choosing to go private may be the same for both genders the factors that go to make up these reasons are, in fact, very different. The people who participated in this research are not a representative group of a general population. The sample consists of people who have actually used private health care facilities (rather than those who have the capacity to use such facilities) and is highly skewed towards social classes I and II. The findings are not generalisable to a wider population. Further research is needed to discover the extent to which the type of health care people desire is gendered amongst wider populations, and the impact of further divisions of class, age and race. Without this, improvements to public services may not occur. It is not adequate to state, as the *Citizen's Charter* has done, that people have the right to 'privacy' without examining what 'privacy' means to different groups. In addition, it is not adequate to talk about the rights of the NHS consumer as if they are a homogeneous group whose needs and wants are all the same. Consumers of health care are both men and women and their health care needs, and indeed underlying reasons for and interpretations of these needs, are likely to be very different.

The New Reproductive Technology: Problem or Solution?

JENNIFER STRICKLER

The feminist response

Feminist literature in the last two decades has criticised the increasing medicalisation of reproduction (Gordon, 1977; Ehrenreich and English, 1978; Ruzek 1978; Petchesky, 1980). To many feminist scholars, reproductive technologies are just a new form of medical interference with women's bodies. In this chapter I examine the arguments of a variety of books and articles which present the feminist analysis of technology and procreation. In addition, I draw on the proceedings of several conferences which have dealt with the impact of reproductive technologies on the lives of women.

Definition of the problem

While infertile women see IVF as one of the many medical treatments for infertility, most feminists who write on the topic see a qualitative difference between infertility treatment, which 'needs to be recognized as an issue of self-determination' (Rothman, 1989, p. 140), and the new procreative technologies, which threaten women's role in procreation (Corea, 1985; Rothman, 1989). One of the best-known feminist health books *Our Bodies, Ourselves* (Boston Women's Health Book Collective 1976), has one chapter on infertility which encourages treatment, and another, fairly critical, chapter on reproductive technology.

While few feminists come out in support of procreative technology, there is extensive debate among feminist scholars about similar

From Jennifer Strickler, 'The New Reproductive Technology: Problem or Solution?', *Sociology of Health and Illness*, 14 (1) (1992).

issues such as parental leave, surrogate motherhood and women's participation in the military, where privileging motherhood is posed in opposition to equality with men. In fact, these policy debates can be seen as real-world applications of two threads of feminist theory: the 'essentialist' view which sees women as inherently different from men; and the 'structuralist' view which sees male–female differences as products of social interaction and/or social structure.

These two lines of feminist analysis translate into two separate critiques of IVF and similar technologies. First, the investment in and emphasis on new technologies which facilitate biological parenthood reinforce the idea that women need to be mothers in order to feel fulfilled. Since motherhood has historically been an important justification for limiting women's opportunities in society, many feminists are very apprehensive about technological developments which place motherhood at the centre of women's lives.

Second, technological conception transfers reproductive control from women to physicians. While recognising that some women who are unable to conceive may benefit from IVF, the feminist literature asserts that on a societal level this technology harms women as a collective group more than it helps them. From this perspective, feminists who put a high value on motherhood find the technologies threatening, since women lose control over conception, as well as gestation. IVF pregnancies are very closely monitored by physicians, and in fact are more likely to be delivered by Caesarian section (Cohen, Mayaux and Guihard-Moscato, 1988). While the individual women who undergo the procedure may appreciate the availability of medical resources, the concern is that such involvement will legitimate increasing medical involvement in 'natural' pregnancies.

Robyn Rowland writes:

> For feminists, these new techniques mean rethinking our attitudes toward motherhood, pregnancy, and most important, the relationship between an individual's right to exercise choice with respect to motherhood and the necessity for women to ensure that those individual choices do not disadvantage women as a social group... Increased technological intervention into the processes by which women conceive is increasing the male-dominated medical profession's control of procreation and will lead inevitably to greater social control of women by men, (Rowland, 1987, pp. 513, 524).

To feminists, the problem is not a woman's inability to bear children (which is seen as an individual, not social, problem) but the structure and institutions of society which reinforce the necessity of childbearing for women's fulfilment on one hand, and physicians' increasing power in managing procreation on the other.

Technological solutions

This literature treats medical technology as a development which decreases women's control over reproduction and exploits the vulnerability of the infertile:

> Control over one's body is perhaps the central feminist credo. It is what is now feared will be lost through the new reproductive technologies. It was perhaps inevitable in our technological age that conception, the last of the cottage industries, will be taken out of the home and placed in the antiseptic factory of the lab. The fear is that all reproduction will become artificial, given the technical means for it. (Baruch, 1988, p. 136)

Gena Corea states:

> Reproductive technology is a product of the male reality. The values expressed in the technology – objectification, domination – are typical of the male culture. The technology is male-generated and buttresses male power over women. (Corea, 1985, p. 4)

There is expressed concern about the potential routinisation of in vitro fertilisation, following the examples of Caesarean section, ultrasound and foetal monitoring, all of which started out as responses to particular conditions and have become routine procedures (Rothman, 1984). A striking example of this pattern is the use of IVF in cases where the male has a fertility impairment (Lorber, 1989). The least invasive procedure to solve this problem is artificial insemination, which involves non-surgical insemination with sperm from a donor. However, it is becoming more common to use IVF (which involves surgery, drugs and a much higher financial cost) in these cases, in spite of the fact that the woman's reproductive system is unimpaired (Cohen *et al.*, 1988).

A related concern of the feminist literature is the extent of iatrogenic (physician-induced) infertility. Caesarian section, the

IUD and DES (an anti-abortifacient prescribed from 1940 to 1970) are all associated with increased risk of infertility (Overall, 1987; Poff, 1987). Pregnancies from IVF are more likely than naturally conceived pregnancies to result in ectopic pregnancy, a condition which is potentially life-threatening and further damages the reproductive tract (Cohen *et al.*, 1988). In these situations, physicians themselves are responsible for the very condition which they are treating. In light of the fact that several studies (Collins *et al.*, 1983; Correy *et al.*, 1988) estimate the incidence of spontaneous pregnancy among infertility patients at approximately 40 per cent, feminists question the benefit of technological intervention.

The possibility of using reproductive technologies for selection of the sex or other characteristics of a child also concerns many feminists (Powledge, 1981; Corea, 1985; Overall, 1987). IVF could be used for sex preselection through the implantation of embryos of the desired sex. Gena Corea (1985, p. 206) describes this procedure as gynaecidal: 'If many women in the Third World are eliminated through sex predetermination, if fewer firstborn females exist throughout the world, if the percentages of poor women and richer men rise in the overdeveloped nations, then it is indeed gynecide we are discussing.'

Thus, new procreative technology is attacked on four principal grounds: (i) it takes reproductive control away from women and gives it to (mostly male) physicians; (ii) it is physically and emotionally harmful to women; (iii) it reinforces the importance of motherhood in women's lives; and (iv) it carries with it the potential for eugenic uses.

Psychological and social factors

To structural feminists, the psychic pain of infertility comes from two sources: the inability to fulfil their socially constructed desire to have children, and the stress of going through infertility treatment. They point out that women are trained from childhood to be mothers and have few alternatives for fulfilling lives (Chodorow, 1978; Overall, 1987). The importance of genetic ties to children is culturally and historically specific (Zelizer, 1985; Stanworth, 1987), and to assert otherwise 'is a remnant of biological deterministic thinking (akin to "mother-right") that should have no place in feminist thought' (Petchesky, 1980).

While recognising that the infertile do suffer emotionally, feminists deny that medical intervention is the appropriate response:

> The suffering infertility causes women is enormous and deserves to be treated seriously. I do not think that those who respond to the suffering by offering to probe, scan, puncture, suction and cut women in repeated experiments are taking that suffering more seriously than I. They are not asking how much of women's suffering has been socially structured and inflicted and is therefore not inevitable. (Corea, 1985, p. 6).

In many cases medical treatment only exacerbates the suffering of infertile women, since treatment is lengthy, painful and generally ineffective. Furthermore, by offering increasingly extreme technologies, physicians make it more difficult to choose non-motherhood, thus reinforcing the status quo (the idea that women need to be mothers to feel fulfilled). As the feminist philosopher Deborah Poff (1987, p. 113) explains:

> A precondition for choice is a meaningful alternative. This requires that men and women cease to believe that childbearing is essential to the definition and nature of being a woman. It also requires that women have equal access to education, equal career or job choices, equal pay for the same jobs and equal pay for work of equal value.

Bibliography to Section VII

Arditti, R., Duelli-Klein, R., and Minden, S. (1984) *Test-tube Women: What Future for Motherhood?*, London: Pandora Press.

Barrett, M. and Roberts, H. (1978) 'Doctors and their Patients: The Social Control of Women in General Practice', in C. Smart and B. Smart (eds) *Women, Sexuality and Social Control*, London: Routledge & Kegan Paul.

Baruch, E.H. (1988) 'A Womb of His Own', in E.H. Baruch *et al.* (eds) *Embryos, Ethics, and Women's Rights: Exploring the New Reproductive Technologies*, New York: Haworth Press.

Boston Women's Health Book Collective (1973 and 1976) *Our Bodies, Ourselves: A Book by and for Women*, New York: Simon & Schuster.

Burgoyne, J., Ormrod, R. and Richards, M. (1987) *Divorce Matters*, Harmondsworth: Penguin.

Calnan, M. and Williams, S. (1991) 'Please Treat Me Nicely', *Health Service Journal*, 17 January.

Calnan, M., Cant, S., and Gabe, J. (1993) *Going Private: Why People Pay for their Health Care*, Buckingham: Open University Press.

Chodorow, N. (1978) *The Reproduction of Mothering: Psychonalysis and the Sociology of Gender*, Berkeley: University of California Press.

Clarke, L., Farrell, C. and Beaumont, B. (1983) *Camden Abortion Study*, Solihull: British Pregnancy Advisory Service.

Cohen, J., Mayaux, M.J. and Guihard-Moscato, M.L. (1988) 'Pregnancy Outcomes after In Vitro Fertilization', *Annals of the New York Academy of Sciences*, 541, pp. 1–6.

Collins, J.A., Wrixon, W., Janes, L.B. *et al.* (1983) 'Treatment-independent Pregnancy among Infertile Couples', *New England Journal of Medicine*, 309, pp. 1201–6.

Corea, G. (1984) *The Mother Machine: Reproductive Technologies from Artificial Insemination to Artificial Wombs*, New York: Harper & Row.

Correy, J., Watkins, R.A. *et al.* (1988) 'Spontaneous Pregnancies and Pregnancies as a Result of Treatment in an In Vitro Fertilization Program Terminating in Ectopic Pregnancies or Spontaneous Abortions', *Fertility and Sterility*, 50, pp. 85–8.

Davies, P. (1987) 'Private Sector is Bedding in', *Health Service Journal*, 9 April.

Department of Health (1989) *Working for Patients*, London: HMSO.

Department of Health (1991) *Health and Personal Social Services Statistics for England*, 1991 Edition, London: HMSO.

Department of Health (1992) *Maternity Services: Government Response to the Second Report from the Health Committee, Session 1991–92*, Cm 2018, London: HMSO.

Department of Health (1994) *Changing Childbirth*, London: HMSO.

Donnison, J. (1977) *Midwives and Medical Men: A History of Inter-professional Rivalries and Women's Rights*, London: Heinemann.

Doyal, L. (1987) 'Infertility – a Life Sentence? Women and the National Health Service', in M. Stanworth (ed.) *Reproductive Technologies*, Cambridge: Polity Press in association with Blackwell.

Duelli-Klein, R. (ed.) (1989) *Infertility: Women Speak Out about their Experiences of Reproductive Medicine*, London: Pandora.

Ehrenreich, B. and English, D. (1973) *Witches, Midwives and Nurses: A History of Women Healers*, New York: Feminist Press.

Ehrenreich, B. and English, D. (1978) *For Her Own Good: 150 Years of the Experts' Advice to Women*, New York: Anchor Press.

Fallowfield, L. and Clark, A. (1991) *Breast Cancer*, London: Tavistock.

Feldman, R. (1987) 'The Politics of the New Reproductive Technologies', *Critical Social Policy*, Issue 19, Summer, pp. 21–39.

Finch, J. and Groves, D. (eds) (1983) *A Labour of Love: Women, Work and Caring*, London: Routledge & Kegan Paul.

Foster, P. (1995) *Women and the Health Care Industry: An Unhealthy Relationship* Buckingham: Open University Press.

Gordon, L. (1977) *Woman's Body, Woman's Right: A Social History of Birth Control in America*, Harmondsworth: Penguin.

Graham, H. and Oakley, A. (1981) 'Competing Ideologies of Reproduction: Medical and Maternal Perspectives on Pregnancy', in H. Roberts (ed.) *Women, Health and Reproduction*, London: Routledge & Kegan Paul.

Halpern, S. (1985) 'What the Public Thinks of the NHS', *Health Service Journal*, 6 June.

Higgins, J. (1988) *The Business of Medicine: Private Health Care in Britain*, London: Macmillan.

Holmes, H.B. and Purdy, L.M. (eds) (1992) *Feminist Perspectives in Medical Ethics*, Bloomington: Indiana University Press.

Horne, D. (1984) 'A Survey of Patients in the Private Sector', *Hospital and Health Services Review*, March.

House of Commons (1992) *Maternity Services, Health Committee Second Report, Session 1991–92*, London: HMSO.

Kelley, J., Evans, M.D.R., and Headey, B. (1993) 'Moral Reasoning and Political Conflict: The Abortion Controversy', *British Journal of Sociology*, 44 (4), pp. 589–611.

Kfir, N. and Slevin, M. (1991) *Challenging Cancer: From Chaos to Control*, London: Tavistock.

Lorber, J. (1989) 'Choice, Gift or Patriarchal Bargain? Women's Consent to In Vitro Fertilization in Male Infertility, *Hypatia*, 4, pp. 23–36.

Lennane, K. and Lennane, R. (1973) 'Alleged Psychogenic Disorders in Women: A Possible Manifestation of Sexual Prejudice', *New England Journal of Medicine*, 288, pp. 288–92.

Major, John (1991) *The Citizens' Charter, Raising the Standard*, London: HMSO.

Martin, J. (1990) 'A Better Life after Cancer', *The Guardian*, 25 May.

Nicholl, J., Beeby, N. and Williams, B. (1989) 'Comparison of the Activity of Short Stay Independent Hospitals in England and Wales, 1981 and 1986', *British Medical Journal*, 298, pp. 239–47.

Oakley, A. (1979) *Becoming a Mother*, Oxford: Martin Robertson.

Oakley, A. (1980) *Women Confined: Towards a Sociology of Childbirth*, Oxford: Martin Robertson.

Oakley, A. (1984) *The Captured Womb: A History of the Medical Care of Pregnant Women*, Oxford: Blackwell.

Office of Population, Censuses and Surveys (OPCS) (1995) *Abortion Statistics 1992, no. 19*, London: HMSO.

Overall, C. (1987) *Ethics and Human Reproduction: A Feminist Analysis*, Boston: Allen & Unwin.

Petchesky, R.P. (1980) 'Reproductive Freedom: Beyond "a Woman's Right to Choose"', *Signs*, 5, pp. 661–85.

Poff, D. (1987) 'Content, Intent and Consequences: Life Production and Reproductive Technology', *Atlantis*, 13, pp. 111–15.

Powledge, T (1981) 'Unnatural Selection: On Choosing Children's Sex', in H.B. Holmes, B. B. Hoskins and M. Gross (eds) *The Custom-made Child?: Women-centered Perspectives*, Clifton: Humana Press.

Reid, I. and Wormald, E. (eds) (1982) *Sex Differences in Britain*, London: Grant McIntyre.

Roberts, H. (ed.) (1981) *Women, Health, and Reproduction*, London: Routledge & Kegan Paul.

Roberts, H. (1985) *The Patient Patients*, London: Pandora Press.

Roberts, H. (1990) *Women's Health Counts*, London: Routledge.

Rothman, B.K. (1984) 'The Meanings of Choice in Reproductive Technology', in R. Arditti, R. Duelli-Klein and S. Minden (eds) *Test-tube Women: What Future for Motherhood?*, London: Pandora Press.

Rothman, B.K. (1989) *Recreating Motherhood: Ideology and Technology in a Patriarchal Society*, New York: Norton.

Rowland, R. (1987) 'Technology and Motherhood: Reproductive Choice Reconsidered', *Signs*, 12, pp. 512–29.

Ruzek, S.B. (1978) *The Women's Health Movement: Feminist Alternatives to Medical Control*, New York: Praeger.

Salter, B. (1995) 'The Private Sector and the NHS: Redefining the Welfare State', *Policy and Politics*, 23(1), pp. 17–30.

Savage, W. (1986) *A Savage Enquiry: Who Controls Childbirth?*, London: Virago.

Smith, J. (1990) *Misogynies*, London: Faber.

Spallone, P. (1989) *Beyond Conception: The New Politics of Reproduction*, London: Macmillan.

Spallone, P., and Steinberg, D.L. (eds) (1987) *Made to Order: The Myth of Reproductive and Genetic Progress*, Oxford: Pergamon Press.

Speedling, E. and Rose, R. (1985) 'Building an Effective Doctor–Patient Relationship: From Patient Satisfaction to Patient Participation', *Social Science and Medicine*, 2, pp. 115–20.

Stanworth, M.D. (1987) 'Reproductive Technologies and the Deconstruction of Motherhood', in M.D. Stanworth (ed.) *Reproductive Technologies: Gender, Motherhood and Medicine*, Cambridge: Polity Press in association with Blackwell.

Stewart, M. (1984) 'What Is a Successful Doctor–Patient Interview? A Study of Interactions and Outcomes', *Social Science and Medicine*, 19, pp. 167–75.

Timmins, N. (1985) 'US Group Buys GP Service', *The Times*, 31 July.

Ungerson, C. (1987) *Policy is Personal: Sex, Gender and Informal Care*, London: Tavistock.

Willcocks, D., Peace, S. and Kellaher, L. (1987) *Private Lives in Public Places*, London: Tavistock.

Williams, B., Nicholl, J., Thomas, K. and Knowelden, J. (1985) *A Study of the Relationship between the Private Sector of Health Care and the NHS in England and Wales*, Sheffield: Department of Community Medicine, University of Sheffield.

Young, G. (1981) 'A Woman in Medicine: Reflections from the Inside', in H. Roberts (ed.) *Women, Health and Reproduction*, London: Routledge & Kegan Paul.

Zelizer, V. (1985) *Pricing the Priceless Child: The Changing Social Value of Children*, New York: Basic Books.

VIII

Women and the Personal Social Services

Introduction

CLARE UNGERSON

The term 'personal social services' is taken to include all those services traditionally provided by Social Service Departments (Social Work Departments in Scotland) and thus includes social work, domiciliary services such as home care, respite services, day centres, aids and adaptations, and, occasionally, money. The position of women in relation to these services has traditionally been a complicated one. On the one hand, as Mary Langan points out in her chapter, women predominate as employees in Social Service Departments, even though they tend to be heavily concentrated in the lower status and less well paid jobs in the social services than their male counterparts. Women's predominance in these 'caring professions' reflects the historical role that women have played in the establishment of social work as a profession (Prochaska, 1980; Lewis, 1991) and in the traditions of nurturance associated with femininity (Abbott and Wallace, 1990). On the other hand, most of the recipients of social work services tend to be women (Hallett, 1989). Thus within the personal social services, women social workers, care assistants, home carers and wardens encounter predominantly female clients.

Relations between professionalised female providers and stigmatised female recipients have historically been difficult (Lewis, 1985) and continue to be so to the present day (Comley, 1989). However, second wave feminism has led to the acknowledgement and analysis of these difficulties with a view to developing a new form of feminist social work practice where relations between social workers and their clients are placed on a more equal footing (Hanmer and Statham, 1988; Dominelli and McLeod, 1989; Langan and Day, 1992). This literature has led to the widespread introduction of training in feminist social work practice and to 'anti-sexist' procedures at the workplace. These are very important changes and should not be downplayed. However, Dominelli and McLeod argue that feminist social work practice depends as much on the political support of feminists working in the higher echelons of local and central government as it does on the existence of feminist social workers, and they suggest that the existence of 'women's units' in local government will provide a basic support network for feminist social work practice. They write within a frame of relative optimism. But since their book was published, many of these 'women's units' have disappeared or been radically reduced in powers and resources. While it is unlikely that the impact of feminism on social work education and practice can be totally expunged, it is also probably true that it is the structure and objectives of social work, with its complex mix of controlling and provisioning functions, that will always be the basis for conflict over rights and resources between women, as social workers, and women as clients, who are in totally different positions of power and legitimacy.

As well as intrinsic conflicts between women as providers and women as users of social services, there are external forces within central and local government and the polity beyond which are at least as powerful, and as radical, as the political efforts of feminists, and which themselves have a considerable gendered impact on the personal social services. These wider forces coming from the polity (particularly since 1979 when the Conservative Party first came to power with a radical agenda for the public sector) have meant that the 1990s have seen the introduction of radical changes in the organisation of the personal social services, particularly in relation to the delivery of so-called 'community care'. The National Health Service and Community Care Act 1990 (implemented in 1993) has made it compulsory for local authorities to withdraw from most of their provisioning functions as far as domiciliary services are concerned. This so-called 'mixed economy of welfare' brings with it a radical restructuring of the tasks and organisation of much of traditional provisioning social work. As far as community care is concerned, most local authorities have divided functions between, on the one hand, 'purchasers' of private and voluntary services, and, on the other hand, 'providers' of services who compete with each other in a market and employ personnel to deliver services at as cheap a rate as possible. Social workers working in the community care arena are renamed 'care managers' and expected to act as organisers of services from a wide variety of sources, and as advisers to their 'users' (the new word for clients) as to where they should best look for self-provisioning.

The ideas behind these reforms are complicated and controversial and, as yet (writing in 1995), their gendered impact is unclear. According to the rhetoric, service provision is to be 'needs led' and sensitive to individual circumstance, 'consumers' or 'users' are to be 'empowered'. Hence it is possible that the predominantly female constituency of users will find themselves in receipt of more efficient and higher quality services than previously. Much of the new system, while recognising the contribution of informal carers, also expects them be the primary carers in most instances (Griffiths, 1988). Yet that rhetorical recognition of carers' needs has in turn made it possible for legislation in the form of the Carers' Recognition and Support Act 1995 to receive all party support and provide for at least some rights to support for carers. If these good intentions are put into practice then in theory the new regime of community care should be more 'user and carer friendly' both to women and to men.

However, Hilary Brown and Helen Smith argue here that there will be important changes in gender relations within the personal social services and that these will impact adversely on women both as carers and users. Their central argument is that gendered inequalities at work will worsen under the new community care regime. If they are right, then it is particularly unlikely that female care-managers working in relatively lowly positions will be able to resist the overwhelming pressure, coming down the managerialist line, to keep costs down, use low-paid or unpaid female labour where they can, and to allocate services only to those whose housekeeping skills and physical abilities are minimal. Moreover, Brown and Smith suggest that 'managerialism' itself is essentially masculine, and that restructuring along managerialist lines is likely to embed men in positions of authority even further. This is a position of relative pessimism.

There is, though, an alternative scenario that is somewhat more optimistic. As a result of the development of line management and devolved budgeting, management, as an occupational task, will spread and diversify (Halford and Savage, 1995). It then becomes possible (other things being equal) that a number of women will be able to demonstrate their managerial aptitudes and move onward and upward into higher managerial positions. Nevertheless, at the same time, other women – the actual service deliverers – will find themselves in increasingly casualised occupations (Baldock and Ungerson, 1991). If more women move into management, even if, in general, the positions of women at work in the personal social services become more unequal, then it becomes possible that women in authority, particularly those who support feminist values, will be in a position to support feminist practice both in the workplace and in relation to users and carers. The need for support for feminist social workers from outside Social Service Departments would no longer be so essential, since the support could come from women working in the higher echelons of the Social Service Departments themselves.

But this more optimistic scenario still faces immense problems. Ruth Eley, an Assistant Director of Social Services, has argued that any woman manager will be relatively isolated and will have considerable problems with her male colleagues (Eley, 1989). Moreover, in a system committed to heavy expenditure constraint at a time of rapidly increasing demand, arising largely out of demographic trends (Baldock, 1994), both women managers and women working at the 'coal face' of personal social service delivery are likely to find themselves under very heavy pressure to cost-cut and ration tightly wherever possible. Women workers within the social services, at whatever level in the occupational hierarchy, will then be sorely tempted to work with rather than against the prevailing norm that women within households should be the primary source of welfare for the people they live with, and that they should do this work relatively unsupported and certainly unpaid. Thus the problem of conflict between those who allocate scarce resources and those who need them is not likely to go away – a gendered sense of unity across social and occupational divides is always extremely vulnerable to problems of scarcity and to the managerial pressures to which that scarcity gives rise.

Who Cares? Women in the Mixed Economy of Care

MARY LANGAN

The restructuring of the personal social services

A number of commentators have argued that the term 'mixed economy of welfare' implies a false counterposition between the (private) sphere of the capitalist economy, which operates according to rigorous free market principles, and the (public) world of welfare which caters simply to social need (Walker, 1984; Knapp, 1989; McCarthy, 1989). Ever since the emergence of the welfare state in the 1940s, the profitable expansion of private capital has always set an external limit on public expenditure on welfare. For the same period, welfare benefits and services have been provided through a mix of private and public mechanisms. Walker writes of a continuum in which the two extremes rarely appear in a pure form, and of 'vague and shifting' borderlines in a complex 'social division of welfare' (Walker, 1984, pp. 19–26). Knapp distinguishes four sectors of supply (public, voluntary, informal and private) and six varieties of demand, producing a '24-cclled matrix' offering 'a bewildering variety' of ways of delivering and financing welfare (Knapp, 1989, p. 23). What is less well recognised is that all sectors of the mixed economy of welfare rely heavily on the labour of women, whether paid in diverse caring occupations, or more commonly, unpaid in the home (Pascall, 1986).

Two key factors have changed the framework of the welfare state and shifted the boundaries between public and private, formal and informal. First, ever since the end of the long post-war expansion in the recession of the mid-1970s, successive governments have

From Mary Langan and Lesley Day (eds) (1992) *Women, Oppression and Social Work*, London: Routledge, pp. 73–8.

squeezed public expenditure in an attempt to reduce the burden on private profitability. The decline of British capitalism has constrained the provision of welfare across the board. Secondly, since Mrs Thatcher's first general election victory in 1979, the government has proclaimed a strong ideological commitment to rolling back the state sector, opening up nationalised industries and welfare services alike to the wider operation of private market forces, and to an even greater contribution from the voluntary and informal sectors.

For a time the personal social services were protected from the full impact of government austerity measures by local authorities which cut housing and education first. However, the combined effect of the continuing financial squeeze and measures to curtail the autonomy of local government resulted in a steady decline in the rate of growth throughout the 1980s. The practice of imposing cash limits led to underspending and undermined planning and innovation (Baldock, 1989; NALGO, 1989). This sluggish growth in resources must be set against the steady increase in demand resulting from demographic and economic trends and from the increasing scale of child abuse, family breakdown, domestic and racial violence, drug abuse and HIV/Aids infection.

The first indication of a major government offensive on the personal social services came in a speech by health minister Norman Fowler in Buxton in 1984. In this speech Fowler first outlined the government's project of fostering an 'enabling role' for Social Service Departments in planning, monitoring, supervising, regulating and supporting a range of private, voluntary and informal welfare services, rather than playing a major role as service providers. He also emphasised the need to use existing resources more efficiently and recommended attempts to attract resources from businesses, charities and voluntary groups. He proposed the more extensive use of charges (for services such as home helps and day centres) and the privatisation of particular services (McCarthy, 1989).

The message of Buxton was amplified in the Audit Commission's 1986 survey of community care, which, although highly critical of the government's poorly planned closure of long-stay institutions, echoed Fowler's demand for greater 'value for money' in social services departments. In 1988 the Griffiths report on community care outlined a comprehensive programme based on the application of the spirit of Buxton to local authority Social Service Departments. What are the consequences of these developments for social work?

By the close of the 1980s the personal social services and the mainstream social work profession were in a state of shock:

> It is hard now to remember the sense of optimism, the belief in the capacity of social workers to make a real impact on the lives of the vulnerable, disadvantaged and disturbed, that characterised the time between the publication of the Seebohm Report (1968) and the advent of the social services departments (1971). (Bamford, 1990, p. ix)

The emergence of the 'generic' social worker as the key figure in the newly created local authority social services departments was one by-product of the liberal social reforms of the 1960s. Twenty years later the world of social work had become more sceptical in its outlook and more pessimistic about the scope for progressive social change.

Conflict and demoralisation were already becoming widespread in social work in the late 1970s, when the tensions between growing demand and stagnating resources became more and more apparent (Clarke, Langan and Lee 1980; Smith, n.d.). Public debate polarised between right wingers who blamed social workers for subverting individual responsibility and social cohesion, and radicals who accused them of facilitating the reproduction of oppressive capitalist social relations. While social service managers took advantage of the cuts to reimpose discipline and to restrict the scope of services, radical social workers looked to community groups, women's organisations, anti-racist movements and diverse self-help organisations to pursue their transformative ideals. The emergence of a feminist perspective on social work, followed in the 1980s by the development of the anti-racist movement in social work, marked the beginning of the new era of anti-discriminatory practice (Wilson, 1977; Dominelli, 1988; Langan and Lee, 1989).

By the early 1980s the ideological attack on social work had become increasingly virulent (Anderson 1980; Brewer and Lait, 1980). Right-wing social policy commentators denounced social workers as hopelessly ineffective, and demanded their abolition or radical reorganisation. When the proposals of Thatcher's Family Policy Group were leaked in 1983, it appeared that the cabinet itself endorsed these views. Prominent social policy academics, such as LSE professor Robert Pinker (1985), adopted a notably defensive posture, making major concessions to the new right critique. In the climate of austerity and vituperation that surrounded social work in the early 1980s, the Barclay Committee attempted to bridge the gap between Seebohm's radicalism and the rampant reaction of the 1980s, and inevitably failed. Its compromise concept of the 'community social worker' was rejected by Pinker, in a minority of one on the committee (Barclay, 1982).

Though Pinker was dismissed as an 'emasculated social democrat' and more recently as 'a lone voice', as the 1980s proceeded his approach converged with that of the government (Leonard, 1982, p. 79; Baldock, 1989, p. 47). Pinker now proposes that social workers reduce their horizons to 'task-centred, problem-solving, crisis intervention, and behaviour modification methods' (Pinker, n.d.). Despite the unpopularity of many of his views within social work, it is likely that Pinker anticipates the trends of the 1990s. Government pressures to curb local authorities, and its determination to extend market forces, as well as the general reaction against the legacy of the 1960s, all point in a similar direction. If social work does have a role in the 1990s it is, at least in the eyes of the government and influential policy experts, as a more specialised service, with a more restricted vision of its role in promoting empowerment and equality, but with a more active role in regulating family life and promoting the mixed economy of welfare. There is little place in this perspective for developing the feminist or anti-racist dimensions of social work practice.

The restructuring of the personal social services by the more rigorous application of market principles is likely to reinforce the existing hierarchical sexual and racial division of labour. Though women constitute only 63 per cent of all local authority workers, they account for 87 per cent of social services staff (Hallett, 1989). Howe's survey of the state of affairs in the late 1970s drew attention to the tendency for women to be concentrated at the lower levels of the social services hierarchy, while men dominated senior positions. In 1977 some 83 per cent of social work assistants and 64 per cent of social workers were women; at every other level from team leader/senior (49 per cent women), through area officer (29 per cent women), divisional area officer (17 per cent), men predominated (Howe, 1986).

More recent figures show that little has changed. Still, more than 90 per cent of directors are male and more than 70 per cent of area officers are men (Popplestone, 1980; Foster, 1987). The LACSAB/ ADSS 1988 survey shows an increasing feminisation at the lower levels of the social services hierarchy: 74 per cent of social workers and 90 per cent of social work assistants are women. This marks the culmination of a trend already noted in the early years after Seebohm, when the 'young Turks' influenced by the radical social work movement began to replace the 'old Maids' associated with traditional casework (Davis and Brook, 1985). This trend has been reinforced by the (male) managerialism of the 1980s. Paradoxically, the growing feminisation of welfare has been accompanied by the further masculinisation of the social services hierarchy.

At the very lowest level of the social services hierarchy – care and domestic staff in homes and day centres, home helps, and other domiciliary care workers – women make up around 75 per cent of staff (Howe, 1986; Jones, 1989). In many areas, manual employment in Social Service Departments provides poorly paid work for white women. In other areas, especially in the inner cities, significant numbers of black women are employed in these jobs (Jones, 1989).

Black people appear to be underrepresented at every level of the social services hierarchy. Though no national statistics are available on the ethnic composition of the social services workforce, local surveys suggest that relatively few black workers are taken on, especially at higher levels (Rooney, 1982; 1987; Hughes and Bhaduri, 1987). Statistics on minority ethnic entrants into relevant training courses confirm continuing racial bias. Though there has been some increase of black recruitment on to social work courses: 'For candidates holding similar qualifications, applicants from the majority ethnic group are more likely to be successful in taking up a place on a course than those from minority ethnic groups' (CCETSW, 1985, p. 17). There is still a marked underrepresentation of minority ethnic students on post-qualification specialist courses (CCETSW, 1986–9).

Changes in training and qualifications for social services staff may consolidate the existing gendered and racialised hierarchy. In addition to the new Diploma in Social Work, an 'advanced award' in social work can now be conferred upon 'advanced' practitioners and social services managers. This award is intended to ratify trends towards more specialist social workers, particularly in the fields of child protection and mental health, where post-qualification courses and dedicated teams are already widespread. The advanced award is intended to encourage the emergence of staff trained in the managerial and commercial skills necessary in the new-style 'enabling' Social Service Department. Meanwhile, for social care staff, a new Certificate in Social Care is planned.

Attempts to raise professional standards and to provide better vocational training for manual staff are undoubtedly to be welcomed. One of the virtues of the new proposals is the way that they begin to recognise care as a skill, rather than as a taken-for-granted female attribute. However, it is important to point out the danger that they may simply reinforce the prevailing polarisation between an overwhelmingly white male management and a predominantly female staff. It is striking, for example, that although many women social workers have moved into the child protection speciality, their advance has been paralleled by that of their male colleagues into the managerial hierarchy where they retain power and authority. Though social work authorities have proclaimed a commitment to providing improved access to minority ethnic applicants, this may not counteract the structural discrimination that tends to prevail in the existing system.

Women Caring for People: The Mismatch between Rhetoric and Women's Reality?

HILARY BROWN AND HELEN SMITH

Women are familiar with the fragmentation of power and responsibility at the heart of the purchaser–provider split; they are, after
all, used to servicing the nation's breadwinners and providing for
dependants within a relationship to their own personal 'purchaser',
whom convention allows to exert emotional, economic and sometimes physical sanctions if their work is not 'up to scratch'. It is an
arrangement which both borrows from, and leans on, traditional
family structures and, like these structures, it shields from view the
immense and ingrained inequality on which it rests.

Thus the hidden agenda behind the new legislation undermines
both women workers and women carers.

The impact on women workers

The physical location of services for people with disabilities has
already moved from hospitals to less formal structures in the community; the NHS and Community Care Act (1990) further dis-
perses the organisational locus of service delivery, by removing it
from the statutory into the private and voluntary sector. This move
was justified by a need to regulate the financing and rationing of
care; however, it is increasingly clear that these aims are to be
achieved through deprofessionalisation and the deregulation of
the terms and conditions of service of people who work in the
service (see Glazer, 1990).

From Hilary Brown and Helen Smith, 'Women Caring for People: The Mismatch between Rhetoric and Women's Reality?', *Policy and Politics*, 21 (3)
(1993), pp. 188–91.

Historically, the professionalisation of caring work allowed some middle-class women to emulate their male colleagues in striving for status and autonomy although in reality the mostly female professions, such as nursing, social work and the therapies, have tended to occupy a twilight zone between the status of their male counterparts and the lowly position of women manual workers. This has created tensions, splitting women from each other, paid from unpaid carers, trained from untrained, black from white and middle from working-class women. Nevertheless, the professions have resisted the characterisation of women's work as unskilled and have had some success in maintaining the rate of women's wages.

New services, particularly those based on the philosophy of normalisation, have sought to present a more 'ordinary' image of the service and the people who use it, but this has cut across the professional definition of roles and tasks, jeopardising the respect shown to people employed as 'support workers', 'care staff' and 'home leaders'. The emphasis on ordinariness, coupled with the unstated but pervasive belief that caring is 'only women's work', led Griffiths (1988) to assume in his report, prefacing the 'Caring for people' legislation, that unskilled and unemployed young people would be able to take over caring work. Thus there is a vicious circle: the fact that women do the work makes it appear unskilled and undemanding, the fact that they are skilled enough to care without straining the appearance of an 'ordinary' relationship further undercuts their need for proper recompense.

The changes envisaged in the new National Health Service are going to have a profound impact on the opportunities open to women, not only for those who aspire towards the top (see, for example, Opportunity 2000), but more significantly for the army of women who work in low-paid and demanding jobs in direct care and other service functions. The National Health Service has a bad record to date on Equal Opportunities (NAHAT, 1988) and the changes are being implemented on shaky foundations.

Theories of occupational discrimination differentiate between *horizontal* segregation, whereby women and men workers are recruited into quite separate professions or groups, and *vertical* segregation which sees women recruited into, but denied promotion in, the same jobs and professions as men (see Crompton and Sanderson, 1990). These groupings remain remarkably intransigent, and as Leidner remarks:

One of the most striking aspects of the social construction of gender is that its successful accomplishment creates the impression that gender differences in personality, interests, character, appearance, manner, and competence are natural – that is they are not social constructions at all. (Leidner, 1991, p. 155)

Davies and Rosser (1986) investigating women's clustering at the bottom of the NHS hierarchy found that there were, in fact, two quite separate hierarchies with different cultures and expectations. The crossover point, at the level of administrator, was inhabited either by mature, experienced women, who had risen from the secretarial ranks or junior graduates, usually men, mobile and able to work long and sometimes inflexible hours, who were on the way up, demonstrating the adage that 'one woman's ceiling is another man's floor' (see also Moss-Kanter, 1977).

Forecasters differ about how the new organisational structures will impact on this bottleneck and about the likely course of women's career paths. Our concern is that the provider–commissioner divide will institutionalise this ceiling effect, eroding women's options for advancement, leaving low-paid and static workers located in provider agencies while the 'high fliers' move around interchangeably from one agency to another. Meanwhile, Goss and Brown (1991, p. 19) are concerned that women managers will face a situation wherein:

men predominately move into 'hard' management roles within the provider units, concentrating on business and financial skills, and women managers are concentrated in 'soft' management roles within the purchaser units, focusing on public health, analysis, monitoring and service development.

The new structures also cut across women rising to management roles within their own largely female professions as these are increasingly brought under the aegis of general management. Goss and Brown (ibid.) remark that: 'restructuring may inadvertently strip out a number of levels of management where women predominated, for example within nursing and the therapies, without creating alternative career paths'. The costs of advancement for women in senior positions are often prohibitive. Goss and Brown (ibid.) note that 93 per cent of male senior managers have children, whereas only 20 per cent of women in such positions do. It is clear that the expected working patterns of managers of care preclude their meaningful presence as carers in the lives of their own families.

Meanwhile, women make up the bulk of the workforce in terms of the actual delivery of care and their reliance on a newly deregulated sector does not bode well for conditions of employment commensurate with the responsibility and arduousness of the work they do. Home helps, for example, are almost exclusively women. Reducing the costs of domiciliary care, while improving productivity, inevitably means reducing wages and job security, destroying the continuity which was established by national pay bodies (Smith, 1991). The consequence of this change may mean that women working in the provider agencies have nowhere to go, work under increasing stress and have to deal additionally with stress in their own lives as a result of low pay, long hours and job insecurity. After all, carers and workers are often the same people! (see Allen, Pahl and Quine, 1988; and Heseldon and Sharrard, 1989.)

Moreover, there is a growing market in individualised packages of care which involve women being 'semi' employed as neighbours or friends to carry out personal tasks for particular individuals. Such work, while portrayed as a flexible and cheap option for meeting service users' needs, again begs the question as to what is proper recompense for women doing this work. Baldock and Ungerson (1991) comment that schemes which pay 'informal' carers make the assumption that 'it is not only possible but morally right to recruit workers who are willing to work unsocial hours for very little pay'.

Crucially then, what the shift in language signifies is a new figuration of power relationships. Beneath the studious gender neutrality of the rhetoric of both community care and new organisational structures are sexualised assumptions about who will do what and about the use of power and resources. These assumptions are implicit in the costing of community care on the basis that women will do it for nothing or for low pay but they also leak into the culture and practices of the new commissioning role. Within commissioning circles, new voluntary and private agencies are sometimes referred to as 'virgin' organisations, while bids for funding are evaluated in terms of how 'sexy' or 'seductive' they are. Such language shows clearly where power lies and with whom. New agencies may naively believe that they can flirt with these powerful organisations from an equal position, but they ignore their relative powerlessness and dependence at their peril and may more cynically conclude that they and the workers who depend on them are vulnerable to being exploited by those who within the new structure 'hold all the cards'.

Thus women workers at all levels are likely to suffer considerable discrimination within the new frameworks. The ideology and the new organisational frameworks act together to confirm women at the lower end of the occupational ladder and to ghettoise those women's professions which previously provided a career path for some women. The deregulation of agencies employing large numbers of women manual workers and the increasing tendency to employ women on piece work contracts in a kind of 'no man's land' risks driving down women's wages at a time of recession. The 'reforms' work by concealing the extent to which they recreate, maintain and exploit a secondary labour market of women.

The impact on carers

How are women, despite their increased participation in the workforce, so easily coopted into caring roles? The 'desire' to care is constructed through what Arendt (1978) has termed 'the existence of relationism'; this relationship-centredness makes others the centre of a woman's life and not her own self. Graham (1990) argues that gender is lived out through the everyday routines of caring and that gender identities are socially constructed and confirmed through such caring. These powerful experiences are integral to women's self concept, as Aronson (1990, p. 76) notes:

> the feelings – guilt and shame – associated with women's concerns at not living up to socially approved notions of giving and receiving care reflect their profound internalisation of cultural prescriptions. Their incorporation and the resulting self-criticism and self-control represent highly effective – and invisible – forms of social control. Motivated to reduce feelings of guilt and shame, women implicitly suppress assertion of their own needs, so that the broad pattern of care [of old people] goes unchallenged – rather it is sustained and reproduced.

Punishment may await those women who do reject this prescribed role. Traustadottir (1988) found that carers of a relative with a learning difficulty received support according to how 'worthy' the Community Mental Handicap Team deemed them to be. In fact, these assumptions were based on gender stereotypical notions that men caring for relatives were 'extra worthy' and so received a high degree of support. Women were assumed to be 'natural' carers and so received less support; those women who preferred not to care and/or wanted to work outside the home were deemed to be 'unworthy' and subsequently received very little statutory support. Thus women quickly learn what they 'should be like'. Traustadottir concludes that it is unsurprising that so few women reject the traditional role of 'natural' caregiver. Yet the enormous cost to individual women is not spoken about – the sacrifice remains invisible, as women remain silent.

Their isolation prevents them from forming an effective lobby as Raymond (1986, p. 154) reflects: 'The rootlessness of women in their own group identity as women contributes more than anything to the wordless, unrealistic and nonpolitical perception that many women have of the world'.

But there are other factors which prevent women recognising a class interest in issues around caring. Graham (1990) cautions against an analysis of caring that focuses solely on gender and does not address issues of class and race. She cites Glenn (1985) who details how black women's lives have been shaped historically by a colonial labour system in which their work outside the family has taken precedence over the needs of their own families. For black women then, caring can be seen 'as a way of resisting racial and class oppression'. Experience of caring is mediated by class and race, as well as gender. As Glazer (1990) notes:

> Women cope differently, depending on class. Women from the upper strata are less likely than others to care continuously for their elderly parents (who also rely on friends) and are less likely than the poor to be in the same community as their parents. Women from households with high incomes may hire substitutes for themselves... In contrast, working class women rarely rely on home care nurses and home health aides.

The impact on women using services

The gender neutrality of the community care rhetoric also obscures the tensions *between* women in their experiences of caring and being cared for (see Brown and Smith, 1992). Aronson (1990, p. 72) in her study of women giving and receiving care noted that women who are caring strive to balance meeting others' needs and meeting their own: 'They face a constant tension between self-enhancement and self-denial. For women being cared for, tension lies between their wish for security and confidence that their needs will be met, and their wish to conform to cultural imperatives to be self-reliant, undemanding.'

Lonsdale (1991) describes how the specific circumstances of women who are disabled, and their unique needs arising out of these circumstances, are not addressed. This may be because the social consequences of disability – passivity, docility and dependence – are assumed to be more easily accepted by women and often considered 'natural' characteristics. Loss of paid employment is seen as less traumatic for women and services more usually focus on them readapting to a role in the home.

When support is offered it tends to replace, rather than complement, their expertise. The male-centredness of much service delivery is highlighted by domiciliary services. The model of care offered by the virtually exclusively female staff group is one that directly replicates normal patterns of labour within the home: home helps do the cleaning, shopping and cooking, yet most of their clients are women, who may feel doubly disempowered by losing some faculties through disability and then having their traditional skills as women usurped. What many elderly or disabled women need is for the roles and responsibilities previously undertaken by their husbands or sons to be offered by the service.

In the acute sector, women's specialities have suffered first, with many abortion, sterilisation, infertility, varicose vein treatment and menopause clinics under threat of contraction or offered only under certain conditions (Newbigging, 1990). This testifies to the fact that women service users do not constitute a powerful lobby and are the first to be jettisoned. Women using long-term care services have to contend with these limitations in their generic health service, as well as face cut-backs in very specific services set up to cater to their particular needs as women with disabilities or mental health problems. These closures in the face of women's needs highlight the fact that this is not in any sense a 'free' market. It is a market controlled by a small, political lobby of mostly white men. (See for example Goss and Brown, 1991, p. 25 showing the minimal numbers of women appointed as non-executive directors of Trusts and Regional Health Authorities.)

Meanwhile, individual women who need services continue to be asking for them from a one-down position with no sense of deserving support as of right and no hope of consultation which taps into their own needs and aspirations.

Bibliography to Section VIII

Abbott, P. and Wallace, C. (eds) (1990) *The Sociology of the Caring Professions*, London; New York: Falmer Press.

Allen, P., Pahl, J., and Quine, L. (1988) '*Staff in the Mental Handicap Services: A Study of Change*, unpublished paper, Health Services Research Unit, University of Kent.

Anderson, D.C. (ed.) (1980) *The Ignorance of Social Intervention*, London: Croom Helm.

Arendt, H. (1978) *The Life of the Mind*, New York: Harcourt.

Aronson, J. (1990) 'Women's Perspectives on Informal Care of the Elderly: Public Ideology and Personal Experience of Giving and Receiving Care', *Ageing and Society*, 10, pp. 61–84.

Baldock, J. (1989) 'United Kingdom – a Perpetual Crisis of Marginality', in B. Munday (ed.) *The Crisis in Welfare: An International Perspective on Social Services and Social Work*, Hemel Hempstead: Harvester Wheatsheaf.

Baldock, J. (1994) 'The Personal Social Services: The Politics of Care', in V. George and S. Miller (eds) *Social Policy Towards 2000: Squaring the Welfare Circle*, London; New York: Routledge.

Baldock, J. and Ungerson, C. (1991) '"What d'ya want if you don't want money?": A Feminist Critique of Paid Volunteering', in M. Maclean and D. Groves (eds) *Women's Issues in Social Policy*, London; New York: Routledge.

Bamford, T. (1990) *The Future of Social Work*, London: Macmillan.

Barclay, P. (1982) *Social Workers: Their Roles and Tasks*, London: Bedford Square Press.

Brewer, C. and Lait, J. (1980) *Can Social Work Survive?*, London: Temple Smith.

Brown, H. and Smith, H. (1992) 'Assertion not Assimilation: A Feminist Perspective on the Normalisation Principle', in H. Brown and H. Smith (eds) *Normalisation: A Reader for the Nineties*, London: Routledge.

CCETSW (1985) 'Ethnic Minorities and Social Work Training', Paper 21.1, October, London: CCETSW.

CCETSW (1986–9) *Data on Training and Reports on Applications*, London: CCETSW.

Clarke, J., Langan, M., and Lee, P. (1980) 'Social Work: The Conditions of Crisis', in P. Carlen and M. Collison (eds) *Radical Issues in Criminology*, Oxford: Martin Robertson.

Comley, T. (1989) 'State Social Work: A Socialist–Feminist Contribution', in C. Hallett, *Women and Social Services Departments*, Hemel Hempstead: Harvester Wheatsheaf.

Crompton, R. and Sanderson, K. (1990) *Gendered Jobs and Social Change*, London: Unwin Hyman.

Davies, C. and Rosser, J. (1986) *Processes of Discrimination: A Report on a Study of Women Working in the NHS*, London: Department of Health and Social Security.

Davis, A. and Brook, E. (1985) 'Women and Social Work', in E. Brook and A. Davis (eds) *Women, the Family and Social Work*, London: Tavistock.

Dominelli, L. (1988) *Anti-racist Social Work*, London: Macmillan.

Dominelli, L. and McLeod, E. (1989) *Feminist Social Work*, Basingstoke: Macmillan.

Eley, R. (1989) 'Women in Management in Social Services Departments', in C. Hallett (ed.) *Women and Social Services Departments*, Hemel Hempstead: Harvester Wheatsheaf.

Foster, J. (1987) 'Women on the Wane', *Insight*, 2 (50), pp. 14–15.

Glazer, N. (1990) 'The Home as Workshop: Women as Amateur Nurses and Medical Care Providers', *Gender and Society*, 4 (4), pp. 479–500.

Glenn, E. (1985) 'Racial Ethnic Women's Labour: The Intersection of Race, Gender and Class Oppression', *Review of Radical Political Economics*, 17, pp. 86–108.

Goss and Brown (1991) *Equal Opportunities for Women in the NHS*, London: Office for Public Management/NHS Management Executive.

Graham, H. (1990) 'The Concept of Caring in Feminist Research', *Sociology*, 25 (1), pp. 61–78.

Griffiths, R. (1988) *Community Care: Agenda for Action: A Report to the Secretary of State for Social Services* London: HMSO.

Halford, S. and Savage, M. (1995) 'Restructuring Organisations, Changing People: Gender and Restructuring in Banking and Local Government', *Work, Employment and Society*, 9 (1), pp. 97–122.

Hallett, C. (1989) 'The Gendered World of the Social Services Department', in C. Hallett (ed.) (1989), *Women and Social Services Departments*, Hemel Hempstead: Harvester Wheatsheaf.

Hallett, C. (ed.) (1989) *Women and Social Services Departments*, Hemel Hempstead: Harvester Wheatsheaf.

Hanmer, J. and Statham, D. (1988) *Women and Social Work: Towards a Woman-centred Practice*, Basingstoke: Macmillan Education, in conjunction with the British Association of Social Workers.

Heseldon, T. and Sharrard, E. (1989) 'Staff development and training for mental handicap services in Medway/Swale Health and Social Services', unpublished paper.

Howe, D. (1986) 'The Segregation of Women and their Work in the Personal Social Services', *Critical Social Policy*, 15, pp. 21–35.

Hughes, R.D. and Bhaduri, R. (1987) *Social Services for Ethnic Minorities and Race and Culture in Social Services Delivery*, Manchester: DHSS Social Services Inspectorate, NW Region.

Jones, G. (1989) 'Women in Social Care: The Invisible Army' in C. Hallet (ed.) *Women and Social Services Departments*, Hemel Hempstead: Harvester Wheatsheaf.

Knapp, M. (1989) 'Private and Voluntary Welfare', in McCarthy, M. (ed.) *The New Politics of Welfare: An Agenda for the 1990's?*, London: Macmillan.

Langan, M. and Lee, P. (1989) 'Whatever Happened to Radical Social Work?', in M. Langan and P. Lee (eds) *Radical Social Work Today*, London: Unwin Hyman.

Langan, M. and Day, L. (eds) (1992) *Women, Oppression and Social Work: Issues in Anti-discriminatory Practice*, London; New York: Routledge.

Leonard, P. (1982) 'Review of "the Essential Social Worker": A Guide to Positive Practice', *Critical Social Policy*, 1 (3), pp. 78–80.

Leidner, R. (1991) 'Serving Hamburgers and Selling Insurance: Gender, Work and Identity in Interactive Service Jobs', *Gender and Society*, 5 (2), p. 155.

Lewis, J. (ed.) (1985) *Labour and Love: Women's Experience of Home and Family, 1850–1940*, Oxford; New York: Blackwell.

Lewis, J. (1991) *Women and Social Action in Victorian and Edwardian England*, Aldershot: Edward Elgar.

Lonsdale, S. (1991) 'Out of Sight, Out of Mind', *Community Care*, 9 May.

McCarthy, M. (1989) 'Personal Social Services', in M. McCarthy (ed.) *The New Politics of Welfare: An Agenda for the 1990's?*, London: Macmillan.

Moss-Kanter, R. (1977) *Men and Women of the Corporation*, New York: Basic Books.

National Association of Health Authorities and Trusts (1988) *Action not Words*, Birmingham: NAHAT.

National Association of Local Government Officers (NALGO) (1989) *Social Work in Crisis: A Study of Conditions in Six Local Authorities*, London: NALGO.

Newbigging, R. (1990) *Suffering the Cuts: A Survey of Cuts in Health Services for Women*, London: London Health Emergency Group.

Pascall, G. (1986) *Social Policy: A Feminist Analysis*, London: Tavistock.

Pinker, R. (1985) 'Family Services', in R. Berthoud (ed.) *Challenges to Social Policy*, London: Policy Studies Institute.

Pinker, R. (n.d.) 'Planning the Mixed Economy of Care', unpublished paper.

Popplestone, R. (1980) 'Top Jobs for Women: Are the Cards Stacked Against Them?', *Social Work Today*, 12 (4), pp. 12–15.

Prochaska, F. K. (1980) *Women and Philanthropy in Nineteenth Century England*, Oxford: Clarendon Press.

Raymond, J. (1986) *A Passion for Friends*, London: Women's Press.

Rooney, B. (1982) 'Black Social Workers in White Departments', in J. Cheetham (ed.) *Social Work and Ethnicity*, London: NISW/George Allen & Unwin.

Rooney, B. (1987) *Racism and Resistance to Change: A Study of the Black Social Workers' Project, Liverpool Social Services Department 1975–1985*, Liverpool: Department of Sociology, University of Liverpool.

Smith, D. (n.d.) 'From Seebohm to Barclay: The Changing Political Nature of the Organisation of Social Work', discussion paper, Manchester: Department of Social Administration, University of Manchester.

Smith, H. (1991) 'Caring for everyone? The Implications for Women of *Caring for People*', *Feminism and Psychology*, 1 (2), pp. 279–91.

Traustadottir, R. (1988) '*Women and Family Care: On the Gendered Nature of Caring*', paper for International Conference on Family Support Related to Disability, Stockholm, Sweden.

Walker, A. (1984) 'The Political Economy of Privatisation', in J. Le Grand, and R. Robinson (eds) *Privatisation and the Welfare State*, London: George Allen & Unwin.

Wilson, E. (1977) *Women and the Welfare State*, London: Tavistock.

IX

Women and Informal Care

Introduction

CLARE UNGERSON

One of the most important contributions of British academic feminism to social policy analysis over the past 20 years has been the identification and analysis of the activity of 'care' as part of unpaid domestic labour. Early British analysis was concerned both with describing care (Finch and Groves, 1983; Briggs and Oliver, 1985) and with counting the number of 'carers' (Equal Opportunities Commission, 1980; 1982). Policy analysis also developed: this looked at the way in which government policies for the decarceration of people with disabilities and policies for 'community care' contained within them assumptions about the availability of women to care for their relatives, neighbours and friends (Land, 1978; Finch and Groves, 1980). As a result of this work, a number of studies were undertaken to look at the processes whereby people became carers, in particular women (Ungerson, 1987; Lewis and Meredith, 1988; Qureshi and Walker, 1989), while others looked at the problem of developing policies of collective provision for care that avoided the exploitation of women (Finch, 1984; Dalley, 1988). Thus a gendered perspective on care contained within it the implicit assumption that 'informal care' (as it rapidly became known within the literature) was a world filled by women, and that analysis of the consequences for policy and for the caring relationship should be based on that assumption (see, for example, Ungerson, 1983; 1990b).

Since that early literature, a number of things have happened which have qualified that perspective. The first is that the British Office of Population Censuses and Surveys (OPCS) decided that the annual General Household Survey – a national sample survey – should in 1985 contain questions designed to identify carers, and

343

ask them about aspects of the work they undertake. The questions that were used to identify carers are reprinted in Table 1 of the excerpt from Arber and Ginn presented here, and from these it will be clear that people were asked to identify themselves if they provided 'special help' and took on 'extra family responsibilities'. Clearly there are some problems of definition here (Ungerson, 1993) and, indeed, there has been some criticism of the way in which the questions were posed such that men were more likely than women to identify themselves as people providing 'special help' (Gibson and Allen, 1993). Nevertheless, when the first publication arising out of that survey appeared in 1988 (Green, 1988) many of those writing about care at that time were given something of a surprise. It seemed, using this data, that proportionately almost as many men (11 per cent) as women (15 per cent) were carers. Indeed, for carers aged over 65, there were proportionately more men carers than women, the reason being that most of them were caring for their frail elderly wives (Central Statistical Office, 1989). Leaving aside the questions of definition of 'care' and taking the dataset as given, there were two major implications: first, that men, as Sara Arber and Nigel Gilbert put it, were 'the forgotten carers' (1989b), and, second, that the feminist analysis had over-emphasised the way in which caring obligations worked across the generations between, for example, daughters and parents and parents-in-law, and underemphasised the way in which caring obligations worked within marriage (Parker, 1990). A literature on the care undertaken by spouses developed, largely carried out by Gillian Parker (see, for example, Parker, 1993). At the same time, further analysis of the General Household Survey dataset revealed that substantial gendered differences did occur in caring, but in qualified ways. For example, women carers on the whole spent more time than men carers engaged in caring tasks and women predominated in the more personal and messy aspects of care (Parker and Lawton, 1994). The piece by Sara Arber and Jay Ginn excerpted here uses the General Household Survey data to look specifically at the informal care of elderly people over 65 years of age and teases out some of the gender differences that occur in the care of different kinds of elderly relatives, within different kinds of informal settings.

The second 'event' in the caring literature was the development, in the late 1980s, of a critique of the feminist literature on care. Part of the critique came from feminists who had themselves been important contributors to the earlier literature. Janet Finch and her colleague Jennifer Mason argued that the early feminist writing had been over-deterministic, and that while there were frameworks of obligations arising out of the culture which were gendered, there were also processes of negotiation occurring within families which mediated those frameworks (Finch, 1989a; Finch and Mason, 1993). Hilary Graham argued that British feminists had overemphasised the gender dimension of care and had been uninformed by currents in mainstream feminism which were developing an integrated analysis of difference, that took account of 'race' and class as well as gender (Graham, 1991). At the same time, a very strong critique of feminist writing on care was mounted by disabled women. Writers such as Jenny Morris (1989; 1991; 1993) and Lois Keith (1992) used the same framework of subjectivity and the critique of 'invisibility' and 'passivity' that had been developed by academic feminism to argue that the feminist caring literature had treated disabled people as themselves invisible, passive, homogenous and dependent. Thus was the biter bit. The excerpt by Jenny Morris presented here provides a summary of her position and that of others writing within and from the subjective experience of being disabled feminists.

The feminist literature on care is now at a further stage of development. Both Hilary Graham (1991) and Clare Ungerson (1995) have pointed out that it is important to qualify the traditional distinction made between, on the one hand, the private domain of informal care delivery where the caregivers are unpaid and, on the other hand, the public domain of social services where the caregivers are paid. Graham has argued that the case of domestic service demonstrates the way in which care has historically been delivered in the private domain by paid workers, and particularly in the United States, by black women. Ungerson has looked at changes taking place in the funding of informal care both here and in other developed countries (Evers, Pijl and Ungerson, 1994) and argued that informal care is increasingly being 'paid' or 'commodified', with important social and economic implications for carers and care recipients. Carol Thomas, in considering the work of Graham and Ungerson and delineating the ways in which these two authors differ, has further suggested a way of analysing 'care' that both includes child care, and also begins to dissolve the conceptual boundaries between formal and informal care (1993). In the piece by Clare Ungerson excerpted here, she presents some of the reasons as to why care within the private domain increasingly has cash attached to it, and suggests some ways of evaluating these trends both for carers in general and for women carers in particular.

Informal Care-givers for Elderly People

SARA ARBER AND JAY GINN

The highlighting of 'carers' as a social group sharing a common problem and a common interest was born out of feminist writing on the domestic labour of women. Caring for elderly people and other dependants was seen as an instance of unpaid work. Because of this, the dominant concern of the literature on care-giving has been the burden faced by women caring for frail elderly relatives (Biegel and Blum, 1990), rather than the preferences, needs and contributions of elderly people themselves. The focus of Equal Opportunities Commission research (EOC, 1980; 1982) and feminist writing (Finch and Groves, 1983; Dalley, 1988) has been on how caring responsibilities disadvantage women, with less attention devoted to gender inequalities among elderly people themselves. On both sides of the Atlantic, caring has been portrayed primarily as work done by daughters for parents (Land, 1978; Finch and Groves, 1980, 1982, 1983; Brody, 1981; Graham, 1983), while care by spouses or other relatives has received less attention (Parker, 1989). There has been little examination of the concept of caring, or questioning of the stereotype of 'carers' as middle-aged women.

Literature on the burdens of care falling on daughters has tended to give a one-sided account, objectifying elderly people as a social problem 'to be cared for', and fuelling the alarmism and moral panic over the growth in the proportion of elderly people in the population. British terminology reflects this orientation in the use of the value-laden term 'dependant'. We follow American practice

From Sara Arber and Jay Ginn (1991) *Gender and Later Life*, London: Sage, pp. 130–40.

(Biegel and Blum, 1990) in using 'care-recipient' to signify a potentially more equal relationship. While acknowledging the constraint of care-giving on individuals' lives, elderly people should also be conceptualised as a resource.

Elderly people have been marginalised as a dependent and unproductive group, partly because of the invisibility of informal work as a contribution to society. Elderly people are givers as well as receivers, through their caring for other elderly people, their unpaid domestic work, care for grandchildren, and voluntary work. Caring is generally only one part of a complex dynamic of reciprocity (Finch, 1987; 1989a; 1989b). We reanalyse data from the OPCS Informal Carers Survey to study the characteristics of carers for elderly people – their gender and age – as well as whether the 'caring capacity of the community' extends beyond the immediate family.

The OPCS Informal Carers Survey

The OPCS Informal Carers Survey, a nationally representative government survey of carers of sick, handicapped and elderly people (Green, 1988), was conducted as an integral part of the 1985 GHS. It provides an invaluable complement to the large number of small surveys and qualitative studies which have been based on localised samples (EOC, 1980; Charlesworth *et al.*, 1984; Wenger, 1984; Qureshi and Walker, 1989) or specific subgroups of carers (Nissel and Bonnerjea, 1982; Wright, 1983; Marsden and Abrams, 1987; Lewis and Meredith, 1988).

Our knowledge about the characteristics of informal carers depends on the questions used to identify them, and how these questions are interpreted by different respondents. The phrasing of the OPCS questions distinguishes 'caring' from 'normal' family care and domestic provisioning work; this may introduce some gender bias because the latter is performed more often by women. The first screening question refers to 'extra family responsibilities': see Table 1. Men may include shopping and cooking for their disabled wife as 'extra family responsibilities', but a woman caring for her disabled husband may not. It may be particularly difficult for a woman to separate time devoted to 'normal' domestic provisioning from the 'extra' care categorised in the survey as 'caring'.

Table 1   *Percentage of adults caring for persons aged 65 and over, by gender, in the Informal Carers Survey, 1985*

		Women	Men	All adults
Qu. 1	Some people have *extra family* responsibilities because they look after someone who is sick, handicapped or elderly. … Is there anyone **living with you** who is sick, handicapped or elderly whom you *look after or give special help to* …? (Co-resident care)	2	2	2
Qu. 2	And how about people not living with you, do you provide *some regular service or help* for any sick, handicapped or elderly relative, friend or neighbour **not living with you**? (Extra-resident care)	10	7	9
	Percentage of all adults who are carers	12	9	10
	N (100%) =	9,846	8,484	18,330

Bold – emphasis in the original; italic – our emphasis.
Source: General Household Survey, 1985 (authors' analysis)

The second screening question identified people with caring responsibilities outside the household, asking whether the individual provided 'some regular service or help'. This may be no more than regular gardening or purchasing some item of shopping for a relative. Such help would be included as 'caring' in the OPCS survey, yet may be unrelated to the dependency of the recipient, and could be considered part of the usual reciprocal help, support and assistance among relatives, friends and neighbours. Thus, the range of activities through which a respondent is classified as a 'carer' for someone in another household is more inclusive than for co-resident care, where 'normal' services are excluded. Ten per cent of women and 7 per cent of men provide such extra-resident care to elderly people, according to the OPCS definition, and 2 per cent each of women and men report providing co-resident care to elderly people.

The two OPCS screening questions identify a total of 12 per cent of women and 9 per cent of men as providing informal care to elderly people. These figures reflect the inclusive definition used for extra-household caring (Arber and Ginn, 1990) and are much higher than other estimates (e.g. Parker, 1985; Martin *et al.*, 1989).

Co-resident and extra-resident care

Informal care provided within the same household (co-resident care) differs on a number of dimensions from care provided to an elderly person living in a separate household (extra-resident care), suggesting that these two locations of care should not be confused in policy debates.

A similarity is that parents and parents-in-law represent about half the elderly people cared for both in separate households and in the same household (Table 2). A difference between the two care settings is that 40 per cent of people caring for an elderly person in the same household support their spouse, whereas over a quarter of people providing informal care outside the household care for friends or neighbours.

Table 2 *Informal care provided to elderly people, by relationship of care-receiver to care-giver (column percentages)*

	(a) % of care-givers			(b) % distribution of total hours of informal care		
	Same household	Other household	All	Same household	Other household	All
Care-receiver						
Spouse	40	–	8	48	–	30
Parent	36	39	39	34	51	40
Parent-in-law	11	15	14	8	15	11
Other relative	18	18	18	10	17	12
Friend/neighbour	–	27	22	–	17	7
Total	100	100	100	100	100	100
N =	(380)	(1497)	(1877)			
Percentage of carers	20%	80%	100%			
Total hours of care provided				20,234	13,012	33,246
Percentage of total hours of informal care				61%	39%	100%

Source: General Household Survey, 1985 (authors' analysis)

Although 80 per cent of informal carers identified in the OPCS survey support an elderly person living in another household, they spend much less time providing informal care than co-resident carers. On average, co-resident carers spend 53 hours per week providing informal care to an elderly person (Figure 1a). This is almost six times

Figure 1 *Average hours of informal care provided by (a) co-resident carers, and (b) carers in a separate household, by relationship between carer and cared for and by gender of carer*

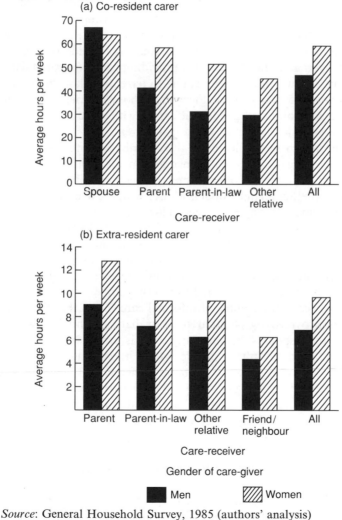

Source: General Household Survey, 1985 (authors' analysis)

greater than the average nine hours a week spent by those caring for an elderly person in another household. The amount of time spent varies according to the relationship between the care-giver and care-recipient, and the gender of the care-giver. The greatest time is spent by carers who support their elderly spouse, averaging 65 hours per week with a negligible gender difference. In other relationships women providing care in the same household spend nearly 50 per cent more time caring per week than male carers. Men who care for a parent report providing an average of 40 hours care per week, compared with nearly 60 hours provided by women caring for a parent.

Much less time is spent providing informal care to elderly people in another household (Figure 1b). Those caring for elderly parents spend on average 11 hours per week providing care, compared with an average 8 hours provided by carers to parents-in-law and other relatives, and 5.5 hours to an elderly neighbour or friend. In each case there is a consistent gender difference with about 40 per cent more care provided by female than male carers.

As a more rigorous indicator of the contribution made to informal care by women compared to men and by different age groups, we use a measure of 'time commitment', which combines information about whether an individual is a carer with the average amount of time they spend caring each week. This shows that 61 per cent of the total time spent providing informal care for elderly people is within the household (Table 2b). Half the total time is spent caring for parents and parents-in-law, and 30 per cent for a spouse. Caring for friends and neighbours represents only 7 per cent of the total volume of informal care provided to elderly people.

This analysis of the volume of informal care shows that the bulk of care is provided by children to their parents and by elderly people to their spouses. 'Community care' is a phrase which suggests integration of infirm people within their neighbourhood, supported by a wide network of 'family, friends and neighbours'. Yet our results show how unequally a 'heavy' caring commitment is distributed among the population. Informal care is concentrated within the family, and especially within households.

The age and gender balance of informal care provision

The prevailing negative view of elderly people as a 'social problem' emphasises the 'burden' on the rest of society of the increasing number of elderly people in the population. The provision of care by elderly people themselves has been largely ignored, although there are some notable exceptions (Wenger, 1984; Parker, 1985; Ungerson, 1987). Elderly people provide 35 per cent of the total volume of informal care to people over 65 (Table 3). This is a conservative assessment of their overall contribution, since the 'normal' domestic support and family help which is provided by elderly people as part of everyday reciprocal exchanges is omitted from the Informal Carers survey. The OPCS Disability Survey estimated that 40 per cent of main carers for disabled adults were themselves over 65 (Martin *et al.*, 1989; table 8.20).

Table 3 *Percentage distribution of total hours of informal care provided to elderly people, by age and gender of carer, and by place of residence*

	Co-resident care			Extra-resident care			All		
	Gender of carer			Gender of carer			Gender of carer		
	Men	Women	All	Men	Women	All	Men	Women	All
Age of carer									
Under 45	6	9	16	11	25	36	8	16	24
45–64	11	26	37	15	32	47	13	28	41
65+	23	24	47	5	12	17	16	19	35
Row %	40	60	100	31	69	100	37	63	100
Total care provided (row %)	25	36	61	12	27	39	37	63	100
Total hours of care (= base)	8,142	12,092	20,234	3,978	9,034	13,012			33,246

Source: General Household Survey, 1985 (authors' analysis)

Elderly people provide almost half the co-resident care (47 per cent) for elderly care-recipients, with elderly men and women each contributing nearly a quarter (Table 3). This confirms earlier findings of gender equality in care for a frail elderly spouse (Arber and Gilbert, 1989a), and shows that, in terms of time spent, spouse care by elderly people breaks 'normal' gender boundaries of caring. Elderly people contribute a smaller proportion (17 per cent) of the informal care to elderly people living in separate households, with over twice as much provided by elderly women (12 per cent) as men (5 per cent), which mirrors the gender difference in provision

of informal care among younger age groups. Overall, women provide 63 per cent of all informal care to elderly people, with middle-
aged women making the greatest contribution. Elderly men play a
larger role in providing informal care than middle-aged men, with
men under 45 contributing only 8 per cent of all care for elderly
people.

The attention given to daughters caring for their parents and
parents-in-law needs to be complemented by acknowledging the
volume of care provided by spouses, most of whom are themselves
elderly. Ageist views, especially those which portray elderly people
as dependent and passive, conceal the activities of elderly people as
informal carers, and the diversity of household situations in which
they live. We turn next to the ways in which caring constrains the
lives of informal carers.

Constraints of providing informal care

Caring may have profound consequences for the carer, including
direct and indirect financial costs, disruption of employment
opportunities and social activities, and adverse effects on mental
and physical health (Nissel and Bonnerjea, 1982; Braithwaite, 1990;
Wenger, 1990). However, the nature and extent of the constraint
depends primarily on the carer's gender, age and relationship with
the care-recipient.

Married women below retirement age are most constrained by
caring for elderly people and are particularly likely to experience it
as burdensome (Nissel and Bonnerjea, 1982; Brody *et al.*, 1988;
Qureshi and Walker, 1989; Braithwaite, 1990). For these women
caring may interfere with the marital relationship and conflict with
responsibilities for children, resulting in role strain and role conflict. Such middle-aged women can be seen as caught 'in the middle'
(Brody, 1981) between the caring needs of two generations. Caring
may be the final straw which prevents them developing their own
self-identity and achieving independence in occupational or other
chosen spheres, and has implications for their personal financial
well-being in later life, since caring responsibilities lead to a lesser
attachment to the paid workforce, and consequently lower contributions to occupational or private pension schemes.

Married men below retirement age are the group least likely to be
involved in informal care. The primacy of the ideology of the male-

breadwinner role largely protects them from all but a minimal involvement in informal care, such as providing support at times which fit into their own work routine. If a married man's own parents require care his wife is likely to provide the bulk of it, and where married men do provide informal care to an elderly parent living elsewhere, they have the added support of a wife to assist in caring and to service their own domestic needs. Pollitt's (1991) study of informal care for dementia sufferers over 75 contrasted married sons and daughters providing care for their mothers living nearby. Married sons provided similar levels of care to married daughters but were happier and less stressed by their care-giver role. They had different ways of coping; the majority were task-centred while daughters were more concerned about the emotional needs and well-being of their mothers. The sons' 'businesslike' approach to caring was similar to that of retired husbands caring for their wives (Ungerson, 1987).

Caring for an elderly spouse is less likely to be perceived as a constraint on other commitments, since these tend to lessen in later life, especially where the occupational role has already been relinquished. Even spouses caring for a severely demented partner may find gratifications from care-giving, for example in terms of companionship and satisfaction at being able to keep the spouse at home (Motenko, 1989). Wenger (1987; 1990) has shown that the caring experience of elderly spouses is associated with intimacy and companionship, but that caring may increase loneliness as the carer's contact with their own friends decreases and other valued social activities have to be curtailed. The experience of caring differs for men and women. Elderly women tend to find the isolation and loneliness most stressful, while elderly men complain more about the physical strain and unfamiliar domestic tasks. Elderly sibling carers are similar to spouse carers in that the caring relationship is likely to have been based on longstanding co-residence and reciprocity. Elderly carers are less likely than those who are younger to complain of stress and they are more likely to continue to provide care in the face of severe disablement (Wenger, 1990). 'For elderly carers, therefore, caring is more likely to be the focus of their lives, while in the case of younger carers caring may displace or distort the previously existing balance of relationships' (Wenger, 1990, p. 199).

Unmarried children caring for a widowed parent, usually in the parent's own home, fall between the two extremes of married child and spouse carers. Unmarried carers include a high proportion (40 per cent) who are sons (Arber and Gilbert, 1989b). Martin *et al.* (1989) found that 64 per cent of sons caring for disabled adults had never married. Caring is often based on long-term co-residence and mutuality and in many ways is more similar to the provision of care by a spouse than care by a married child. The major difference is that for the adult child caring may conflict with paid employment and adversely affect their social life and leisure activities (Wright, 1983; Lewis and Meredith, 1988). Another difference is that caring is based on a parent–child relationship rather than one of marital equality. The unmarried child may be the less powerful partner in this relationship, particularly if they have never left the parental home. The care-giver role may become particularly stressful where the child continues to try to meet the parent's wishes, however irrational these may have become (Pollitt, personal communication). There are few differences between unmarried sons and daughters who are carers in terms of the nature of the care provided and the ways in which caring constrains their own lives. However, sons are more likely to have the financial resources to buy in care (Pollitt, 1991).

Caring, dependence and autonomy

Both material resources and access to caring resources mediate the relationship between functional disability and dependence. Sociological and feminist literature on disability (Bullard and Knight, 1981; Matthews, 1983; Deegan and Brooks, 1985; Fine and Asch, 1988; Lonsdale, 1990) provides insights into the relationship between disability and dependence.

Dependence should be seen as socially constructed. There is a need to shift the focus away from disability as a personal tragedy, and to recognise the extent to which the social, economic and political structures which govern people's daily lives are responsible for the adverse effects of disability, especially dependence (Oliver, 1990; Begum, 1991). The restrictions which usually accompany disability, such as lack of mobility and privacy, are imposed not by the disabilities themselves, but by a society which denies disabled people the means to exercise the capabilities they do possess (Sutherland, 1981). Financial resources can be used to minimise the risk of becoming dependent on others, but elderly women have fewer financial resources, as well as higher levels of physical disability, than men.

One of the prime requirements for minimising the dependence of disabled people of all ages is sensitive and accessible personal care services. Begum (1991, p. 6) argues in relation to disabled women:

> Personal care services are the key to a dignified and productive life in the community. However, the mechanisms through which they are provided can lead to dissatisfaction, a loss of self-esteem and despair. ... Personal care brings out into the open and challenges a myriad of social rules and cultural expectations governing interactions of adults. It touches upon deep-rooted feelings about the nature of bodily functions and the interpersonal relationships between adults.

Both informal and formal care for disabled people in later life must take account of the feelings and attitudes of the person being cared for. Stacey (1981, p. 189) writes: 'We must admit the importance of feeling states ... It has been a major contribution of the recent women's movement to put feelings, experiences, consciousness on the agenda for political action.' Caring is an example of 'people work'. The elderly person must be seen as the subject rather than the object of that work. Caring involves not only physical and emotional labour, but is often embedded in personal relationships whose history influences the meaning of caring to the participants involved.

When help is essential, the question arises of who should provide it, and what elderly people themselves would prefer. Forecasts of escalating costs of meeting the health and welfare needs of elderly people have reinforced the government's preference for community care (Department of Health, 1989), which in practice transfers many of the costs of care from the state to individuals. In spite of the view of the Conservative government (Jenkin, 1977; DHSS, 1981) that the family is the most natural and preferred source of care for those needing help, there is evidence that elderly people would often prefer to rely on state services than on their children (Sixsmith, 1986). The minority of recent British research which has taken the perspective of elderly people (e.g. Wenger, 1984; Qureshi and Walker, 1989; Aronson, 1990) demonstrates that they are anxious not to become dependent on their children. Qureshi and Walker (1989, pp. 18–19) state: 'Elderly people do not give up their independence easily; with few exceptions they are reluctant subjects in caring and dependency ... Elderly people desire, often more than anything else, the preservation of their independence.' Similarly in the USA, the majority of elderly people would prefer to go into a nursing home than to move in with adult children (Crystal, 1982).

There is little research on the preferences of elderly people for different types of care (Wagner Report, 1988a, 1988b). A survey of Scottish adults found that sheltered housing was preferred for frail elderly people compared with moving to live with a relative, or into residential care, and for over three-quarters of people the least acceptable option was to move in with relatives (Thompson and West, 1984; West *et al.*, 1984). However, two-thirds of respondents advocated residential care for an elderly person with senile dementia. The authors conclude: 'In respect of confused elderly persons there is the strongest evidence of public preference for service and professional involvement of the most intensive kind' (West *et al.*, 1984, p. 293). Salvage *et al.* (1989) found that a small minority (15 per cent) of a community sample over age 75 were not averse to entering some form of residential care, and saw this as preferable to the struggle to remain at home.

Feminist Research and Informal Care

JENNY MORRIS

Social science research has an important role in informing policy debate and challenging public attitudes. Unfortunately, a significant amount of the research which has informed the public debate on community care – feminist research on informal care – has both silenced the voice of those who need personal assistance and failed to challenge general social attitudes about old age and impairment.

Laying the foundations for feminist research on informal care

Research on, and theorising about, informal care has emphasised its significance for women as carers and the effect that this role has on their participation in the labour market. When feminist academics started to address this issue in the late 1970s and early 1980s, they initially drew on the statistical evidence of the extent to which women were caring for elderly and disabled people which had been published in two surveys by the Office of Population Censuses and Surveys; one on women's employment in 1968 (Hunt, 1968), the other on elderly people living at home in 1978 (Hunt, 1978). Hilary Land (1978) and Mary McIntosh (1979) had both started to articulate the impact of community care policies on women's role as carers within the family, but Janet Finch and Dulcie Groves's paper at the 1979 Social Administration Policy Conference clearly argued that such policies were incompatible with equal opportunities for women. The Equal Opportunities Commission backed up

From Jenny Morris (1993) *Independent Lives: Community Care and Disabled People*, London: Macmillan, pp. 40–9.

this conclusion by asserting that women's role of caring for older and disabled people was inhibiting their full participation in the labour force (Equal Opportunities Commission, 1982).

The increasing attention which started to be paid to the issue of informal carers came at the end of a decade during which a strong women's movement had highlighted the way the sexual division of child care within the family disadvantaged women in the labour market, and the way that the social security system both assumed and reaffirmed women's economic dependence on men. The debate on informal care was initially informed by the feminist analysis of women's role as the primary carers of children. The discussions on child care had taken children's dependency on adults for granted and the focus was on the way that the sexual division of child care made women economically dependent on men, and what steps could be taken to change this state of affairs. When feminists turned their attention to the sexual division of caring for older and disabled people, they similarly assumed the dependency of this group and focused on the way in which women were made dependent by their caring role, searching for ways in which their economic independence could be achieved.

However, in the course of identifying women's role as carers of older and disabled people, the terms 'care' and 'carers' have come to be used in a way which excludes child care and women's role as carers of children (unless they are caring for disabled children) from the debate. This was neatly illustrated when a conference was held at Kent University in 1985 whose purpose was to 'bring together academics from the countries of Scandinavia and Britain who had for some time been studying and theorising on the concept of "care"' (Ungerson, 1990a, p. 1.) As Clare Ungerson (ibid., p. 179) wrote:

> there was some puzzlement on both sides of the linguistic and geographical divide as to why a conference on 'Cross-national perspectives on gender and community care' should bring together, on the part of the Scandinavian participants, both child-care analysis and commentators on the care of the dependent elderly, whereas, amongst the British participants, the term 'caring' had come to have a much narrower and more specific meaning, referring to the care of the incapacitated only.

Undoubtedly, part of the explanation for these different interpretations was that the feminist debate in Britain addressed itself to a particular set of British government policies on community care which are concerned with older and disabled people, and not with issues of child care. However, it is also significant that British feminist research and theorising on 'caring' was solely motivated by the assertion that community care policies were against the interests of 'women' (by which was meant non-elderly, non-disabled women). While the 1980s saw increasing attention in Britain on the rights of children, it was not until the end of the 1980s that the disability movement started to make an impact on the academic consciousness in terms of the rights of disabled people. The failure to recognise the interests of older and disabled people meant that British feminist academics were able to discuss community care as an issue solely in terms of its effects on non-disabled, non-elderly women who were identified as shouldering a 'burden of care'. In contrast, Scandinavian countries have a longer history of recognising the civil rights of disabled people and in Sweden in particular, personal assistance services have been available since the 1930s (Ratzka, 1986). Kari Waerness's contribution to the 1985 conference, entitled 'Informal and Formal Care in Old Age [in Scandinavia]' was notable for including a much clearer representation of the voice of older people than that contained in any of the British contributions.

Unspoken prejudices

From the early 1980s onwards, with the interests of non-disabled, non-elderly women firmly at the centre of the debate, British feminist academics who turned their attention to community care constructed older and disabled people as 'dependent people', focusing on the 'burden of care' which was imposed on women within the family. Before looking at the way that this research developed and its implications for the public debate on community care, we need to confront the assumptions which influenced both the theory and the research methodology.

We have already discussed the prejudicial social attitudes which are commonly held about older and disabled people. Feminist academics are no more immune from these prejudices than any other social group. At the core of attitudes towards older and disabled people is the feeling that their quality of life is often so poor that their lives are not worth living. This assumption is rarely articulated within the academic literature but it is nevertheless often there in the background. Duleie Groves, who co-edited the key feminist text on informal care which is discussed below, wrote in 1979:

> If inadequate care is available to frail elderly people, some might prefer death as an alternative to cruel and pointless suffering. It seems a logical alternative... In the absence of protective legislation for elderly and handicapped people, perhaps the least that can be done is to offer them a dignified way of ending what, after all, must be a living death. (Groves, 1979)

Miller and Gwynne (1972) in their research on residential care, categorised disabled people as 'socially dead', asserting that bringing about physical death was the logical course of action. Such a conclusion is only possible because of the assumption that impairment itself is the cause of such 'social death' rather than society's reaction to impairment. The same assumption often underlies research on informal care, namely that old age and impairment inevitably bring with them a poor quality of life and an inability to participate in society. Taking this for granted, attention is then focused on the difficulties experienced by family members who provide help and support to older and disabled people.

The construction of 'women' and 'dependent people'

When Janet Finch and Dulcie Groves edited *A Labour of Love*, a book published in 1983 which brought together the thinking at that time on the issue, it was subtitled *Women, Work and Caring*, illustrating the way that the key theoretical and political questions were focused on how caring restricted women's opportunities for paid employment. The dependency of those being cared for was taken for granted and the emphasis of the book was 'upon the tension between women's economic independence... and their traditional role as front-line, unpaid "carers"'. The book was concerned with exploring the 'different facets of women's experience of caring, the dilemmas which caring poses for women, the tension between paid work and unpaid caring (which can be hard work) and the social policy issues raised by the particular topics under discussion' (Finch and Groves, 1983, p. 2). There was no room here for exploring either the experiences of older and disabled people or the social policy issues from their point of view.

A companion book to *A Labour of Love* was published, edited by Judith Oliver and Anna Briggs, both of whom were involved in the Association of Carers. While this book, *Caring: Experiences of Looking after Disabled Relatives* contained powerful and moving accounts of the reality of 'community care' for those who had to care with little or no support from public services, it also clearly represented those who are cared for as 'dependants'. In asserting that informal carers were an oppressed group, ignored by policy-makers and service-deliverers, neither books left any room for the voices of those who were receiving care.

There followed a number of pieces of qualitative research (e.g. Ungerson, 1987; Hicks, 1988; Lewis and Meredith, 1988; Glendinning, 1992) which did much to explore and bring out into the open the experience of what it was like to be an informal carer. However, although this research purported to explore the 'caring relationship' not one study actually interviewed those who were cared for; instead such research was entirely confined to the subjective reality of informal carers.

The absence of the voice of older and disabled people from the research confirmed them as dependent people and undermined their humanity. This was reflected also in a number of articles and books which further developed a feminist analysis of caring and community care. Hilary Graham, in discussing what was meant by the term 'caring', emphasised that it involved not just 'feeling concern for' but also 'taking charge' of others (Graham, 1983, p. 13). What was not made explicit was that this 'taking charge of' element in the definition of caring is predicated on an unequal relationship between carer and cared-for (echoing the unequal relationship between service-providers and older and disabled people). The terms in which feminist academics wrote about older and disabled people, the way that they were given no voice and were constructed as dependent people, flowed naturally from both the shift away from looking at child care issues to looking at issues around the care of adults, and from the general assumption that older and disabled people are 'other', not normal, not 'one of us'. Indeed, the language that was used clearly identified the interests of the feminist academic with the interests of the woman carer whilst there was no similar identification with the interests of older and disabled people (see Morris, 1991, pp. 154–6). In the process, not only were disabled and older people constructed as dependent people but the category, women, was constructed as non-disabled and non-elderly. There was no recognition that women make up the majority of disabled and older people, nor indeed that many disabled and older people are also informal carers.

Residential care as an equal opportunities solution

This failure to identify with the interests of older and disabled people was clearly illustrated when feminists came to articulate what they perceived to be the equal opportunities issues raised by community care policies. If women's caring role made them economically dependent, and community care policies were likely to confirm women's role as carers, should such policies be supported, they asked? As Janet Finch wrote in an article published in 1984:

> We are clear what we want to reject: we reject so-called community care policies which depend on the substantial and consistent input of women's unpaid labour in the home, whilst at the same time effectively excluding them from the labour market and reinforcing their economic and personal dependence upon men.

She then went on to ask, 'Can we envisage any version of community care which is not sexist?' Finch has consistently argued that it is not possible to do so.

Feminist academics' identification of the equal opportunities issues raised by community care policies was entirely concerned with the interests of those women identified as informal carers. The attention paid to community care during the early-to-mid-1980s failed to consider whether there were equal opportunities issues for those who needed assistance (a majority of whom are women) and it is perhaps not surprising therefore that some feminists, such as Janet Finch and Gillian Dalley, found themselves advocating residential care for older and disabled people (see Morris, 1991, pp. 152–3, 157–63, for a discussion of Gillian Dalley's work).

Janet Finch, in a paper published in 1990, argued that feminists should concern themselves with promoting what she called 'different models for the care of dependent people' (Finch, 1990, p. 54). She acknowledged that one obvious response to the identification of the sexual division of caring within the family is to encourage men to take on more of the earing tasks, and recognised that this might be done partly through increasing the financial support to carers and partly through challenging the notion of caring being women's work. However, Finch is sceptical about whether this would ever be possible, and even if it were, she says,

> it might not necessarily be a state of affairs which feminists would want to support, partly because it keeps caring for dependent people in the family domain as a privatised activity, and partly because one would want to defend the right of women who need care to be cared for by other women, not by men. (Ibid.)

Significantly, this latter point is not based on any research about whether women who need assistance would rather receive that assistance in a family (where it may often be given by male partners) or a residential setting; in fact Qureshi and Walker's research indicates that spouses/partners are the preferred carers of both men and women (Qureshi and Walker, 1989).

Finch goes on to argue that the feminist challenge is the assertion that 'community care need not mean family care' (Finch, 1990, p. 55). Although this statement seems similar to those made by activists within the independent living movement, what Finch actually means by this is 'new' forms of residential care. Thus:

> Policies devised on the basis of non-family care 'in' the community would have to concern themselves with how to provide a range of residential facilities, with nursing and domestic support attached, which would enable elderly and handicapped [*sic*] people to lead as independent and normal lives as possible, but in which the care would be provided by people who are properly paid for doing so. The de-emphasising of family care as the central feature of community care might well receive the support of handicapped people themselves, for whom personal independence is a key goal... Of course within such settings attention would need to be paid to enabling people to maintain links with people (relatives or friends) to whom they are emotionally close, that is, people who care 'about' them: but in my view, removing the compulsion to perform the labour of caring 'for' one's relatives is likely to facilitate rather than to obstruct that. (Ibid.)

While the construction of older and disabled people as dependent people developed partly out of the identification of child care as an equal opportunities issue for women, the subsequent development of research and analysis on caring as solely concerning the care of older and disabled people is also reflected in the different policy implications which feminists such as Finch and Dalley have identified. Feminists have not advocated that the solution to the sexual division of child care within the family is to confine children to residential care (unless they have a physical or intellectual impairment). Instead they have focused on the need to challenge men's attitudes to childcare, and have pressed for better nursery and after-school provision and for workplace practices to change to take account of the need for parents to look after their children. Undoubtedly, the generally prejudicial attitudes towards older and disabled people – which undermine their human and civil rights – had an important influence on the ability of feminists such as Finch and Dalley to feel that a denial of a home and family life were appropriate social reactions to growing older or experiencing physical, sensory or intellectual impairment.

An analytical straitjacket

Finch and Dalley, in their explicit espousal of residential care, do go further than many other feminist academics writing about community care. Other writers have tended to shy away from what is in fact merely the logical conclusion of the way their analysis is shaped solely by the economic interests of non-disabled women. Indeed, in the past few years, feminist academies have started to acknowledge the interests of disabled people in response to the growing political voice of the disability movement (e.g. Baldwin and Twigg, 1991). However, the way in which the analytical framework for research on informal care has developed has acted as a straitjacket, as a limitation on how far feminists are able to go in recognising the interests of older and disabled people.

The construction of older and disabled people as dependent people means that they are treated as incapable. The focus therefore remains on informal carers and the only alternative to residential care which is suggested by this framework is the payment of informal carers. Ungerson (1990), in advocating this as a way forward, discusses the advantages and disadvantages solely in terms of the implications for women as carers, failing to consider what the implications are for those who are cared for. And Glendinning dismisses the disability movement's demand for resources to go directly to the person needing personal assistance, saying 'It is not appropriate for reasons of both principle and practicality, to consider a system whereby benefit is paid to the disabled person to enable her/him to pay an informal carer for the care s/he provides' (Glendinning, 1988, p. 139).

Glendinning and others reach this position – echoing that of the Carers' National Association – because they are still focusing on what they see to be an issue concerning women's economic independence: there is no consideration of economic independence being an issue for those who need help with the tasks of daily living, of the way that such economic independence would enable people to influence the quality of their lives, or of the way that it would diminish the vulnerability to abuse. There is no recognition that disabled people may see the right to choose who should provide them with assistance 'as potentially liberating not only for themselves but also for carers such as family members who feel bound by duty to look after parents, spouses or disabled children' (Keith, 1992, p. 172).

Unfortunately, therefore, in giving voice to the experience of informal carers, or rather in the particular way that this experience was represented, feminist research has further legitimised the denial of the human rights of older and disabled people. Moreover, this research has significantly failed to challenge the social and economic oppression experienced by informal carers because it has failed to challenge – and indeed has done much to reaffirm – the social construction of dependency of old and disabled people.

The failings of the feminist research and analysis on informal care must also be put in the context of the fact that the academic sociology community generally has failed to develop a sociology of disability or of old age; instead both are conditions identified in the context of the problems they pose for society, for government, for other people (see Fennell *et al.*, 1988, pp. 172–3). Disabled and older people are treated as social policy issues and there has been very little challenging of the public attitudes which are held on impairment and old age, and a significant failure to explore the experiences in terms of the subjective reality of those who are old and/or disabled.

Conclusion

Both the public representation of carers as a pressure group and the feminist research which attempted to articulate their interests have failed to confront the fact that informal carers only exist as an oppressed social group because older and disabled people experience social, economic and political oppression. The consequences of old age and impairment include a high risk of poverty, a disabling experience of services, housing and environment, and the general undermining of human and civil rights by the prejudical attitudes which are held about old age and impairment. These are the factors which create a dependence on unpaid assistance within the family. The sexual division of labour within society in general and the family in particular explains why it is that two-thirds of informal carers are women; it does not explain why the role exists in the first place.

By taking the need for care for granted and by assuming the dependency of older and disabled people, feminist research and carers as a pressure group have not only failed to address the interests of older and disabled people but they have, unwittingly, colluded with both the creation of dependency and the state's reluctance to tackle the social and economic factors which disable people. In so doing they have failed to challenge either the poverty of older and disabled people, or the discrimination and the social prejudice which characterises their interaction with individuals and social institutions.

Payment for Caring – Mapping a Territory

CLARE UNGERSON

The issue of payment for care is, as I shall argue in this chapter of increasing interest to the social policy community. It raises traditional questions of equity, quality, professionalisation, as well as being a topic that is appropriately addressed by the now well-established feminist perspective on social policy. I will outline why the topic is growing in importance in Britain, and also point up some of the dilemmas (many of them moral) that arise from considering the issues involved.

Definitions

It is, as I think this chapter will make clear, rather difficult to delineate what constitutes payment for caring. In many ways it is easier and simpler to decide what we are not interested in. I am not interested in the payment, organised within a private market, between individuals, one a care-giver and the other the care-receiver; in other words, I am not talking about domestic service, privately organised and generally, unless the payments come to the notice of the tax authorities, invisible. What does concern me are the caring relationships involving the receipt of income, from whatever source, on the part of the care-giver, and the receipt of care on the part of the person with needs, with some element of public intervention, organisation, subvention. A wide variety of

From Clare Ungerson; 'Payment for Caring – Mapping a Territory', in Robert Page and Nicholas Deakin (eds) (1993) *The Costs of Welfare*, Aldershot: Avebury, pp. 149–64.

such public interventions may exist: they could include tax allowances for those who receive payment; tax allowances for those who give payment; social security payments for those who give care (but not, I think, social security payments for those who receive care – such as an Attendance Allowance or Disability Premium – unless it is specifically tied to the costs of paying for care as is the case with the British Independent Living Fund); payments, generally nominal and/ or called 'expenses', given to volunteers, either directly paid by a voluntary or statutory agency, or paid by the care- receiver, but organised and regulated by a voluntary or statutory agency.

It should already be clear that it makes little sense to use the term 'payment' in the singular since there may be such a variety of forms, levels, organisation and origins of payment. Moreover, although there is an element of exchange in these relationships, in the sense that care is given and taken, and at some point the carer's income is raised as the result of that giving of care, these are not ordinary exchange relationships where, in return for services rendered, payment is made. There are some forms of 'payment' which are not explicitly designed to pay for caring services; items like payment for 'out of pocket' expenses, the 'hotel' costs of caring, compensation for not participating in the labour market, may well have originally been intended for some other purpose but have come to be regarded by many care givers as a form of pay.

As if this were not complicated enough, we also need to establish what, in the context of this discussion, is meant by 'care'. Mindful of the claims made by many feminists, for example, that 'care' should be defined by its personal, individualised nature and the dyadic relationship between carer and cared for rather than the way in which it is organised, who delivers it, or the demographic profile of who receives it (Ungerson, 1990a; Thomas, 1993), it is arguable that we should include the care of children without special needs when they are cared for by their parent/s. There are, for example, countries where there are very substantial payments by municipalities to mothers who care for their pre-school children (Finland for example); and it might well be possible to make an argument that universal Child Benefits such as exist in Britain constitute, at least partially, a payment for care. Ultimately, largely for expedience and simplicity's sake, I have decided to exclude the care of 'normal' children when they are cared for by their own parent/s. In contrast, because of the nature of the public organisation, intervention and subvention of fostering, I include the care of children when they are cared for by publicly recognised surrogate parents (but not adoptive parents).

Why is the topic of payments for care important?

In a recent study of payment for caring funded by the Joseph Rowntree Foundation, Diana Leat found an extraordinary mixture of arrangements, rationales for and levels of payments for care in this country (Leat with Ungerson, 1993). Much of the mixture (a polite word for 'muddle') results from the variety of sources of payment – from social security to local authorities to voluntary organisations; but it also arises out of apparently genuine confusions as to whether such payments are for work, compensation for out of pocket expenses incurred by volunteers, the 'hotel' costs of caring rather than the caring itself, and whether, significantly, they are compensations for not working – but caring. At the core of these difficulties is a central issue about what constitutes 'work' and what constitutes 'care' and whether the two activities are distinguishable.

One might well ask if there is much point in trying to make sense of this muddle. Are we not trying to knit together transactions which, empirically, have nothing in common in terms of objectives, assumptions, beneficiaries, institutional setting, and construe them as a single issue, and then attack them, unfairly, for inconsistency, and contradiction? Of course that is possible. But I want to suggest that there are contextual factors, both practical and conceptual, why they should both be addressed as a single issue, and are of growing importance.

First, there are practical contextual reasons, deriving both from social and economic trends, and from policy trends. In the case of the social and economic trends, it is the way in which these trends threaten the supply of unpaid informal carers which leads to the consideration of payment for care as a way of generating further and possibly different sources of supply. The most important of the social trends is the entry, over the past thirty years, of the vast majority of women of working age into the paid labour market. While much of this paid work is on a part-time basis, hence not necessarily preventing women from spending at least some of their time in informal care, this 'economic activity' nevertheless raises the question about the security of future supply of informal carers and the competition between the world of paid work and the world of care for women's time. Moreover, it is possible that for the women themselves, many of whom are employed in the personal services, it raises the question as to why they should be paid for carrying out certain tasks in the public domain but not in the private domain. Secondly, the changes in family formation and biography brought about by the loosening, through divorce and cohabitation, of marriage, raises a question about the future operation of family obligations (Finch, 1989a). It seems likely that as families increasingly contain members who are related by the marriage of their parents rather than by blood, there will be concomitant loosening up of kinship and care obligations between step-relations. There may have to be some counterweight in the form of monetary remuneration in order to generate the same supply of care, based on traditional kinship obligations, as can currently, with safety and empirical evidence, be assumed to exist (Ungerson, 1987; Qureshi and Walker, 1989).

The policy, as opposed to the social, trends are rather less to do with supply of carers and are due more, as we shall see, to the reorganisation of demand. However, there is one interesting exception to this statement: this is the recent decision, by the British government, to abandon altogether the earnings disregards for old age pensioners. While this decision was taken within a context of a fear of imminent labour shortage in the late 1980s, and the perceived need, therefore, to encourage pensioners to remain in the paid labour market, the recession and high unemployment of the early 1990s have not led to a reversal of this policy. Indeed, it is extremely unlikely that once an earnings disregard has been dropped, particularly for such a large group of recipients, it can with any political impunity be reimposed. Hence it may be that in future, should the economy recover, the supply of informal carers from active pensioners is also threatened by competition with the paid labour market, and that payment for care, even for those above the 'official' retirement age, will also have to be carefully considered. But rather more important as far as policy trends are concerned are the implications of the National Health Service and Community Care Act 1990. As far as community care is concerned, there are two main changes: first is the switch from social security funding of private residential care to the local authority funding of domiciliary care; second is the change in role for local authority Social Service Departments from being mainly concerned with provision of services to being mainly concerned with enabling the development of non-statutory providers, and ensuring that those who need services are maximally provided with income (usually from benefits) to purchase and pay for them, and optimally provided with a 'package' of services from statutory, non-profit, and for-profit providers. Many local authorities have also introduced purchaser–provider splits within their Social Service Departments and devolved care-purchasing budgets to frontline social workers, now known as 'care managers'.

The effects of these changes in the organisation and financing of social care are yet to work through, especially since the full changes have only just been implemented in April 1993. But one particular aspect is already clear: they are likely to (indeed, they are intended to) commodify the personal social services; and most of these services consist of caring labour. A number of pressures are likely to lead to the recruitment of such labour using a 'quasi kin' model of care, but with a form of payment attached. First, the switch away from the funding of residential care to the funding of domiciliary care means that there will be rapidly increasing numbers of very frail individuals, living in their own homes, and without the insurance of 24-hour surveillance provided by residential care. Typically the frail are most in need of care at times outside 'normal' working hours – early in the morning, late at night, and at meal times. It is for these reasons that informal care, which is often proffered by co-residents of the person being cared for (Green, 1988), is generally assumed to work best as a substitute for residential care, because care can be provided on a 24-hour basis and at these crucial moments in a care-recipient's day. But if, as a result of the social trends outlined above, the availability of kin-based informal carers is reduced or non- existent then how can reliable and continuous care be assured? One of the obvious ways is to introduce the idea of flexible labour willing to work as the need arises and at unusual times, and contracted to do so. In these circumstances any underlying idea of moral commitment, whether taking the form of generalised altruism or a personalised form of commitment through a weak relationship as neighbour, friend or family, has to be reinforced. The development of the contract to provide caring services, reinforced by the linkage of nominal pay, in combination with labour (usually women's) that is prepared to be especially flexible, is a growing feature of British social care thinking, if not yet a widespread feature of practice (Qureshi,

Challis and Davies, 1989). While at the moment generally restricted to the recruitment and maintenance of caring strangers, there is no conceptual or practical reason why the idea of the contract linked with payment should not be used to pay 'informal' carers, where the originating informality of the relationship appears to need more formal and regularised reinforcement.

A second pressure to pay for care arises out of the idea that payment can at least introduce an element of control. As residential care declines, or remains static relative to the expected growth in domiciliary care, care workers will increasingly work on their own and will be able to act independently, invisibly (except to the person they are caring for), and hence, potentially – unaccountably. Payment can be used to enforce reliability, introduces the power to hire and to fire, to formulate job descriptions, and to establish occupational hierarchy and structure. How well payment does in practice introduce control over quality of service delivery depends on many factors, not least the way in which the payment is organised and who is responsible for monitoring and evaluation: the client, the agency or the social service department (for a discussion see Leat and Gay, 1987). Nevertheless, the introduction of payment into caring relationship does, at least in theory, offer a sanction – the withdrawal of payment and the ending of a contract – should the care prove to be inadequate and/or unreliable.

A third pressure for payment is that, as a result of the new financial regimes being introduced in Social Service Departments, social workers will, through devolved budgets and purchaser–provider splits, increasingly have the means as well as the responsibility to purchase care from whatever source they can find. Payment for care will almost inevitably ensue, whether it be directly to the care-provider or to an agency such as a voluntary organisation. If the payment is made in the first instance to a contracted voluntary organisation or private for profit agency, then they in turn, in order to maintain control and reliability, will tend to have to pay the care-providers even if, in the case of voluntary organisations, they call these care workers 'volunteers'. Moreover, in a severely cash limited situation, rather than pay the full cost of care provided by personnel employed by the local authority, voluntary organisations or for profit private agencies, there will be considerable pressure to find care which can be provided at less than full cost and for nominal payments – hence, the presentation of such care as 'quasi kin' and 'quasi voluntary', and the potential search for carers claiming benefits, such as Income Support, or even Invalid Care Allowance, for which small 'top-up' payments are all that is needed, or, indeed, desired by the care-giver.

Thus there are strong, possibly irresistible, pressures both as a result of the perceived shortages of unpaid informal carers, and as a result of the reorganisation of the financing of demand, that are likely to lead to payment for care. For that reason alone, if we are interested in how payment for welfare will look in the early twenty-first century, the subject is worthy of treating as a single topic – even though the justification for such payments, their level and their institutional context may vary considerably. The signs that such a trend is already in place are everywhere: payment for care schemes are becoming more and more widespread (see for example, Leat and Gay, 1987; Qureshi, Challis and Davies, 1989; Thornton, 1989; Horton and Berthoud, 1990) and apply to a wide variety of caring relationships, from foster care for children and elderly people, to payment for carers to live in the homes of people with special needs arising out of age and/or disability. Similarly there are signs that informal carers in receipt of Invalid Care Allowance are increasingly treating ICA as a form of payment (and a very inadequate one at that); in a recent study of ICA by McLaughlin (1991, p. 48), 'most carers and ex-carers...perceived ICA to be "payment" for caring'.

But quite apart from the way in which social and policy trends are encouraging payment/s for care and are likely to continue to do so, there are also conceptual contextual factors which mean that the issue should be treated as a single one, and it is to these issues that we now turn.

Contexts and concepts: two traditions

The feminist perspective

The first conceptual reason is to do with twentieth-century feminism. The distinction between the 'public' domain and the 'private' domain, which has run like a deep fissure through European and North American thought and social practice since the industrial revolution, has been for almost as long a period subject to the fierce and critical scrutiny of feminist writers – ranging from the so-called 'material feminists' of the turn of the century in north America (Hayden, 1981) to the socialist feminists of the 1970s and the 1980s. For all these feminists there was a central understanding: what took place in the home was (i) a social construct and not a natural event and (ii) was similar to and, some would argue, the same as the paid work which took place in the public domain. Hence the efforts of the material feminists to design housing and urban settlements that collectivised housework, and the efforts of later socialist feminists to analyse domestic labour as productive labour in the Marxist sense. Some feminists of the second wave went beyond Marxism and developed a campaign for 'wages for housework'. The history of the practical impact of the North American material feminists, whose ideas were actually translated into concrete, most notably in Britain in the quadrangle Ebenezer Howard and his wife lived in in Letchworth Garden City, is a sorry one (kitchens have long since been installed in all the experiments in kitchenless housing) (Pearson, 1988). But the idea of the social construction of domestic labour has a more lasting quality, and within social policy has been translated into mainstream (I earnestly hope) thinking by, for example, the classically and resonantly titled collection *A Labour of Love: Women, Work and Caring* (Finch and Groves, 1983). Debates about the relationship between care and work have continued since then (see for example, Ungerson, 1990a; Graham, 1991; Thomas, 1993) although it is noticeable that this debate tends to take place in sociology journals rather than those of social policy, reflecting perhaps the founding paper of the sociologist Margaret Stacey (1981). Thus an interest in payment for care derives directly from this tradition of breaking down the conceptual boundary between public and private in both feminist sociology and social policy thinking. It has to be said, though, that the emphasis in this tradition, when it comes to look at caring, is on what is normally known as 'informal' care, carried out by kin, in their own homes or in the home of the relative for whom they are caring. So far, little of feminist thinking has addressed the question of care given by strangers which is also traditionally unpaid but is increasingly paid – namely, that of volunteers (for an account of paid volunteering, analysed from a feminist standpoint, see Baldock and Ungerson, 1991). Yet there are interesting developments of payment for such volunteers, many of whom work with one needy person in their own home. These volunteers are often treated in the literature and in practice as quasi kin. Challis and Davies

(1986, p. 142) note with approval the way boundaries can shift between 'formal' and 'informal' care in the context of paid volunteering:

> The social workers saw helpers as having a separate and distinct contribution to make to the care of the elderly. It was not simply care to meet basic instrumental needs of daily living, however important this was, but care with an affective basis which in many respects resembled informal care... For these people, a relationship had developed with the elderly person whom they helped and the tasks and activities undertaken had broadened out, albeit within the original planned approach.

And Tinker (1984, table 4.1) quotes one such scheme's job description for volunteers paid £10 a week as: 'to give help to one elderly person (usually a close neighbour) on a flexible basis, i.e. as and when needed in conjunction with statutory help e.g. home help if needed'. Thus the difficulty of establishing a conceptual boundary between public and private, care and work, is as applicable to voluntary caring as it is to kin-based care.

The social administration perspective

The second conceptual context derives from the way in which the topic raises questions traditional to mainstream social administration. A fundamental question is whether cash relationships are incompatible with care relationships, an argument that has roots back to the work of Octavia Hill and other nineteenth-century female philanthropists, and, more recently, Titmuss (1970). But if one assumes such payments, then, secondly, there are questions as to whether their basis should be general, universal and citizenship based, or particular, selective and conditional. Moreover, arising out of the wide variety of routes to and organisation of payment/s for care, there are questions about fairness and equity between different kinds of care workers, and different kinds of caring relationship and dependency. Finally, the development of such payments raises the question both of the working conditions of those who deliver welfare, and of whether and how an occupational structure should be developed for those engaged in this caring work.

The feminist and traditional issues: laying out the territory

Using feminism for making judgements

The feminist issue concerning the relationship between the public and private domains, and the allied attempt to break down the division between public and private worlds both conceptually and empirically, raises the question about 'wages for housework' which has dogged and divided feminism throughout the century (Malos, 1980). The arguments for and against translating the conditions of the public world of work into the private world of the home are now so sewn into the fabric of feminism that it is verging on the banal to repeat them: against are the arguments that payments for housework would trap housewives and carers in the home; that the payment of one person to service the household would ensure that demeaning and isolating tasks are never shared; that women ought to find financial autonomy through the labour market rather than perpetuate their dependency on either male partners or the state. In favour of such payments are the arguments that they recognise the unpaid work currently undertaken in the home; that they provide carers, particularly women, with their own reliable source of income; that they compensate for not undertaking paid work in the conventional labour market.

In my view the longevity of this debate, with its heady mixture of value judgement combined with few empirically testable questions, indicates that it is a fruitless exercise to attempt to decide, in general, whether or not 'wages for housework' (or payment for some subset of caring relationships within the home) is, in general, in women's interests or against them. The most one can do is attempt to agree on a general set of criteria for judging whether or not a particular scheme of payment (be it a social security payment or from a social service agency) is in the interests of all those involved in the caring relationship; and, if one uses a specifically feminist analysis, whether a particular scheme is in the interests of women carers. If one accepts this point, then I tentatively suggest below some, at least, of the criteria we must be concerned with:

- Does the scheme specifically seek out carers on the grounds that they are likely to be available and willing to undertake care for less than full pay because they have an income from another source – their male partner, benefits from the state with low earnings disregards, part-time paid work which does not reach tax and national insurance thresholds?

• Does the scheme specifically exclude women – or particular subsets such as married women – on the grounds that they are likely to provide unpaid care anyway?

• Is the level of payments to carers, whether they are informally caring for kin, friends or neighbours, or recruited as caring strangers, simply a reflection of the minimum pay thought necessary to ensure the supply of and control of carers, where caring is presented as something different from work?

• Or is it a reflection of prevailing wage-rates for similar fully paid work; does it reflect the amount of time spent caring and the 'unsocial' hours involved; does it reflect the complexity and difficulty of the tasks involved?

This is by no means a complete list of possible criteria for which much more thought and space is needed; it does not, for example, include any criteria for judging the scheme as far as the care recipient is concerned. However, I do suggest that if one is trying to judge a scheme and its related payments as far as carers are concerned, and within a feminist framework, then, if the answers to any one of the first three questions are in the affirmative, then the scheme is not in the interests of carers in general and women carers in particular. Indeed, such a scheme would be positively bad, particularly for women carers, since if any of these three criteria are fulfilled then women are likely to be further embedded into a way of life – and a life course – so graphically described by Laura Balbo (1987) as 'piecing and patching'. Answers in the affirmative to the fourth question indicate a scheme which is arguably positively in the interests of all carers since a level of payment is indicated that reflects both the social and economic value of such work. Such payments may of course raise other problems, not least of the professionalisation of care.

Bibliography to Section IX

Arber, S. and Gilbert, N. (1989a) 'Transitions in Caring: Gender, Life Course and Care of the Elderly', in B. Bytheway, T. Keil, P. Allatt and A. Bryman (eds) *Becoming and Being Old: Sociological Approaches to Later Life*, London: Sage.

Arber, S. and Gilbert N. (1989b) 'Men: the Forgotten Carers', *Sociology*, 23 (1), pp. 111–18.

Arber, S. and Ginn, J. (1990) 'The Meaning of Informal Care: Gender and the Contribution of Elderly People', *Ageing and Society* 10 (4), pp. 429–54.

Aronson, J. (1990) 'Women's Perspectives on Informal Care of the Elderly: Public Ideology and Personal Experience of Giving and Receiving Care', *Ageing and Society*, 10 (1), pp. 61–84.

Balbo, L. (1987) 'Crazy Quilts: Rethinking the Welfare State Debate from the Woman's Point of View', in A. Showstack Sassoon (ed.) *Women and the State: The Shifting Boundaries of Public and Private*, London: Hutchinson.

Baldock, J. and Ungerson, C. (1991) ' "What d'ya want if you don't want money?": A Feminist Critique of Paid Volunteering', in M. Maclean and D. Groves (eds) *Women's Issues in Social Policy*, London: Routledge.

Baldwin, S. and Twigg, J. (1991) 'Women and Community Care: Reflections on a Debate', in M. McLean and D. Groves (eds) *Women's Issues in Social Policy*, London: Routledge.

Begum, N. (1991) 'At the Mercy of Others: Disabled Women's Experiences of Receiving Personal Care', paper presented to the BSA Annual Conference, University of Manchester, March.

Biegel, D. and Blum, A. (eds) (1990) *Aging and Caregiving: Theory Research and Policy*, Beverly Hills: Sage.

Braithwaite, V. (1990) *Bound to Care*, Sydney: Allen & Unwin.

Briggs, A. and Oliver, J. (eds) (1985) *Caring: Experiences of Looking After Disabled Relatives*, London: Routledge & Kegan Paul.

Brody, E. (1981) ' "Women in the Middle" and Family Help to Older People', *The Gerontologist* 21 (5), pp. 471–9.

Brody, E., Kleban, M.H., Hoffman, C. and Schoonover, C.B. (1988) 'Adult Daughters and Parent Care: A Comparison of One-, Two-, and

Three-generation Households', *Home and Health Care Services Quarterly*, 9 (4), pp. 19–45.

Bullard, D. and Knights, S. (eds) (1981) *Sexuality and Physical Disability*, St Louis: C.V. Mosby.

Central Statistical Office (1989) *Social Trends 19*, London: HMSO.

Challis, D. and Davies, B.P. (1986) *Case Management in Community Care*, Gower: Aldershot.

Charlesworth, A., Wilkin, D. and Durie, A. (1984) *Carers and Services: A Comparison of Men and Women Caring for Dependent Elderly People*, Manchester: Equal Opportunities Commission.

Crystal, S. (1982) *America's Old Age Crisis: Public Policy and the Two Worlds of Aging*, New York: Basic Books.

Dalley, G. (1988) *Ideologies of Caring: Rethinking Community and Collectivism*, London: Macmillan.

Deegan, M. and Brooks, N. (eds) (1985) *Women and Disability: The Double Handicap*, New Brunswick, NJ: Transaction Books.

Department of Health and Social Security (1981) *Growing Older*, Cmnd 8173, London: HMSO.

Department of Health (1989) *Caring for People: Community Care in the Next Decade and Beyond*, Cm 849, London: HMSO.

Equal Opportunities Commission (1980) *The Experience of Caring for Elderly and Handicapped Dependants*, Manchester: EOC.

Equal Opportunities Commission (1982) *Who Cares for the Carers? Opportunities for Those Caring for the Elderly and Handicapped*, Manchester: EOC.

Evers, A., Pijl, M., and Ungerson, C. (eds) (1994) *Payments for Care: A Comparative Overview*, Aldershot: Avebury.

Fennell, G., Phillipson, C. and Evers, H. (eds) (1988) *The Sociology of Old Age*, Milton Keynes: Open University Press.

Finch, J. (1984) 'Community Care: Developing Non-sexist Alternatives', *Critical Social Policy*, 9.

Finch, J. (1987) 'Family Obligations and the Life Course', in A. Bryman, B. Bytheway, P. Allatt and T. Keil (eds) *Rethinking the Life Cycle*, London: Macmillan.

Finch, J. (1989a) *Family Obligations and Social Change*, Cambridge: Polity Press.

Finch, J. (1989b) 'Social Policy, Social Engineering and the Family in the 1990's', in M. Bulmer, J. Lewis, and D. Piachaud (eds) *The Goals of Social Policy*, London: Unwin Hyman.

Finch, J. (1990) 'The Politics of Community Care in Britain', in C. Ungerson (ed) *Gender and Caring: Work and Welfare in Britain and Scandinavia*, Hemel Hempstead: Harvester Wheatsheaf.

Finch, J. and Groves, D. (1980) 'Community Care for the Elderly: A Case for Equal Opportunities?', *Journal of Social Policy*, 9 (4): pp. 487–514.

Finch, J. and Groves, D. (1982) 'By Women for Women: Caring for the Frail Elderly', *Women's Studies International Forum*, 5, pp. 427–38.

Finch, J. and Groves, D. (eds) (1983) *A Labour of Love: Women, Work and Caring*, London: Routledge & Kegan Paul.

Finch, J. and Mason, J. (1993) *Negotiating Family Responsibilities*, London: Routledge.

Fine, M. and Asch, A. (eds) (1988) *Women with Disabilities – Essays in Psychology, Culture and Politics*, Philadelphia: Temple University Press.

Gibson, D. and Allen, J. (1993) 'Parasitism and Phallocentrism in Social Provisions for the Aged', *Policy Sciences*, 26, pp. 79–98.

Glendinning, C. (1988) 'Dependency and Interdependency: The Incomes of Informal Carers and the Impact of Social Security', in S. Baldwin, G. Parker and R. Walker (eds) *Social Security and Community Care*, Aldershot: Gower.

Glendinning, C. (1992) *The Costs of Informal Care*, London: HMSO.

Graham, H. (1983) 'Caring – a Labour of Love', in J. Finch and D. Groves (eds) *A Labour of Love: Women, Work and Caring*, London: Routledge & Kegan Paul.

Graham, H. (1991) 'The Concept of Caring in Feminist Research: The Case of Domestic Service', *Sociology* 25 (1), pp. 61–78.

Green, H. (1988) *Informal Carers*, OPCS Series GHS, no. 15, Supplement A, OPCS, London: HMSO.

Groves, D. (1979) Letter in *New Society*, 20 September.

Hayden, D. (1981) *The Grand Domestic Revolution: A History of Feminist Designs for American Homes, Neighborhoods, and Cities*, Cambridge, Mass.: MIT Press.

Hicks, C. (1988) *Who Cares: Looking After People at Home*, London: Virago.

Horton, C. and Berthoud, R. (1990) *The Attendance Allowance and the Costs of Caring*, London: Policy Studies Institute.

Hunt, A. (1968) *A Survey of Women's Employment*, London: HMSO.

Hunt, A. (1978) *The Elderly at Home*, London: HMSO.

Jenkin, P. (1977) Speech to the 1977 Conservative Party Annual Conference, quoted by A. Coote and B. Campbell, *Sweet Freedom*, London: Pan Books.

Keith, L. (1992) 'Who Cares Wins? Women, Caring and Disability', *Disability, Handicap and Society*, 7 (2), pp. 167–176.

Land, H. (1978) 'Who Cares for the Family?', *Journal of Social Policy*, 7 (3), pp. 357–84.

Leat, D. (1990) *For Love and Money: The Role of Payment in Encouraging the Provision of Care*, York: Joseph Rowntree Foundation.

Leat, D. and Gay, P. (1987) *Paying for Care*, PSI Research Report No. 661, London: Policy Studies Institute.

Leat, D. with Ungerson, C. (1993) *Creating Care at the Boundaries: Issues in the Supply and Management of Domiciliary Care*, Canterbury: University of Kent.

Lewis, J. and Meredith, B. (1988) *Daughters Who Care: Daughters Caring for Mothers at Home*, London: Routledge.

Lonsdale, S. (1990) *Women and Disability*, London: Macmillan.

McIntosh, M. (1979) 'The Welfare State and the Needs of the Dependent Family', in S. Burman (ed.) *Fit Work for Women*, London: Croom Helm.

McLaughlin, E. (1991) *Social Security and Community Care: The Case of the Invalid Care Allowance*, Department of Social Security Research Report No. 4, London: HMSO.

Malos, E. (ed.) (1980) *The Politics of Housework*, London: Allison & Busby.

Marsden, D. and Abrams, S. (1987) '"Liberators", "Companions", "Intruders" and "Cuckoos in the Nest": A Sociology of Caring Relationships over the Life Cycle', in P. Allatt, T. Keil, A. Bryman and B. Bytheway (eds) *Women and the Life Cycle: Transitions and Turning Points*, London: Macmillan.

Martin, J., White, A., and Meltzer, H. (1989) *Disabled Adults: Services, Transport and Employment*, OPCS Surveys of Disability, Report 4, London: HMSO.

Matthews, G. (1983) *Voices from the Shadows – Women with Disabilities Speak Out*, Toronto: Women's Press.

Miller, E.J. and Gwynne, G.V. (1972) *A Life Apart*, London: Tavistock.

Morris, J. (1989) *Women's Experience of Paralysis*, London: Women's Press.

Morris, J. (1991) *Pride Against Prejudice: Transforming Attitudes towards Disability*, London: Women's Press.

Morris, J. (1993) *Independent lives?: Community Care and Disabled People*, London: Macmillan.

Motenko, A.K. (1989) 'The Frustrations, Gratifications, and Well-being of Dementia Caregivers', *The Gerontologist* 29 (2), pp. 166–72.

Nissel, M. and Bonnerjea, L. (1982) *Family Care of the Elderly: Who Pays?*, London: Policy Studies Institute.

Oliver, M. (1990) *The Politics of Disablement*, London: Macmillan.

Parker, G. (1985) *With Due Care and Attention: A Review of Research on Informal Care*, London: Family Policy Studies Centre, Occasional Paper no. 2 (new edition 1990).

Parker, G. (1989) 'A Study of Non-elderly Spouse Carers', University of York: Social Policy Research Unit Working Paper.

Parker, G. (1990) *With Due Care and Attention: A Review of Research on Informal Care*, 2nd edn, London: Family Policy Studies Centre.

Parker, G. (1993) *With This Body: Caring and Disability in Marriage*, Buckingham: Open University Press.

Parker, G. and Lawton, D. (1994) *Different Types of Care, Different Types of Carer: Evidence from the General Household Survey*, London: HMSO.

Pearson, L.F. (1988) *The Architectural and Social History of Co-operative Living*, London: Macmillan.

Pollitt, P. (1991) 'Senile Dementia in the Family and the Response of Male Relatives', paper presented at the British Sociological Association Annual Conference, University of Manchester, March.

Qureshi, H. and Walker, A. (1989) *The Caring Relationship*, London: Macmillan.

Qureshi, H., Challis, D., and Davies, B. (1989) *Helpers in Case-Managed Community Care*, Aldershot: Gower.

Ratzka, A. (1986) 'Independent Living and Attendant Care in Sweden: a consumer perspective' (monograph).

Salvage, A., Vetter, N. J. and Jones, D. (1989) 'Opinions of People Aged over 75 Years on Private and Local Authority Residential Care', *Age and Ageing*, 18, pp. 380–6.

384   *Women and Informal Care*

Sixsmith, A. (1986) 'Independence and Home in Later Life', in C. Phillipson, M. Bernard and P. Strang (eds) *Dependency and Interdependency in Old Age*, London: Croom Helm.

Stacey, M. (1981) 'The Division of Labour Revisited or Overcoming the Two Adams', in R. Deem, J. Finch and P. Rock (eds) *Practice and Progress: British Sociology, 1950–80*, London: Allen & Unwin.

Sutherland, A. (1981) *Disabled We Stand*, London: Souvenir Press.

Thomas, C. (1993) 'De-constructing Concepts of Care', *Sociology* 27 (4), pp. 649–69.

Thompson, C. and West, P. (1984) 'The public appeal of sheltered housing' *Ageing and Society* 4(3), pp. 305–326.

Thornton, P. (1989) *Creating a Break: Home Care Relief for Elderly People and their Supporters*, London: Age Concern Institute of Gerontology.

Tinker, A. (1984) *Staying at Home: Helping Elderly People*, Department of the Environment, London: HMSO.

Titmuss, R.M. (1970) *The Gift Relationship: From Human Blood to Social Policy*, London: Allen & Unwin.

Ungerson, C. (1983) 'Women and Caring: Skills, Tasks and Taboos', in E. Gamarnikow, D. Morgan, J. Purvis and D. Taylorson (eds) *The Public and the Private*, London: Heinemann.

Ungerson, C. (1987) *Policy is Personal: Sex, Gender and Informal Care*, London: Tavistock.

Ungerson, C. (1990a) 'The Language of Care: Crossing the Boundaries', in C. Ungerson (ed.) *Gender and Caring: Work and Welfare in Britain and Scandinavia*, Hemel Hempstead: Harvester Wheatsheaf.

Ungerson, C. (ed.) (1990b) *Gender and Caring: Work and Welfare in Britain and Scandinavia*, Hemel Hempstead: Harvester Wheatsheaf.

Ungerson, C. (1993) 'Commentary: "Measuring the Impact of Informal Caring" by S. Orbell', *Journal of Community and Applied Social Psychology*, 3 (2), pp. 165–8 (see also 3 (3)).

Ungerson, C. (1995) 'Gender, Cash and Informal Care: European Perspectives and Dilemmas', *Journal of Social Policy*, 24 (1), pp. 31–52.

Wagner Report (1988a) *Residential Care: A Positive Choice*, vol. I, London: HMSO (chair: Gillian Wagner).

Wagner Report (1988b) *Residential Care: The Research Reviewed*, vol. II, London: HMSO (chair: Gillian Wagner).

Wenger, G.C. (1984) *The Supportive Network: Coping with Old Age*, London: Allen & Unwin.

Wenger, G.C. (1987) 'Dependence, Interdependency and Reciprocity after Eighty', *Journal of Aging Studies* 1 (4), pp. 355–77.

Wenger, G.C. (1990) 'Elderly Carers: The Need for Appropriate Intervention', *Ageing and Society*, 10 (2), pp. 197–219.

West, P., Illsley, R. and Kelman, H. (1984) 'Public Preferences for the Care of Dependency Groups', *Social Science and Medicine*, 18 (4), pp. 287–95.

Wright, F. (1983) 'Single Carers, Employment, Housework and Caring', in J. Finch and D. Groves (eds) *A Labour of Love: Women, Work and Caring*, London: Routledge & Kegan Paul.

Index